ALSO BY DON GRAHAM

꙳

State of Minds:
Texas Culture and Its Discontents

State Fare:
An Irreverent Guide to Texas Movies

Kings of Texas:
The 150-Year Saga of an American Ranching Empire

No Name on the Bullet:
A Biography of Audie Murphy

Lone Star Literature: A Texas Anthology

Giant Country: Essays on Texas

GIANT

ELIZABETH TAYLOR,
ROCK HUDSON, JAMES DEAN,
EDNA FERBER,
and the
MAKING OF A
LEGENDARY AMERICAN FILM

DON GRAHAM

ST. MARTIN'S PRESS
NEW YORK

www.stmartins.com

Designed by Kathryn Parise

The Library of Congress Cataloging-in-Publication Data
is available upon request.

ISBN 978-1-250-06190-4 (hardcover)
ISBN 978-1-4668-6797-0 (ebook)

Our books may be purchased in bulk for promotional, educational,
or business use. Please contact your local bookseller
or the Macmillan Corporate and Premium Sales Department
at 1-800-221-7945, extension 5442, or by email at
MacmillanSpecialMarkets@macmillan.com.

First Edition: April 2018

10 9 8 7 6 5 4 3 2 1

For the Betsola

CONTENTS

Texas is a world in itself.

—Zane Grey, *West of the Pecos*

I have said that Texas is a state of mind, but I think it is more than that. It is a mystique closely approximating a religion.

—John Steinbeck, *Travels with Charley: In Search of America*

Geographically and economically nature had thrown two hazards at the Texans: unlimited space, seemingly unlimited wealth.

—Edna Ferber, *A Kind of Magic*

Of course it's a story about Texas. But only because Texas, right now, represents the American dream in a special way—as the place where there is perhaps the most dramatic realization of material possibilities.

—George Stevens, interview

sugar. An accordionist played "The Eyes of Texas Are Upon You," and composer "Dimmy" Tiomkin cracked that George Stevens cried every time he heard that song.

Jack Warner, or "the Colonel," as many called him, the nattily dressed, mustachioed majordomo of Warner Bros., hurried in and made a few brief remarks, including a couple of bad jokes. Not even his closest friends could ever recall the Colonel's telling a funny one. Jack Benny quipped that "Jack Warner would rather tell a bad joke than make a good movie." Nobody ever forgot his toast to Madame Chiang Kai-shek at a gala party at his Hollywood mansion: "Madame, I have only one thing to say to you—No Tickee, No Laundry." When a flat-footed joke fell flat, as it invariably did, he would break into a soft-shoe routine—a throwback to his teenage days on the vaudeville circuit in Ohio. But he was truly funny when he played his best role, a tough Jew who knew how to deal with filmmakers who thought they were creating art. When Warren Beatty tried to sell a skeptical Warner on the merits of *Bonnie and Clyde*, Beatty said to him, "This is really a kind of homage to the Warner Bros. gangster films of the '30s, you know?" And the clown prince of Hollywood said, "What the fuck's an homage?"

Warner handed out copies of Ferber's novel, signed by members of the cast, to the press. "I know I won't have to tell you the wonderful story because you'll all stay up nights reading it," he said. He closed with a remark addressed specifically to his strong-willed director: "I want to thank you all for coming. I hope we will all meet again when the picture's over—in the not TOO-long-distant future!" That did draw a laugh.

Coming in on time and under budget was always the Colonel's goal, and he hated overruns. With a schedule pegged at seventy-seven days and a budget of $2.7 million, Warner had reason to be concerned, because the man at the helm, the often inscrutable George Stevens, might have been listening or he might have been whistling under his breath "The Yellow Rose of Texas." Earlier that year, as *Giant* moved inexorably toward its as-yet-undetermined starting date, Jack Warner wrote Stevens a memo expressing his acute anxiety: "Is there some way in your rewriting and polishing that you can maintain the same dramatization and still aim for

PROLOGUE

❧❧❧

On May 12, 1955, director George Stevens and producer Henry Ginsberg
sent a folksy telegram inviting members of the press to attend an Off-
to-Texas Luncheon. Six days later, the "Chuck Wagon" opened at 12:30
at Warner Bros. Studio, and some thirty-odd journalists forgathered to celebrate, at long last, the launching of *Giant*, the much-ballyhooed film that
was going to be made from Edna Ferber's bestselling novel. It had taken
Stevens and Ginsberg only three years to reach this point, and everybody
was in a festive mood. Besides the local press, journalists from *Life, Time,
Look, Good Housekeeping, Seventeen*, and *Newsweek* were on hand. Some
names were semifamous: Sheilah Graham, "Bow-Wow" Wojciechowicz,
Joe Hyams.

Entering the commissary, the guests filed through glass doors into a
smaller and more formal dining area where photographs of stars adorned
the walls. This was the fabled Green Room, the inner sanctum, with ban-
quettes and tablecloths and fancy silverware and waiters so that the stars
and executives didn't have to stand in line. It was a sign of status to dine
in the Green Room.

On this day, a Texas flag graced every table, and guests were treated to
huge slabs of Texas steaks and an enormous cake in the shape of Texas,
dotted with tiny trees, candy sagebrush, and oil derricks made of spun

a two hour show rather than the length I am sure you're going to wind up with; namely, two hours and twenty-five or thirty minutes?" Warner was only about an hour short of what the immovable Stevens would deliver.

It was well known in the industry that Stevens would almost certainly take as long as he thought necessary to make the film he envisioned. Indeed, members of the press were already making wagers on how far behind schedule the production would fall. At age fifty, resolute, stubborn, and assured in his craft, Stevens had been directing films since the silent era and had to his credit early hits like *Alice Adams* (1935), *Gunga Din* (1939), and *Woman of the Year* (1942). More recently, he had snagged an Oscar for directing *A Place in the Sun* (1951) and was nominated for *Shane* (1953). He was at the top of his game. He also enjoyed great prestige within the power elite circles of the industry, twice serving as president of the Directors Guild and receiving the Irving Thalberg Award in 1953. During the worst days of the blacklist, Stevens had put up a stiff, principled fight, and according to Fred Zinnemann, younger members of the Guild regarded him as "a sort of pope or certainly a cardinal."

Introduced as "the giant behind *Giant,*" Stevens read aloud an affectionate telegram from Edna Ferber. Addressed to "Henry and George and all you boys and girls gathered together at the Warner studio," it expressed how much she would have liked to have been there for the start of the filming. *Giant* interested and fascinated her "much more than the screen career of my other novels or plays," which was saying a good deal, because twenty-one of her works had been filmed so far. She went on: "Under George Stevens' magic direction the stone and mortar and beams that hold the structure will not show at all but they'll be there." Finally, she wished everybody good luck, "which is really just slang for hard work."

Then Stevens presented the cast. There was Rock Hudson, a dark horse borrowed from Universal, where he had made films like *Taza, Son of Cochise*, in which he played a very tall, very bronzed Apache, and, most recently, *Magnificent Obsession*, a Douglas Sirk melodrama that augured a bright future for the rising star. But *Giant* offered the best role yet. Rock was twenty-nine and top-of-the-mountain stardom was within reach. One correspondent underlined the role's importance for Rock's future: "There's better than an even chance that under Stevens' guidance Hudson might take on the dramatic stature he so badly needs. In short, Stevens may do for Hudson what he did for Miss Taylor at a vital point in her career." According to several scribes, Hudson was wearing a "ten-gallon" hat to hide the attempt by makeup men to make him look bald as he aged toward the end of the film. This method of aging Hudson was shelved later on, and it's very doubtful that he was wearing a ten-gallon hat, the tall-crowned western headgear that went back to the days of Tom Mix and was reincarnated by Hopalong Cassidy. In all likelihood, Rock was wearing a Stetson like the one he wears in the film, but the tenderfoots in the press saw all western hats as ten-gallon ones.

His costar, Elizabeth Taylor, had already made one picture with Stevens, *A Place in the Sun*, a film that luminously transformed her from an adolescent star to a leading lady. But four lackluster films had followed, and now at age twenty-three, married (number two), with two young children, talented, stunningly beautiful, and very ambitious, she was eager to play a role of greater maturity and depth. Moreover, she believed that under Stevens's direction, she could achieve the next level—an Oscar. This was her first day in the public eye since the birth of her second child on February 27—her birthday. When one columnist asked what it meant to work for Stevens, she sounded like a love-struck young girl, purring, "Oh, he's just the end." Another columnist described her as "a summer dream in snow-white dimity demurely fashioned." Another said she looked like a teenager. And a fourth reported that she "looked as unbelievably beautiful as ever in a frosty-white dotted swiss dress with a neckline plunging just low enough to give a ladylike *suggestion* of cleavage." Red roses adorned her place setting, and there was a surprise gift from her husband, Michael Wilding, an alarm clock to remind her of how much she hated getting up in the morning, a pointed but affectionate reminder of her cavalier attitude toward time. Taylor did the honors and cut the huge cake.

Going down the roster, there were familiar character actors like Chill Wills, an actual Texan in this most Texas *über alles* movie, and gravelly voiced Academy Award–winner Mercedes McCambridge (*All the King's Men*), cast as Bick Benedict's prickly, mannish sister. Years later, her guttural rendering of Satan's rantings in *The Exorcist* would scare the daylights out of a generation of moviegoers. There were also promising newcomers like Method actress Carroll Baker, fresh from New York, who would herself win an Academy Award nomination for *Baby Doll* two years later, and a clean-cut young actor named Dennis Hopper, who was just nineteen and bursting with ambition, and the former child star Jane Withers (another Texan), coming out of retirement after seven years of marriage to a Texas oilman. Rounding out the cast present that day were Robert Nichols, tagged for Jane Withers's husband, and Paul Fix and Judith Evelyn, two veteran character actors who play the parents of Leslie Benedict. All in all, a very impressive lineup, though casting was, in fact, still going on. The country-western singer Monte Hale signed on May 19 and the Mexican beauty Elsa Cárdenas on May 27. Screenwriter and Stevens confidant Fred Guiol was also present, along with Mort Blumenstock, head of the publicity department.

But one actor, the third lead, was noticeably late. When he finally did show up, he came slouching in, wearing blue jeans and a worn red flannel shirt, scruffed cowboy boots, a braided belt with a big silver buckle, and a weathered-looking cowboy hat. Already in character as the surly, resentful ranch hand Jett Rink, James Dean was, as usual, playing himself, the aloof rebel whose disdain for ordinary social protocols was typical of his behavior on and off sets.

Stevens joked that it was time for the studio head and the young star to meet, but Dean made no effort to acknowledge the introduction.

All the other actors smiled when their names were called and embraced the applause. Not Dean. "Instead, he squirmed a bit in his seat, fiddled with his big horn-rimmed glasses and stared at the floor," wrote Kendis Rochlen. When he seemed unwilling to honor even the simplest request, Rochlen needled him, saying, "It wouldn't kill you to stand up," to which he responded with an "Aw" and a shrug, and she fired back, "Who do you think you are—Clark Gable?"

When a photographer wanted to take Dean's picture, the actor snapped on dark lenses and never looked up from his preoccupation with his boots. When the photographer asked him to please remove his glasses, Dean ignored him, prompting Rochlen to point out that the guy had a job to do, to which Dean replied that he didn't have any makeup on and hadn't shaved yet. He went on to defend himself archly: "What counts to the artist is performance, not publicity." This self-important utterance was typical of the brooding young actor, but it was only half true, for there was hardly anybody who pursued publicity more ardently than Dean—both in his personal and professional life. Dean was into selfies long before the technology or the word existed. He loved being photographed and cultivated photographers throughout his career.

Studio regulars were all too aware of Dean's attitude. He often ate alone in the Green Room, dressed like an indigent street person, sometimes barefooted, sometimes shod, almost always surly. He would show up shirtless, hunched over his plate, wolfing down a sandwich. His body language nearly always said Keep away. So it was natural that a studio representative who observed Dean's rudeness that day at the luncheon remarked, "That's typical of the guy. I hope the Army drafts him and teaches him a little cooperation."

When the luncheon broke up, Dean spoke to two of his fellow cast members, Mercedes McCambridge and Elizabeth Taylor. He would always seek out potentially sympathetic mother figures, and both would become his friends in the months ahead.

As everybody began to leave, the press moved in and snatched the sugary oil derricks and the Texas flags that adorned the tables and departed to write their stories. *Giant* would provide them with great copy for the next two years.

The make-believe cowpoke dominated most of the publicity generated by the event. He laid down his personal gauntlet at the luncheon. He hadn't changed his recalcitrant behavior a jot since his first two films. He was still equal parts brilliant and a royal pain in the neck.

After the luncheon, Dean joined friends Joe Hyams, a journalist, and Lew Bracker, an insurance salesman and automobile enthusiast, for coffee at the Smoke House across the street from the studio. (Both later wrote books about Dean.) When Jimmy took off his sunglasses, he looked terrible, with large black bags under his eyes. Lew asked him what was going on, and Jimmy said, "Just can't get any goddamned sleep. I still have the same dreams about my mother and they're driving me crazy." James Dean had been locked in that psychic prison since 1940, the year of his mother's death, when he was nine years old.

Emotionally, he was twenty-four going on twelve. As an actor, however, he was something else. Photographer Roy Schatt found him "miserable, a squinty-eyed runt." Then he added, "But he was like an electric bulb—you plug him in and there's all this light, a battery or something inside him, generating this incredible light."

George Stevens and the cast and crew of *Giant* would see the full wattage of that glow, and like everybody who came into contact with Jimmy, they would never forget him.

Jimmy would spend the rest of his surprisingly foreshortened days trying to usurp *Giant* and make it his own. And in the decades to come, he would succeed to a remarkable extent—even if he wouldn't be around to enjoy it.

1

Long Story Short

The story of *Giant* the movie begins in May 1952, when George Stevens instructed his secretary to obtain an advance copy of Edna Ferber's new novel. He wanted a big, serious subject, a worthy follow-up to *A Place in the Sun* and *Shane*, which he had recently completed editing. Now he was looking for another property, and he thought that Ferber's latest opus might be the ticket. It was likely to be a bestseller, because Ferber rarely missed, and its subject was Texas, a state that Stevens, like many other observers in the fifties, viewed as a unique reflection of postwar America.

But he soon learned that Ferber adopted a tough stance regarding Hollywood, as reported in a May 21 *Variety* article. She had long used magazine serialization to build up interest in her novels, and she preferred leasing rather than selling the rights to the studios. That is exactly what she was doing with "The Giant," as the press tended to mistitle the novel, and on May 28, Stevens's secretary reported that all requests for "The Giant" were being met with a "blanket 'no.'"

Undeterred, Stevens had his secretary read the first installment (the first four chapters of the novel) in the *Ladies' Home Journal*, and she reported that the novel would be "based on character sketches of these 'giants'—their intrigues—great wealth—race hatred for the Mexicans—and one central figure called Jett Rink—who is more fabulously wealthy than all the others." That was enough to fan her boss's interest.

In Hollywood, the Ferber name was as surefire a brand as there was among novelists of that era. And there seemed to be an especially strong demand for Ferber films during the Eisenhower years. Five of her works appeared over a nine-year period: A remake of *Show Boat* (1936, 1951) featured Kathryn Grayson, Ava Gardner, and Howard Keel; a third remake of *So Big* (1924, 1932, 1953) starred Jane Wyman and Sterling Hayden; and a remake of *Cimarron* (1931, 1960) starred Glenn Ford and Maria Schell. Her last novel, *Ice Palace* (1958), came out in 1960, featuring Richard Burton, Robert Ryan, and Carolyn Jones. And of course there was *Giant* in 1956. From the silents through the talkies, Hollywood made twenty-five films from Ferber's works—an astonishing run.

Stevens knew that the book was stirring up a lot of ire in Texas, but he thought all the back-and-forth in the press augured well for bringing the novel to the screen. He embraced the hostile reaction: "All of this bombast meant controversy, a healthy and provocative thing. And as such, it served to add to my enthusiasm for putting the subject onto the screen in the best and most forceful possible form." He felt that the brouhaha over the book would stimulate audiences to see the film, and in early 1953 he took steps to make that happen. He also had confidence that Texans would embrace his film: "Despite their fierce pride in their state, Texans have a great sense of humor—I hope. That's what we're counting on."

For years, going back to his involvement with Frank Capra and William Wyler in forming Liberty Films in 1945 as an independent production company, Stevens had been interested in breaking the studios' stranglehold on deciding which films got made. Although Liberty folded after making only one film, Capra's *It's a Wonderful Life*, the dream of independent production remained.

In an unusual move, Stevens teamed up with producer Henry Ginsberg and Edna Ferber to form their own production company. Stevens had known Ginsberg for a long time, and although they had clashed when both were at Paramount in the late forties, it was Ginsberg who had offered

Stevens the *Shane* project. A respected figure in the film industry, Ginsberg was also friends with Ferber.

On May 4, 1953, Stevens, Ginsberg, and Ferber signed a partners' agreement to produce a film based on Ferber's novel. They called it Giant Productions and opened an office at 4000 West Olive Avenue, Burbank. The agreement allotted 33 1/3 percent of profits to each partner, and for her story, Ferber would receive no compensation. She had concluded years earlier that it was better to lease her works for film development rather than sell them. That way, rights eventually reverted to her. In this instance, she agreed to a ten-year license, while retaining stage and musical comedy rights. The risk for all three was considerable, but the prospect of riches was also great. They were nothing as much as wildcatters setting forth to drill for oil in the fabled wilds of West Texas.

Opposition in Texas appeared as soon as news reports about the deal were published. Upon hearing that the novel might be made into a film, a man in Beaumont told a Hollywood columnist, "If you make and show that damn picture, we'll shoot the screen full of holes." And in Houston, Carl Victor Little, Ferber's most indefatigable critic in the Lone Star State, unleashed an attack at the end of that May. Little had scoffed at the book when it started appearing in the *Ladies' Home Journal* the year before and had devoted several columns of denunciation when it hit bookstores. Now here he was again. He renewed his mockery of Ferber's insistence that Texans owned DC-6's and flew them everywhere. He applauded the fact that it had taken eighteen months for the author to sell her "shoddy piece of defamatory merchandise." He joked that the film was going to be shot in England and star Charlie Chaplin as "the Big Rich rancher."

The columnist had already upset Ferber over his call for a public hanging of the author. It frightened her, she said, but it was simply an example of the very type of humor—Texas exaggeration—that she satirized in her novel. Faced with hostile criticism, she fought back and called for a truce. She pointed out that there were novels by Texas authors published that same year that were very critical of the state and yet they had drawn no ire at all. But the truce she sought wouldn't happen until the film appeared. When it did, Texans embraced it from the Red River to the Rio Grande.

On December 14, 1953, Giant Productions secured from Warner Bros. a budget of $2.5 million, subject to approval by Warner if it exceeded that figure.

The next step was to boil down the hefty 447-page novel into a treatment and ultimately a shooting script. Stevens signaled his intentions in a lunch conversation with John Rosenfield, a friend who was also the entertainment editor of the *Dallas Morning News*. Ferber, who also knew Rosenfield, considered him "a man of taste, intelligence, and vitality in writing." According to Rosenfield's column in March 1954, Stevens asked him for advice. "Shall I produce '*Giant*' as pure Ferber and make most Texans sore or shall I tone it down and get a pretty story out of it?" But the question was rhetorical; Stevens already knew exactly what he was going to do. He explained to Rosenfield that he intended "to follow the Ferber book, only clarifying and linking episodes for smoother screen narrative." He argued that Texans were "so state-proud that none of them would pay attention to a mere glorification." Finally, he thought that the film, if faithful to Ferber's vision, would have more "impact in Texas and elsewhere."

Ferber's novel told the story of a Texas ranching empire and the clash between old ranch aristocracy and the new breed of oilmen. The head of the vast Reata Ranch (2.5 million acres), Jordan (Bick) Benedict, travels to Virginia to buy a horse named My Mistake to put out to stud. There he meets Dr. Lynnton, the horse's owner, and his lively, intellectual daughter, Leslie, a "tall slim girl. Not pretty." After an almost overnight courtship, they marry and he takes her back to Texas, where she is both fascinated and appalled by the "state of mind" she finds there, along with proud Anglos who like to think of Texas as "a world in itself." She loves her husband but finds his mannish sister, Luz, rude and domineering. What bothers her most, though, is the wholesale discrimination against the Mexican-American workers on the ranch. Besides that, a sullen ranch hand, Jett Rink, shows her something about class structure, as well. He is resentful of the few acres of scrubland that Bick had given him and exclaims at the size of Bick's ranch: "Who gets hold of millions of acres without they took it off somebody!"

As the years pass, Jordan and Leslie produce two daughters and a son.

Jett Rink strikes oil and amasses the kind of wealth that surpasses the Benedicts'. During World War II, Jordan finally submits to drilling on his land, and the Benedicts benefit from this new source of revenue—airplanes, a swimming pool. As the Benedict children grow up, it becomes painfully clear to Jordan that his son, Jordan Benedict III, will not follow in his footsteps and take over management of Reata. Instead, "Jordy" wants to become a doctor and open a clinic for Mexican-American citizens living in deplorable conditions. He further frustrates his father's patriarchal desire by marrying a Mexican-American woman, Juana Guerra. They have a baby, Jordan Benedict IV, but Bick can't accept that his grandson and heir to Reata is half Latino. Everything comes to a head when the Benedicts reluctantly travel to the grand opening of Jett Rink's airport in the imaginary city of Hermoso (Spanish for "beautiful"). There Jordy's wife is turned away from a beauty parlor because of her race, and Jordy loses a fight with Jett Rink. The novel ends with Leslie's assertion that "after a hundred years it looks as if the Benedict family is going to be a real success at last." She defines success in human capital, a different kind of Texas that will eventually result from their son's rejection of ranching in favor of medicine and, to cap it off, his marriage to Juana and the birth of little Jordy. Success is not about bigness—ranches, oil, and wealth; it's about racial equality and justice. But Bick is never permitted any moral growth in the novel. He's almost the same benighted patriarchal figure at the end as at the beginning.

This bare-bones outline comes nowhere close to indicating the exhaustive amount of criticism directed against Texas in the novel. Striding into this desert of the beaux arts, Leslie offers opinions on everything. Hardly a day passes without some disquisition on the shortcomings of Texans—their boorishness, their insularity, their arrogance, their addiction to coffee, fried food, and barbecue, their supposed racism, xenophobia, and cultural illiteracy. Texas women are shrill, empty-headed, and dominated by the gigantic oafs they marry—Texas men.

In a newspaper column, Stevens went public on what he hoped to accomplish in *Giant*. He called Ferber's novel "admittedly a provocative book" and promised to present a balanced view that would "depict the warmth, beauty and nobility of character as well as the weaknesses as we see them." The film, he insisted, would not be a diatribe against Texas, but it also would not ignore the "conditions that many Texans themselves are sensitive about." He never mentioned race in this article, but that was the principal "condition" that his film would confront straight on.

Stevens considered Ferber's novel big and brash, a troubling touchstone of modern America, and for all of her exaggerations and personal pique, the ingredients of an epic film were right there in her book, waiting for lights, camera, and action.

From a filmmaker's viewpoint, Ferber's work was rather like the state it lampooned: spread out and sprawling. And getting this into shape for a film was not going to be a quick or easy task, and so Stevens turned to a couple of old friends, both of whom had worked with him before—Fred Guiol and Ivan Moffat.

Fred Guiol (pronounced Gill) remains something of a mystery man. Of Mexican descent, he was born in San Francisco in 1898 and got into the movie business early, beginning as a prop boy for D. W. Griffith and then, in 1917, moving to the Hal Roach Studios, where he became a cameraman and director. By 1927, he was directing the early efforts of Laurel and Hardy. He and Stevens became pals during those Hal Roach days, and when the talkies came along, they worked together first at Universal and then at RKO. They churned out shorts with titles like *What Fur* (1933) and *Bridal Bait* (1934).

After Stevens hit the big time with *Alice Adams* in 1935, he took Guiol along with him as a screenwriter on *Gunga Din* and *Vigil in the Night* (1940). Freddie, as Stevens called him, also worked as an associate producer on several Stevens films in the 1940s and on *A Place in the Sun* and *Shane*. Although Guiol was not always very articulate in explaining his thinking, Stevens trusted his instincts for storytelling. Besides that, Stevens felt very comfortable with Guiol. They both liked the outdoors and both liked to hunt. Ivan Moffat thought that Guiol had a "moderating influence on George." An Academy Award nomination for Best Adapted Screenplay for *Giant* marked the apex of his career. Guiol died in 1964.

Ivan Moffat came from a cosmopolitan background. He was born in Havana, Cuba, in 1918, the son of a New York photographer and artist

named Curtis Moffat. His mother, Iris Tree, was also artistic—and famous.
As a young woman, she was much sought after as an artist's model. Au-
gustus John painted her, as did some of the Bloomsbury crowd, including
Duncan Grant, Roger Fry, and Vanessa Bell. Jacob Stein sculpted her,
Man Ray photographed her, and Nancy Cunard went around with her in
Paris. She published two volumes of poetry, was the subject of a famous
Modigliani nude in 1916, and, later in life, appeared in both *Moby Dick*
(1956) and as herself in a scene in Fellini's *La Dolce Vita* (1960).

Moffat had an international upbringing, living in the United States,
Australia, and England, where he attended school, eventually studying at
the London School of Economics and joining the Communist Party. In the
late 1930s, his father moved back to the United States, and in 1943, Moffat
enlisted in the U.S. Army, working in the Signal Corps as a writer. It was
through this posting that he met George Stevens and worked for him as a
writer and assistant director. He was with Stevens during the liberation of
Paris and later at concentration camps in Germany. A handsome, witty,
and sophisticated man, Moffat had impressive friends, including Aldous
Huxley, Dylan Thomas, Jean-Paul Sartre, and Simone de Beauvoir.

After the war, Moffat moved to Hollywood and put his writing skills
to work in the motion picture industry. Stevens made him an associate
producer on *I Remember Mama* (1948), *A Place in the Sun*, and *Shane*.
Moffat once declared that "associate producer can mean anything from
writing scripts to producing the coffee." He also played a creative role with
Stevens by rewriting some scenes and providing ideas for others. For his
work on *Giant*, Moffat received an Academy Award nomination for Best
Adapted Screenplay. Besides *Giant*, other notable Moffat efforts include
D-Day the Sixth of June and *Bhowani Junction* (both 1956), *They Came to
Cordura* (1959), *The Heroes of Telemark* (1965), and *Black Sunday* (1977). A
rather dashing figure, he associated with the expatriate crowd, was twice
married, twice divorced, and had affairs with beautiful women, including
Lady Caroline Blackwood—married first to painter Lucian Freud and then
to poet Robert Lowell—and the young actress Elizabeth Taylor.

Stevens and Moffat were on the same wavelength most of the time, and
Stevens was the only director Moffat ever felt enthusiastic about.

The three of them spent nine months, from March 1954 to December of that year, putting together a treatment. Moffat recalled how the trio went about their task: "Most of the writing was done at George's house on Riverside Drive. He attended every story conference. He paid more attention [to the script] than any other director I worked with. We spent a lot of time making tea in the morning to avoid getting down to work." Sometimes they would take a break to have lunch at a nearby golf course. It was a laborious process with a lot of frayed nerves, as Moffat remembered.

The McCarthy hearings were on television that year, a distraction amounting to an addiction. The trio took lots of breaks to watch the unfolding real-time drama. But looking back on that span of time from March to December 1954, Moffat said that the role of Stevens in the completion of the final product was quite extensive: "For Fred Guiol you might read George Stevens, and perhaps George Stevens too for Ivan Moffat."

The earliest indication of Stevens's thinking can be seen in the remarks and annotations with which he peppered his copy of the novel, which became so worn that it fell apart, a broke-back book. He had marked passages throughout, underlined whole scenes of dialogue, and made notes in the margin reflecting his responses to Ferber's text.

Stevens made some pertinent observations on the principal female character, Leslie Lynnton. At one point, he conveyed his sense of the stridency of Ferber's portrait. To Stevens, Ferber's Leslie is a "mordant tongue, a bluestocking Foreign reading books—opinions of her own—argued with distinguished father. A tomboy." Stevens obviously thought she was rather unlikable—mouthy and opinionated—and, in fact, the Leslie of the novel is an incessant critic of all things Texan, a busybody with an opinion about everything, a bit of a nag who rarely stops talking. (Ferber loved her.) Many male reviewers—and not just those in Texas—mentioned these annoying attributes in their reviews. Female reviewers, on the other hand, tended to admire Leslie. She was saying things they actually thought— how men are vain, how their stubbornness and self-assurance mask their actual weaknesses, how they need the moral insight that women seem to come to naturally.

For the film to succeed, Leslie would have to be made more likable and far less of a scold. Stevens had already made a movie about a very modern woman, played by the very modern Katharine Hepburn, in *Woman of the Year;* and, commenting on the scene where Bick and his wife have a major quarrel, Stevens noted, "Woman of the year kind of love affair." And later, when Bick and Leslie argue at length over her having rebuked him for the exclusion of her and the other women from a conversation about politics, Stevens noted, "Make This One Hell of a Fight, The Best Since Shane."

Stevens also paid close attention to Bick Benedict and the necessity for his character to change during the course of the film. Bick could not remain a static figure of stubborn resistance to everything Leslie represents, as he does in Ferber's novel. It had to be a dynamic relationship, and in his marginalia Stevens entered a rather elaborate analysis of Bick's awakening of conscience in the diner scene. This is a major departure from the novel. The fight scene is not in the novel. Bick is not at Sarge's Place. Instead, in Ferber's handling it's a depressing scene of racial discrimination without any answer or resolution. Stevens gave careful thought to this moment and its effect upon Bick: "Bick comes in just in time to hear this— this is the roughest thing that has ever happened to him—and as his blood pressure soars he reacts in the only way he possibly can—physical violence." After this typical reaction of Bick's, Stevens grants him a moment of self-realization: "Bick is old for this sort of thing and in with a couple of blows he is humiliated—the little boy cries loudly and Bick his grandfather— feels as if he would like to cry to [sic]—Leslie comforts the remains of her empire—and now love is the important thing in Bick's life."

Stevens made other brief notations of points that caught his attention. Jett Rink's angry remark, "Nobody's king in this country—no matter what they think," in response to Bick Benedict's lordly manner moved Stevens to write, "Memorable line. Should register on some people later on."

Stevens tagged momentous plot events: "Aha! Oil" and "War."

The treatment ran to 366 pages, and now they needed a script. Stevens and Guiol produced a first draft of 260 pages (undated) and then, with Moffat's input, a revised screenplay, dated April 16, 1954. At this point, together with Henry Ginsberg's help, Stevens persuaded Ferber herself to try her hand. It was the first time in her career that she had undertaken such an assignment. She had been making suggestions all along, putting in her two cents' worth, and now she agreed to travel to L.A. One of her insights was quite to the point. In a letter to Stevens back on December 7, 1954, she had criticized the wholesale use of "aint's, gonnas, and you was-es." Instead, she accurately pointed out that for the "Texans who talk and behave like comic-strip Texans," there are also "Texans who behave with taste and intelligence," while adding, "even though their outlook may be narrow." In a letter to Ginsberg on April 23, 1954, she summed up her view of the treatment. She considered it "powerful, dramatic and often compelling." But she also saw deficiencies. "Its faults are, for the most part, in dialogue, characterizations, and (in a very few cases) scenes such as the tea-drinking bit." This last is the scene, much admired, in which Jett Rink serves tea to Leslie Benedict in his little shack. Ferber could never reconcile herself to that scene.

She flew to California on June 20, 1954, and set to work on June 28. Working six days a week, sometimes with Stevens, Guiol, and Moffat, she finished the job on August 23. The "White Script," as it was called, weighed in at 285 pages.

Moffat got a kick out of Ferber, "a funny, frisky woman." To Moffat, she "had sort of girlish ways which were at ill with her appearance, which was rather stern—I used to think she looked like Frederick the Great, or something." Moffat remembers that she objected mightily to the "wake scene at the ranch that gets out of hand and turns into a Texas whoop-de-doo." She told Moffat, "You're a bunch of necrophiliacs." In a letter to her pal Ginsberg, Ferber told him what she really thought of Moffat: "He is 36, charming, talented, sensitive; he has taste, a feeling for words." However, she added, "He is indolent and can't do a real day's work. He knows as much about Texas as I know about Iran. Less. If I get out of this town without killing him it will be the greatest known triumph of restraint against honest impulse."

The big problem that Stevens had not solved by the end of his reading of the novel was where, exactly, the film should begin. Ferber's novel began near the end, with the Benedict family and other filthy-rich Texans flying to Hermoso to attend the grand opening of Jett Rink's Conquistador hotel and airport.

These opening chapters give an exaggerated account of Texans' preoccupation with size, wealth, history (the Alamo and all that), and indifference to the rest of the world. And Ferber began her script along the same lines—a panoramic array of images that would have seemed like a tired documentary:

Huge Map of the State of Texas
Sky-line of Dallas
A Mexican shack in the Dust Bowl
An Oil well coming in
Kilgore Drum Majorettes
Texas 72; Notre Dame 0

In his copy of the novel, Stevens had noted, "We might use just the airplane scene for the opening—before retrospect it tells everything with explanation of Jett Rink." Stevens also thought about starting the film in another place—when the child Jordy announces that he wants to be a doctor and not a cattleman like his father. He wrote in the margin, "This scene with the boy could be the start of the picture & retrospect back from there." This idea was never developed. Clearly, Stevens had not yet settled on where the film would begin.

Only later did he realize that it had to begin at the beginning, with Bick Benedict traveling to Virginia (Maryland in the movie) to buy a horse. The year is 1925, the date clearly signaled in the novel during a family discussion around the dinner table when Leslie and her family talk familiarly about what was culturally important that year. They mention the Scopes Trial in Tennessee, which occurred in 1925, and there are references to both Theodore Dreiser's *An American Tragedy* (1925) and Eugene O'Neill's *Desire Under the Elms* (1924). The novel was quite explicit about the dates—twenty-five years, 1925 to 1950. Stevens viewed the film as a commentary on the transition from America of the 1920s to the 1950s—Eisenhower's America.

Stevens made notations on Ferber's script, as he had done with her novel. One seemed cryptic: "Honda Knot one of the great subjects of our times, big to mothers—wives—and young men who are to die for their communities." Only years later would Stevens explain the Honda Knot reference.

There were details in the White Script that would be changed in the film. For example, the good-old-boy ranchers want Bick to pay $2,500 to buy out Jett Rink's little parcel of land bequeathed him by Madama, but the film lowers this to $1,200. The size of Jordan Benedict's Reata ranch is reduced from an absurd 2.5 million acres to 595,000 acres.

Over all, Ferber's script did not meet the expectations of Stevens, Guiol, and Moffat. It was too long, and it was too novelistic, too much prose description; too much telling and not enough showing. A film was moving pictures, or "moom pitchers," as Stevens sometimes called it, but it was not moving words. A typical response of Stevens to Ferber's script was her handling of a moment when Jordy Benedict tries on a hat, a Christmas gift from his father, and it is much too large. She felt compelled to explain the point, with Jordy saying, "They never did fit me, did they dad?" Stevens, whose apprentice years had been spent making physical comedies full of sight gags, reacted sharply in a note in the margin: "Let the picture say this— Do all our jokes need explaining?" He objected just as strongly to Ferber's having Jett Rink, in his drunken near stupor in the hotel banquet scene, say to himself, "Stand up. . . . Ought to stand up." Stevens wrote an emphatic "NO!" in the margin and added that this bit of overexplanation was as "Bad as the Chinese stage hand that comes on and hands the dagger."

Months later, on December 7, 1954, Ferber wrote Stevens a letter indicating that she was obviously missing those weeks in L.A. when she had worked on the script. She told him that she considered *Giant* easily the most interesting and important of the films made from her novels. She praised his "strengthening" of the "book's weaknesses" and his clarification of its theme. By that, she meant the treatment of racial issues: "That theme (I regret in a way, to say) is truer, more vital, more prevalent today in the United States than it was when I began to write the novel." Obviously, she had in mind the recent Supreme Court decision and the roiling opposition that was beginning to course through the South and elsewhere. Near the end of her letter she asked, making a stab at Texas talk, "How are yo'all?"

They were, in fact, still wrestling with that gnarly script, and Stevens,

Guiol, and Moffat found themselves forced to reduce, alter, and invent—a not uncommon process in pruning a novel into a film. As the old song has it, they biled that cabbage down. They went from Ferber's 285 pages to 218 (December 5, 1954). Under increasing pressure to get a working script finished, Stevens asked his friend Fred Zinnemann (*High Noon*) to look for places to reduce or cut. Zinnemann's one-page letter of December 16 was a minimalist notation of six points in the screenplay where things could be trimmed. He pointed to the arrival of the married couple in Texas, the barbecue scene, a bit of dialogue that seemed "a bit expository," and so on. All of his suggestions involved pacing. It was now late 1954, and filming was scheduled to begin early in the new year. The pressure of time felt like an iceberg in front of this slow-moving *Titanic* of a script.

Jack Warner had already submitted an estimating script to the Production Code Administration—a requirement in those days. Geoffrey M. Shurlock detailed their findings in a letter to Warner on December 13. He itemized certain changes that must be made if the script were to be approved. The censors didn't like the honeymoon scene on the train when the two newlyweds are shown wearing "night clothes." Their recommendation was to "suggest that, if the principals were in a sitting position rather than prone on a bed, and if the room were lighted, much of the excessive sex suggestiveness might be eliminated." As for language, nobody could say "damn" and nobody could say "Good Lord," "Lord," "*Madre de Dios*" or "*Madre Dios.*" The censors also cautioned that the fight scene should avoid any "sadistic love of brutality for its own sake" or any hint of sadism.

Stevens had to deal not only with the Production Code but with rumblings within Warner Bros., as well. In addition to all the usual problems of reducing a novel to a script, Stevens and his screenwriters had to keep an eye on Ferber's sources and avoid too close an association with the King Ranch and wildcatter Glenn McCarthy. In fact, Carl Milliken of the Research Department at Warner Bros., in league with the Legal Department, sent Henry Ginsberg a detailed interoffice communication on December 14, 1954, concerning the whole question of the "specially worrisome property."

The "Censorship Memo" pointed out that "in the public mind" there was little doubt about Ferber's reliance on the King Ranch as a source for her novel. Yet in the same breath, the letter quoted a paragraph from a review in the *Saturday Review* that argued exactly the opposite: that Ferber had taken measures to assure any reader that she was not talking about the ranch or the wildcatter, that in fact the names Kleberg and McCarthy both appeared in the novel as separate and apart from Reata and Jett Rink. The *Saturday Review* was exactly right on this point. The novel contains several references to the Klebergs, King Ranch, and Glenn McCarthy as a means of distancing the characters from identification with real-life prototypes.

Even so, Milliken and his team worried about too close a similarity between Bick Benedict and Robert Kleberg because they both ran huge operations and both had married women from Virginia following a very short courtship; because they both lived in grand houses; and because they both owned very large ranches. Stevens and company took care of such parallels by reducing the size of the ranch and changing the state where Leslie Lynnton lives from Virginia to Maryland.

Milliken also worried about Glenn McCarthy. He pointed to the oilman's rise from poverty to riches, his building a great hotel to celebrate his status, and the extravagant party he threw to highlight his success— indeed, a party attended by many Hollywood celebrities. With every sentence he wrote, Milliken seemed more nervous about the real-life sources and their representation in the film. He even worried about the color green, which figured so prominently in McCarthy's Shamrock Hotel, and argued that the film should employ a "disguise" to avoid any such associations.

Ferber had taken care of such problems, or so she thought, by bringing McCarthy and his hotel directly into the novel. At one point, Luz, one of the Benedict daughters, is discussing a recent evening: "We were having dinner at the Shamrock, Glenn McCarthy came into the Emerald Room with a bunch of Big Boys and Jett Rink was one of them. He looked quite handsome in a Mississippi Gaylord Ravenel way." This was a little inside joke for Ferber's fans, who would recall Gaylord Ravenel as the handsome, reprobate gambler in *Show Boat*.

In the end, Stevens thought they had done enough to distance the film from any legal problems, and Milliken's memo disappeared into the moun-

tain of paper being generated day by day as the film crawled to its starting date.

Finally, on April 4, 1955, Stevens, Guiol, and Moffat had arrived at the
final version of 178 pages. To mark its completion, it was bound in hand-
tooled leather, with the name of George Stevens on the cover.

A Warner Bros. production description from years later (1972) summa-
rized the three plotlines that Stevens and his screenwriters had wrought.
First: "The saga of three generations of a wealthy Texas ranching family
and the land they inhabit is an intimate story of a marriage, in which the
romantic dreams of youth are replaced by the resolution and unswerving
commitment of adulthood." Second: "It is a searching social commentary
on the racial and ethnic discrimination arising from a border-state culture
with stupendous natural resources." And finally: "It is a fascinating look
at the obsessive drive and greed of a hot-tempered and determined outsider whose achievements and failings reflect many people's view of the
entire state of Texas."

Just as it had taken a considerable stretch of time to get the script in
shape, Stevens foresaw a lengthy shooting schedule, and this, too, made
Jack Warner and his executives nervous. Eric Stacey, in a private memo to
Warner on January 20, 1955, predicted, "I believe that once the green light
is given to go ahead with this picture it will be impossible to control the
costs, due to Mr. Stevens's methods of shooting." Stacey cited the fact that
Stevens had "interviewed 1,500 horses before selecting Alan Ladd's horse
in *Shane*." Mel Dellar, production manager, estimated that the film would
run over schedule by about thirty-five days—a very accurate calculation,
as it turned out. Warner also wanted, rather desperately, a film of two hours
instead of the proposed two and a half hours. Warner felt that the longer
a film, the more likely an audience's restlessness. But Stevens contended
that "[s]hort pictures also have restless audiences."

There was still the question of when shooting in Texas would com-
mence. In a memo of February 4, 1955, Stevens asked Mel Dellar to give
him "the information on a map at what point the sun rises and sets in
Marfa during the months of April and May." Those dates, too, would be
pushed forward.

2

Beefcake Baron

When George Stevens picked Rock Hudson to play rancher Bick Benedict in the big new film that everybody in Hollywood was buzzing about, the actor couldn't have been happier. He was "walking in clouds," he wrote Stevens in late November 1954.

It was a long road that led to Hudson's selection. Stevens began casting near the end of 1953 and didn't arrive at a decision on who would play Bick Benedict until a year later. Stevens went about the process with his usual thoroughness. He created a kind of Texas bazaar in his office at Warner Bros., with photographs and articles about Texas posted on the walls. He wouldn't have any trouble finding materials. As Edna Ferber wrote, "Texas of the 1930s and 1940s was constantly leaping out at one from the pages of books, plays, magazines, newspapers. Motion pictures of Texas background were all cowboys and bang-bang, Texas oil, Texas jokes, Texas money billowed out of that enormous southwest commonwealth." Ferber was right on all counts. Texas had been a movie state from the earliest days of film, going all the way back to 1908's *Texas Tex* (shot in Copenhagen, Denmark!). In the run-up to *Giant*, Hollywood pumped out sixty-three films about Texas from 1950 to 1956, almost all of them shot on studio backlots.

Stevens, however, wasn't sure how to represent the Texas type, and in October 1954, he placed a call to John Rosenfield, longtime arts critic of the *Dallas Morning News.* He thought Rosenfield might be able to help. "You know, I don't know what a Texan looks like. I'm afraid that if I follow my ideas I will show types that Texans will hoot at." What he wanted, he went on, was "a good portrait artist who will visualize six leading characters for me." Furthermore, he added, "I want him to do this without any reference to established movie stars."

Rosenfield knew just the man, Edward Bearden, a Dallas artist and former member of the SMU faculty. At Stevens's bidding, Bearden drew the six key figures: rancher Bick Benedict; his wife, Leslie Lynnton; Jett Rink, the poor ranch hand who strikes it rich; Luz Benedict, Bick's cantankerous sister; Uncle Bawley, a wise old bachelor; and Old Polo, the vaquero *caporal* (foreman). Stevens felt it was imperative to have a Texas perspective, and Bearden gave him that. Delighted with the sketches, Stevens posted them outside his office and distributed copies to casting agents and the press.

Stevens also valued Ivan Moffat's incisive prose profiles of the principals in the story. Moffat's insights into character and motive were striking. Typical is this probing analysis of Bick Benedict: "Perhaps deep down Bick had long known that some of his views were wrong, and that Leslie was right in her point of view, but he never admitted it. He indulged to his own considerable satisfaction in unfavorable comments about the appearance of his half-Mexican grandson, and relished doing so all the more because he had a sneaking feeling that in actual truth the mixture of his blood would be a pretty good one."

With Bearden's drawings and Moffat's verbal descriptions as guides, Stevens directed his search for actors along those lines. He preferred choosing actors instead of holding auditions. Having grown up in a family of actors, he knew the humiliations associated with auditions. And in casting *Giant,* he had an abundance of eager talent. Just about every leading man in Hollywood felt he was perfect for the role of Bick Benedict.

After all, most of them had already played Texans in one film or another. Clark Gable, Gary Cooper, Charlton Heston, William Holden, Robert

Mitchum, Joel McCrea, Sterling Hayden, Errol Flynn, Robert Taylor, and Forrest Tucker—all had donned chaps and Stetsons, holstered their side-arms, mounted their trusty steeds, and ridden off to some studio backlot Texas town to save it from desperadoes waiting for a train.

And so the suitors presented themselves. They telephoned, they wrote, and they visited the Warner Bros. lot. Early hopefuls included Gable, Cooper, Holden, Mitchum, and Hayden. With all that talent around, Rock Hudson wasn't even in the running in the beginning. But from Stevens's perspective, all the other aspirants faced an insuperable problem. They were too old. The story line of *Giant* covered twenty-five years and whoever played Bick Benedict would have to transition from a young man courting a young woman to a graying middle-aged grandfather. For established male stars, it was a canyon too far.

Stevens believed it was easier to age a younger man than to make an older one appear younger. And he most certainly did not want to use two actors to convey the sense of aging.

Among the actors that Stevens did consider in the beginning are a few surprises. He briefly entertained the idea of Forrest Tucker, a rugged six-foot-four action star in not-so-great Westerns. The lead in *Giant* would have been a bigger boost for his career even than it was for Hudson.

Budgeting problems expanded the range of possibilities. Already worried about cost overruns, Warners had the studio casting department draw up a list based on box-office appeal. With John Wayne at the top, the roster included sixteen names, among them Jimmy Stewart, Henry Fonda, and Jeff Chandler. Some seem very implausible: Victor Mature and Cornel Wilde, for example. Edna Ferber's favorite, Burt Lancaster, was never considered.

For a time, it appeared that Sterling Hayden might have the inside track. His agent lobbied hard for Hayden: "He has the great robust charm these 'Texians' seem to have," but there again was the question of age. The agent thought that with a little makeup and the right clothes, his client could pull off the younger Bick Benedict. But Stevens rejected this argument: "It's easier to believe a romance between young people than among older, more established stars."

Gradually, Rock Hudson emerged as the pick. Earlier that year, he had achieved a level of stardom playing a handsome hunk in Douglas Sirk's "weepie" hit, *Magnificent Obsession*. But it was a routine Western, *The Lawless Breed* (1953), that won Stevens over. His secretary, Joan McTavish (later, his second wife), urged Stevens to screen the film (originally titled *The Texas Man*), and when he did, he was impressed with Hudson's performance. The movie opens with Hudson as a graying gunfighter who, freed from prison, appears as a man more than twice the actor's age. In the rest of the film, he is his younger self, and Hudson showed up very well in both parts.

Many were profoundly disappointed when Hudson got the lead, especially William Holden. Although he had given close attention to Moffat's character sketch and had had several conversations with Stevens, it was not to be. When Holden heard the news, he was depressed and decided to take comfort in a steam bath at the Universal lot. When he walked in, there was Rock Hudson, and Holden congratulated him. "I wish you a lot of luck with the picture," he said, and added, "It's a *very* good role."

Looking back in 1981, Hudson remembered that "every actor in town wanted the role—Gable, Alan Ladd, but they were too old. Holden was borderline. I was 29 when I did it, so I could play the young man, the middle-aged and then the old man with the rubber face." Holden was a creaky thirty-seven.

Excited about landing the part, Hudson was very impressed with Stevens's confidence and thoroughness. "He so inundated himself in Texan and 'Texanism' that whatever decision he made was absolutely right." Rock also began asking around among other actors who had appeared in Stevens's films about what to expect, and they told him, "Just make yourself a piece of putty and put yourself in his hands, and rely on him."

That was easy. Rock's entire career had been based on putting himself in people's hands and letting them chart his career path. That was how he had become Rock Hudson in the first place.

Upon being discharged from the navy in May 1946, Roy Fitzgerald (born Roy Harold Scherer, Jr., in 1925) returned to his hometown of Winnetka, Illinois, took and passed the postal exam, and became a certified mail carrier. Life in Winnetka was as boring as ever, and he'd been dreaming of Hollywood since he was a teenager. He loved movies and he fantasized about being a movie star. One of his favorite films from those days was *The Hurricane* (1937). One scene made a particularly strong impression on the teenage boy: the handsome star, Jon Hall, diving into a lagoon and swimming toward Dorothy Lamour. It turned out that Roy was more interested in Hall than he was in Lamour. It was around age nine, he later stated, that he had feelings that he knew were different from those of other boys. Roy Fitzgerald was a good diver himself, and he could fantasize about being that swimmer, that star.

Since his father resided in L.A., in 1946 Roy decided to go to California and take his chances. He hoped to study acting at USC but lacked the grades to be admitted. He moved in with his father, who was chilly on the idea of acting and promptly put him to work selling vacuum cleaners. Instead of insisting on yes from prospective housewives, Roy always took no for an answer and never sold a one, and then his father got him a job driving a delivery truck. He held that job for six months before making a move to get into films. In 1947, a man whom Hudson happened to know advised him to get some photos made and present himself to Henry Willson, the head of talent for David O. Selznick Productions. It was the only practical career advice that Fitzgerald had yet received in sunny Southern California, so he followed up on it. Though there are other versions of how he wound up in Willson's office, the main fact is that he did, and it would change his life.

Hardly anybody greener or more unpromising could have appeared at Willson's door. Roy Fitzgerald was an awkward, culturally illiterate Midwestern bumpkin when he slouched his six-five frame into Willson's presence. He sort of stooped to hide his height, he had bad teeth, he was shy, and he was largely uneducated. His voice was high-pitched and squeaky, and he had zero acting talent. But he was handsome, and Willson had an eye for comely young men. They were his stock-in-trade, in the full sense of that word. Willson used the casting-couch method as a recruiting tool, and in Roy Fitzgerald he found an enthusiastic Pygmalion. The Illinois ingenue was eager to learn.

The first thing Henry did was to give his client a new name. Hereafter, Roy Fitzgerald, rube, would be Rock Hudson, putative movie star. Willson explained his thinking: "I tried to think of something strong and big. Rock of Gibraltar. Hudson came from the Hudson River, for no reason." Douglas Sirk, the director who made seven films with Hudson, associated the last name with the Hudson automobile, a swank and durable car popular in the late forties and fifties. In any event, Rock Hudson it was, though for a brief period at the outset of his career with Universal-International, the studio spelled his name "Roc," a misstep, instead of the more manly Rock. Rock Hudson maintained throughout his life that he hated his made-up name, but he kept it and it kept him.

The studios were all about makeovers and branding, and Willson possessed a genius for naming unknowns. The roster of lesser stars in his crown included Rory Calhoun (Francis McCown), Troy Donahue (Merle Johnson, Jr.), and Guy Madison (Robert Moseley). His best female remake was Rhonda Fleming (Marilyn Louis), but Natalie Wood remained Natalie Wood. The aim was simple: straightforward Anglo-Saxon names. John Saxon, born Carmine Orrico, was a perfect example of Willson's method. But Rock Hudson was his greatest creation.

Henry Willson devoted himself twenty-four hours a day to furthering the careers of his clients. He told them how to dress, how to eat, how to smoke a cigarette, how to sit, how to conduct themselves in expensive restaurants like Chasen's and nightclubs like the Mocambo. Henry scarcely had any life outside of his work. Tab Hunter described Henry's skills well: "He convinced unsure talent they were going straight to the top; he made casting directors and producers believe he had the ideal lead for their production; and most important, he made everyone around him believe that Henry Willson was one of the most hard-charging, high-powered players in Hollywood." He surrounded himself with handsome males and held forth on all things Hollywood. He loved gossip, possessed a sharp wit, and gave off an air of louche sophistication.

Physically, he was the opposite of his stunning boy clients. According to one of his secretaries, "His face was a misshapen mask: the weak chin, the fleshy lips, the bulbous nose, the wide-apart lifeless eyes, heavy eyebrows, and receding black hair. You could understand why he made a career of discovering and exploiting beauty." His biographer, Robert Hofler, described him as "a beefy, tough-talking, chronically phobic, archconservative homosexual."

Everybody in Hollywood knew Henry Willson's MO. Roddy McDowall stated that Willson "sought sexual favors from many young men. I'm so glad I didn't become a Willson client." Tony Curtis, painting with a broad brush, said, "Everybody who went with him had to sexually express himself to Henry, I'm putting it nicely. With Henry, it was almost mandatory." Farley Granger put it this way: "It was awful what he made his clients do, men like Rock." Robert Wagner labeled him "grossly unethical but unsavory as well."

Despite all of the negative criticism of Willson, many regarded him as a good agent. Robert Osborne, a client in the 1950s and best known as the voice of Turner Classic Movies, considered him "the most powerful agent in Hollywood" at that time. Natalie Wood had nothing but praise for Willson.

❦

Casting went on through the spring of 1955, right up until the start of the film—and afterward, too. There was no lack of candidates. In October 1953, Warner Bros. sent Stevens a list containing dozens of names of potential actors for eight major roles in the film. But Stevens went his own way, in the end choosing only one name from those submitted. In making his choices, Stevens kept uppermost in his mind whether the actors selected would be convincing as Texans. He wanted authenticity in every way he could achieve it.

Many of the second-tier parts were as much desired as the starring roles. Actors throughout the industry hoped for a nod from Stevens; opportunities to appear in an important film didn't come along every day.

Texas native Chill Wills, from Seagoville, a small town south of Dallas, walked off with a prize part, Uncle Bawley, a lovable old bachelor based on another King Ranch figure, Caesar Kleberg. Wills was shrewd. He visited Stevens's office and studied the Bearden drawing of the character. A few days later, he returned to the studio dressed like Uncle Bawley, and it was enough to convince Stevens. To play a Texan, Wills certainly didn't have to work on a Texas accent. If anything, he had to tone it down. He had a very recognizable voice (made famous in the Francis the Talking Mule series), and he liked to call himself "Mr. Texas." He said, "Even Rock Hudson calls me Uncle these days instead of braying like Francis every time I pass by." Wills had already made a movie filmed in the Marfa area, *High Lonesome* (1950), a low-budget Western, and although it had drawn some attention, it was nothing compared to what the *Giant* invasion would initiate. And Stevens might well have thought that an outgoing Texan like Wills would be a good evangelist for the film once they were on location in the Lone Star State. Wills was excited about the role; it would be a Texas-size boost to his career. The part turned out to be one of the most memorable in Wills's long career.

Only a few of the actors could speak like an authentic Texan, and Stevens needed a good Texas-born dialogue coach if the accents were going to sound convincing. He got lucky. Robert Hinkle was a real Texas cowboy, born and raised in Brownfield, Texas, a little agricultural town in the Panhandle. Bob had come out to California hoping to get into films and had signed on with Henry Willson. So far, he'd worked as a stuntman and a double in several films, and he'd one small credited part in a forgettable Western. When Willson sent him over to Warner Bros., Stevens turned him away, saying he wouldn't be casting the smaller roles until the next month. Yet just a day later, Bob got a call saying Stevens wanted to talk to him. Elated, Hinkle felt sure Stevens meant to cast him as Jett Rink, never mind the scuttlebutt that James Dean had already landed the part.

When he got to the office, there was Stevens, a man "about fifty years of age, a little shy of six feet, and well fed." When Stevens brought in Fred Guiol and Henry Ginsberg to meet him, Bob just knew he was going to get the Jett Rink role. Guiol, a tall, thin man dressed in cowboy boots and hat, looked "like a Randolph Scott–type character," and Ginsberg "looked like a stereotype of the Jewish movie executive, neatly dressed in a suit and tie."

But Stevens had something else in mind.

"Do you think you could teach Rock Hudson to talk like you do?" he asked.

"Mr. Stevens, to tell you the truth, I've been going to a speech coach to try to lose this damn accent."

At this, the three men burst into laughter. Then, promised a job as dialogue coach for the length of filming, Bob exclaimed, "Hell yes, I can teach Rock Hudson to talk like a Texan."

Immediately, the "Texas Talk Man," as he was listed on the payroll, was driven over to Universal to meet Hudson, who was filming *Battle Hymn* there. (Hudson worked all the time, it seemed.) Hinkle and Hudson hit it off, and Hinkle spent some time showing him the wonders of Texspeak, such as "bob wahr" for barbed wire, "awl bidness" for oil business, and "far" for fire. And Hinkle was right; that's how a lot of Texans used to say those words. Returning to Warner Bros., Hinkle reported to Stevens that Rock Hudson would be able to pass as an authentic Texan.

Luz Benedict, Bick's tough-talking old-maid sister, was another choice role. Actors in the running included Jo Van Fleet (who had just played James Dean's prostitute mother in *East of Eden*), Claire Trevor, Agnes Moorhead, and Angela Lansbury. Both Stevens and Ferber, however, favored Judith Anderson, but she wanted too much money, and late in the proceedings the name of Mercedes McCambridge popped up. Many of her friends who'd read the book thought she would be perfect for the role, but she said she didn't want to "play another dowdy part." Upon learning that George Stevens was directing, she changed her mind.

Stevens was a little bit worried about her, given her over-the-top performance in Nicholas Ray's ultraweird Western, *Johnny Guitar* (1954). He still wasn't sure she could handle the Texas-inflected dialogue, and he sent Bob Hinkle to meet with her. He told Hinkle, "She has a tendency sometimes to overdo it. I want her to be a pure Texan, and I don't want her to get in there and go all syrupy sweet on me, you know, like she's from the South." Stevens could not have been more right. In film after film about Texas, directors relied on dialogue coaches from states in the Deep South, such as Georgia, Alabama, or Mississippi, and the results were often off-putting, at least to Texans. Hinkle found her a quick study, but he critiqued some aspects of her speech. He told her that Texans didn't say "Mex-i-cans"; they said "Mes-kins." (Some did, but it was considered highly offensive.) A Texas accent lacked the heavy honeysuckle notes of southern pronunciation. It was twangier and more inclined toward nasality. After a couple of sessions, Hinkle confidently reported that McCambridge would be able to handle the Texas accent.

Hinkle's next project was Carroll Baker, for whom big things were expected. She was awfully good-looking and she had Method credentials from having studied at the Actors Studio. She'd been on the stage in New York and knew James Dean from those days, and she'd had one very brief screen role (listed eighth in the credits) in an Esther Williams water ballet, *Easy to Love* (1953). Stevens saw in her possibilities for the role of Luz Benedict II, one of Bick and Leslie's daughters. The only question was, could she manage the accent?

Stevens introduced Hinkle, "a real live Texan," to Baker and told her to hang out with him and listen and observe. "When we run the test, I want you to be as Texas as he is," Stevens said.

For the screen test, Stevens chose the scene with Jett Rink during the hotel sequence near the end of the film, when Jett and Luz have a soulful talk and she realizes he really loves her mother, not her. The day of the screen test, Hinkle was surprised to see that Tab Hunter was going to read the Jett Rink part. Hinkle never knew why Dean wasn't there that day. Baker performed like somebody who "had come from the flat plains of west Texas," but Tab Hunter seemed not to have a clue as to how to be a Texan, and, worst of all, he affected a southern accent without any trace of a western edge. Also, Hinkle thought, he was too pretty to be a Texan.

The part was Baker's. She would play Luz II, the second daughter of Elizabeth Taylor, though she was almost a year older than Taylor.

For Vashti Snythe, Bick Benedict's neighbor and onetime potential spouse, Stevens plucked Jane Withers out of retirement. A celebrated child star in the 1930s, Withers had left the movie industry in 1947, when she married Texas oilman William P. Moss, Jr. The marriage produced three children but ended in divorce in 1954. *Giant* would rekindle her film career and she would also play an important role off-camera in the wilds of Texas.

Alexander Scourby was cast as Old Polo, patriarch of the Obregón family. Known for his strong, deep voice, he recorded 422 audiotapes for the blind, though he hardly has a word in the film.

Earl Holliman was an up-and-coming young actor who landed a part in *Giant* that he didn't think he wanted. Stevens had admired his work in *Broken Arrow* (1954), and when Holliman heard by the grapevine that Stevens had said, "When I do *Giant* I want to use this boy," he immediately set to reading the novel and fell in love with the Jett Rink part. But then he heard that Stevens wanted him for Bob Dace, a much smaller role. The Dace character (Dietz in the novel) appears only twice in the whole of the story, and, with a dozen films already to his credit, Holliman wasn't interested in taking something that small. He told his agent that it "wasn't much of a part" and that he didn't want to do it. But the agent urged him to meet with Stevens anyway, and so he agreed to do so but without much enthusiasm. Later, Holliman recalled their meeting: "Well, I went up to Warner Bros. and George came over and . . . began to tell me how he saw this part . . . as a Booth Tarkington character, real shit-kicking." Stevens quickly won him over: "He was so charming, I never once had a chance to say I didn't want to do his movie."

Stevens chose Texan Fran Bennett, a native of Fort Worth, to play Judy, one of the Benedict daughters. The summer of 1953 she was staying on vacation at the Ambassador Hotel in L.A. with her mother when the indefatigable Henry Willson spotted her and urged her to become an actress. A year later, she took him up on his offer, and before long she had appeared in forty-two television shows. She told a reporter that the proudest thing in her Hollywood experience was being a client of Henry Willson's. While other agents sent over long lists of actors, Willson's note to Stevens on Bennett was precise and helpful: "Texas Girl . . . One year from home."

As late as April 1955, agents were still putting forward their clients for parts, no matter how small. Henry Willson continued to send photos and notes for his clients, including one on Natalie Wood: "strong acting quality, age 17."

Although Wood was never considered for the film, three of her fellow actors in *Rebel Without a Cause* landed roles. In addition to James Dean, teenager Sal Mineo, a Sicilian, would play Angel Obregón, the first youth from the ranch to enlist at the onset of World War II. Dennis Hopper, a clean-cut, very ambitious young actor, would play the part of Bick Benedict's son, who rejects the patriarchal mantle in favor of becoming a doctor. For these young actors, the transition from the ultrahip Nicholas Ray to George Stevens would not be easy. A fourth, Nick Adams, would famously be brought in at the end to dub Dean's voice in the drunken scene in the banquet hall.

"You don't know much, do you," Henry said after he'd talked to Roy Fitzgerald for a few minutes.

"I don't know nothing," said Roy.

Henry realized he would have to begin with grammar. He would have to teach him everything.

Obviously, it would take considerable instruction and time to turn the eager but very limited Hudson into a screen presence. When Willson took him to meet Walter Wanger, a top producer, Hudson appeared flummoxed when Wanger asked him how old he was.

"How old am I?" Roy asked Henry.

Even so, Henry had faith in his young ward and spent his own money to develop Rock's potential. Rock was so innocent of any acting experience that everything had to be taught except the jitterbug, a dance he had learned back in high school. In a 1952 article in *The Saturday Evening Post*, Rock, speaking about his early training, revealed how green he was: "We used to do whole scenes from plays and scripts and especially something called *Hedda Gabler*—you know, like Hedda Hopper—by a guy named Ibsen. It was the dullest stuff you ever heard."

Raoul Walsh, the eye patch–wearing former silent movie actor turned director who had discovered John Wayne, thought he saw something in the neophyte Hudson and gave him a role with four lines in *Fighter Squadron* (1948). Rock managed the first three lines but had so much trouble with the fourth that it became a source of permanent embarrassment to him. As it happened, Henry Willson visited the set that day with his latest acquisition, handsome, chisel-chinned Art Gelien at his side. They watched Rock butcher a line referring to the squadron's success. Instead of "Pretty soon, you're going to have to get a bigger blackboard," it came out in Rock's delivery as "bligger backboard." Thirty-eight times it came out that way. Walsh finally rewrote the line and it was delivered off-camera. Meantime, Art Gelien was thinking, "*Thank goodness I've already got a good, short, strong name: Art.*" He felt certain that he wouldn't be called something as ridiculous as Rock Hudson. But before he knew it, Art Gelien would morph into Tab Hunter and become the second-biggest star in Willson's stable.

Together, Willson and Walsh spent $9,550 ($97,441 in today's money) on Rock's development, for which expenses they were reimbursed a year later when Rock signed with Universal-International, where the development of Rock's education in acting proceeded. Near the end of his life, Hudson recalled, "I had it lucky. Any kinds of lessons you chose were free—drama, diction, voice, horseback riding, ballet, sword fighting, gymnastics."

A year later, he appeared in numerous films, and in six more in 1950. They were all small parts: a truck driver, a store detective, an Indian named Young Bull, a villainous Arab, a nightclub doorman, and a football star in *Peggy,* the only one that had any import for his career. Teenage girls, a new demographic, noticed the handsome actor with the easy-to-remember name, and they liked what they saw, a manly young beefcake with an infectious smile. Suddenly, Rock was getting fan mail.

In 1951, he appeared in five films, all his roles still minor. He played a boxer in *Iron Man,* starring Jeff Chandler, and Rock had to overcome a disadvantage. He was left-handed, and director Joseph Pevney insisted he had to use his right hand. He was impressed with Rock's work ethic and the fact that he learned to use his right hand very convincingly in the fight scenes. Once again, the girls fixed their attention on Hudson. He looked good with his shirt off, and studio publicity flacks started picturing him sans shirts in the fan mags. *Bend of the River* in 1952 confirmed his growing popular appeal with young females. At a premiere in Oregon, teenage girls shouted "Rock Hudson! Rock Hudson!" and paid no attention to the star, Jimmy Stewart. Studio suits took notice as the letters poured in.

The next year, he got his first starring role, billed second to Piper Laurie in Douglas Sirk's *Has Anybody Seen My Gal*. Sirk saw something in Hudson: "The camera sees with its own eye. It sees things the human eye does not detect. . . . The only thing which never let me down in Hollywood was my camera. And it was not wrong about Hudson." Theatrical posters for the film featured Hudson in a dance pose, and in one scene he engaged in a spirited jitterbug with Laurie.

In 1953, Rock appeared in seven films and was slowly but surely moving up the pecking order at Universal. Henry Willson was moving up, too, opening his own firm that same year, Henry Willson Management.

Nineteen fifty-four was Hudson's biggest year yet, despite a misfire with Douglas Sirk in a Western titled *Taza, Son of Cochise*, in which Rock played a bronzed and very tall Apache. The role gave Rock some of the most ludicrous dialogue in his career, and he never tired of repeating such lines as the one he uttered to his costar, Barbara Rush, playing the equally bronzed Indian maiden named Oona: "Taza will build Oona a wickiup." Rock recalled that he "looked like Joe College with a long wig and dark makeup. It was ridiculous."

In another film directed by Sirk that year, *Magnificent Obsession*, Rock found himself on the verge of stardom in this splashy over-the-top melodrama. Phyllis Gates, Henry Willson's secretary, reacted to the film in a way typical of many American women: "I had seen him on the screen only once, with Jane Wyman in *Magnificent Obsession*, a movie that made me weep like a schoolgirl." She went on to say, "As I studied his almost-perfect face, with a crinkle at the eyes denoting he was not stuck-up about it, I could understand why he was such a favorite with teenage girls." Willson was counting on Rock: "He had good looks, strength and a certain shyness that I felt would make him a star like Gable."

Written on the Wind, Hudson's second major melodrama with Douglas Sirk, was released in December 1956, a month after *Giant*, and curiously, Rock played another Texan, Mitch Wayne, an upright oil geologist whose moral rectitude is as solid as Hudson's first name. Sirk liked to present

Hudson "as a straight, good-looking American guy. A little confused, but well-meaning." Hudson would go on to star in three more Sirk melodramas.

But of all his films, it was *Giant* that meant the most to Hudson. Over the years, he invariably listed it as his favorite film, and it was the only one for which he received an Academy Award nomination. He should have won.

⁕

Rock Hudson led a complicated double life.

Nobody was more aware of the danger of being exposed as a homosexual in Hollywood than Henry Willson. But Henry was not worried about himself. Everybody knew he was gay, and he acted the part with brio. Although Henry wasn't in front of the camera, his livelihood did depend upon the public's favor. If a gay actor like Rock Hudson were exposed, Henry would suffer financially, and he would do just about anything to prevent that from happening. When Henry discovered that Rock and another man were living together, he put an end to that in a hurry. Rock was in grave danger, he told him. The young man would have to move out, and Rock complied.

Henry laid down three rules for living gay in Hollywood. 1. "Don't ever let a man park his car in your driveway overnight." 2. "Never sit down at a restaurant with another man without a young lady being present." 3. "And never live with another man."

One of the best ways to create a traditional masculine image was to go on arranged dates with starlets. The resultant press coverage was essential in validating one's heterosexual identity. Rock did whatever Henry Willson asked him to, and they both prospered.

But doubts lingered in the public's mind, and during the summer and fall of 1955, while *Giant* was being filmed in Virginia, Texas, and Burbank, questions surrounding Rock Hudson's offscreen identity were beginning to circulate in L.A. and beyond.

In the 1950s, being openly gay was like being a Communist. In Hollywood, Rock Hudson acted a part in real life just as he acted parts in the movies. He was as good off-camera as he was on. Just about everybody inside the industry knew that he was "musical," a code word used by both gays and straights in that period, but he didn't act gay in a stereotypical sense—except when he was among other gays at parties, or at popular haunts like the Tropical Villa, a gay bar on the boardwalk at Santa Monica. Here, wrote John Gilmore, "it wouldn't have been unusual to spot Rock Hudson or Dan Dailey dancing somewhere deep in the place." Rock also liked to throw private parties at his home, and they were just as revealing as those gatherings at the bar in Santa Monica. "Before a Rock Hudson party was over, there was always someone (and more often than not it was Rock) who ended up dressed in a ballerina outfit twirling about the living room," reported one Dean biographer.

Hardly anybody in the general moviegoing population had any notion at all of Rock's secret life. This was especially true of women. To them, he was divine, a heartthrob. Males liked him, too. He was tall, handsome, and quietly commanding—a man's man. In the movies, he got all the girls.

But there remained many doubts about his private life, and the real Rock Hudson continued to intrigue the staff of a certain magazine that was everybody's guilty pleasure in the industry. *Confidential* not only raised eyebrows; it could damage, if not destroy, a career. So while Rock was away in Texas, Henry Willson plotted a course for his burgeoning star's survival in L.A.

3

Tell Mama All

At age twenty-three, a mother with a two-year-old and a new infant born on her birthday three months before shooting on *Giant* began, Elizabeth Taylor had been in the movies since the age of ten and had made twenty-four films. There was hardly anything about studio culture that she hadn't experienced—and sometimes battled. Intuitive and intelligent, she understood the studio system from the ground up: "It was like a big extended *factory* . . . I was *used* from the day I was a child, and *utilized* by the studio." She had long reached the point where she didn't want to be used anymore, and she was also fiercely ambitious. She had few illusions about being a movie star. "I don't remember ever not being famous," she once remarked.

She was also an incurable romantic and tended to believe the scripts that MGM churned out—the ones about marrying and living happily ever after. She fretted constantly about the roles they were assigning her. She was determined to escape the fate of other child stars and not have to see the rest of her life slow-dissolve into the past. She had wanted out of the Lassie movies, playing second fiddle to a dog. Horses were another matter. *National Velvet* had made her a child star, and she always seemed to do well when there were horses in a picture.

Giant, of course, had horses. It had everything, really, that she hoped for—a major role in a major film with the great George Stevens. But she knew from the trades and industry gossip that Stevens had been pursuing a number of actresses, and she was very worried that he would overlook her.

At the outset, Elizabeth Taylor was just one of the thirty-one names on a roster of possible candidates prepared by Warner Bros. The list began with Jane Wyman and ended with Janet Leigh. But Stevens never paid much attention to studio suggestions. Instead, he had his heart set on Audrey Hepburn, and he courted her like a suitor. He talked to her about the role as early as October 1953, and then on July 2, 1954, he mailed her a copy of the screenplay. He also sent along Ivan Moffat's character sketches, by which he set great store. He journeyed to New York to press his case, hoping that their conversation "can bring before us a visualization of *Giant* as a film." It did not, and his July 9 telegram to Hepburn stated that while they were not always in agreement, he respected her views on the story and said they would be "helpful in final development." Whatever her objections were, she was no longer a possibility. Would Hepburn have made a good Leslie? Doubtful. She appeared in only one Western in her career, John Huston's fretful *The Unforgiven* (1960), filmed in the rough country of Durango, Mexico. It was a particularly personal film for her because she fell from a horse and broke her back.

Grace Kelly, the top female star at the time, was Stevens's second choice, and she wanted very much to do the film. She had been quite effective in *High Noon* (1952) playing a proper, educated Quaker bride from the East who journeys to the West and offers strong criticism of the violent culture she encounters there, until at the end she takes up arms to save the life of her husband. It wasn't a stretch at all to visualize her getting off that train in the middle of the Texas prairie, a bride from Maryland come to her new home, Reata.

But Kelly was at loggerheads with her studio, MGM, because she had turned down several films MGM had picked out for her, and when Warners approached MGM with an offer for Kelly, it was rejected. Despite Stevens's confidence that MGM would eventually come around, the studio wouldn't budge and the possibility for a deal fell apart. Kelly left

Hollywood to assume her new real-life role as princess the year *Giant* was released.

In the meantime, agents implored Stevens to pick *their* client. Anne Baxter's agent argued that she was perfect for the part, since she "is practically described by Ferber in the book except, of course, for the height, weight and cast in her eye which are not vital elements in your story." But Stevens kept his own counsel.

Ferber, as usual, weighed in, lobbying for Patricia Neal. And it would appear that Ferber was never on board with Elizabeth Taylor. As late as January 1955, she wired Ginsberg that she had reliable information (probably from her friend Katharine Hepburn) that Grace Kelly might still be available for *Giant*.

And so it went, agents and their clients vying for the most desirable female role of the year.

Stevens didn't choose Taylor so much as she chose him, he recalled in 1967. "Liz Taylor cast herself into *Giant*. She wanted to play that part. She called me to talk [about it]. But she was about to have a baby. Her doctor called me and said [she was] in great shape, obstetrically, and she'd be able to work four weeks after the baby was born."

Even so, Stevens also said that he would have preferred Grace Kelly, "the most important female star at the time." At one point, however, he extolled Taylor in glowing terms: "She has extraordinary talent and is potentially the best female star in Hollywood. There is more acting in that girl than anyone has ever gotten out of her."

Taylor chafed that MGM was content to put her in one inconsequential film after another. The year 1954, for example, saw her in *Rhapsody*, *Elephant Walk*, and *Beau Brummel*—all forgettable costume dramas. But another film that same year gave a hint of things to come. Taylor later recalled, "A rather curiously not-so-good picture, *The Last Time I Saw Paris*, first convinced me I wanted to be an actress instead of yawning my way through parts." In this film, based on F. Scott Fitzgerald's great story "Babylon Revisited," she played a character who was "off-beat with mercurial flashes of instability—more than just glib dialogue." She was ready for something big, challenging, and important—like *Giant*—which is why she fought so hard to land the part. In late January 1955, the part went to her.

In retrospect, Taylor seems a perfect choice, though there is little doubt that Grace Kelly could have shone, as well. In giving the nod to Taylor, Stevens was going with someone he already knew well. After all, he had plucked her out of MGM entertainments to play the stunningly beautiful and spirited Angela Vickers in *A Place in the Sun*. It was her breakout role from the children's movie ghetto, and whatever ups and downs her relationship with Stevens would entail in the future, she was always grateful to him for having helped her make that crucial transition. *Giant* would be another huge step in that direction.

George Stevens's conception of Leslie Benedict would challenge Taylor, stretch her talents as an actress, and allow her the opportunity to portray a wife and mother for the first time in her career. Stevens felt very keenly the importance of the marriage plot: "So many of our romantic pictures just lead up to the altar and leave you with a general assumption of inevitable unhappiness. But this is a story about the hazards of the marriage relationship." Moreover, Elizabeth Taylor as Leslie Benedict would have to carry a heavy thematic burden: "The character development herein is the story of the change of Texas. Leslie is the agent of this." For Ferber, in terms of her novel, the stakes were even higher, as she wrote her editor: "Do you really think that I imagine a Leslie could make a dent on the hard hide of Texas! She wins—or will in the end win—through her son and daughter." Clearly, it was a major role, and Taylor had her work cut out for her.

The complexity of the part was defined succinctly in Ivan Moffat's sketch of the character. He depicted Leslie as someone who had fallen in love with a romanticized view of the West, only to find that she had been quite wrong about that: "She was soon to discover that Texas was as different from what she had imagined as her own brand of nonconformity was different from what Bick had imagined. Each of them had been guilty of self-deception, and each was to be shocked and surprised at the consequences."

Giant would prove to be a major turning point in Elizabeth Taylor's life. It would contribute to the breakup of her second marriage, it would bring her into new, intense friendships with two of the period's most famous stars—Rock Hudson and that doomed figure James Dean—and it would mark her most successful screen appearance yet. It would also prefigure a string of adult roles that would solidify her standing in the film industry as a star of the first magnitude, or in Kitty Kelley's view, the last of the great screen goddesses.

Even as a youngster she showed steely determination in fighting for parts and standing up to bullies like Louis B. Mayer, the feared head of MGM. Taylor wrote that Mayer "alarmed her terribly" and "looked rather like a gross, thick penguin." At fourteen, she told him to go to hell after he cursed out her mother in a fight over a silly film called *Sally in Her Alley.* Of the MGM operation, she called it an iron lung, where "the executives tell you just how to breathe."

Puberty brought a new dimension to Elizabeth Taylor's image. She changed from a tomboyish girl to a precociously voluptuous woman. She developed breasts purportedly admired widely in the industry. It was as if at once there was an irresistible erotic charge to the child star who was on her way to becoming a star of the first magnitude. Orson Welles recalled the impact her presence had on him. He said that he had never been attracted to child actresses and considered them off-limits, with one exception. He explained, "When I read *Lolita,* I understood what he [Nabokov] meant—because of Elizabeth Taylor as a child. I just never saw anything like her. She was so unbelievable." She was five two and had large feet and arms covered with hair. But still, she drew everybody's admiring gaze. A Hollywood producer, Joe Naar, described the stunning contrast between her age, sixteen, and her appearance at a party: "Draped head to toe in yellow chiffon and looking like a delectable lemon meringue pie, Elizabeth Taylor suddenly walked through the door. She appeared sixteen going on thirty."

Ned Wynn, son of actor Keenan Wynn, offered perhaps the most eloquent description of her impact when, at the tender age of eight, he saw her for the first time. She was seventeen. "I never understood why people claimed her eyes were violet. They were the color of the skin of an eggplant. Aubergine. Garnet. But then only women and gays discussed the color of her eyes. It was her breasts. Oh, Jesus, the breasts. Those breasts fueled my fantasies for decades to come." Ivan Moffat described what happened when she appeared at Paramount to begin filming *A Place in the Sun*: "When she first came into the Paramount commissary before making a costume test, she was only seventeen, most people had never seen her in the flesh before, but she looked pretty smashing and people were subdued when they looked at her." When she came over to the writers' section of the commissary, Billy Wilder cracked, "How the hell did *she* ever get into the movies?"

A Place in the Sun marked a turning point in her career and proved to be an education in itself. Taylor, at seventeen, had little curiosity about anything unless it related to the mechanics of achieving stardom. All she read were the trades and movie magazines, and all she was interested in was the next boy or man she was going to fall in love with and marry. Her stand-in on *A Place in the Sun* itemized her insularity from everything except the culture of making movies: "She was not one to read the newspaper, and she never listened to the news on the radio. Her whole life was making movies, having fun, and wearing pretty clothes. She was too young to know what a Communist was. All she knew about was cashmere sweaters." So she was in many ways a typical teenager of the time, except that she had exceptional beauty and exceptional ambition. She was already famous, but she wanted to be more famous and she wanted a happy marriage to a particular sort of man: "I want someone who can keep me in horses."

Making *A Place in the Sun* taught her to take her profession seriously; it also taught her that acting was an art. Her two mentors were George Stevens and Montgomery Clift, her costar. To a teenage girl, Monty Clift was dreamy handsome. She'd never met anybody so handsome. Not even John Derek or Glenn Davis or Peter Lawford, all of whom she'd had crushes on, could match Clift's beauty. So of course she fell in love with him. But he didn't want that kind of love. Monty was a tortured soul. His guru acting coach, Mira Rostova, said he "was totally split sexually. That was the core of his tragedy, because he never stopped being conflicted and he never stopped feeling guilty about being conflicted."

Clift was a New York actor who liked very little about Hollywood culture, and he had no clear idea in the beginning who Elizabeth Taylor was, only that she was very young and very beautiful. When Paramount insisted that he attend the premiere of *The Heiress* with her, he balked, saying he didn't want to go. But the studio was adamant, and so he went, along with the ever-present Rostova, and a press agent named Harvey Zim. On the way, they picked up Taylor, and according to Zim, "She looked ravishing, and she was so foul-mouthed and unconcerned about going to this premiere that everybody else relaxed in the limousine too." Though still in her teens, she was an old pro at such events and embraced the limelight. Clift, on the other hand, was the tortured artist, shy, difficult, complicated, brooding, aloof. After the film was over, he told Taylor they had to leave, that he couldn't stand the whole scene. Only he didn't call her Elizabeth; he called her "Bessie Mae." He told her that it made her unique in his eyes. It was also a way to deflect the yearning teenager's romantic feelings for him.

The actress Diana Lynn gave a wonderful description of Elizabeth Taylor and Montgomery Clift as they appeared that night at a reception given by the William Wylers: "The combination of their beauty was staggering. Elizabeth was hypnotically beautiful—almost embarrassingly so. She was a perfect voluptuous little doll. And those great violet eyes fringed by double lashes." Taylor, she went on, possessed "an enigmatic power and magnetism behind her looks which gave her beauty—and his—a sultry depth. One could see her as a goddess, mother, seductress, wife. One could see him as prince, saint, and madman."

Clift was the first Method actor Taylor had ever encountered, and his dedication to craft had a pronounced effect upon her. To enhance his performance, Clift insisted that Rostova be put on the payroll to assist him in creating his character. Rostova functioned as a kind of second director, and there are many stories about her strange presence on sets. Most directors didn't like it, and Elia Kazan threw her off the set of *Wild River* in 1960. Stevens put up with her in *A Place in the Sun*, as he did with another ever-present woman on the set, Elizabeth Taylor's stage-managing mother, Sara Taylor. Stevens did not, however, let the youthful Taylor get away with just being beautiful. He had her do retake after retake in scenes with Clift, and he could be bitingly critical, telling her on one occasion that she wasn't making *Lassie Comes Home to a Place in the Sun*. She left the set weeping after that put-down. Taylor had a serious temper, and more than once she got very angry with Stevens. She had also to deal with her hovering, watchful mother, who didn't want her meeting Clift alone in his dressing room. She complained about her mother all the time, calling her "a real pain in the ass."

Stevens and Ivan Moffat would have agreed with that assessment. They both found Sara Taylor's presence such a nuisance as to be almost laughable. Stevens recalled, "When we had lunch in the studio commissary, Mrs. Taylor would preface most of her remarks with 'Elizabeth thinks' or 'Elizabeth says' until I finally felt like shouting 'Why don't you let Elizabeth say it for herself?' " And once when Moffat said hello to Elizabeth and asked how she was, the ubiquitous mother replied, "Oh, hello, Mr. Moffat. Elizabeth is fine. She's having a wonderful time." Like most red-blooded males, Moffat wanted to date Elizabeth, and there are reports that he did date her during the making of that film. In his own words, all he said about her, apart from extolling her great beauty, was, "I once began kissing her and she seemed to like it, but unfortunately there was no time for more, she's always so busy."

Taylor's propensity for salty language contrasted so sharply with her beauty and youth that everybody was always a little bit stunned by it. She swore like a longshoreman. Blaine Waller, a young photographer friend of Clift's, described Taylor pretty completely: "She wore an awful lot of makeup, she smoked like a fiend, and she used more four-letter words than any of us put together, and boy was she gorgeous!" Another time he said, "The fun thing about her was that dirty, filthy, foul mouth of hers. The things she said were so shocking because you didn't expect any kind of coarseness to pass those gorgeous lips." Clift cursed a lot, too. When he was trying to break free once and for all from a strong-willed mother who disapproved of his sexual predilections, he began every sentence directed to her with "fuck" or "shit." Oddly, the two stars also shared another thing. They were both unusually hirsute. Because of his excessive body hair, Clift refused to do a swimming scene in *A Place in the Sun*. People thought they looked like twins, and Clift himself, who had a twin sister, felt he was closer in looks to Elizabeth than to his sister.

Nobody knows whether they ever consummated their love for each other. The answer is probably not, although Clift was certainly keenly aware of her physicality. During a scene in the film when Elizabeth was wearing a white strapless evening gown, Monty told her sotto voce, "Your tits are fantastic, Bessie Mae, just fantastic." Taylor was crazy about Monty and wrote him passionate love letters, which he routinely shared with a gay boyfriend. In any event, Taylor's lifelong friendship with Monty would become part of the pattern of her life, a selfless display of her generous spirit and loyalty.

The film was shot in the fall of 1949, and after completing studio scenes, they went on location, shooting outdoor footage at Cascade Lake and Lake Tahoe in late October, when there was already snow on the ground, which had to be hosed off. Mira Rostova thought that Stevens didn't like having her around, but he didn't say much to her or to the actors. Ivan Moffat, Stevens's friend and associate producer, who came up with the title *A Place in the Sun*, said that Stevens at first objected to Rostova's presence but realized that she boosted Monty's self-confidence.

Stevens liked to play recordings of music to create a mood or atmosphere for the actors. Rostova remembered that "he communicated with them through body language and facial expressions." "Stevens," she said, "had the reputation of being a kind of fearsome fellow—very severe. There were times he played his role to the hilt."

Taylor never forgot a scene that Stevens made them do over and over. Standing on a float in the middle of Lake Tahoe, Monty had to drop Taylor into the freezing water again and again. As the retakes continued, Sara Taylor reported that Elizabeth was menstruating and couldn't go on any longer. Stevens told Clift to drop her into the icy lake one more time. Taylor said she could have killed him.

Stevens insisted on seemingly endless retakes of her scenes with Clift. Stevens wanted Angela Vickers to be warmer, more caring, more loving than the cold, materialistic rich girl of Dreiser's novel. And Stevens would get from Taylor her best performance to date. When he stayed up late rewriting dialogue, Taylor would balk at having to learn new lines the next day. And one famous line in the film that she didn't like at all was the one Stevens wanted her to say when she realizes the depth of her love for George and George for her. Stevens had added a line of dialogue the night before, just five words: "Tell Mama . . . tell Mama all." But upon seeing those words, the seventeen-year-old angrily asked, "Forgive me, but what the hell is this?" She didn't believe a girl her age would say that, but Stevens insisted she do it his way, and the line stayed in. Stevens said later, "Elizabeth dissolved when she had to say 'tell Mama.' She thought it was outrageous she had to say that—she was jumping into a sophistication beyond her time." Biographer William Mann sees that moment in *A Place in the Sun* as the turning point in Taylor's career: "With that one radiant scene, she became one of the great movie stars."

More recently, a feminist critic, using language only a brain surgeon would understand, claims that the "Tell Mama" line "overrides our prefrontal cortex. Like a heat-seeking missile, it hones in on that aft-brain. Scan the brain of a viewer during that scene, and you would likely see the amygdala light up."

What seems more to the point is that those words, "Tell Mama all," became, in fact, a kind of mantra for Taylor in her real life. She had a particular gift for listening and sympathizing with men like Rock Hudson and James Dean, who found in her the wisdom and nonjudgmental sympathy to understand and accept them. In Texas, both men would, in fact, tell Mama all.

Years later, Stevens summed up his impressions of Taylor at that time in her life. "If she thought I was more severe [with her] than needed, she'd spit fire." But, he continued, she'd forget about the whole episode by the next morning. "The only thing," he said, "was to prod her a bit into realizing her dramatic potential."

Due to the combination of Clift's meticulous preparation and professional intensity, coupled with Stevens's craftsmanship and story sense, Taylor gave an incandescent performance. And she knew it, too. In *Elizabeth Taylor: An Informal Memoir* (1965), she stated, "The first time I ever considered *acting* when I was young was in *A Place in the Sun*." From watching

Clift, she came up with her own definition of Method: "They evidently sort of work themselves into a thing by transplanting themselves out of reality and making the fiction reality." She thought the key was concentration.

But she also credited Stevens for his direction, saying, years later, "He didn't make me feel like a puppet. He was an insinuating director. He gave indications of what he wanted but didn't tell you specifically what to do or how to move." Instead, she explained, "[h]e would just say, 'No, stop—that's not quite right,' and make you get it from your insides and do it again until it was the way he wanted it."

Montgomery Clift, like James Dean after him, never gave Stevens his full due. Ever the perfectionist, Clift considered Stevens a craftsman, not an artist. Clift, after all, had spent a night on death row in a prison as preparation for the final scenes of the film, when his character is awaiting execution. That's how serious and artistic he was. Method-inclined actors and auteur critics were always categorizing Stevens in that manner— craftsman, not artist; journeyman, not auteur. Method actors like Clift tended to underestimate Stevens. To see the kind of intellect and depth that Stevens brought to the study of actors, is there a better, more accurate picture of Elizabeth Taylor than what Stevens said about her? "She has been kept in a cocoon by her mother, by her studio, by the fact that she's the adored child who has been given everything she ever wanted since the age of eight. What most people don't realize is there has been a smoldering spirit of revolt in Elizabeth for a long time." And Stevens was able to use that kind of insight to get the results he wanted.

Clift introduced both Stevens and Taylor to their first taste of Method acting and its handmaiden, angst, and both director and actress would find themselves encountering the Method once again, in spades, in the next movie they would make together, this one down in Texas.

✢

In her private life, Elizabeth Taylor seemed to embody the ideals and romanticism of MGM's version of reality. *Father of the Bride* (1950), starring Spencer Tracy, featured Taylor as a beautiful, naïve, conventional young woman whose wedding is based upon a love-conquers-all fantasy. Audiences ate it up, as well as the sequel, *Father's Little Dividend*, which came out the next year. What was troubling, however, was that the young star seemed to believe the premises of such films: that a girl's ideal destiny was to marry, have babies, and live happily ever after.

In making *Father of the Bride*, Elizabeth Taylor lived out every girl's dream—or so she believed. She would marry and become a fulfilled person. She had several motives, chief among them that she wanted to escape the omnipresent, ever-monitoring eyes of her mother. On sets, Sara Taylor was almost a parody of a stage mother. She had a complex set of hand signals to advise her daughter when to raise her voice, how to move, how to build a scene.

By this time, Taylor had been through several widely publicized romances—one with football star Glenn Davis and another with rich boy William Pawley. But naïve as she might have been, she was not receptive to the lucrative advances made by one of the strangest men in Hollywood, Howard Hughes. The forty-four-year old Texan had spotted her on the cover of *Life* (August 22, 1949) and courted her, or tried to, in his usual manner. First, he ingratiated himself with her parents by buying some paintings from Francis Taylor's gallery, and then he treated the whole family to a weekend in Reno. Over dinner, Hughes, worth a fortune of $150 million, offered a million of it as dowry and promised to finance Elizabeth's pictures. Elizabeth's father said no, but later he told his lover, Adrian, that he had been very close to agreeing to Hughes's deal. His daughter was adamantly against it. The next day, when Hughes had his aide, Johnny Meyer, take her an attaché case filled with jewelry, Elizabeth exclaimed, "Tell that madman to stay away from me. He bores me with all his talk about money. He reminds me of L. B. Mayer," whom she despised.

Then she met somebody who seemed to have it all. Nicky Hilton, the very rich son of multimillionaire hotelier Conrad Hilton, was handsome, debonair when he wasn't falling-down drunk, and something of a "sexual athlete," as Joan Collins would later claim. He was also a habitual gambler, as a newspaper columnist tried to warn Sara: "I told her myself that all Nicky ever did was drink until he was drunk and shoot craps with

Glen[n] McCarthy"—the selfsame Texas oilman who had a similar taste for excess.

When Nicky laid eyes on Elizabeth Taylor, he ran and told his father he had met the most beautiful woman in the world. After a brief, much-photographed romance, they were married in a ceremony attended by Hollywood royalty while thousands of fans crowded the street outside the church. Their marriage of true love lasted, Taylor later said, a grand total of two weeks. She didn't know how to be a wife, and Nicky certainly didn't know how to be a husband. She was utterly helpless in all the practical requirements of a wife, and Nicky couldn't stop drinking himself senseless, and, worse, he had a particularly nasty habit of physical abuse. Or as Taylor put it in an interview with Larry King decades later, "Nick kind of got a kick out of beating the shit out of me." They stormed across Europe in a seemingly endless honeymoon of misery and suffering, and not quite a year later, the bride divorced him.

Waiting in the wings was husband number two. Michael Wilding was a leading British cinema actor, an urbane and kind man nineteen years her senior. He knew he was too old to marry this girl, and then there was this other woman in his life, Marlene Dietrich, the Blue Angel herself, whom he also loved. Taylor was nineteen, Dietrich forty-nine. One could give him children, the other not. But he loved them both.

At age nineteen, Elizabeth Taylor was more eager than ever to get married a second time. Wilding was, by his own admission, a fairly passive person, and he remained conflicted, torn between his affection for two strong women. Sam Marx, a producer (it was he who had put Elizabeth in *Lassie Comes Home*) recounted an evening in New York when he observed all the principals in action: "I saw Elizabeth at the St. Regis. She and Montgomery Clift were together, slugging vodka. I joined them and the atmosphere was very tense. Later that evening I saw Elizabeth with Wilding. He looked so bored. And later that same night I was in '21' and I saw Wilding with Marlene Dietrich. And he was so alive. The difference was astonishing. I wondered then what Elizabeth was getting into."

In the end, Wilding succumbed to Elizabeth's entreaties. He could not help but be pushed into marrying this beautiful, voluptuous, and spirited young woman. She pressed him at every opportunity, she bought her own engagement ring, she proposed to him ("Dear Mr. Shilly-shally, will you marry me?"), and she set the date for the marriage, February 21, 1952. That day, Wilding got his first taste of what it meant to be with Elizabeth Taylor when he saw thousands of Londoners waiting outside the Caxton Hall registry office for a glimpse of his bride and later when they gathered outside the couple's hotel and clamored for them to come to the window and wave, like royalty.

Wilding arrived in Hollywood trailing clouds of British film glory; he was the most popular postwar British actor for three straight years, but he failed to gain traction in Hollywood. This despite the enthusiasm of Jack Warner, who told the *Hollywood Reporter*, "I believe Michael Wilding is the biggest romantic male discovery since Rudolph Valentino." Instead, Wilding was utterly wasted in movies like *The Egyptian* (1954), in which he played a skin-darkened pharaoh. The director, Michael Curtiz, had once, back in 1946, had an affair with Elizabeth Taylor's mother. Hollywood was a very small town.

Soon, Wilding held the same opinion of the studio system as his wife, writing in his memoir, *Apple Sauce: The Story of My Life* (1982), "In 1952 Hollywood was still the film capital of the world and still run, as it always had been, like a slave city. The producers were dictators, the agents were ten-per-cent spongers, while the actors were treated like blancmanges, to be cast in any mould which suited the studios' politics." And those politics— this was the era of blacklisting—were depressingly reactionary.

Michael Wilding was in several ways a version of Elizabeth's father, Francis Taylor. He was quiet, a homebody, a man of taste and judgment, and a man who could be eclipsed pretty easily by a strong-willed woman. The marriage to Wilding brought a pleasing, calm, stay-at-home interlude in Elizabeth Taylor's life. They had two children within two years, and Elizabeth surrounded herself with a menagerie of three dogs, three cats, and a duck, all of which had the run of the place and relieved themselves whither they pleased. Her husband told one guest, "Our home is like an animal shelter." The house was typically a mess, and Elizabeth Taylor was never going to be a housewife in any conventional sense. But they both knew how to drink and they kept up a steady flow of wine and spirits.

Life in Hollywood was no cup of tea. The blacklist mood seeped easily into accusations of homosexuality, a charge as damaging as being labeled a Communist. When Hedda Hopper, a family friend, learned of the forthcoming nuptials, she warned Taylor in person that Wilding was gay and linked him with his longtime friend and fellow British actor Stewart Granger. Although Taylor brushed off the accusation and Wilding himself dismissed the charge as risible ("What an allegation to make about two of the greatest womanisers in the business!"), there remains considerable speculation that perhaps he was bisexual. In any event, it didn't matter to Elizabeth.

Their marriage produced two children: Michael Howard Wilding, born on January 6, 1953, and Christopher Edward Wilding, born on his mother's birthday, February 27, 1955.

Giant offered Taylor the prospect of a kind of vacation from marriage as well as the opportunity to work under Stevens's direction again. They'd had some rocky moments in *A Place in the Sun,* but making that film had been crucial to her development as a serious actress. Now *Giant* promised to recharge her career just as *A Place in the Sun* had.

4

Plantation Life

On May 19, 1955, the day after the Off-to-Texas luncheon, shooting on *Giant* began on Sound Stage 15 on the Warner Bros. lot. The glamour of location shooting would come later, and all of the interiors in the film would be shot at the studio in Burbank. The schedule would closely follow the narrative set forth in the script, and over the next six months filming would take place at the studio, on two locations, and back at the studio again. For a film with all those sweeping vistas, *Giant* was a very intimate indoor drama, as well.

The only stumble that first day was Bick Benedict—that is, Rock Hudson. His shaky start was a bit surprising because Stevens had already laid the groundwork for how to play the rancher patriarch.

Earlier that spring, Stevens and Hudson had had lunch together in the Green Room, and afterward, Stevens, quiet, deliberative, even "hypnotic," asked Hudson if he would like to see the house he would own in the film. Hudson said yes, of course, though in fact there were many houses on any movie studio lot, and he had been in many fake houses at Universal, from small-town Americana homes to tepees, so he didn't understand the importance of Stevens's point until they came to the "house": "And there it was, in sections, the raw lumber." Then Stevens asked him what color he wanted it painted, and Hudson replied, "Well, Victorian . . . I don't know. Tan with brown trim, I guess." Stevens said okay and ordered the workmen to paint it just as Hudson had decided. "Well, it was my house," Hudson said, and he always gave full credit to Stevens. In 1983, two years before Rock's death, he recalled, "He was like a god to me. I mean, I followed him around like a puppy. . . "

Stevens defined Hudson's character so effectively that Rock in a sense became Bick Benedict on that very day: "I was rich and strong and bigoted and powerful, so I didn't have to play it. I was there." Stevens also asked Rock who he thought should play opposite him: Grace Kelly or Elizabeth Taylor. Rock picked Taylor. In any event, Stevens's cagey directorial method made Rock feel very empowered.

Still, he was nervous on the first day of shooting and overdid the dinner table scene in the Lynnton dining room, where all eyes are trained on him, a tall stranger from Texas dressed in a western-cut suit and high-heeled boots. His name is Jordan Benedict, implying status and power, a kind of pope of the range. He has come to Virginia to buy a stallion for breeding purposes on his ranch in faraway Texas. To the rest of those at the dinner table, he is an object of curiosity, someone who hails from a place they know little about. Leslie's ditzy mother (Judith Evelyn) thinks he's from Nevada, the Englishman, Sir David Karfrey (Rod Taylor), is very curious about the size of his ranch—a subject Texans are supposedly close-mouthed about—and Leslie, who is engaged to Karfrey, seems more than a little interested in everything about Mr. Benedict.

Rock, however, did not respond the way Stevens wanted, and Stevens took him aside and reshot the scene with Hudson by himself at the table and the other actors in the background, off-camera. Ivan Moffat said he was "soft, petulant" in an early take. Stevens, who earlier had filled Rock with soaring confidence, telling him he was a wealthy rancher used to everybody's bowing to his will, now wanted him to be surprised and intimidated by the superior-seeming status of the Lynntons and the Englishman—hence the strategy of isolating him without the other actors and making Rock seem distant and wary. According to Rock, "He spoke quietly to me through a megaphone. I didn't have to act the scene because I felt strange and uneasy."

On the sixth day of shooting, May 24, Rock was still having trouble with his interpretation of Bick. According to dialogue coach Bob Hinkle, both Rock and Taylor bungled the scene where Leslie challenges Bick at the breakfast table. She has stayed up all night reading books about Texas, and armed with her new knowledge, Leslie comes to the breakfast table eager to question Bick. She shows her intelligence by challenging the hagiographic history she has been reading, saying straight out, "Why, we really stole Texas from Mexico, didn't we, Mr. Benedict? I mean away from Mexico." Bick bristles at this heresy and defends the honor of Texas.

But Stevens didn't like the way they played the scene. Again, Bob Hinkle: "Rock overacted a bit, almost as if he were in a silent movie—using broad gestures and facial expression, practically mugging for the camera." Elizabeth was off, too: "Liz, for her part, was a little too flighty when she poked at Rock. The tone just wasn't right."

At this point, Stevens stopped the filming of this scene and told Hinkle, Hudson, and Taylor to meet him in his office, which was nearby. Then he had Hinkle read Rock's lines while Rock listened, and, strangely, he had Elizabeth read her mother's lines. (They read through the scene, then did it again at Stevens's orders, but when Stevens said to read it a third time, Elizabeth burst out, "Damn it, George, what the fuck do you want me to do? I don't understand what you're trying to do here.") But they did it again, and then Stevens ordered them to return to the set and shoot the scene without explaining anything. The next day, when he showed the rushes, the results were obvious: "Bick Benedict was royally PO'd at Leslie Lynnton, with tension in his face and curt answers to her questions, because Rock Hudson was royally PO'd at George Stevens." Taylor was much better, too, because Stevens "had taken the edge off of Elizabeth Taylor." Hinkle, who saw Stevens as a "master psychologist," was very impressed. Stevens had achieved his goal not by directing but by "*allowing* people to do what you want them to do by making them think it was their idea." And Rock saw it as well, telling Hinkle, "I'm never gonna question that man again."

In the meantime, the two costars quickly became fast friends. During that first week's filming, Elizabeth invited Rock and his date, Phyllis Gates, to dinner at her home with her husband, Michael Wilding. After a few drinks, Rock was emboldened to ask, "How can you stand being so beautiful?"

"Beautiful? Beautiful! I'm Minnie Mouse," Taylor replied. She then bounded into her bedroom, only to return a few minutes later transformed into Minnie Mouse, with her hair pinned back and wearing a little red skirt and black pumps. It was the beginning of a beautiful friendship. Everybody kept drinking, and they didn't stop until 4:00 A.M. It was one of those nights. Rock and Liz had to be at the studio at 6:00 A.M., in just two hours, to film the scene where Leslie's younger sister gets married. The nuptials of Bick and Leslie were not part of the script, and instead Stevens used the sister's wedding to dramatize Rock's return to Maryland to collect his slightly estranged wife and their children and take them back to Texas. In a wordless scene, Bick comes up behind Leslie while the ceremony is going on, and, feeling his presence, Leslie turns to enfold herself in his arms. The brilliance of the scene lies in the fact that we never saw their wedding. So this wedding reminds us even more forcefully of the power of the ceremony that we have not seen. Hudson remembered the reaction as the scene was being shot: "All the women on the set—seamstresses, wardrobe women, hairdressers—were all sobbing. 'Oh, what a moving scene.'"

Both Hudson and Taylor reflect a sense of longing and anguish, but as Rock explained later, "We were both so hung over we couldn't speak." Their misery can clearly be seen on-screen—the blank, glazed punishment of hangovers. They threw up several times before the whole sequence was completed. They were pros. That was Rock's memory.

Elizabeth remembered something else—the first evidence that she was no longer the shielded adolescent of *A Place in the Sun*. Apart from the hangover that day, May 27 (the eighth day of shooting), her experience foreshadowed things to come.

Taylor had lunch and waited in her dressing room to be called to the set, but nobody called her. Eventually, she came out, to find everything eerily quiet on the set, the lights off, the extras standing around, and Stevens slumped over in his chair before suddenly erupting, "Just who the hell do you think you are to keep these people waiting? Just how far do you think you can go? Just how much do you think you can get away with?" When she explained what she had been doing, getting her makeup right and a dress ironed, Stevens kept up his derisive comments, mocking the idea that her makeup and her costume were more important than that of other actors in the scene. As it turned out, the person who was supposed to summon Taylor had not done so, but Stevens never apologized, and she did the scene under great emotional duress, wondering later if Stevens's angry outburst had been calculated, if he had done "all that deliberately for the sake of the scene."

Her main solace in days to come was the burgeoning friendship with Rock. They developed their own private intimacies. He called her "Bessie" (much as Montgomery Clift called her Bessie May), and she called him "Rockabye." They talked a kind of comic southern pidgin, one saying "I daz" and the other "No you dazn't." They laughed a lot. Blinded by her beauty, most men were surprised and delighted by Elizabeth Taylor's playfulness and down-to-earth manner.

ᛦ

After nine days of shooting interior scenes, ending on May 28, Stevens and cast and crew flew to Charlottesville, Virginia, to begin filming the outdoor scenes depicting Bick Benedict's arrival in the lush green horse-breeding country of Albemarle County. Jack Warner had lobbied Stevens to use the Colonial house on the Warner Ranch, at Calabasas, near L.A., for the exteriors. It would save $27,000 (around $216,000 in today's currency). But Warner couldn't get Stevens to forgo his idea of shooting the opening sequence in Virginia.

Whenever possible, Stevens wanted the reality of the actual place, not a simulacrum. The studio system was very adept at converting settings in California into whatever location was called for. Douglas Sirk's *Written on the Wind*, another Texas-based film of 1956, was shot entirely on studio sets, and it shows. Nothing looks authentic. The film has its admirers (especially in France), but no one has ever celebrated its granular depiction of a place.

Stevens had his reasons for filming on location. First, he was being faithful to Edna Ferber's novel. After all, by the time the film was released, millions of people had read the novel, and they would expect Leslie's home territory to be a recognizable Virginia. Second, he wanted a vivid contrast between two very different landscapes, Virginia versus Texas. Third, he wanted a southern belle aura, a kind of update of *Gone with the Wind*, a film Stevens much admired. Finally, he had always enjoyed shooting on location.

The trip to Virginia put Stevens further behind schedule. Now it was May, and here they were in Virginia, when, originally, he had expected to be in Texas by March or April. Stevens was probably very lucky that they didn't start shooting in Marfa in the spring, because from February through May, it's so windy in the desert that it feels almost like a fifth season.

Stevens chose Albemarle County because of its beauty and its historical associations with the Old South. The Belmont horse farm, seven miles east of Charlottesville, was an estate dating back to about 1730. An adjoining estate had belonged to Peter Jefferson, Thomas Jefferson's father. The whole area was marinated in history. Monticello was only a few miles away, and the homes of two other presidents, James Madison and James Monroe, were close by, as well.

The first day of shooting, May 31, occurred at Keswick, a small railroad station that Stevens used for the opening shots of the Virginia background. The name was changed to Ardmore in the film.

Stevens saw dramatic visual possibilities in choreographing the arrival of the train with the fluid movements of horses in a fox hunt flowing over hill and dale. He had employed a similar technique in the famous opening scene of *Shane*, when Alan Ladd rides into a valley in Wyoming where the boy Joey (Brandon de Wilde) gazes at horse and rider, who are framed by the antlers of a real deer drinking from a pond.

Grover Vandevender, a former hunt master, was a key figure in the difficult action shots that Stevens imagined. It was his job to coordinate the train's progress with that of the horses. But it was devilishly hard to film. To get it right, Stevens instructed Vandevender to ride the course while they timed him. Then the railroad engineer had to synchronize the train's speed with the running of the horses. And the smoke from the old steam engine had to be exactly the right color or the whole thing would have to be done all over again. Speed, smoke, timing—it wasn't easy, but Stevens had all the patience in the world. They would do it and redo it until he said it was right. Even by this time, so early in the shooting, Stevens was running behind schedule. The original seventy-seven-day shooting schedule, once breached, would be virtually impossible to recover.

The first shots are of a train puffing white smoke into the sky as it rolls through the verdant landscape. Outside, in the rich, green pastures of Virginia, a fox hunt is in progress, horses and riders flashing by, men and women dressed in the traditional color of British foxhunting equestrians. It seems right out of England (or the Old South). The riders were members of the Farmington Hunt Club, a famous foxhunting organization in Albemarle County that counted William Faulkner among its members.

Inside the train, a figure looks out the window. He is wearing a brown business suit and a white Stetson. As he descends from the train, the camera focuses on his western-style cowboy boots, or "high heel boots," a leitmotif in the novel. Indeed, Ferber once considered titling her novel *High Heel Boots*, the footwear that made Texas males look even taller.

After Dr. Lynnton picks up Bick at the train station, they drive down a country lane bordered by white fences. All the while, the horses and their red-jacketed riders are flashing by. At one point, Dr. Lynnton brings the automobile to a halt so that Mr. Benedict can get a better look at War Winds, the horse he has come to view, whereupon Dr. Lynnton's daughter Leslie trots over to greet her father and the visitor beside him. As she returns to join the other riders, Bick and Dr. Lynnton gaze at the departing figure, and Bick comments, "That sure is a beautiful animal." Obviously, he's not talking about the horse.

The magnificent black stallion that she is riding would have been familiar to filmgoers who had seen *Black Beauty* (1946), and although owner and trainer Ralph McCutcheon had originally named the horse Highland

Dale, he now simply called him Beauty or Beaut. For some viewers, seeing a grown-up Elizabeth Taylor on horseback would have evoked memories of her as a twelve-year-old in *National Velvet* (1944).

Although Elizabeth Taylor was an accomplished rider, having learned as a child growing up in England, she was too valuable a property to ride a horse at top speed, so Stevens turned to a local girl, Valley Keene, who everybody in the area knew was the best rider in Albemarle County. Keene had to ride Beaut at a breakneck pace to get the imagery that Stevens wanted.

On the next day, June 1, the filmmakers descended upon the plantation grounds at first light and worked until dusk. All the shooting was outside, since the rooms in the house were too small to accommodate the lighting equipment and cameras, and besides, they had already shot the interior scenes in L.A. They used just one room in the house, for costumes and makeup.

Immediately, Stevens and his team began adjusting reality to fit the script. Belmont had been freshly painted and looked sparkling in the late-spring sunlight, but the script called for the house to be a bit dowdy and run-down, so at Stevens's bidding, technicians sprayed the four gleaming white columns with dirty water. It needed to look aged and redolent of the past. In the film's dynamic, the Virginia plantation would belong to an eclipsed historical moment: The Old South was truly gone with the wind; the future resided in the Southwest, in Texas.

But a significant vestige of southern history resides within the Lynnton family household—the black butler, played by veteran character actor Napolean Whiting. A native of Mississippi, Whiting had a long career in Hollywood playing stereotypical servant roles. In *Giant*, he appears to be almost family, and there are numerous reaction shots reflecting his understanding of the domestic dramas unfolding around him. In the novel and the film, Leslie seems unaware of this servant's status, as compared to her intense interest in the Mexican servants at Reata, but Bick, in the novel at least, likes to point out the prevalence of "nigger shacks" in Virginia to counter Leslie's criticism of conditions in the Mexican village.

Thanks to Stevens's open-set policy, people from Charlottesville came out to Belmont in droves, eager to get a glimpse of Elizabeth Taylor and Rock Hudson—both at the height of their physical attractiveness. Police were brought in to prevent trespassing and to keep overeager sightseers from disrupting the shooting.

At times, though, the gorgeous black horse stole the show. During breaks, the horse's owner would sit down near the horse and ask him if he was tired, and Beaut would lay his head in McCutcheon's lap and relax. The horse's reward for an especially good take was a Coca-Cola, his favorite beverage. Stevens said if all his actors and actresses were as easy to manage as Beauty, it would take no time at all to shoot the film. If only.

But there is one odd thing about the Virginia location. In the film, it's not Virginia; it's Maryland, the first indication of which is the Maryland license plate on Dr. Lynnton's car at the "Ardmore" train station. The reason for the change from Virginia to Maryland is quite simple. The Warner Bros. legal team wanted to steer clear of anything having to do with the powerful Kleberg family. Stevens commented on this in an interview with a film critic from *The Washington Star*: "It is a touchy sort of story, you see, and without changing any of the details, we are getting as far away as possible from any resemblance to actual people living or dead."

The shoot in Virginia was wrapped up in four days. Everybody got along splendidly and there were no problems whatsoever. Stevens got the footage he wanted, and Jack Warner liked it, always a positive.

But when Edna Ferber, never one to withhold an opinion, saw the rushes, she didn't like them one bit. What she "liked least of all" was the sequence of early scenes in the Lynnton house. In a letter dated August 15, 1955, she expressed her disappointment to her friend Henry Ginsberg: "I found Taylor a simpering mess, Dr. Lynnton dull, and the Lynnton dining room a sort of apartment house dinette instead of the candlelit, crystal, silver thing of spacious elegance I had expected." Ferber's classist assumptions come into play here, as usual. Leslie and the doctor represent for her the best ideals of liberal values backed by good taste and quiet money. But it's clear that the Lynnton home and the family's economic circumstances reflect a reduced version of the grandeur of the plantation mansions celebrated in many southern-based films. Economically, the Lynnton family needs to get those daughters married, and Leslie's marriage to Bick is, from Ferber's perspective, a step down rather than a step up. But the Old South and its genteel world belong to the past. Marrying Karfrey would guarantee Leslie a comfortable, conventional, and complacent life. Instead, she's drawn to the romance and challenge of leaving all of that for a new life in Texas.

Ferber also objected to the name War Winds (My Mistake in the novel). She thought it "difficult to enunciate and hard to hear." She suggested alternatives—Swift Winds, Follow Me, Care Free, High Boy, and Green Light—and declared that her choice was Swift Winds. Based on the frequency of errors regarding the horse's name in numerous critical studies, Ferber might have been onto something. One critic, for example, insists that the horse is named Whirlwind. In any event, Stevens stuck with War Winds, probably because the war was still much on his mind.

The Virginia shoot was short and sweet—four days, May 31–June 3—but Texas awaited. Leaving Virginia's verdant landscape for the wide-open prairie would feel like a nineteenth-century journey to the unknown West—except it was made by plane, not wagon train, and in a matter of hours, not weeks, they would enter an altogether new republic.

5

Lone Star

The role of wildcatter Jett Rink, the brooding ranch hand who becomes a wealthy oilman, looked like a surefire cinch for an Oscar nomination, and the scramble to land that part even outpaced in interest and intensity the search for the rancher and the rancher's wife. Stevens said as much in a newspaper interview: "Of all the roles, that of Jett Rink has been the subject of much speculation, report and discussion," and, he added, "More actors have bucked for this part than for any of the others."

But in the beginning, Stevens knew exactly whom he wanted, and before casting any other parts, he offered the role to Alan Ladd, fresh from his outstanding performance in *Shane*. Ladd credited his success in *Shane* entirely to Stevens: "I learned more about acting from that man in a few months than I had in my entire life up until then. Stevens is the best in the business. He knows exactly how to handle actors, how to relax them and win their confidence." Like a lot of other actors who angled for a role in *Giant*, Ladd read Ferber's novel and fell in love with the role of Bick Benedict. But to his chagrin, Stevens wanted him for Jett Rink, the second male lead, a role that, in Stevens's view, might well overshadow that of the rancher. Although Ladd was older than many seeking the part,

Stevens believed that with proper lighting in the early scenes, Ladd would age quite naturally as the story unfolded over a span of twenty-five to thirty years. At five six, he was used to being altered by the alchemy of film.

But as much as Ladd admired Stevens, he turned down the offer because he didn't think he could afford to give up his hard-earned leading-man status. As he was soon to realize, that pride led to the worst decision of his career. One day at the studio commissary as filming was nearing its end, Stevens happened to run into him and commented, "You know, you could have spared me all this aggravation if you had taken the role." That aggravation had a name: It was James Dean.

With Ladd out, Stevens, as usual, had a roster of candidates suggested by the studio, including everybody from Marlon Brando to Gordon Mac-Rae. Somebody suggested Frank Sinatra on the basis of *Young at Heart* and *Suddenly.* That went nowhere. But among the most unlikely of candidates, Richard Burton probably took the prize. Although he wanted the part badly, he took himself out of the running, writing Stevens in March 1955, "I have worked at the 'Texas' material, but to no avail. I just don't seem to drawl in the right places and my 'You-alls' don't quite come off."

As for other possibilities, Robert Mitchum was the most obvious choice. "Mitchum any good for Jett?" asked Edna Ferber in a letter to Henry Ginsberg. Mitchum was a natural; he owned surly; he could do outsider resentment with a curl of the lip. Eventually his agent got in touch with Stevens to tell him his client's schedule was closing fast, and Stevens let it close.

Ferber also passed along an intriguing suggestion from her niece, Janet Fox Goldsmith, who thought that they might cast Jett "against type, for a kind of sympathy." Specifically, someone "smallish, compact, quick on his feet—a sort of Gene Kelly with a quick punch." Gene Kelly seemed sort of ridiculous, but the description did fit a rising young star named James Dean.

Stevens was already aware of Dean, having secured a copy of "The Capture of Jesse James," a teleplay from CBS's program *You Are There!* (February 8, 1953). He screened it on September 28, 1954. Dean played the assassin Robert Ford. Stevens was impressed but kept his own counsel.

In the spring, Dean launched a concerted effort to land the Jett Rink role. According to Stevens, "My secretary, Leona, had a war started with Jimmy Dean because she was afraid of beatniks and he came and sat in her office with those dirty blue jeans on and those boots, itchin' and scratchin' and bothering her an awful lot." Jimmy's persistence paid off in the end, Stevens recalled. "Freddy Guiol and I got a kick out of him. We used to talk to him and got very well acquainted. He was a smart guy. Whatever your kind of atmosphere, he fits into it."

In *Screen Stories* (November 1956), Stevens commented on how Dean landed the part. "Physically and temperamentally," he wrote, "Jimmy Dean was wrong for the part. Jett was a tall, powerful, extroverted character. There were a dozen actors who seemed more likely choices." But, Stevens continued, "[w]e felt that the part needed an extremely good actor, and so we gave the script to Jimmy to read." He read it and came back and said, "That guy's me, I could do that." At the top of his copy of the script, Dean had written above the name of Jett Rink, "That's me, that's me because I can convince myself that it will be me, really me."

Meanwhile, the excitement about *East of Eden*, released on March 9, was growing louder and louder, and when Stevens viewed the film with his son, George, Jr., both were impressed with Dean's performance.

Jimmy's friend Lew Bracker sheds light on Dean's maneuverings in the early days of negotiations regarding *Giant*. In March 1955, before Jimmy signed on the dotted line, he invited Bracker to lunch at the Green Room, and shortly after Bracker arrived, the two were joined by George Stevens and Henry Ginsberg. Jimmy introduced Bracker by name but didn't indicate who he was or why he was there. As the luncheon got under way, it became clear to Bracker that the director and producer were trying simultaneously to sell Jimmy on *Giant* and making clear to him who was in charge. Jimmy's tactic was to listen, then look at Bracker, who never said a word. But his presence conveyed the idea, unspoken, that he was some kind of adviser whom Jimmy trusted. The whole luncheon was a duel between Jimmy and his overlords, as he saw them. He was trying to set up the idea that he could not be expected to go along with Stevens's "autocratic ways on the set," and Bracker's suit-and-tie presence helped tilt the discussion in Jimmy's favor. Or so Jimmy believed. What Ginsberg said of Dean might have been said by dozens of producers and directors: "There were many things about this boy that many people wouldn't have overlooked. I overlooked them because he had talent."

On March 16, Warner Bros. announced that Dean had landed the role. At one point, Stevens offered a very perceptive comment about why Dean was his choice: "There is a lot in this character that Jimmy Dean presumes to be." A description of the Jett Rink character in Warner Bros. production materials might have applied to Dean himself: "Discontented, cheated out of his birthright, feeling deeply the inequality and unfairness of his position, it must have been hard for Jett Rink." Whatever the final reason, Stevens decided to gamble along with the mercurial young actor.

Dean's meteoric rise to the pinnacle of Hollywood stardom occurred in a very short period of time, from winning the part of Cal Trask in *East of Eden* in 1954 to completing *Giant* in September 1955—eighteen months of passionate work and accelerating fame. To Dean, though, his success seemed much too slow. He had expected it to happen literally overnight. At the same time, he was a nervous bundle of volatile polarities, of open aggression and little-boy wounds, of brash bad-boy behavior and exposed nerve endings. Admirers called him a rebel; others said his initials stood for juvenile delinquent.

꧁

Born on February 8, 1931, in Marion, Indiana, to parents ill-suited to each other, the boy spent his early childhood wrapped in the warmth and love of his mother, Mildred Dean. The family moved to Fairmount, Indiana, then to Santa Monica, California. James Dean was emotionally healthy and happy the first nine years of his life. Though his father, Winton Dean, was noncommunicative and remote, his mother made up for it with her total devotion to her son. She pampered him, encouraging him to express himself through playacting and dancing and singing. They were everything to each other, and then suddenly it all ended when she died of cancer on July 14, 1940. The loss to Dean was devastating. Now he was alone with his strange, cold, distant, emotionally inarticulate father. Almost overnight, Winton Dean abandoned him, too, sending him back to Indiana to live with an aunt and uncle. The child was put on the same train in California that carried his mother's coffin to Indiana, and every time the train stopped, he jumped off and ran to make sure her coffin was secure and still on it. It was like a scene from *As I Lay Dying*, like the little boy Vardaman drilling holes in his mother's coffin so she can breathe.

The boy's childhood in Indiana was like a Booth Tarkington novel, but with darker tones. His uncle, Marcus Winslow, and his aunt, Ortense, were good, solid people, and they did the best they could to raise the young boy. Marcus taught him all the duties required of a young farm youth, and Ortense cooked hearty country fare and kept a clean, wholesome Quaker household. But a boy's life on a farm was rough-and-tumble. One time, Jimmy fell out of the barn loft and knocked out two front teeth, necessitating that he wear a dental bridge for the rest of his life. Popping out that bridge became a staple part of the grown-up Dean's way of shocking people and getting attention. He had very poor vision, myopia, and was always breaking his glasses as he tore through the world. Such things could happen to anybody, but in the case of Dean, everything that happened to him became heightened, revelatory in the light of his developing personality.

In high school, the wiry little kid with poor eyesight showed considerable skill in basketball, baseball, and track. He was a lot stronger than he looked and was also fiercely competitive. Despite his weak eyesight, he was one of the stars on the basketball team, and in one game he scored fifteen of the team's total of thirty-four points. The Fairmount High yearbook tagged him as a "brilliant senior guard" and "one of the main cogs" on the team. His grades, however, were unimpressive, as reflected in a report card during his junior year: English, D; U.S. History, C; Geometry, C+; Art, A; and, one to take note of, Safety Driving, C+.

Long before he ever heard of Marlon Brando, the boy evinced a passion for riding motorcycles. At age fifteen, he owned a Czech-made CZ motorcycle, which he raced up and down the farmland and through the main street of Fairmount at a top speed of fifty miles per hour while lying flat on the seat. Everybody in Fairmount knew the daredevil sound of "One-Speed" Dean roaring into town.

Jimmy also showed an aptitude for acting, and appeared in several dramatic productions. One of his teachers, Adeline Nall, thought she saw something special in the young boy and encouraged his early training in speech and theater. A hopeful thespian herself, trapped in the boondocks, she found in Dean someone who, she believed, possessed extraordinary gifts. In 1949, Dean won two prizes in drama competitions with his rendition of "A Madman's Manuscript" from Dickens's *The Pickwick Papers*—a first at the state level and a sixth at the national. The poorer finish in the national competition made him furious at his teacher. But it was his refusal to stay within the allotted time limit that brought him down. Despite being warned by Nall and by a judge, he kept all the ad-libs in, and it cost him. But, as he nearly always did, he blamed his failure on an authority figure—in this case, Nall. He laid everything at her feet, saying she hadn't supported him before the judges.

In that not-so-idyllic Indiana boyhood, the boy fell under the influence of the Reverend James DeWeerd, pastor of the Wesleyan Church in Fairmont. A decorated veteran, DeWeerd lived with his mother and liked to act as an unofficial counselor and guide to young boys. He introduced a little bit of bohemia to rural Indiana. He took boys to a nearby YMCA swimming pool, where he encouraged them to swim nude. As might be expected, he was known as "Dr. Weird" within the community of upright Quakers.

The Reverend DeWeerd invited Jimmy over to listen to classical music and read Shakespeare. He also introduced the boy to bullfighting, showing footage of bullfights from his trips to Mexico. He drove Jimmy to the Indy 500 one time. Thus two of Dean's lifelong obsessions—bullfighting and automobile racing—were fostered in that otherwise-quiet community. There was something weird about DeWeerd, though; on at least one occasion he invited Dean to place his hand in the permanent hole in his stomach, the result of a wound at Monte Cassino in World War II. Years later, DeWeerd spoke of himself and Jimmy in a very suggestive manner:

"Jimmy never mentioned our relationship nor did I. It would not have helped either of us." Joe Hyams, a journalist and close friend of Dean's, claims that DeWeerd and Dean had a "homosexual relationship that would endure for many years."

Upon graduation from high school in 1949, Jimmy headed west to Santa Monica to join his father and stepmother, Ethel. The boy hoped to kindle something with his father, and he stayed with Winton and Ethel until it was evident that neither wanted him. Winton Dean was as cold as ever and unable to acknowledge his son's emotional needs. Later on, Dean told Jonathan Gilmore, "I knew within five minutes of being back in Santa Monica at my father's house that it was a miserable, rotten mistake." Winton regarded actors as unmanly and dissolute, dismissing his son's career goals, urging him instead to major in something practical at Santa Monica City College, which he attended in 1949–1950. He majored in physical education, apparently to please his father.

In September 1950, he transferred to UCLA as a prelaw major with a minor in theater arts. Prelaw was probably a crumb for his father. He landed a major role, Malcolm, in a production of *Macbeth*, but the only published notice he got was quite negative. One of Dean's friends, Larry Swindell, later a biographer of Hollywood movie stars and book editor of the *Fort Worth Star-Telegram*, said Dean's performance in *Macbeth* was "terrible." Fellow student William Bast saw the play and thought to himself that this James Dean fellow would never go anywhere as an actor.

At UCLA, Dean joined a fraternity, Sigma Nu, which seems as odd as Lee Harvey Oswald joining the marines. For a short time, he lived at the frat house, where he went through the usual fraternity hazing rituals. Mainly, he kept to himself and didn't participate in other activities. James Bellah, son of author James Warner Bellah, knew why Dean didn't get along in Sigma Nu. "He was too eccentric. . . . He was a born performer; he loved to take the stage. But Sigma Nu was establishment, and Dean was not establishment. He was just undesirable." After getting into a fight with a frat brother, he was kicked out. James Dean, frat boy, is the strangest identity he ever inhabited, however briefly. It didn't matter, though. He dropped out of college altogether in January 1951, later claiming to Hedda Hopper that he "couldn't take the tea-sipping, moss-walled academicians, that academic bull."

William Bast, who died in 2015, would get to know Dean better than most. For a time, they shared an apartment while both scrambled for odd jobs to pay the rent. They spent a lot of time together, and thus began a lifetime for Bast of explaining James Dean. They both dated girls off and on. Beverly Wills, an actress who was the daughter of comedian Joan Davis, told a friend that Dean was "the worst mannered and rudest person" she'd ever dated. He could be the "absolutely cutest guy" one moment and a complete "asshole" the next.

Both Bast and Dean were also dancing around the subject of their own relationship. Bast didn't seem to know if he himself was gay or not, and Dean was open to experimentation. How close they were was not revealed in Bast's highly regarded biography of Dean, published in 1965, but in the second one, in 2006, he filled out the story with an account of a sexual week with Dean in Borrego Springs, in the desert south of Palm Springs, after Dean had returned to L.A. to prepare for his breakout role in *East of Eden*.

Over the years, Bast has appeared in numerous documentaries on Dean and seems to have known him about as well as anyone did in those early days. According to Bast, it was he who prompted the Actors Studio alumnus James Whitmore to offer an informal class in the Method for young actors like himself and James Dean. Whitmore agreed to do so, and in turn he became part of the James Dean narrative by telling the driven young actor that he must go to New York to hone his skills and then come back to Hollywood instead of trying to breach the studio parapets on the ground in L.A. The advice made sense to Dean, especially since he wasn't getting anywhere much knocking on doors and going to casting calls. When he did get something, he usually made the most of it, but that wasn't enough, for it didn't lead to where he wanted to go. In a Pepsi commercial shot in Griffith Park on December 13, 1950, Dean performed a couple of smooth dance moves, standing out from the other kids, one of whom was Nick Adams, but nothing came of that appearance, except he earned a few bucks.

Done with college, it was acting or nothing. Yet he wasn't having much luck in landing parts. One reason was that he would lash out at the simplest request. Once when a producer asked him to read something so they could check his voice, he told him, "Go fuck yourself! I don't do readings." Another actor called him a "mixed-up misfit."

⚜

Picking up bit parts in Hollywood was hit-or-miss at best, but it was mostly miss, and there were depressing dry spells when nothing was happening and Dean had to take odd jobs to help pay the rent. In June 1951, he took one that was a staple of out-of-work actors—parking cars at the CBS studio in hopes of catching the eye of a producer or director. The plan worked like a plot in a B movie. Almost immediately, he met Rogers Brackett, a producer and director of radio drama. Brackett, thirty-five, was a sophisticated, well-dressed, well-connected figure. He was one of those Hollywood types who always had a tan, and he prided himself on his wit. He was always "on," and one friend considered him a kind of Noël Coward figure. He knew everybody in the film industry, and one of his friends was the well-known gay agent Henry Willson, the man who invented Rock Hudson. Brackett was himself gay. James Bellah described him as "an elegant, Clifton Webb type homosexual. There's no question he was a swish." Actor Phil Carey captured the relationship: "Here was Jimmy, the boyish farm boy when it suited him, and Rogers Brackett—older, suave, *très chic* and influential."

Bast was not happy when Brackett entered the picture. Like a spurned lover, he profiled Brackett as "an arch, pompous villain out of Dickens or a haughty Max Beerbohm dandy." To Bast, Brackett had the air of "affected bitchy queens."

In his heterosexual life, Dean was still sort of dating Beverly Wills, and almost farcically he asked his agent, Isabelle Draesemer, what he should do: marry Wills or live with a successful producer?

The drive to succeed won out. Dean saw in Brackett a path to success, and almost immediately he moved into Brackett's spacious apartment in the Sunset Plaza Hotel in West Hollywood. With that, Bast felt, "life was never the same again for any of us."

Moving in fast circles now, Jimmy started putting on airs and became a name-dropper and spoke knowingly of the stars they cavorted with—Franchot Tone and Barbara Payton, for example, who were having a torrid affair that season. Dean got to hang out poolside with Payton, one of the top blond beauties of that era and as wild as they come. In Brackett's circle, Dean heard firsthand the kind of lurid gossip that propelled the scandal magazines—which starlets were performing which sexual favors to win parts, which actors were closeted, all the louche, underground, au courant chatter that made Hollywood Hollywood.

Brackett took him to fancy restaurants like La Rue, where Jimmy discovered fine cuisine, including vichyssoise, though he insisted on calling it "swishy-swashy." Isabelle Draesemer noticed changes in her client. Taking him to lunch, she was surprised that he got upset because the restaurant didn't have Roquefort dressing. "I asked him, 'Why are you upset at that, when last week you'd have been glad just to have a sandwich?' He said, 'I've been getting around, and I have some new clothes.'" Being "kept" clearly had its upside.

Bast watched in amazement and a bit of envy as Dean took on the trappings of Brackett's manner. Still, he conceded that "Rogers did manage to facilitate the metamorphosis of James Dean from an unsophisticated shit-kicker into an urbane and polished bicoastal sophisticate, or at least a good facsimile thereof."

Brackett had connections throughout the industry. On a weekend jaunt to Mexicali to see the bullfights, he introduced Dean to Budd Boetticher, a bullfight aficionado and director best known for a series of taut Randolph Scott Westerns in the late fifties. Boetticher gave Dean a pair of horns and a matador's cape. The bloody cape was a treasured talisman, and everybody who visited Dean's various living quarters mentioned it—a defining James Dean objet.

Under Brackett's aegis, Dean made some headway, landing a few minor parts in films. He appeared briefly (uncredited) at the end of Samuel Fuller's *Fixed Bayonets* (1951), with one line, which was cut. He notched a small, uncredited part in a Dean Martin–Jerry Lewis comedy, *Sailor Beware* (1952). Although many commentators report that "First Sailor—#210" did not have a speaking part in that film, Dean in fact delivers one line in the locker room scene and also appears in a boxing scene as a handler for one of the boxers.

In the only feature film where he actually got to say something substantive, however brief, he did an excellent job with some tricky lines. The film was *Has Anybody Seen My Gal* (1952), and it starred someone who would never warm to him, an actor on the way up named Rock Hudson. They would meet again in Texas. In a very brief scene, Dean bops onto a drugstore stool, dressed in period 1920s collegiate gear, white pants, a checkered vest sweater, a boater, and a bow tie. All he needs is a raccoon coat to be the complete 1920s college boy. With carefully marcelled hair— that great James Dean hair—he's the cat's meow as he reels off a mouthful of verbiage: "Hey, Gramps, I'll have a choc malt, heavy on the choc, plenty of milk, four spoons of malt, two scoops of vanilla ice cream, one mixed with the rest and one floating." Hearing this, Rock Hudson might have recalled all the trouble he had had with the "bligger backboard" fiasco of his first screen appearance. Dean hoped to connect with director Douglas Sirk, but he did not. Sirk, who made seven films with Rock Hudson, could not recall ever having met Dean.

Dean's friend John Gilmore (author of two books on Dean) stated that "there seemed to be a barrier around Rock Hudson—a number one boy in the business—that was like an invisible no-trespassing sign." Bast, however, gives another version of what Dean thought. "It was after his first day of shooting on that picture that Jimmy confided in me his contempt for Mr. Hudson, based on nothing more than Hudson's hypocritical pose as straight on the set while privately trying to hit on him." Bast felt that his friend was being somewhat hypocritical himself, considering his relationship with Brackett.

Even from the briefest appearances on film, Dean created a compelling presence. There were early signs of his appeal. In "Hill Number One," his first TV drama (March 25, 1951), he played the apostle John and had to deliver such lines as "Rejoice! He has risen as He promised." Forty-six million people saw that Christian-themed program, the largest crowd Dean would ever have in his lifetime. Among them was a klatch of schoolgirls at a Catholic high school in Los Angeles who formed the Immaculate Heart James Dean Appreciation Society and invited him to a meeting—and he went! It was his first fan club. There would be many more in the years to come, over four hundred in the wake of his death.

Brackett's circle of gay friends wasn't as impressed with his ward as he was. They considered Dean a rude, pouty, unsophisticated toy boy. They called him "Hamlet," mocking his ambition to be a great actor. Brackett sometimes called him Hamlet, too. The screenwriter Leonard Spigelgass, a friend of Brackett's, characterized Dean as "an ill-mannered, boorish young fellow and a great deal sharper than he allowed to be seen beneath the 'Aw, shucks' country-boy façade."

But being Brackett's protégé offered Dean opportunities that he might not have been able to find otherwise, although it came at a cost. At some level, Dean was deeply embarrassed by the relationship. As time went on, he grew tired of being used. Later, he would talk around the topic, telling Bast when they met up again in New York, "I did a little dancing myself" and "I paid my way." If there was ever any doubt about the relationship, what Brackett himself said years later should make everything perfectly clear: "My primary interest in Jimmy was as an actor. His talent was so obvious. Secondarily, I loved him, and Jimmy loved me. If it was a father-son relationship, it was also somewhat incestuous." The only part of that statement one might have doubts about is the "Jimmy loved me" bit. Biographer Donald Spoto offers an explanation of Dean's actions: "Rogers Brackett did not, then, seduce an innocent victim. Twenty-year-old James Dean was primed for a sexual relationship with a man he trusted." Ultimately, Brackett was a means to an end. Dean's future resided in Brackett's address book, the names the older man could give the younger, the contacts that would lead to parts that would lead to stardom. It was networking not so pure and not so simple.

One of the things about Dean that most irritated Bill Bast was his inability or unwillingness to acknowledge the truth about himself. According to Bast, Dean "felt that he was above having to kiss anyone's ass in order to get a part, and whenever he saw his friends in this situation, he put them down for it, said he lost respect for them. The truth, though, is that Dean kissed a lot of asses, and he hated this about himself. That's why he took it out on others."

⋇

In October 1951, Brackett's work took him to Chicago, and Dean went with him. After a few days there, Dean visited his hometown for a five-day visit, then returned to Chicago, driven by his old minister, the Reverend De-Weerd. Later that month, Brackett put Dean on a bus to New York. Dean was itching to go to New York. James Whitmore had advised him to go east, young man, where television drama was exploding. Whitmore told him he needed to study at the Actors Studio if he really wanted to become a serious actor. Clearly, New York offered the best possibilities. Bit parts in L.A. weren't going to do it.

Upon arriving in the city, Dean had very limited funds to live on and spent much of his time watching films. It was the year of *A Streetcar Named Desire* and *A Place in the Sun*, films that Dean virtually worshipped. He watched each five times in four days, studying his idols, Marlon Brando and Montgomery Clift. Brando and Clift were the two poles of Jimmy's professional aspirations. He sometimes signed his letters "Jim (Brando Clift) Dean." Dennis Hopper liked to quote Dean on the subject: "He said he had Clift in his lowered left hand saying, 'Please forgive me,' and Brando in his raised right hand saying, 'Go fuck yourself.' "

He would eventually star in films made by both directors—Elia Kazan and George Stevens. As he told his friend John Gilmore, "Shit, man, Stevens even made Elizabeth Taylor look good," and added, "If I ever meet that woman I'd like to fuck her in the ass."

The hungry young actor had one contact in New York, the composer Alec Wilder, a close friend of Brackett's. Soon after his arrival in New York, Jimmy called Wilder and announced, "It's the Little Prince." Wilder, of course, knew what Dean was talking about; the children's book *The Little Prince*, by Antoine de Saint-Exupéry, was a work much prized in Brackett's circle. Brackett had introduced the book to Dean, who loved it so much that he gave away numerous copies and often quoted his favorite line: "It is only with the heart that one can see rightly; what is essential is invisible to the eye."

Wilder helped him get a room at the Iroquois Hotel, on West Forty-fourth Street, a down-market poor relation a couple of doors from the famous Algonquin, where Wilder stayed. Dean liked to hang out in the lobby of the Algonquin, the fashionable site of the Round Table back in the 1920s. In an unpublished manuscript, Wilder gave a vivid description of Dean: "He was short, physically strong, weak-eyed to the extent that he needed glasses, cheerful, uninformed, a prankster, and most certainly not a reader." Wilder continued: "He came from a poor farming family, had no money, but was possessed by the desire to act. He behaved in a very masculine manner, but was homosexual." Wilder considered him "a pleasant companion, a cheerful, noisy kid"—that is, until he had success on the stage. Then he became insufferable.

Most of Brackett's friends were homosexuals, and Dean spent a lot of time in their midst, but he also mocked them to his straight friends. He called them "mother hens" and ridiculed their fancy lives with its chatter about this maître d' and that sommelier. Among themselves, they called him the "Marshmellow Brando." David Diamond, a composer, and a member of the Wilder–Brackett circle, was a keen observer of Dean. He said there was an "agony" in the boy and that "he was the loneliest person I ever knew." Among gays, Dean was taken as gay; among heterosexuals, as straight. Joe Hyams, who became friends with Dean in 1955, concluded, "Depending on which of his ex-lovers I interviewed he was either heterosexual, asexual, bisexual, or homosexual." And Dean's most famous statement about this question, widely quoted, was, "Well, I'm certainly not going through life with one hand tied behind my back."

In mid-November 1951 Dean got the news he'd been praying for: a 4-F deferment from the U.S. Selective Service. How he managed to avoid being drafted and sent to Korea has long been debated among biographers. Some believe that he declared his sexual orientation as homosexual, and others do not. The latest to weigh in on this mystery was William Bast, whose second book on his friend, *Surviving James Dean* (2006), argued unequivocally that Dean did make that declaration and that he was worried about its being disclosed at some point later in his life. He feared such exposure as much as Rock Hudson did.

An employee at the Iroquois saw Dean in action many times and said, "He's the type of guy you wouldn't like." He said that Dean always walked behind Brackett and that when Brackett and his friend Wilder were sitting at a table in the lobby, Dean would not sit with them; instead, he would be by himself in a corner. "He always had that snarl, that sneer. That wasn't acting. That was James Dean." The employee said he never saw Dean smile or laugh and that he would say to anybody who looked at him, "You-son-of-a-bitch," and that he was always "alone in a crowd."

The heterosexual side of Dean's psyche comes into relief in his relationship with Liz Sheridan, or "Dizzy," as she was called, a dancer and later actress (best known as Jerry Seinfeld's mother on *Seinfeld*). Her memoir, *Dizzy & Jimmy* (2000), traces the history of her affair or relationship or whatever it was she had with the feral young actor. They met by chance early in 1952 in the lobby of the Rehearsal Club, a kind of hostel for out-of-work actresses, and began to talk about each other's dreams and aspirations, and eventually he showed her his bloody bullfighting cape and talked about how he wanted to be both an actor and a matador. And Dizzy wondered "if this shy, mumbling, crumpled little guy could act at all." They continued to see each other and eventually decided to move in together and share the rent. They had successful sex and she got the special Dean treatment, a copy of *The Little Prince* with Jimmy's commentary thrown in for good measure.

Liz's mother was fine with her daughter's living arrangements, but her father, a prominent composer, was not. He wanted to know why he should pay for her piano lessons and private schools when she was shacking up "with some child with the breeding of a cow chip." Dean rarely made a good impression on fathers or other representative older figures who were successful.

While things were going well between Dizzy and Dean, Brackett's arrival in New York led Jimmy, either from guilt or guile, to tell Dizzy about their relationship. He reviewed all that Brackett had done for him and stated that in a private compartment on the train to Chicago Brackett "came on" to him. "I succumbed to him. I felt bad afterward. Really strange, like a whore," he told Dizzy, much to her dismay. Naturally she wanted to know why he hadn't told her earlier. He said that of course he was ashamed. Thinking about it, Dizzy reminded herself, "I knew Jimmy had an experimenter's heart. He'd told me he wanted to try everything." Things escalated; she called him the *q* word, he called her the *c* word, and so much for young love.

As if this emotional turmoil weren't enough, Dizzy and Jimmy were kicked out of their living quarters for being behind on the rent. Each turned to friends for help, and a few days later they had, she reports, "the greatest sex of my young life." But it wasn't enough. Jimmy wanted her to meet Rogers Brackett. He wanted to maintain his friendship with Brackett because of "his connections and all," but he wanted the older man to stop hitting on him. Perhaps the most interesting thing he told Dizzy is, "I keep telling him that I'm not that way. He says he isn't so sure." Carlton Hale, one of Brackett's associates, put it this directly: "Rogers babied Jimmy, who desperately needed babying, and sucked his cock and fell in love." Hale also felt that Brackett did help Dean's career.

Dizzy agreed to meet Brackett, and things went about as anyone would have expected. She noted that he lived in "a building famous for its notable occupants over the years" [the Algonquin], and she noticed also that "Rogers Brackett was color-coordinated with his own hallway: casual but elegant in beige shirt, beige trousers, beige loafers." He called Jimmy "James," which no one did. Dizzy and Brackett exchanged pleasantries and Brackett asked her a lot of questions about herself, but neither liked each other, and all in all, it felt like a bad play. She said Brackett "was really like an old woman—he even looked like an old woman made-up to look like a man." Like Bast, she had absolutely nothing good to say about Brackett. After that meeting, "Brackett seemed to fade out of the picture," she wrote. And as for Jimmy, she concluded, "I don't believe that Jimmy was gay in his heart, at least not at that time. I'm sure of that. But I knew how driven he was to become an actor."

Most women who had any kind of relationship with James Dean, sexual or otherwise, arrived at conclusions similar to those of Dizzy Sheridan: "One of his favorite roles was the child who had to get his way, and if he didn't he could be despicable." Also: "It was so evident that he was turning to me to make up for some emptiness inside of him, to fill him up and heal his wounds." The actress Betsy Palmer, with whom he had a brief fling, said much the same: "Nurturing was really the thing about our relationship. He was a lost lamb. I never felt he would live to be old. Something hovered around and shrouded him, an air of 'I've got to get this done quick.'" But there were other women, ones who never bedded him, who thought that everything he did was a performance. In L.A., actress Karen Sharpe was one: "Later I came to understand that his notorious 'strangeness' was just an act. But he played that part so long, maybe he became the act." Terry Moore was another: "I believed his mannerisms were premeditated. I think his behavior was an act."

In May 1952, Dean decided he was ready to make a run at the Actors Studio, the sine qua non of Method legitimacy. He and another aspirant, Christine White, using original material that she had written, were both accepted on their first try. It was a real coup, but the Actors Studio, with its constant program of collaboration and performances under the withering scrutiny of Lee Strasberg, was not going to be very important in James Dean's development. When it came time for Dean to perform alone, he turned to one of his favorite subjects, bullfighting, and developed a monologue based on Barnaby Conrad's novel *Matador*. It was a disaster, as he realized about halfway through, so he broke it off and then had to endure a blistering critique from Strasberg. As in other encounters with authority figures, Dean could not stand to be criticized. Kazan remembers that he sat "in a sort of poutish mess in the front row and scowled." Dean never again performed at the Actors Studio and seldom attended any of its functions.

That same month, his old buddy William Bast moved to New York and they resumed their friendship. Bast, Dizzy, and Dean made a mostly compatible threesome, and one week in October 1952, Jimmy came up with a typically loopy idea: The three of them would hitchhike back to Jimmy's hometown in Indiana and breathe some fresh air and eat some hearty down-home food. They had great luck finding a ride and spent several days at the Winslow farm, where Jimmy had grown up. Dean's father happened to be on a visit to Fairmount at the same time, and Jimmy took advantage of his dental skills to have a new plate made for his missing front teeth. Dizzy had much the same impression of Winton Dean that most people did: "There was no sign that he participated in any of the joys of life; even simple affection seemed beyond his reach."

Near the end of their stay in Fairmount, Jimmy got the phone call that altered everything. He was going to read for a part in the play *See the Jaguar.* Dizzy felt something shift; she felt, as Jimmy did, that the big break had come. And though Dizzy didn't know it, Brackett and Brackett's address book had been behind the breakthrough. Brackett was friends with a wealthy producer named Lemuel Ayers. Ayers owned a yacht, and every summer he took friends on a cruise up the Hudson River. Upon meeting James Dean, Ayers invited him to come along as a deckhand. Dean knew nothing of boats or sailing, but he knew a main chance when he saw one. It was like James Gatz becoming Jay Gatsby—a boy boards a boat and everything changes. The feeling among Ayers's associates is that, though married, he was gay, and rumors, whether true or not, circulated that Dean's boat ride was what got him a shot at his first Broadway production. Bast spilled the beans many years later: "Jimmy later conceded grudgingly that, while Shirley [Ayers's wife] turned a blind eye, he put out for Lem."

Dean's forays into gay circles were producing promising results in New York compared to less successful ones in L.A. He told his friend Jonathan Gilmore, "You know, I've had my cock sucked by five of the big names in Hollywood. I think it's pretty funny because I wanted more than anything to get some little part, something to do," but all they offered was fancy dinners and drinks in beautiful settings along the coast. In New York, things were looking up.

With rehearsals under way, Dean became impossible around Dizzy. He didn't want to be bothered with anything concerning her; he wanted to enjoy the ride to the top. Upset, she saw where things were headed. He was on a different trajectory, and both knew it.

For once, James Dean got along reasonably well with his director and cast, especially the star, Arthur Kennedy. *See the Jaguar* opened on December 3, 1952, at the Cort Theatre on Broadway and closed only three days later. Although the play proved to be one that just about every reviewer agreed made little sense, it gave a huge boost to Dean's standing. He garnered good reviews for his portrayal of a strange kid confined to a cage. The performance lifted his profile and led to numerous offers to play similar roles of troubled youths in TV dramas all that year and the next. Bill Bast and Dizzy Sheridan attended opening night of *See the Jaguar* and witnessed the liftoff of their immensely complicated and talented friend and lover.

Bast had found congenial work at CBS in New York and had begun to feel comfortable in a circle of young professionals who were homosexual and well educated. Although he yearned to introduce his friend Jimmy to this group, he "knew instinctively that it wouldn't work." The reason, he explained, is that Jimmy's role as "an older homosexual's toy-boy" would be incongruent with the style and class of the gays among Bast's new friends, and Jimmy would have hated being a square among progressive young gays. Also, Bast could see that Dean was still struggling with the Brackett relationship. One day, Dean drew a sketch of a lizard that unmistakably bore the head of Rogers Brackett.

In the meantime, his career in TV was gaining momentum. He appeared in an impressive number of television dramas: thirty in all from February 1952 through May 1955. All were on CBS, NBC, or ABC. So before Dean became a movie star, there was lots of footage of him on the small screen.

James Dean's success on TV didn't change his behavior one whit. At one time or another he treated just about everybody with contempt and bad manners. "Undisciplined" and "irresponsible" were common descriptions of the difficult young star. And, perhaps most telling of all, he still relied on a juvenile tactic to get attention: In response to criticism or stress, he would urinate in front of everybody. He would even do this onstage. He urinated on the stage of *The Thief* in January 1954. Mature actors were exasperated by his intemperate antics. Paul Lukas, a veteran character actor, told the director of *The Thief,* "This young man is crazy."

Dean's next—and last—Broadway play would bring him into conflict with the director, the star, and assorted minor figures. *The Immoralist,* adapted from a novel by André Gide, explored a controversial topic for that era, homosexuality. The star, Louis Jourdan, was coming to Broadway from film, the opposite route Dean would take. Jourdan clashed with Dean, and like most of the other actors, he hated Dean's habit of never saying a line the same way. Dean also profoundly irritated the play's coauthor, Ruth Goetz: "The little son of a bitch was one of the most unspeakably detestable fellows I ever knew in my life. The little bastard would not learn the words, would not really try to give a performance, would not really rehearse. He drove us up the wall."

The only actor Dean got along with was Method-trained Geraldine Page, another mother figure for little boy Jimmy. On opening night, Dean transfixed the audience and reviewers with his portrayal of Bachir, a homosexual Arab boy. Dressed in a rather ridiculous-looking bathrobe, Dean played a flute and clicked scissors while he danced around the stage. He later told his friend Jonathan Gilmore that the scissors bit was meant to "cut more and more at the man's hopeless respectability" and that Louis Jourdan never had a clue as to what he was doing. Although the dance electrified many in the audience, one actor had an entirely different take on the performance: "Jimmy played Bachir like a Third Avenue faggot. He had no sense of the period. He played it like an American prostitute." Was this role of blatant homosexuality also a coming-out for Dean? Logically, if everything he did was a reflection, Method-wise, of previous recalled experience, then it could certainly be viewed in that light.

Among the young crowd of actors and artists that Dean hung out with in New York, he stood out for his unpredictable and eccentric behavior. One of Dean's standard fantasies, and one that he embellished in relating his passion to others, was bullfighting. Michael Gordon, director of *See the Jaguar,* said, "I often saw him make daring passes and fariñas at onrushing taxicabs while crossing Broadway or Seventh Avenue." Mark Rydell saw

Dean take off his jacket and use it like a cape to make a pass like a toreador, with a bus going down Madison Avenue at forty miles an hour: "You know, I was shocked because I said to myself, this guy is going to kill himself and it was a year before he died."

Life seemed to him a kind of absurdist play, and he would do whatever it took to gain attention. Photographer Roy Schatt met Dean in February 1954, just as his career was taking off. "What a shock. He slouched, was unkempt and squinty," Schatt recalled. Then he performed the castanet dance from *The Immoralist* for Schatt, and the photographer saw the "small lump on the couch . . . become a thing of beauty." And for a finale, Dean plopped out his two front teeth, reverting like a vaudeville hack to an old standby—the midwestern rube.

At this point, on the verge of stardom, Dean still desperately craved attention and would take risky chances to get it. At a party at Schatt's apartment, Jimmy suddenly disappeared, only to resurface on the street below, sitting on a chair in the middle of the street with angry motorists shouting at him. It was stupid, it was dangerous, but the tactic accomplished exactly what Dean sought: "I just wanted to spark things, man, that's all." And there was always the competition with Brando; as Dean told the photographer repeatedly, "I had a motorbike before he did." One time, Schatt opened his apartment door and found Jimmy standing there stark naked. Schatt called him "a man with a great emergent talent, a screwball sense of humor, a flair for daredevilry."

And regarding Dean's sexuality, always a matter of interest to those who knew him, Schatt wondered if Jimmy was gay or bisexual. He concluded, "Well, maybe. His nuttiness and constant attempts at breaking from the humdrum could have led him into it."

On another occasion, Schatt watched as Jimmy sped away on his motorcycle at top speed. Schatt never would get on the bike; he was too afraid, he told Jimmy. Or too smart. But daredevil Jimmy wasn't afraid at all. "I'm not going to live past 30," he told his friend, smiling.

Having stolen the show with his rendition of the Arab street hustler, Dean next did something nobody could believe. He gave notice and walked out of the play. He didn't explain why; he just quit.

But the why was one to conjure with: Elia Kazan, a Greek, whose birth name was Elia Kazanjoglous. Cofounder of the Actors Studio in 1947, Kazan directed Marlon Brando in *A Streetcar Named Desire* (1951), *Viva Zapata* (1952), and *On the Waterfront* (1954). Kazan, in 1954, had artistic cachet and his films made money. On the basis of *Streetcar* (a Warner Bros. production), he was able to sell Jack Warner on the proposition of filming John Steinbeck's *East of Eden*. Warner didn't need to read the book to agree on the spot to Kazan's proposal.

Next, Kazan had to find a lead, and one of his associates suggested the kid who was playing the Arab boy in *The Immoralist*. Kazan called the actor in for a meeting and at the appointed time walked into the New York office of Warner Bros., where he found Dean "slouched at the end of a leather sofa in the waiting room, a heap of twisted legs and denim rags, looking resentful for no particular reason." According to Kazan, "He was guarded, sullen, suspicious, and he seemed to me to have a great deal of concealed emotion. He looked and spoke like the character in *East of Eden*." Kazan waited him out, but Dean wasn't really able to talk—"conversation was not his gift." Instead he communicated by taking Kazan on a scary motorcycle ride through the streets of New York. Immediately, Kazan knew that this "country boy" was Cal, the hurt, embittered brother to Aron in the Cain and Abel parable of Steinbeck's novel.

In March 1954, Kazan wrote Steinbeck, a personal friend, explaining his choice. "I looked thru a lot of kids before settling on this Jimmy Dean. He hasn't Brando's stature, but he's a good deal younger and is very interesting, has balls and eccentricity and a 'real problem' somewhere in his guts, I dont [*sic*] know where or when." He went on to say that he thought Dean was "a real good actor" and concluded, "Dean has got a real mean streak and a real sweet streak." Nobody ever put it better. Sure of his choice, Kazan sent Dean to meet Steinbeck himself, who lived nearby. "John thought Dean a snotty kid. I said that was irrelevant; wasn't he Cal? John said he sure as hell was, and that was it."

During this period, Jimmy suffered a fall on his motorcycle, and Kazan ordered him to "stay off that fucking motorcycle!" So instead of taking a cross-country trip on his bike, Jimmy flew out with Kazan. It was Dean's first time on an airplane, and carrying his meager belongings in packages wrapped with string, he looked like an immigrant. Upon leaving the airport in L.A., Dean asked if they could stop at an office building where his father worked. Kazan saw in the father exactly what he needed in order to understand the son. Winton Dean "had no definition and made no impression except that he had no definition. Obviously there was a strong tension between the two, and it was not friendly. I sensed the father disliked his son." Kazan knew that that's where the "real problem" in Dean's guts had its origins—the cold, remote father.

Kazan wanted Dean to get a tan and put on some weight for his role in *East of Eden*, and so on April 10, Dean and his friend Bill Bast drove 150 miles south to Borrego Springs and checked into the best hotel in the small desert town. And there, the first night, it happened. In bed together, Jimmy uttered one of his signature lines from his Indiana upbringing, "Well, then, there now," and as Bast tells it, "I slipped under the sheet beside him, my heart beating so hard I was sure he could hear it."

"What took you so long?" he asked.

"Scared, I guess."

"Nothin' to be scared about."

And so, Bast wrote, "there wasn't."

In the early tests, Jimmy impressed Kazan, but no one else. The crew thought he was a stand-in, that the real star would show up later. One of the tests pitted Dean against another young actor out from New York, Paul Newman. Kazan began the test by saying, "All right, you two queens." Kazan had them make up their own banter, and when Jimmy said to Newman, "Kiss me," the flustered Newman had been out-Methoded. Richard Davalos, a client of Henry Willson's, and something of a James Dean look-alike, got the role of Cal's brother, but unlike Dean, the break for Davalos did not lead to a successful career.

Once filming began, Kazan, though often irritated by Dean, knew he had made the right choice. In a letter of July 5, 1954, Kazan observed, "Jimmy is inventive and true. Amazingly he takes to movies like it was HIS medium." And he predicted, "He'll be a big star." While Dean's erratic behavior annoyed much of the crew and some of the cast, Kazan made allowances for him and catered to Dean's idiosyncrasies because of the intensity the actor brought to his performance. Kazan even worked out a system whereby Dean could go off by himself and charge himself up for a scene, and when the actor was ready, he would blow a whistle to alert the cast and crew. Very few directors would have put up with such nonsense.

During filming, Dean's tactics sometimes amused but mostly infuriated other members of the cast. The most sympathetic figure was Julie Harris, another alumnus of the Actors Studio. Though only slightly older than Dean, she assumed the familiar role of the mothering female, and the two of them got along fine. Kazan pronounced her an "angel" and said that she was "kind and patient and everlastingly sympathetic" and that Dean might not ever have gotten through the film without her. "She would adjust her performance to whatever the kid did," wrote Kazan. Patience was certainly required to deal with Dean.

One day, Dean's agent at that time, Dick Clayton, and his friend Beverly Linet visited the set. Linet was anxious to meet Dean, and seeing him leaning against a tree, she wanted to go over and introduce herself, but Clayton said no, the actor was preparing for a scene. For fifteen minutes, Jimmy stood there in intense concentration, then walked up to Julie Harris and asked, "Are you going to the carnival tonight?" and she replied, "Yes, I'm going." It took fifteen minutes of prepared angst for thirty seconds of screen time.

Dean's antics infuriated old pros like Raymond Massey. A veteran character actor (Abe Lincoln, Sherlock Holmes, various generals), Massey blamed Dean's mannerisms on the Method: "Jimmy never knew his lines before he walked on the set, rarely had command of them when the camera rolled and even if he had was often inaudible. Simple technicalities, such as moving on cue and finding his marks, were beneath his consideration." Massey recognized that "Gadge" (Kazan's nickname) "endured the slouchings, the eye-poppings, the mutterings and all the wilful eccentricities" because he was "getting solid gold."

Still, it bothered Massey. During one scene, Dean had to express anger and shove a bunch of blocks of ice from an icehouse down a chute, but when the scene was ready to be shot, he kept pacing back and forth. Massey, looking on, asked Burl Ives what the holdup was. "Jimmy's got to get to hate the ice," Ives said. "It takes time."

But the scene that ripped it for Massey was the one where the father orders his son to read a passage from the Bible, and when the boy doesn't do it properly, the father tells him to read it again. This time Dean, reading off-camera, interjected obscenities when introducing the verses, and Massey lost it, yelling "Cut" (always the director's prerogative, not the actor's) and storming off to his dressing room. In a few minutes, most of the crew came to his dressing room to thank him, and then Kazan himself came to confess that he had put Jimmy up to the profanities to get the angry reaction shot from Massey that he wanted. Massey held no grudge against Dean personally; he just didn't like the lack of professionalism exhibited in the young man's behavior.

Although Dean's rebellious behavior on-camera was exactly what Kazan wanted, off-camera it was a different story. Being so near to the success he had dreamed of seems not to have helped Jimmy in the way he conducted his life. He was pretty miserable most of the time and seemed unable to comprehend his own actions. In L.A., he continued both to fascinate and bewilder fellow actors with his rude, erratic behavior. He acknowledged as much in a letter to Barbara Glenn, a girlfriend in New York: "Must I always be so miserable? I try so hard to make people reject me. Why? I don't want to write this letter. It would be better to remain silent. Wow! Am I fucked up." Stewart Stern, screenwriter for Dean's next film, observed that "he was constantly fucking himself over by behavior designed to alienate people."

And he certainly began to irritate Kazan. When Dean bought a horse (which he named Cisco) and put it in a corral on the lot, he kept leaving the set to go fool around with Cisco, to the point where Kazan had the animal removed to a distant farm in the San Fernando Valley. Jimmy's hair-raising motorcycle riding was another problem, and Kazan laid down the law: no more goddamn motorcycle riding until the shoot was over. Next thing you know, Dean bought an expensive camera and brought it to the set, and Kazan had to tell him not to do that. Then Dean showed up late for work a couple of times, and Kazan had Jimmy move into a star dressing room on the Warner lot and the director did the same so he could keep an eye on the boy's comings and goings. Kazan claimed that he could hear Dean and his new girlfriend, Pier Angeli, alternately "boffing" and arguing.

Although Dean was dating Angeli, that came to an end when she married singer Vic Damone, who was much more suitable for Angeli, according to her fierce mama, who hated Dean and didn't want her daughter having anything to do with him. The story of this intense romance of lost love dominated biographers' portraits of Dean for several decades, but it no longer does. It was a brief affair and marriage was discussed, but some close to Dean, like Bill Bast, believed that losing the competition with the mother hurt Dean the most, not losing the daughter to Damone. Dean's bad-boy persona couldn't take losing, period. Typical of the ambiguity surrounding this entire episode is that on the day of the wedding, as the newly minted couple walked out of the church, a supposedly heartbroken James Dean revved his motorcycle to a high pitch and roared away down the street. It made irresistible magazine copy, but Dean later told Bast that he had hired someone to impersonate him and perform the motorcycle stunt. Fact, publicity, and legend are nearly always intertwined when the story involves James Dean. Bast summed up the whole episode as a "decades-long myth that she was the romance of Jimmy's life."

In retrospect, this widely publicized narrative of young love and heartbreak may have inoculated Dean from other, more dangerous narratives pointing to homosexuality. Instead of whispers and printed innuendos, Dean's "broken heart" over Angeli would reinforce the heterosexual theme. The effect of the romance and breakup with Angeli was similar to the cover that Rock Hudson's arranged marriage would later provide him. The studio assiduously pushed the love story/boo-hoo narrative—a soapy saga of young love that persisted for about twenty to thirty years before it began to be challenged by the Rogers Brackett homosexual/bisexual narrative.

Kazan, for one, was pleased with the breakup. "Now I had Jimmy as I wanted him, alone and miserable," he wrote in his autobiography, *A Life*. Bereft, Dean would pose in front of a mirror and take photograph after photograph of his face and then show Kazan the "goddamn contact sheets" and ask him what he thought. Kazan thought they all looked alike but kept his thoughts to himself. In any event, he considered the camera a better hobby for Dean than his romance with Angeli.

It was this kind of setup: All Kazan cared about was the film, and all Dean cared about was himself. Dean seems at times to have thought Kazan was his pal, but apparently Jimmy never knew how Kazan used him and played upon his fragile psyche to get the performance he wanted. Kazan projected an image of sympathy and concern but was just as hard-boiled about his goals as any of the tough-guy directors were. The fact is, Kazan didn't like Dean very much at all, but he made Dean think he really cared. Kazan considered Dean "twisted": "He was actually a very disturbed young man—sick. He was in bad need of some help—some psychological help."

In a sense, Kazan outacted James Dean in the private little movie they enacted together. The truth is that Dean never acknowledged the pivotal role that Kazan played in his career. Nor did he really trust Kazan. There was hardly anybody in the industry whom Dean trusted or felt he owed anything to. "In this business," he said to a reporter, "nobody helps you." His credo didn't allow for gratitude. On the set of his next film, Dean entertained the other actors with spot-on parodies of Kazan's manner.

Dean carried within himself the requisite life experience for the character he was playing in *East of Eden*. Kazan's theory of acting, grounded in the Method, was perfectly encapsulated in a few sentences in *A Life* when he speaks of actors' lives: "Their life's experience is the director's material. They can have all the training, all the techniques their teachers have taught them—private moments, improvisations, substitutions, associative memories, and so on—but if the precious material is not within them, the director cannot get it out. That is why it's so important for the director to have an intimate acquaintance with the people he casts in his plays." This is the Method in a comprehensible nutshell.

Kazan considered Dean's stagecraft lacking in technique. Compared to Marlon Brando, for example, Dean drew upon raw, naked self-revelation, whereas, in Kazan's view, Brando was superior because he also possessed a mastery of technique. Dean's method of intense personal anguish worked about 95 percent of the time, Kazan thought, but Jimmy lacked the craft to carry him through the other 5 percent. According to Kazan, if Jimmy missed the first take, he was lost.

During filming, Kazan invited Brando to visit the set of *East of Eden*. Alongside his idol, Dean "was so adoring that he seemed shrunken and twisted in misery," Kazan wrote, and a photograph of the two of them bears out this impression. Alongside Brando, the younger star looks much diminished.

For his part, Brando seems to have been bothered by what he regarded as Dean's copycat emulation. There was the motorcycle riding, the bongo drums, the recorder (an instrument that Dean took up, following Brando's lead), the slurred and mumbling speech, the Levi's, the aura of rebellion against middle-class mores. Like Dean, Brando suffered from insomnia, and he could be just as sullen at parties as Dean could. And there were reviewers who, when *East of Eden* came out, evoked Brando's name either to praise or condemn Dean's performance.

One time when Brando saw Dean arrive at a party, he told Janet Ward, an Actors Studio friend, to watch what Dean did next. Brando predicted Jimmy was going to pull off his jacket and throw it on the floor. When Ward asked him how he knew that, he said, "Because I do it." As if right on cue, Dean tossed his jacket to the floor. When Dean tried to talk to Brando at a party, Brando would usually snub him, though on one occasion he told Dean that he was "sick" and should see a psychiatrist. In his book *Songs My Mother Taught Me* (1994), Brando summed up Dean: "He was hypersensitive, and I could see it in his eyes and in the way he moved and spoke that he had suffered a lot. He was tortured by insecurities, the origin of which I never determined, though he said he'd had a difficult childhood and a lot of problems with his father." Brando told Leonard Rosenman, a mutual friend, "Len, why don't you get him to an analyst? Your friend is nuts!"

As they neared the end of the shooting schedule, Kazan saw early signs of Dean's corruption by success. With people beginning to talk about his breakout performance, the budding star began to act the part of a prima donna. Kazan objected to Dean's rude treatment of a wardrobe man and did not like his complaining about this scene or that. When Kazan couldn't get him to perform convincingly when he was standing on a slanted roof for a second-story-window encounter with Harris, he took them to an Italian restaurant and got Dean loaded on Chianti—"a technique," he said, that he had "used on occasion to supersede Stanislavski." There would be other signs of what Edna Ferber called "success poisoning" during Jimmy's rise to the top. Marlon Brando had perhaps the best perspective of all on success in Hollywood. "It grated on me that movie stars were elevated into icons; Hollywood was simply a place where people, including me, made money, like a mill town in New England or an oil field in Texas."

The more Kazan was around Dean, the more he came to understand the depth of Dean's problems. He thought that Dean was "an extreme grotesque of a boy, a twisted boy," and that in fact he had been made so "by the denial of love." Kazan grew to dislike Dean: "I got to know him and he was an absolutely rotten person. Right away, he was a real cocker and an asshole. But he was the most perfect fucking actor for that part—all bound up in himself with his neurotic problems, lashing out at inappropriate moments; a sulker, an asshole."

The day filming was completed, Dean was a sodden mess. Julie Harris found him weeping in his trailer on the last day. He seemed, she said, "more than ever to me like a little lost boy. The rebel, the boy who wanted to shock and irritate, was gone, and suddenly there was Jimmy Dean, very vulnerable and very sweet."

Jimmy wanted everything on his terms. One of the expectations the studio held was that its newest find would fully participate in generating publicity for the film that would make him a star. But James Dean didn't see it that way. He was either too troubled or too busy appearing to be troubled to bother with ordinary practices like giving interviews. A telegram of February 11, 1955, to Morton Blumenstock, head of publicity, said it all: "He has been absolutely impossible. Has been extremely uncooperative and refused to see fine lineup of newspaper interviews we had set for him." It went on to say that the "way he is acting he can do us more harm than good. He needs good scrubbing behind ears." It also pointed out that Gadge didn't want to be "father confessor to this kid."

When Dean was back in New York after finishing *East of Eden*, he acted the part of a movie star, or so thought Dizzy Sheridan when she saw him wearing a turtleneck sweater. "My God, you've gone Hollywood," she exclaimed. And when he ran into an actor named Don Miele, a fiery Italian who knew Jimmy from the Actors Studio days, Miele commented, "So, kid, you're now a movie star. They say you gave head to get ahead." He was joking, but there was a dangerous truth in that kind of talk, and there are those like Alec Wilder who believe that Dean was seriously worried about this part of his past being made public. Wilder: "It's my belief that when Jimmy became a star, he was terrified that his homosexual background might be revealed. [The press] swallowed hook, line, and sinker the publicity Jimmy had allowed to be spread about him, and this, in turn, was further distorted by the flagrant lies he himself told about his background."

Whatever the case, he certainly continued to act out in all the same old annoying and adolescent ways. In almost all of his dealings with Warner Bros., Dean played the spoiled brat. One studio executive spoke for many: "You always knew when he was around. In the green room he would hum, sing to himself, talk in a loud voice, drum on the table or with a spoon on a glass. Anything to attract attention." When Warners invited the powerful Hedda Hopper to visit the studio to meet Jimmy, he put on his usual show, and the behatted one was not amused. She wrote, "The latest genius sauntered in, dressed like a bum, and slouched down in silence at a table away from mine." Then he dragged a chair with his toe, propped up his feet in it, and glanced sidewise at her. "Then he stood up to inspect the framed photographs of Warner stars that covered the wall by his head. He chose one of them, spat in its eye, wiped off the spittle with a handkerchief, then like a ravenous hyena, started to gulp the food that had been served him." She dismissed him as another "dirty-shirttail boy in blue jeans." Brando had treated her the same way but, unlike Jimmy, never changed his attitude toward her, remaining both indifferent and insolent. She wrote Brando off as a "supreme egotist."

Even so, Hopper came away a fan of Jimmy's after being persuaded to see *East of Eden* by her friend Clifton Webb. Dean also did his bit to make a better impression on Hopper. He donned a suit for an interview with her and charmed Hopper so completely that she wrote nothing but positive copy about him from then on. In this instance, he did what Brando would not do. Carroll Baker once saw Jimmy literally throw himself at Hopper's feet on the Warners lot. She couldn't believe it; he was so contemptuous of such behavior otherwise. Her husband, Jack Garfein, saw the same kind of behavior on Dean's part. "I loved Jimmy and we were very close to each other, but if I was in a restaurant with him and Hedda Hopper walked in, he would get up and walk over and say 'Hello' . . . and he would stay there with her for forty-five minutes and you're sitting at the table." Jimmy's friend Joe Hyams called Dean a phony to his face because he knew that Jimmy didn't like the feared columnist yet pretended he did. Jimmy told him that Hopper was his "friend in court."

The film's reception confirmed Kazan's faith in having chosen Dean, and *East of Eden* made money and made Dean a star. Although a few critics, such as Bosley Crowther of *The New York Times*, complained that Dean's performance smacked too much of Marlon Brando's influence, most reviewers singled out Dean for praise.

Although *East of Eden* has long been a favorite of Dean fans, it does not hold up well today. It feels like an art-house film, stagy, stilted, and cold. But among die-hard Dean fans, the film is usually rated either his best performance or second to that in *Rebel Without a Cause*. Dean's appeal is most apparent when his face breaks into a smile (although the Deaners prefer the outbursts of rage). He has the eyes of a movie star, the hair, and the androgynous face; above all, he has the androgynous mouth. His first agent, Isabelle Draesemer, said, "To me, his sex appeal lay in his mouth and below—the use of his body."

Among young people, the film hit a nerve. It suggested a restlessness of spirit, an unpinned set of emotions. Moody, at times almost hysterical, needy, bursting with physical energy, and, above all, angry and unloved, Dean seemed to tap into a social phenomenon that the movies were just discovering: the youth market. Emotionally, the film is a kind of rural anticipation of the juvenile delinquents in *Rock Around the Clock* and *Rebel Without a Cause*. But to those who knew Jimmy back in Fairmount, like his old drama teacher Adeline Nall, "[m]any of the movements of the character Cal Trask—his funny laugh, the quick, jerky, springy walk and actions, and the sudden changes from frivolity to gloom—were all just like Jim used to do." After viewing the film, Bill Bast said what others who knew Dean were probably thinking: "I had just watched Jimmy relive the sad reality of his own existence."

꽃

Now Dean was faced with the question of a second act—a film worthy of the quality and predicted success of *East of Eden*. His new status made the selection of his next film especially important in terms of his overall career trajectory, and he would take his time, cat and mouse–style, before arriving at a decision.

Warner Bros. had owned a property titled *Rebel Without a Cause* since 1946. Producer Jerry Wald had wanted to do the film with Marlon Brando, but Brando turned it down and it languished until 1954, when Nicholas Ray became interested in it. There was no script, but in a mad burst of work, he dictated a seventeen-page treatment, which convinced Warners to produce the film. *Rebel*, the studio believed, would be its answer to MGM's *The Blackboard Jungle*, a socially conscious drama about urban teens in an inner-city public school that proved to be a surprise hit upon its release in March 19, 1955—and justly famous for its electrifying opening with Bill Haley & His Comets pounding out rock's early anthem "Rock Around the Clock." Like *Jungle*, *Rebel* would be shot in black and white and targeted at the new youth market.

Ray, whose office was next door to Kazan's on the Warners lot, would naturally have heard talk about Dean, with all the buzz surrounding his performance in *East of Eden*. The first time Ray laid eyes on the hottest thing since Brando was at a special screening of his friend Kazan's film. Dean was there in the flesh, looking typically scruffy and standoffish. By that time, Kazan was especially tired of Jimmy: "I got fed up with Dean at the very end of *East of Eden*. He began to abuse people and throw his weight around."

But Ray was intrigued, and one day Dean knocked on his door. Ray later described what it was like to meet him: "The only thing to do with a Siamese cat is to let it take its own time. It will come up to you, walk around you, smell you. If it doesn't like you, it will go away again; if it does, it will stay." Dean circled around Ray and drew closer but took his time reaching a decision. Ray knew that there were people around Dean who were urging him to take nothing less than a film based on a bestseller and directed by one of the top four Warner Bros. heavy hitters, Elia Kazan, George Stevens, John Huston, or William Wyler.

Dean's first appearance at Ray's Chateau Marmont digs was memorable. He rolled in with Maila Nurmi, a gothic-styled TV horror movie host, and Jack Simmons, a groupie, in tow, and his entrance was quintessential Dean: He did a double somersault and gazed up at Ray from ground level. He interrogated the director, an inveterate gambler, as to whether it was true that he had escaped from a fire in a casino a couple of years earlier. It was true, and with this, Ray seemed to have passed some kind of test.

Ray was mesmerized by Dean's persona. And why not, for it wasn't all that different from his own hipster bohemianism. But one friend, Andrew Solt, a British screenwriter who'd worked on *In a Lonely Place*, formed a rather different impression of Dean the first time he laid eyes on him. It was at Ray's cottage at the Chateau Marmont. "There sat in the corner a little boy, emaciated, the whole thing could have been 125 pounds, a little effeminate, dark, the only thing that made him a little interesting was that he had a cat on his shoulder."

But Dean remained uncommitted, and Ray followed Jimmy to New York in December 1954, hoping to coax him to take the part. They spent two weeks in the city, the nights punctuated by all-night bongo sessions in Dean's apartment or those of his actor friends from his New York period, the whole bohemian scene aglow with excited talk, gossip, burning ambition. Dean took Ray on motorcycle rides through the city—his litmus test for those he favored.

A couple of weeks later, Dean took part in the first reading of the script, held at Ray's bungalow. But still he delayed committing to the film. In February 1955, he made the victory-lap trip to Fairmount with photographer Dennis Stock. Having met Dean at one of Ray's gatherings, Stock concluded that he would be a good subject for a photo story for *Life*. Dean agreed but wanted a cover story, which Stock considered a "highly egocentric gesture." Upon being told no, Jimmy "acted like a spoiled kid" for days afterward. The actor and the photographer wound up going to Fairmount and Stock photographed Dean on the farm, among the animals, Dean in town, and, strangest of all, Dean in a coffin at the local funeral home. Stock said he "let him fool around" until he "found a moment that showed the truth—that James Dean was a lost person."

Returning to L.A. in early March, Dean waited until after the release and rapturous reception of *East of Eden* to commit to *Rebel*. One reason he cast his lot with the intense director was that Ray guaranteed Dean that he could create the character of Jim Stark (an anagram of Trask). He would even function, with Ray's tacit approval, as a kind of codirector. Ray was very sympathetic with youth culture and recognized, on the basis of his performance in *East of Eden*, that Dean was its chief exemplar. In the new film, he would let Jimmy Dean play Jimmy Dean, just as Kazan had. He knew Dean was the perfect actor for the part. Dean was always in a lonely place, even in the midst of a crowd.

Nicholas Ray (born Raymond Nicholas Kienzle, Jr.) had led a colorful life, and his counterculture persona appealed to Dean. Ray, too, came from the Midwest (without the Midwest, there would have been no Hollywood as we know it). He grew up in La Crosse, Wisconsin, and had a very checkered high school career, finishing one from the bottom of his graduating class of 153. He excelled, however, in English and public speaking. He spent stints at La Crosse State Teachers College and the University of Chicago, compromised somewhat by an early addiction to alcohol, and met both Frank Lloyd Wright and Thornton Wilder. He studied architecture at Wright's Taliesen and accompanied folklorist Alan Lomax on trips through the South, recording blues singers like Lead Belly. He joined the Communist Party and eventually went west, where he got his first job working in Hollywood with Elia Kazan.

When Dean met him, Ray was a forty-three-year-old nonconformist, a talented filmmaker sympathetic to youth and the disaffected, who mistrusted most forms of power. Ray was a sixties radical a decade before Haight-Ashbury. As a filmmaker, he specialized in edgy naturalistic and noir cinema—*Knock on Any Door* (1949), *In a Lonely Place* (1950), and a twisted Western, *Johnny Guitar* (1954). French critics like Jean-Luc Godard and François Truffaut loved his films. American critic David Thomson summed up Ray as the "American director in whom greatness is inseparable from the refusal to grow up." Thus the actor who would never grow up would work with the director who would never grow up—a perfect pairing.

Ray almost out-Deaned Dean in the outlier game. An alcoholic and sometime drug user with a gambling problem, Ray had a lively marital history. His second wife was the beautiful Gloria Grahame, who starred in two of his films, *A Woman's Secret* and *In a Lonely Place*. The marriage came to a shocking end when Ray discovered his fifteen-year-old son, from a previous marriage, in bed with his wife. (Several years later, Grahame married the son, Tony Ray.) During the filming of *Rebel*, Dennis Hopper, who had been dating young Natalie Wood, found her in bed with Nicholas Ray in his cottage at the Chateau Marmont. She was sixteen, he was forty-three. There was a lot of Freudianism going on in Ray's life.

Casting, according to Beverly Long (Helen in the film), was "nuts." Every teenager in Hollywood was vying for a part, and she herself went to three or four of these cattle calls, where Ray would talk to each candidate about the kid's family life and who the kid really was. "I don't know," she said, "he was so strange; he was a very iconoclastic kind of director." Dean thrived in such chaos, and Ray welcomed his suggestions, even if he didn't always follow them. Dean, for example, wanted his New York friend Christine White for the role that eventually went to Natalie Wood, whom he also knew from having previously worked with her in a TV drama (he gave Wood her first screen kiss).

He also lobbied hard for Jack Simmons, one of the strangest figures in Dean's inner circle. John Gilmore had known Simmons before Jimmy did. To Gilmore, he was "an odd bird" who held a reputation as "one of the most notorious faggots in Hollywood." Simmons got a nose job and started combing his hair like Jimmy's. He was the same height as Dean (five eight) and dressed exactly like him. Stewart Stern, the screenwriter for *Rebel*, offered an emphatic portrait of Simmons: "Jack was gay, and he was very androgynous, and you would have thought he was like a little girl. He was feminine—and pert and puckish and adoring." Stern wanted only a hint of homosexuality for Plato Crawford's character, but at Dean's insistence, Simmons got a background role in the gang. His only moment is when he hands the knife to Jim Stark preceding the famous fight scene. Dean and Simmons usually arrived on the set together and left together.

Instead, the actor chosen for Plato was sixteen-year-old Sal Mineo, who was also gay but much more repressed, which made him perfect for the role. The teenager was quite perceptive in his view of Jimmy: "I did feel there was something behind some of his actions that other people might call cruel or unsympathetic to others—I mean things like there were mornings when he really was awful to people, he'd totally disregard them and not say anything the whole day, and man, I could feel rejected and I'd end up saying, 'What did I do wrong?'" Mineo fell hopelessly in love with Dean anyway.

Filming began on March 25 and finished sixty-three days later, on May 27.

Dean's temperamental dominance, along with Ray's approval, affected just about every scene in *Rebel Without a Cause*. Jim Backus, cast as Dean's weak, apron-wearing father, wrote in his autobiography, *Rocks on the Roof* (1958), that he had never seen anything like it. He was one of the few older men Dean seemed to like. He said Dean was "practically a co-director."

Like the older actors in *East of Eden,* Backus and Ann Doran (the mother) watched with great amusement Dean's method of getting into the right frame of mind to do a scene. The two of them sneaked onto the set of the police station to watch a scene, then stood around waiting while Jimmy "got down in this fetal position." After a long wait, he stood up, and Ray said "Action!" Doran and Backus couldn't stop laughing and had to sneak out. "We had never seen such a bunch of crap in our lives," she recalled.

In one of their scenes together at the police station, Dean tried to tell Doran how to react, and she replied icily, "Look, junior, I've been around a long time, and you're new. Don't tell me how to do it. Let me make my own mistakes." Doran was so disgusted with Dean's foul language that she threatened to quit if he didn't stop. His marijuana smoking on the set also infuriated Doran, who hated the smell and his behavior. And yet, Doran would later see another side of Dean, as he started dropping by her house to talk and calling her "Mom." Dean's search for the lost mother was never-ending.

Another older woman actor, Marietta Canty (the Crawford family's maid), saw just how close to the surface Dean's perpetual hurt lay. In one scene when he couldn't get it the way he wanted, he took out his anger by beating his fists and head on a wall, and when she went over to caution him about a possible concussion, he asked, "Who cares?" She said she did, and his response stayed with her: "Well, God doesn't care. Just look at the dirty trick he played on me with my mother and father."

Brando had urged that the actor's mission was to "turn trauma into drama," and Dean had enough trauma to last him a career, or so it seemed. But how long could Dean have drawn upon that well of loneliness? Age, time, change, experience—all of these awaited him, though at twenty-four he seemed locked into a timeless past that started at age nine and ran like a jagged plumb line straight to the heart of Cal Trask and James Stark.

Teenager Natalie Wood, like many others, was struck by his strange intensity. But his attention-seeking antics also made her nervous. A seasoned veteran child star trying to make the jump to adult roles, Wood was alternately drawn to Dean and rebuffed by his rudeness and his obvious delight in humiliating her. She also seems to have had a profound understanding of the Dean–Ray symbiosis: "But I think Nick just absolutely understood Jimmy, they were just completely in tune, their personalities." She thought that Dean "reminded Nick of himself a great deal." As a result, she concluded, "So there was never any friction, as there was between Jimmy and other directors that he worked with."

Besides Jack Simmons, the person Dean seemed closest to on the set was Nicholas Ray. Dennis Hopper, who didn't like Ray because of the Natalie Wood business, hero-worshipped Dean and stated emphatically that "James Dean directed *Rebel Without a Cause,* from blocking all the scenes, setting the camera, starting the scene and saying 'cut.' Nicholas Ray intelligently allowed him to do this." Hopper was typically overstating the case, but it is true that Ray ceded to Dean a very unusual amount of power in the creative process.

Indeed, Ray and Dean grew closer together as filming progressed, spending a weekend on a quick trip to Mexico on one occasion and watching road races together on another. Ray even began to dress like Dean, wearing jeans and a T-shirt and going barefoot. There was no other director in Hollywood likely to do that. Ray was reliving his youth and sleeping with teenager Natalie Wood the whole time. What a trip.

Dean's unusual codirector role in *Rebel* is nowhere more evident than in the famous knife-fight scene. Dean insisted they use real knives, and when Buzz (Corey Allen), accidentally nicked him, drawing blood, Ray stopped the action, and Dean blew up. "Goddamn it, Nick! What the fuck are you doing? Can't you see this is a real moment! That's what I'm here for!" According to Ray, Dean had to have "a special kind of climate"—one of "reassurance, tolerance, [and] understanding." Translation: He had to be coddled. And according to Marietta Canty, if things went badly and Ray wasn't pleased, Jimmy "would stand there and cry like a baby."

There were other moments when Dean's intensity seemed extreme, as though it sprang from some personal source rather than from the demands of the script. Which, of course, it did. In one scene, a fierce encounter with his parents, Dean grabbed Jim Backus with such strength and ferocity that Backus was helpless as Dean virtually carried him across the room. And in a scene at the police station that called for the actor to express anger,

Dean slammed his fist onto a desktop so hard that they had to take him to the hospital to see if he had broken a bone. He had not, but nobody who witnessed that display of rage, real or Method-inspired, ever forgot it. Photographer Dennis Stock remarked, "When you saw *Rebel Without a Cause*, that was Jimmy you were seeing up there on the screen."

⚜

Off-camera, Jimmy's penchant for Nathaniel West–type lonely hearts ran unabated. He collected them.

Googie's, an all-night coffee shop next door to Schwab's Pharmacy on Sunset Boulevard, was Dean's favorite nocturnal hangout, and here he held court with acolytes and seekers and doppelgangers in that weird group known as "the Night Watch," or, more dismissively, a "crew of creeps." Dean's shadow, Jack Simmons, was nearly always there, and Maila Nurmi was another regular. Nurmi dressed like a witch and called herself "Vampira," her professional name. She hosted horror movies on TV and traveled around in a black hearse chauffeured by Simmons. Nurmi tried to capitalize on her closeness to Dean, and it got to the point where he had to throw her under the hearse. Asked about their relationship, he told a reporter, "I don't go out with witches, and I dig dating cartoons even less."

Another person Jimmy met at Googie's was a girl who had lost part of one leg in a motorcycle accident. Her name was Toni Lee. One night around 4:00 A.M.—prime time for Jimmy—he called at her apartment, and as they talked, he asked her to remove her clothes for him. She did, and he "ran his fingers over the scars on the stump . . . he went over them one by one." After he was finished, he kissed her leg and told her, "It's beautiful and you're beautiful." In her memoir, Toni Lee Scott says there was no romance, that instead "there was friendship; and that, too, is a kind of loving."

Not so surprisingly, Jimmy's kind of loving took various forms.

According to his friend John Gilmore, Jimmy was an "opportunistic explorer" for whom sex was basically an experimental act. In *Live Fast— Die Young: Remembering the Short Life of James Dean* (1997), Gilmore gave a detailed account of his and Jimmy's fumbling attempts at some kind of

sexual rapport, and he summed it up in one taut phrase: "Bad boys playing bad boys while opening up the bisexual sides of ourselves."

It was probably Jimmy's coffee-fueled, insomnia-driven quest for the
outré, the forbidden, the beyond-the-pale that earned him a brief turn in
Hollywood Babylon II. In Kenneth Anger's hands, Jimmy's presumed sexual practices took on masochistic meanings: "sex assorted with beatings,
boots, belts, and bondage—spiced with knowing cigarette burns (which
gave Jimmy his underground nickname: The Human Ashtray)." There is
no evidence of such beyond the fact that Dean did sculpt an ashtray of himself that he called "the Human Ashtray." Jimmy was an experimenter:
John Gilmore, Dizzy Sheridan, and William Bast each attest to that. But
like many other aspects of Dean's life, there are claims and counterclaims
that are likely never to be resolved.

Dean's penchant for exotic foreign types found a new, though brief, out-
let that April when he started seeing Lili Kardell, a young starlet from
Denmark. Lili was a free spirit and would jump on the back of Jimmy's
motorcycle and speed away into the night. She kept a diary in which she
recorded a typical evening: April 10, "had a dinner date with Jimmy at Villa
Capri. Drove home to his place **there." The asterisks were code for sex.
She said Jimmy was often moody, and she mentioned his habit of hopping
up from their table at the Villa Capri to visit with a buddy he'd spotted at
another table, leaving her alone with her thoughts and her bread sticks
while he carried on with his friend for a half hour or more. She was good-
natured about it, but still, it made a girl wonder.

The singer and dancer Eartha Kitt was a favorite of Dean's sleepless
nights. They met for the first time in Hollywood and spent time together
there and in New York. In her autobiography *Alone with Me*, Kitt describes
their relationship as "strictly platonic and spiritual" and "like brother and
sister." Much of their interaction took place in the wee hours of the night.
He would ring her up in the predawn hours and she'd drag herself out of
bed and get on the back of his bike and they'd cruise the quiet streets of
L.A. while the city slept. He never took her to haunts like Googie's, where
the Night Crew operated. In New York, they walked the streets in the post-
midnight hours, and during the day Dean would sometimes join her in a

modern dance studio, where he sought to improve his physical movements. She always called him "Jamie" and wrote that she never saw that side of him described as "a solemn, intense, and troubled young man." Instead, she believed that "each brought out the child in the other." He called most often when he was troubled, and in the summer of 1955, during the filming of *Giant*, he called all the time.

Between motion pictures, Dean continued to appear in TV dramas, and despite his new success and fame, he remained basically unchanged. Some thought he was worse. Don Medford directed Dean in three TV dramas and found him "virtually impossible." "He had no discipline at all," said Medford. Success hadn't changed his appearance or lack of consideration for others. He typically showed up late, wearing dirty clothes and pants with a string for a belt.

The more famous Dean became, following the buzz surrounding *East of Eden*, the crazier he acted. There was a near-death experience on his new motorcycle, a 500 Triumph Trophy. He came within inches of crashing into photographer Phil Stern when he ran the light at Laurel Canyon and Sunset, and screenwriter Irving Shulman saw him barreling down a street and into a gas station driveway at a very high speed. There was no difference between the teenager of Fairmount and the twenty-four-year-old star when it came to speed.

The Sunset Strip was Jimmy's personal playground. Everybody who wanted to be somebody, among the young and the still hungry older seekers, fought it out in this two-mile stretch, a kind of battlefield of ambition and desire. Jimmy took pleasure in harassing and scaring people he knew, such as Shelley Winters, who recounted a particularly harrowing experience. One night she was driving down Sunset toward the Chateau Marmont when Dean appeared on his motorcycle, whizzing in and out of the roadway in a "deadly game of circling us." The other person in the car, Marilyn Monroe, was terrified, as was Winters. When they finally reached Chateau Marmont and parked, Jimmy got off his motorcycle and "stood there like a little boy who had been playing a practical joke."

His friend Arthur Lowe, Jr., recalled nights when he would be driving home on Sunset Boulevard long after midnight, when suddenly Dean would spring into view, riding his motorcycle a hundred miles an hour in one direction, then blaring toward Lowe's car at the same speed from another. It scared the hell out of Lowe. Don Medford recalled a fright he had back in November 1954, when he was directing Dean in "I'm a Fool," a teleplay starring Dean and Natalie Wood. He was driving home on the freeway one night and here came Jimmy on that bike, weaving this way and that with his hands in the air. "It scared the shit out of me," Medford said, and he told Jimmy the next morning, "Don't play with your life like that!" But Jimmy just smiled at him.

Lots of people thought Dean was going to kill himself or somebody else riding what he called that "murdercycle."

Dean also drove his car like a maniac. His friend Joe Hyams got a taste of Jimmy's dangerous driving one night when as a passenger he found himself going with Jimmy up Mulholland Drive and enduring a hair-raising race downhill between Jimmy and Lew Bracker, both cars roaring pell-mell down the winding road with its hairpin curves and breathless glimpses of deep canyons on one side.

Jimmy seemed to make little distinction between ordinary driving and organized racing events. His first car, a red MMG-TD sports car purchased in May 1954, was not fast enough, and in February 1955 he bought a white Porsche 356 Super Speedster. Showing off his new car, Jimmy took his friend Bill Bast on a harrowing drive in the Hollywood Hills, from winding Appian Way at the crest to the high-speed steep mountain drive through Laurel Canyon—a perilous ten-mile-long roadway. "That night I swore I'd never ride with him again."

Two months later, Jimmy drove the Porsche in his first racing competition, on March 26 and 27, in the Palm Springs Road Races, where he finished in third place before being moved up to second place because of another driver's disqualification. In his second race, in Bakersfield on May 1, he placed third. Jimmy's lifelong taste for speed had reached a new level.

⁂

When Carroll Baker arrived in L.A. that April, the first guy she met upon entering the Warner Bros. lot was an old acquaintance from her Method days in New York. He lay in wait for her at the guard's booth, where "a small face peeked out—the eyes a bit too close together, a crooked grin—Jimmy Dean!" He plopped her on the back of his motorbike and gave her a lightning tour of the studio grounds, screeching to a stop at his favorite place on the lot, a replica of an American small town that evoked his upbringing back home in Indiana. Baker was impressed with his demeanor. Jimmy seemed to be a lot more confident than he had been in New York.

Once her tour of the lot was over, James Dean reappeared and together they had lunch in the fabled Green Room. Munching her Betty Grable salad, she watched as Elizabeth Taylor, beautiful but overweight from her recent childbirth, dined with George Stevens. Baker was impressed that Stevens, unlike everybody else in the Green Room, concentrated on his conversation with Taylor and was not constantly swiveling around to see what was happening at another table. She was also amazed at James Dean's behavior. He hopped from one table to another, spreading goodwill. Baker could hardly believe her eyes. And when Hedda Hopper swept into view, he almost threw himself on his knees before the feared queen of columnists. This was definitely a new side of Jimmy.

Hedda Hopper interviewed Carroll Baker but wasn't the least interested in her professional prospects. Instead, she concentrated on coaxing the recently married young actress to admit that she was having an affair with James Dean, which she most decidedly was not. Besides being married, there was never any sexual feeling between the two of them. In fact, Baker considered Dean asexual, as did several of her women actor friends back in New York. Everybody seems to have been interested in Dean's sexual identity, but there was little consensus as to what that identity might be.

On another motorcycle ride with Dean that day, the two of them returned to his favorite place on the lot, the Norman Rockwell–type small town. Only this time, he was furious upon finding Dennis Hopper there. He made Baker go over and meet him, saying bitterly, "It's his place now." Hopper did not impress her. "He looked up only briefly from contemplating his boots and then reassumed his 'James Dean' attitude. But he was only a mimic. There were no thoughts in his head worthy of boot contemplation. The troubled pose was just that: a pose."

Even as shooting on *Rebel* continued, Dean began developing the character he would play in *Giant*. To do so, he sought out the help of Bob Hinkle, and the two hit it off immediately. Jimmy told Hinkle, "I want you to help me create the character of Jett Rink. When I get into a part, I like to stay in that part and never come out of it until the picture's over. I want to be a Texan twenty-four hours a day." This was the beginning of a friendship free of angst, brooding, and complications. Hinkle was a country boy, and so was Jimmy. They got along fine. At Dean's suggestion, Hinkle helped outfit him at a western-clothing store in L.A., and they hung out together. They would sometimes grab a burger at Barney's Beanery, a popular eatery in West Hollywood. A sign hung over the bar: FAGGOTS—STAY OUT. Jimmy told Bob, "That's why I like to come here."

At one point, Nicholas Ray dropped by Hinkle's office (in Alan Ladd's old digs) and asked him to "ease up a bit." What he meant was that "Jett Rink is starting to wear off a little bit on Jim Stark. Here I've got this guy who's supposed to be a big-city juvenile delinquent and he sounds more like John Wayne."

※

Warner Bros. was going to make Dean rich, but he felt absolutely no gratitude to the studio. He told Carroll Baker, "You've got to treat these guys like shit." He remained contemptuous of the system that he had worked so hard to become a part of. He showed up at studio-arranged interviews dressed like a feral homeless person. "Really filthy, with heavy dandruff and a really bad appearance" was how one person in the publicity department described him. His wardrobe typically consisted of torn jeans and a ratty sweater. And there were numerous instances of brattish, ungrateful behavior. Bob Hinkle remembered coming out of the commissary one day with Dean when a reporter asked for an interview and Jimmy said, "Hell no. You're not going to write what I tell you. You're going to write whatever you want to, so why don't you just go ahead and write it?"

Another time, a Warner Bros. executive introduced Dean to an important stockholder, and Dean grabbed all the change in his pocket and flung it at the man's feet. Dean himself was fully aware of his ill-mannered ways.

He wrote Barbara Glenn, telling her how he would like to be close to someone but would be rude instead: "Then I say something nasty or nothing. Or I walk away. The poor person doesn't know what happened." George Stevens, Jr., offered a similar assessment: "He could be warm, entertaining, and fun to be with. And he could be diffident and inconsiderate of those around him."

Jimmy's obsessive need to be the center of attention was evident to everybody, but some thought they saw through the bad behavior. "Those of us who knew Dean in New York know that there was a monotonous sameness about everything he did," said one. "Fame made him uncomfortable and did strange things to him." Leonard Rosenman traced Jimmy's behavior to "his almost pathological vulnerability to hurt and rejection."

Several people saw Dean as looking much older than the troubled teen roles he played in *East of Eden* and *Rebel Without a Cause*, and they were keenly aware of the difference between the on-screen image and the person they knew. Frank Corsaro, a theatrical and opera director who remembered Dean from the Actors Studio days, spared nothing in his analysis of Dean: "Verging on thirty, he was still twelve years old emotionally." Corsaro also saw that "For all the supernal light he radiated on screen, he had a perverse cruel streak in him which negated that image in life." Corsaro also pointed to Dean's androgynous nature: "Jimmy lived a complex, shady existence. Emotionally, he was a male hustler." An actor who knew Jimmy in New York was astonished at the "magic creature" on the screen in *East of Eden*: "He was never pulled together. He was generally quite filthy—I mean, really filthy: heavy dandruff and the whole scene. But really bad. He looked, I'd say, older than thirty."

Even with success firmly in his grasp, Jimmy continued his willful and abrasive behavior. One day at Warner Bros., he saw a huge blowup picture of himself in the commissary and ripped it from the wall. He walked over to a table where some of the publicity staff were dining and tore it to pieces, exclaiming, "Don't ever put my fucking picture up in here! Whatta you think, that I live here or something? You think you own me? Nobody owns me!"

Yet the publicity department continued to do all they could to promote the young actor, though naturally they were worried about his demeanor and unpredictable actions, which seemed to betoken an adolescence without end.

⁂

On the night of May 27, 1955, when they finished the last day of shooting on *Rebel*, nobody wanted it to end, especially Ray. For him personally, *Rebel* would be the high point of his career in motion pictures. To celebrate, he collected Natalie Wood, Dennis Hopper, and a couple of assistants in his old Cadillac and set out for Googie's, with Jimmy Dean leading the way on his motorcycle. As the caravan neared the coffee shop, Jim Stark lay stretched flat out on his British Triumph T-100 motorcycle, with the enigmatic "Dean's Dilemma" stenciled on its side, as it raced toward Sunset Boulevard, and Nicholas Ray told his passengers wistfully that that was how the film should have ended.

⁂

Although George Stevens insisted upon a contractual ban against racing until Dean's work on *Giant* was completed, Jimmy entered his Porsche Speedster in a race in Santa Barbara on May 28–29, reasoning that he hadn't started work on *Giant* yet. He had a shot at fourth place until he blew a piston and had to drop out. This would be Jimmy's last chance to show his stuff on a racetrack until he returned from Texas.

6

West of the Pecos

By reason, luck, or divination, Stevens decided to film *Giant* in a remote, sparsely populated region of far West Texas. Popular novelist Zane Grey had celebrated the area in his novel *The Lone Star Ranger* (1915): "In the valleys of the foothills out across the plains were ranches and farther north, villages, and the towns of Alpine and Marfa."

This isolated stretch of American ranching country is part of the vast Chihuahuan Desert, which reaches from northern Mexico all the way to New Mexico. The great expanse of open prairie, desert, mountains, and the arching sky above captured the imagination of George Stevens, but it would take a good deal of time and travel before he settled on the exact spot.

Stevens had always been drawn to location shooting. A city boy, he loved working in the outdoors, and his preference for outdoor films was evident from the first, as he recalled years later: "When I was a kid in San Francisco . . . I could always tell from across the street whether I wanted to see [a] film. . . . If pictures were outside I would cross the street, but if I could see it all took place inside I didn't want to see it." Plein air shooting served many purposes in his psychic economy. Echoes of the Old West were everywhere, and Stevens had fallen in love with the West working on silent films for the Hal Roach Studio that featured Rex the Wonder Horse. On one of these, *The Devil Horse,* he spent time on a Crow Indian reservation near the Little Big Horn River, where there were Crow Indians who had been involved in, as he said, the "Custer adventure."

Stevens would also have agreed with something John Huston said about the value of shooting on location: "The point about location filming is that if the actors are living in a certain way, it will come out in their performances. Their very hardships give character to the finished film." Earlier in Stevens's career he had shot the popular adventure film *Gunga Din* (1939) in the rugged Alabama Hills of northern California, in the Sierra Nevada range. The area was a good match for the Khyber Pass region in India. What Stevens said about that location would apply to *Giant,* as well: "The one thing that's continually at work in the film is the landscape, which is fine to look at." The plain and the mountain possessed value no fake backdrops could capture: "These visuals go beyond the set itself, and give the audience something rewarding." There was a personal advantage in distant location shooting as well—to be as far away from intrusive studio executives as possible. He appreciated Western locations in particular. "Nothing is more pleasant for me," he said decades later, "than to be on location in the country I love, in any of our western landscapes."

Stevens was bound and determined to shoot in Texas, though he was keenly aware of the general hostility to Ferber's novel in the state. In early 1953, he joked about the possible lengths to which he might have to go: "The story's so hot and Texans object so hotly, we'll have to shoot it with a telephoto lens across the border from Oklahoma."

Warner Bros. had other ideas about where to film, but Stevens, known to be a stubborn man, was also politic enough to entertain alternatives. He listened to various possibilities as they percolated through the system. Somebody proposed Santa Ynez Valley, in the Santa Barbara area, but the accompanying photos in the *L.A. Examiner* (May 23, 1954) showed dude ranchers riding through dense vegetation and canopies of trees, with captions reading "copious rains" and "almost a jungle like setting." It looked nothing like Texas. There were also those lobbying for Arizona, sending copies of *Arizona Highways* to Stevens, who looked them over and said no. He examined photos of the countryside around Tucson and rejected that landscape, too. He screened *Broken Arrow,* filmed in New Mexico, but it didn't appeal to him, either. Not surprisingly, Jack Warner's preference was based on economics. Ever concerned with budget considerations, he favored California.

Apart from Texas, the most intriguing prospect was Mexico, as Stevens wrote to Mel Dellar, unit manager, and Boris Leven, set director, on November 1. "Tenny Wright suggests we might solve our location problem—Reata Ranch, Mexican village, etc.—in Mexico, on the basis that huge houses have been built down there in connection with cattle ranches; one, for instance, having been built by William Randolph Hearst. Let's keep this in mind." The ranch in question was Barbícora in Chihuahua, Mexico, approximately three hundred miles southwest of El Paso. At 1.6 million acres it was the largest on the continent, larger even than the King Ranch in South Texas.

But in the end it was Texas, not Mexico, that exerted a magnetic pull on Stevens's imagination. Nothing, he felt, was more important than authenticity of place, speech, mores, and manners. Obviously, he needed to go and see for himself, and like Ferber a decade before, he went to Texas to take a look around.

Warmly welcomed in every town and city he visited, from Galveston, on the coast, to Amarillo, in the Panhandle, he ricocheted around the state, being feted by mayors and chamber of commerce go-getters who saw dollar signs in the prospect of Hollywood's coming to their town or city. After miles and miles of Texas, Stevens knew that the one place where he wasn't going to shoot was anywhere near the King Ranch, in South Texas, near the coast, forty-five miles northwest of Corpus Christi. He wanted to avoid any associations with the storied ranch because just about everybody knew that the novel was based in part on the Kleberg family and the vast holdings and power and legendary status of the Walled Kingdom.

Ferber had it both ways in her novel, setting the action near the King Ranch and extending its sweep to incorporate the extravagant geography of Texas: "The giant kingdom that was the Reata Ranch lay dozing in the sun, its feet laved by the waters of the Gulf of Mexico many miles distant, its head in the cloud-wreathed mountains far far to the north, its gargantuan arms flung east and west in careless might." In point of fact, the King Ranch consists of four separate divisions, all in South Texas, where the landscape is as flat as an iron and thickened by heavy brush.

In San Antonio, Stevens saw a western painting hanging in the lobby of the Menger Hotel, right next to the Alamo. He fell in love with it and set out to acquire it for his picture. In Dallas, he met with R. J. (Bob) O'Donnell, the powerful head of the Interstate Theatres, which controlled over two hundred venues in Texas and the Midwest. O'Donnell was excited about the prospect of the film premiering in Texas. Any one of the crown jewels in his chain—the Majestic Theatres, large and richly appointed cathedrals of cinema located in Dallas, San Antonio, Houston, and Fort Worth—would welcome such an opportunity. O'Donnell would be heard from later on when screenings of *Giant* were shown to preview audiences in the summer of 1956.

Even after Stevens's travels, the big question remained: Where in Texas? The state is huge, 801 miles from its southernmost point in Brownsville to its northernmost at the top of the Panhandle. It has 254 counties, some bigger than Rhode Island. Brewster County alone is four times the size of Delaware. With an expanse of 268,581 square miles, Texas is large enough to contain ten states. Not only that; by comparison with Europe, Texas is bigger than France and twice the size of Germany. It's plenty big all right, and before the Interstate Highway System (a transformative achievement of the Eisenhower administration), the state felt even bigger in a sense because lower speed limits and two-lane highways meant longer driving times.

In late 1954, Stevens chose Boris Leven, a Russian émigré born in Moscow, to handle the set design for the film. Set designers are usually among the unsung background figures on a movie set. Although very important to directors, they are rarely in the limelight themselves. Leven (1908–1986) enjoyed a long career marked by nine Oscar nominations for his work as a sketch artist, art director, and set director. Stevens selected him based largely on his work in *The Silver Chalice* (1954), a box-office bust remembered in film circles only because it featured the disastrous debut of a very young Method actor from New York named Paul Newman, who was decked out in a ridiculous-looking Roman costume that looked like a cocktail dress.

Despite that movie's problems, Stevens admired what he saw in the set designs—a style that handled space well and juxtaposed ordinary reality with the unexpected. Spatial relationships in *Giant* would be critical to its visual success. Early on, Stevens rejected the new rage, CinemaScope, although that was what Jack Warner wanted. Like many in the film industry, Warner believed that CinemaScope was going to pack theaters and offset the popularity of the invidious new competition—television. But Stevens intensely disliked CinemaScope and argued that it "was better suited for high school graduation photos and profiles of submarines." He wouldn't stand for it, remarking at one point that "the question is whether you want a system of photography that pictures a boa constrictor to better advantage than a man." Instead, he opted for a visual method that conveyed both horizontal space and height to express "man's aspirations." He wanted a system that would capture the size and scope of Texas. Once again, his preferences prevailed over those of the head of Warner Bros.

After surveying the photographs plastered all over the entry to Stevens's office, Leven proposed going to Texas to see for himself, and to that end Stevens dispatched him to scout locations in late November 1954. The mission was to find "a real ranch house in which the Benedicts lived" and to "keep away from the King Ranch because the story was written about them and it wasn't particularly complimentary and so that was out."

Leven arrived in El Paso on November 29, 1954, and returned to L.A. on December 8. Once back in Burbank, he typed up a somewhat caustic account of his journey: "Ten Beautiful Days in Texas."

In El Paso, he noted, "Many pregnant women. Large Mexican population." From there he went southeast into the plains of Presidio County, pronouncing it "monotonous country." He did take note of a small cattle town named Marfa in some detail, though: "Marfa—population 3600. Hotel Paisano. In the lobby the usual stuffed head of a steer and directly below an elaborate display of Copenhagen china, Swedish stainless steel and paintings—contemporary—from New York that sell from $150 to $650."

He liked the old courthouse in Marfa, a "real gem of Victorian era"— half a block from the hotel.

Looking at the landscape with a painterly eye, Leven observed, "Flat country is topped off by low horizontal hills. Dark cattle create an interesting pattern against the bleached grass." This detail would resonate in the eventual sketch that he made of the landscape.

From the Marfa area, Leven traveled to San Antonio, where he observed "40% Mexican. Segregated." On the road to Houston he remarked, "Since we left home have not seen a single attractive male or female." He took note of the "gaudy" Shamrock Hotel, oilman Glenn McCarthy's pride and joy.

In Dallas, he summed up a very stereotypical view of the state: "Texans still have a girl in one hand and a bottle of bourbon in the other."

In all, Leven visited seventeen towns and cities in Texas, from El Paso to Houston, and although he drove 2,500 miles across the state, he found, with one exception, no imposing ranch houses. The single exception that caught his eye was the Victorian house at the Waggoner Ranch in Decatur, 175 miles northwest of Dallas. In an interview years later, he praised its "old beauty" and its "real flair for elegance and scale." "What would happen," he wondered, "if . . . this wonderful Victorian house perhaps stood all by itself and there would be nothing but the field, you know, the ranch and no other buildings."

He was also impressed with county courthouses, and he had the same thought about them as he did about the Waggoner mansion: "I saw quite a number of these sort of Victorian architecture country court houses that were rather interesting. On the way home, I suddenly thought, What would happen if this house, this wonderful Victorian house, stood all by itself, with nothing around it but the field."

The idea appealed to him so strongly that he prepared a color sketch showing a three-story Victorian pile surrounded by flat, pale whitish plains on which brown cattle grazed. The house, on the right side of the sketch, drew one's eye across the emptiness of the landscape, broken only by the brown cattle. And there stood the grand, solitary house and the sky reaching down in the distance. It was a marvelous drawing, and when he showed it to Stevens, the director exclaimed, "Partner, this is the best damn thing that has happened in this film so far. This is it."

It wasn't until early the next year, though, that Stevens made the decision where to film. Leven's sketch seems to have had a lot to do with his choice. Feeling that he needed to see the ground again, Stevens went back to Texas in January 1955, accompanied this time by Leven and three other members of the *Giant* team, sidekick Fred Guiol, location manager Joe Barry, and production manager Mel Dellar. They journeyed to Presidio County and, like early cattlemen, looked at the grasslands, and Stevens concluded that the Reata headquarters would appear to best advantage on the lonely, largely empty prairie of the Marfa Plateau, outside of Marfa, the county seat of Presidio County. It was wide-open big-sky country.

The town was very remote—194 miles southeast of El Paso, the largest nearby city, and 236 miles from Midland-Odessa. Presidio County was a sparsely populated land with slightly more than eight thousand people in the whole vastness of its 3,856 square miles. It was ranching country and had been since Anglos had begun to push into the region in the 1880s, when the last of the Plains tribes, mainly Comanches and Apaches, gave way to the iron horse and the founding of ranches and small towns. Marfa began its existence in 1883 as a water stop on the newly built railroad that connected the region to San Antonio and El Paso. According to legend, the town was named after a character in either a Russian novella, *Marfa Posadnitsa,* or a character in Dostoyevsky's *Crime and Punishment.*

The Marfa Plateau is the easternmost part of the Chihuahuan Desert. The Spanish considered the region so desolate that they called it *desplobado*— "the uninhabited." The American sector stretches seventy-five miles long and thirty-five miles wide and is covered with buffalo grass, grama, and cactus. At night, the plateau, with an elevation of 4,685 feet, gives the feeling of a dais configured to present a world of stars so close, one can almost reach up and touch them.

Beyond the plains to the south lie distant blue mountains where the peaks of the Sierra Viegas, Chinatis, Bofecillos, and Chisos reach heights of six thousand feet or more. They are the northernmost reach of the Big Bend, around eighty miles south of Marfa. To the north, the Davis Mountains, twenty-five miles distant, offer a similar distant bluish allure. Stevens wanted the flatness and endless space, and although mountains appear in a few shots, he essentially shot the Texas landscape as one endless prairie. And there was also the sky, which very much appealed to Stevens. He loved the light and the sky in that region, and artists and photographers still do.

To outsiders, Presidio County looked desolate and uninviting, but for the latter-day pioneer George Stevens, it seemed to be the perfect landscape for his intentions. It offered a spatial dimension that his cameras could dramatize and a remoteness that allowed him to create his own little commonwealth in the Chihuahuan Desert. Stevens explained his choice to a visiting reporter from L.A.: "It has a natural beauty, with the broad sweep of the plains, the mountains in the background, and the striking white clouds against a blue sky." The landscape of Presidio County would long define Texas in the popular imagination.

The place where everything came together for Stevens was the Ryan Ranch, which ran alongside State Highway 90, twenty-one miles west of Marfa. Consisting of 34,880 acres, the Ryan Ranch wasn't the biggest in the county, but it was big enough. (The Brite Ranch, founded in 1885, was the largest, at 88,573 acres.) Wildlife on that prairie included mourning doves and blue quail, pronghorn antelopes and desert mule deer. Because of the elevation, 4,685 feet, it never gets as hot as the Hollywood people or their chroniclers thought it did. Many of the biographies and memoirs report that temperatures soared to 120 degrees, but that never happened. One historian, in fact, states that "in the summer it is often one of the coolest places in the state."

Stevens contracted with Worth Evans, owner of the Ryan Ranch, to grant access to his property. Evans welcomed the economic boon that Hollywood would bring during a time of drought and depressed cattle markets. The country had been in a devastating drought since the beginning of the decade. The lack of rain led to overgrazing and diminished grass, and cattle had to be fed bales of hay if the rancher could afford it, and for those who could not, they used handheld burners to singe thorns off prickly pear to make it edible for their cows. Cattle prices plummeted. A cow that had brought $250 in 1950 sold for $65 six years later. Raising cattle was never an easy proposition. There were only three good years in ranching from 1945 over the next twenty-odd years: 1950, 1963, and 1973.

The drought was so bad, about all you could do was laugh. Locals told whoppers about the dry spell. According to one joke, when it finally rained a little bit and a child felt a raindrop on his head, he fainted, and his folks had to throw a bucket of sand in his face to wake him up. Another joke spoke to churchgoers in the region. How dry was it? It was so dry that the Baptists stopped baptizing and resorted to sprinkling, the Methodists gave up sprinkling and used a damp sponge, and the Presbyterians handed out rain checks.

Yet Worth Evans made certain to inform Stevens about the possibility of rain. Though the drought had begun to take on biblical proportions, someday it would rain, it had to, and when it did, the rancher said, it could really cause trouble. High winds, lightning, and flash flooding were all local features of heavy rain. Stevens listened in that quiet way he had and went right ahead with his plans. Shooting was months away. The weather would take care of itself one way or the other.

Unlikely as it might seem, this small, isolated cattle town in the middle of nowhere held certain advantages that many another town of its size did not. The secret of Marfa's appeal to Stevens was twofold: the landscape of the countryside and, within the town, an infrastructure that met a surprising number of the needs of a visiting army of moviemakers.

First of all, there were two hotels where cast and crew could be housed, along with private residences to be rented for the stars. The El Paisano Hotel, built in 1930–1931 in anticipation of an oil boom that never happened, and now called the Hotel Paisano, is an impressive two-story Spanish Revival building with a large open central courtyard and a ballroom. The Crews Hotel, long since demolished, offered another useful venue for the *Giant* crew. And there were motels as well, not so comfortable as the Paisano, but serviceable: the Toltec Motel, the San Jacinto Motel, the Thunderbird Motel, and, in a pinch, the Bien Venido Motel in Alpine, twenty-six miles east of town on State Highway 67.

The El Paisano was absolutely crucial to the undertaking. The contract with the owner, Mrs. Emma Mallan, was for 118 people for twenty-four consecutive days, at a rate of $16.50 per person. Stevens objected to having to put as many as three persons in a room, but production manager Ralph Black pointed out that it was better than having to go to Alpine (which they would have to do anyway for some crew members and visitors).

Across the street from the Paisano stood the Palace Theatre, which Stevens would use to screen dailies.

Marfa also had transportation assets. The Southern Pacific Railroad came right through town, crossing Highland Street about three blocks from the El Paisano. There was also an airport close by—a necessity because dailies would have to be sent back to L.A. every day by air. The Marfa Municipal Airport, a little over four miles northeast of town, enjoyed regular service from the Trans-Texas Airlines, or Tree Top Airlines, as it was known throughout Texas because of the frequency of landings and takeoffs at cities as small as Marfa and Alpine.

Not everybody at Warner Bros. was happy with the decision to film in such a remote place. C. A. Bonniewell, Jr., the production timekeeper, was sent to Texas to secure union labor, only to find that there were no unions. He cast a disparaging eye at the local segregated Mexican population and sounded like one of the biased whites in the film when he wrote, "I have my own ideas why I find so many of them sleeping under their respective sombreros, against the Marfa State Bank building. Local opinion avers that when hired as laborers, you have to be a Simon Legree to get one hour's work out of eight of them."

Bonniewell mocked Marfa as the "sun-drenched gem of the West"—a place where he couldn't "figure why any soul would take a chance on crossing the Styx from here."

But Stevens liked it and that's what mattered. From his point of view, everything he needed was right there: the remote town, the endless prairie.

Stevens and his team also scouted the even smaller nearby town of Valentine, thirty-seven miles northwest of Marfa on State Highway 90, just inside Jeff Davis County. There the Warner Bros. construction crew would build the impoverished barrio village of Vienciento, where the Obregón family lives in distressing squalor. The Valentine cemetery would be used in a scene of great importance to Stevens. Finally, they built Rink's shack and its Little Reata gate entrance on Ben S. Avant's ranch land alongside State Highway 90, seven miles west of Marfa.

❊

Marfa in 1955 was kind of stalled out. The town had been hard hit by the closing of military installations ten years earlier, and its population of five thousand, the highest in Marfa's history, had dropped by a couple of thousand. The economy was hurting, and the drought wasn't helping. Ranchers scanned the skies, looking for signs, and some wondered if they were going to survive this long dry spell.

The month of June, however, started off very promising. First of all, it did rain, and rain was something grown-ups prayed for and little children were curious about. On June 2, two storms whipped into Presidio County. A windstorm swept eastward out of Mexico, causing considerable damage in the ancient town of Presidio, just across the Rio Grande from Ojinaga. On the roadways to Marfa, the dust was so thick that it "dropped visibility to zero for a few minutes on both highways." With the wind's gusting to an estimated forty miles an hour, it also brought a "smattering of hail" in Marfa. The second storm came from the Southwest and produced a lot of wind and lightning and, above all, "a fine rain which greatly benefited the entire area with much-needed water." Presidio County ranchers received an inch in some areas, less in others.

Oddly, the second cause for hope also carried the sound of *rain*: uranium. A talk at the local chamber of commerce on the possibility of finding uranium in Presidio County had left listeners "spellbound." But for all of its 3,856 square miles, there never has been a single oil strike or uranium discovery in that promising prairie sublime. And the fact remains that from then until now, the county has earned more income from the location filming of *Giant* and subsequent tourism inspired by the film than it ever has from oil or uranium.

In all that excitement about future prospects, there was only one mention in the local paper of the impending Hollywood invasion of their town, an advertisement on page 3: "THE PAISANO HOTEL of Marfa, Texas, is pleased to announce that we have been chosen as headquarters for Warner Brothers Motion Picture Stars and Technicians during the filming of 'The Giant' at Marfa June 4 through June 28." It concluded by inviting everybody to "Come and Dine with the Stars in the Paisano Coffee Shop and Dining Room." Breakfast, luncheon, and dinner ($4.50) would be served by the Leon Gillespie Catering Service of El Paso. The phone number was 311, an indication of how small Marfa was.

Fresh from his successful campaign in Virginia, Lt. Col. George Stevens proceeded to the small, distant town of Marfa. Stevens, cast, and crew landed in Marfa on June 4 at the Marfa Municipal Airport, four miles north of town. A train from L.A. had already brought in the rest of the cast and crew the day before. The skies were clear, the weather sparkling. A delegation of dignitaries and a crowd of about fifteen hundred excited citizens from Marfa and nearby towns had gathered to say howdy to Stevens and forty-three other "notables of the film industry." The high school band played "The Eyes of Texas," and Mayor H. A. Coffield presented a bouquet of roses to Elizabeth Taylor and Stetsons to Stevens and Rock Hudson—traditional Texas gifts, the same that were given to President and Mrs. Kennedy everywhere they stopped during their trip to Texas in November 1963.

Weeks before, a caravan of huge trucks had passed through on their way to the Ryan Ranch, and it took five railroad flatcars to deliver the twenty painted prefab sections that would be assembled and erected to create the incarnation of Boris Leven's sketch. The largest set ever constructed by Warner Bros., it cost $100,000 ($895,548 today) to build and had eighty-one feet of porches. The structure was lashed to telephone poles to prevent it from crashing down in high winds. Three stories high, with its topmost point crowned by a tower looming up sixty-four feet, the great house on the prairie loomed up arrestingly in the dazzling light of that summer, a beacon and an icon, both in the film and in the memory of millions of people who'd never even been to Texas. *The Big Bend Sentinel* dubbed it "Benedict Manor."

Warner Bros. had also seen to it that movies featuring the stars were playing in town that week: Rock Hudson in *Captain Lightfoot* at the Palace and Elizabeth Taylor in *The Last Time I Saw Paris* at the Marfa Drive-In out on State Highway 90. The next week featured Rock Hudson again, this time in *Magnificent Obsession* at the Marfa Drive-In, and James Dean in *East of Eden* at the Palace. "James Dean Must Be Seen," the paper shrieked. Plus, over at the Marfa Drive-In, *Francis Joins the WACS* featured the voice of Chill Wills as the talking mule.

Ferber's novel was generating a lot of local interest, as well. Nearly fifty readers checked out the library's single copy, and with the appearance of a paperback edition, sales at local stores were steady, with 842 copies snapped up in two weeks, and after filming got under way, teenagers bought copies for actors to sign.

-%-

On the ground in Marfa, the Hollywood visitors were kind of stunned at the isolation, which was so different from their usual surroundings. Elizabeth Taylor looked around and asked, "Where are we?" From an L.A. perspective, Marfa was a frontier outpost, a "dusty one-horse town." It was the definition of absence: no heart-shaped swimming pools—in fact, no swimming pools at all—no Romanoff's, no Don the Beachcomber and therefore no mai tais, no Schwab's, no Googie's, no Smoke House, no Mocambo, no Trocadero, no Ciro's, no La Rue, no Cock 'n Bull, no Cocoanut Grove, no Chateau Marmont, no Villa Capri, no gay bars, no beaches, no surf, no palm trees. In her memoir, *The Quality of Mercy* (1981), Mercedes McCambridge described the location as "the ugliest landscape on the face of the earth." The only tourist attraction was the Marfa Lights, a site nine miles east of town, just off State Highway 67, where from around 1880 onward folks had purportedly seen mysterious unexplained lights jumping around in the night sky. In many ways, the Hollywood crowd felt as isolated as if they had landed on the moon. In weeks to come, boredom, along with the exhaustion from long days of work, would set in for some, though for others the days would crackle with tension.

Stevens and company invested the town like an invading army, quartering most of the personnel in the El Paisano Hotel or the Crews Hotel.

Others, like Rock Hudson, James Dean, Chill Wills, Jane Withers, and Carroll Baker, were housed in private "Sunday homes" rented for the duration of the filming. Taylor got special star treatment, a private residence that she shared with her hairdresser, Patricia Westmore.

Once settled in, Stevens took a stroll down Highland Street and dropped into a barbershop near the hotel for a haircut and shave. He seemed like a regular guy at home on the range. The last thing he wanted to do was come off as a Hollywood swell, which he wasn't anyway. Very aware of how much Texans disliked Ferber's novel, Stevens was keenly attuned to the importance of public relations. He wanted to build a solid base of goodwill. Stevens was also always working when he was on location, and at the barbershop he spontaneously hired a local to appear in the film. *The Big Bend Sentinel* wrote the whole thing up, titling the story "Chaney Chosen for Part in 'The Giant,'" Chaney was Grannison Chaney, an African-American man who, according to the paper, was "Marfa's only fulltime professional boot black."

Leaning back in a barber's chair, Stevens jumped up suddenly and shouted, "I want you," indicating Chaney.

The startled man thought Stevens wanted his shoes shined. The newspaper's dialogue provides a racially tinted window into stereotyping typical of the period.

"You does, suh?" he stammered.

"Yup!" yupped Stevens, "I don't want a shine, I want you."

"What's you want me for?" asked Chaney.

"I want you to play in the 'Giant,'" said George.

The paper went on to add that "Chaney had taken his share of the kidding that had been going on around Marfa ever since it was known Stevens would film the movie here."

Marfa had long been segregated not by law but by custom, which amounted to the same thing. Theaters, schools, and cemeteries were segregated. There was a separate dance hall for Mexican-Americans, built in 1926. (The building is now Ballroom Marfa.) Mexican-American children attended Blackwell School, housed in an adobe building, while Anglos attended all-white schools with better facilities. One Latino resident of Presidio County recalls the time a white teacher told him to stop speaking Spanish or he would be sent back to Mexico, where he'd come from. But, he replied, he had never been to Mexico in his life. A white seventh-grade teacher in the segregated Blackwell School came up with a grotesque plan to force Latino students to learn English. She created a document, "The Last Rites of Spanish Speaking," and instructed the children to write Spanish words on pieces of paper and bury "Mr. Spanish" in a grave dug in the schoolhouse yard. The schools would not be integrated until 1964.

Mexican-Americans were buried in one of two cemeteries—the Cemeterio de la Merced and the Marfa Catholic cemetery. Both were located next to the white cemetery on State Highway 90, just outside town. A barbed-wire fence divided the two races, so that in death, as in life, there was segregation. There was no black cemetery, probably because only two African-Americans lived in Marfa: Grannison Chaney and his good friend George Livingston, a chef at the Paisano Hotel, who also operated a barbecue restaurant. When they died, two years apart—1972 and 1974, respectively— they were buried in the "paupers' corner" in the white cemetery, their graves separated from the white graves by a gravel path.

As the citizens of Marfa would discover, the film being shot in their county would present a powerful indictment of racial intolerance in Texas, and in the United States.

❧ 7 ❧

Plein Air

Principal photography began on Monday, June 6, a date that was sure to evoke memories for Stevens. Eleven years earlier, Lt. Col. George Stevens and his cameramen in the Army Signal Corps had filmed the Allied landing at Normandy. Ivan Moffat, who was with Stevens in France, had recently completed a screenplay for *D-Day the Sixth of June*, which would be released the same year as *Giant*. The war was something men who'd been there wouldn't forget, and memories of it would find their way into *Giant* in a moving sequence that tied together several motifs about contemporary Texas, and America.

According to the Daily Production and Progress Report, Stevens was already four days behind schedule, and fourteen days had elapsed since starting. By the end of the month, the studio estimated, he would be over budget by $200,000 ($1,812,231 today). It wasn't bothering him, or if it was, he didn't let on.

The day started at 6:15 A.M. and finished at 6:55 P.M., which was the case on most days. On that Monday, cast and crew gathered at "Benedict siding," seventeen miles west of Marfa, and they had to halt filming several times during the day for trains to pass by. They were using the siding to film the arrival of Bick Benedict and his bride, Leslie Lynnton Benedict, by train from Maryland. This scene parallels the opening scene in Maryland at the railroad station, when Bick comes calling. Now the situation is reversed and the stranger is Bick's youthful, educated, cultivated, and beautiful young bride. She first sees Texas by looking out of the train window, just as her husband had first viewed the place where she lived. She glimpses a strange animal—a coyote—and then, taking a longer look, sees a barren, flat, brown desert, nothing like the green lushness that her husband observed upon arriving in Maryland. Texas is a treeless wasteland marked only by a few tumbleweeds bouncing along. "Is that Texas?" she asks, and Bick says, "We've been in Texas for eight hours."

The script called for a dust storm, and since it was a calm day, Stevens ordered huge wind fans to be brought to the set. Locals familiar with real dusters declared it "a pretty puny attempt. Didn't move more than three or four acres of dirt. Why didn't the Hollywood bunch wait a few minutes, until the real thing came along."

The Hollywood people also imported tumbleweeds to roll around in the manufactured dust storm. They paid local kids a quarter for each tumbleweed they brought to the set.

The first day of shooting at the ranch, June 8 (camera day 16), dealt with the arrival of the married couple at the bride's new home, Reata, which dialogue coach Bob Hinkle taught these Hollywood "Texians" to pronounce as Re-att-a instead of the softer, lovelier, lilting Spanish Reata. Lots of cowboy and cattle lingo derived from Spanish words because the vaqueros originated in Spain.

In the film, the car bearing the newlyweds seems to drive forever (fifty miles to coffee, Bick says), and then suddenly there is the grand headquarters looming on the horizon. Apart from the visual impact in the film, perhaps the best description of this first sighting appears in Billy Lee Brammer's novel, The Gay Place (1961): "Everyone strained to catch sight of the prefabricated Victorian mansion towering about the floor of the ranchland. The mansion loomed on the horizon like a great landlocked whale, ginger-bread bas-relief against the backdrop of bleached dune and mountain and gunmetal sky."

A reporter on hand that day gave a brief sketch of Stevens at work. The simple act of the married couple getting out of the car upon arriving at the Reata mansion drew the director's close attention.

"Cut," he said.

"Liz, honey, don't spring out of the car—walk."

"And Rock, let's get this a little faster. This is plot stuff, but I don't want to make it like driving nails."

This scene took slightly more than one minute and was shot seventeen times. "Before it's over," the reporter noted, "it will have been filmed a staggering 60 times."

This was also the day that James Dean would make his first appearance, a silent entrance, a carefully crafted visual introduction of a major character that avoided using the shopworn technique of a close-up to announce its importance. In a 1965 interview, Stevens commented on the strategy: "In *Giant* there is the big house, there is the couple. There is an insignificant character in the background very remotely." Done right, "the eyes of the audience go with the vanishing point to that little figure."

The audience sees a man working on a car as Bick and Leslie arrive at their destination, the Reata Main House. It is Jett Rink, and as Stevens explained, "Nothing has told them [the audience] that the insignificant figure is an important man, but they have discovered that this fellow is of interest." Ostensibly a ranch hand, he is never once seen on horseback or working cattle or doing anything a cowboy might be expected to do. Instead, he is always associated with gasoline-operated vehicles: a Model T, an old dilapidated pickup, or Bick's elegant Duesenberg touring car. Jett Rink signifies the oil industry's overtaking of cattle and cotton as the dominant engine of economic might in Texas, and Jett becomes the hardest-working person on Reata, and the richest.

On June 9–11 (camera days 17–19), they shot the barbecue scene, involving many extras (including, legend has it, ten millionaires) and memorable because it is the moment when the young bride, unaccustomed to the customs and cuisine of that barbarous land, faints. The calf's brains entrée was quite authentic, a delectable delicacy. Ferber observed such a barbecue during her tour of Texas, and Helen Kleberg Groves recorded a similar

culinary event in her account of life on the King Ranch, writing of an occasion when the chef's menu "included everything that was part of a six-
month-old heifer except for the hide and hooves."

Jane White, an extra, recalled how it took three days to shoot the scene.
She had to get up at 5:00 A.M. and get costumed and ride a bus to the location. "Then we'd be dressed in 20's-style clothing and stand out there in
the pasture. The meat, incidentally, was taken back to Marfa where it was
stored in a meat locker! By the third day it didn't look too appetizing."

Here, as usual, Stevens's meticulous and often expensive attention to
detail prevailed, as a Mel Dellar memo to Art Klein, in charge of transportation, detailed back in February 16, 1955: "Mr. Stevens would like six
of the best and most expensive cars of the 1923 period, that rich cattle
people would drive. This is a new item and was not figured in your original
budget."

The barbecue scene is surpassed, however, by the famous shot of Jett
Rink alone, stretched out in Bick's Duesenberg, hat tilted on his head, feet on
the richly upholstered front seat, while in the distance looms the giant
house that symbolizes all that he desires: land, wealth, status. The image
of Jett Rink/James Dean in the automobile, apart from the community of
ranchers and neighbors, dreaming of wealth (and of Leslie) is pretty close,
as icon and image, to Daisy's green light in Jay Gatsby's imagination—
the have-not fantasizing about having it all, fortune, girl, America. It is
one of the enduring images of American cinema, and it wasn't in the script.
George Stevens added it at the last minute, on June 11 (camera day 19).

Another impressive visual moment in *Giant* is the stunning close-up
of Luz Benedict, Bick's mannish, resentful sister, driving a spur deep into
the flank of War Winds. The scene was shot on June 23 (camera day 29).
In a fit of pique at her realm's being usurped by her brother's new bride,
she takes out her rage on the horse that Bick bought in Maryland and
brought to Texas. Luz hates War Winds, associating the animal in her
mind with the upper-class young bride her brother has married. First we
see Luz from a long shot, the horse bucking, the rider whipping and spurring the stallion. Then the close-up, the spur thrust into the horse's flank,
producing blood.

Stevens himself beautifully explained his intentions in a 1973 interview. It was not something that occurred in the cutting room, he said, but was in his mind "long beforehand." Specifically, he "wanted to see this dowager woman, Mercedes McCambridge, on a bucking horse from a great distance—beautiful landscape, straight horizon, blue sky, and distant image of this contest between a woman and a horse—skirts flying and the horse really breaking it in two." He continued: "I wanted to go from the extreme long shot to the spur going right into the horse's flank, which—if you had sympathy for the woman—gave validity for the horse bucking like that. In two cuts there's a story—how we contribute to our own undoing." J. W. "Bub" Evans, Worth Evans's oldest son, doubled for McCambridge, and he was so pleased with his getup that he swanned around in the skirt and womanly garb an entire day.

The story of the horse's demise is told visually, as well. Beauty had arrived with his owner and horse trainer, Ralph McCutcheon, on June 9. His big dramatic day took place on June 15 (camera day 22). Shortly after the spurring incident, Beauty limps up to the hitching rail in front of Reata, the saddle empty. Beauty's acting is very strong, and the horse should have received an Oscar for best performance by an animal. Unlike a number of actors who did not have anything lined up after *Giant* wrapped, Beauty already had the lead equine part in the television show *Fury,* which would enjoy a five-year run.

When Jack Warner saw the rushes, he exploded. The first take, he said, was perfect, and yet he told Henry Ginsberg, "I will wager that 5,000 feet or more was shot on this horse," adding, "This is an out-and-out waste and someone has to tell Stevens to stop this." But who was going to stop Stevens? No one.

James Dean's only scene alone with Elizabeth Taylor was shot over two days, June 27 and 28 (camera days 32 and 33), at Jett Rink's shack on Little Reata, the old Buffalo Wallow (pronounced *waller*) piece of ground that Luz Benedict had bequeathed to him. Leslie drives up to Jett's place and we hear the sound of a shotgun and then see Dean walking toward her, rifle in hand and a large dead jackrabbit dangling from his side. The most famous still photograph from the film, the so-called crucifixion shot, depicts Elizabeth Taylor kneeling on the ground before Dean, who holds the rifle behind his neck, his arms on either side in a crucifixionlike position (the rabbit has disappeared). It's very artful, a prairie pietà, but it's not in the film.

The scene continues as Dean fumblingly talks to Leslie. What happened next was pure James Dean. Dennis Hopper paints the picture: "Jimmy was doing his first scene with Elizabeth Taylor and it was the first and only time I saw him nervous on set. They were shooting the scene where he fires the shotgun off the water tower, and she stops the car, and he asks her in to tea. He was so uptight he could hardly get the words out." And this is where Dean did something that Hopper never forgot. He walked off the set onto to the prairie, where sightseers were lined up behind the ropes, watching, and Jimmy "got half-way, unzipped his pants, took out his cock, peed, dripped it off, and zipped it up, and walked back into the scene." Dean had a history of such stunts, but the audacity of his performance that day was exponentially larger. Instead of actors and crew on a closed set, his audience consisted of a herd of Texans from near and far watching wide-eyed as he urinated in front of them.

Dennis Hopper marveled at Dean's aplomb and talked about it the rest of his life. On their way back to town that afternoon, Dennis wanted to know why he had done it, and Jimmy explained, "It was Elizabeth Taylor. I can't get over my farm-boy upbringing. I was so nervous that I couldn't speak. I had to pee, and I was trying to use that, but it wasn't working. So I thought that if I could go pee in front of all those people, I would be able to work with her." It was an old trick in Dean's kit bag of self-motivation. He had urinated on the set of *East of Eden* and on the stage of a TV drama in New York, and he had invited Jack Simmons to join him in urinating on the set of *Rebel Without a Cause*. Dean also urinated publicly in Marfa just for the hell of it, explaining to Mercedes McCambridge, "I did it because nothing else was happening."

But whether motivational stimulation was required or not, the scene inside Jett Rink's shack is great. It took two actors and fifty production people to pull it off. Jett Rink, like Jay Gatsby, has been undergoing a self-improvement program, evident by a copy of *How to Speak and Write*

Masterly English, which Leslie takes note of. As one critic puts it, "Jimmy has never been more vulnerable and lovable than in this scene, and inevitably it's a vulnerability—and an innocence—which is lost the second he strikes oil." Also he has learned how to make tea—the sine qua non of class status. And he has put up lacy curtains and tacked up pictures of Leslie from the newspaper.

It is all very touching, and Edna Ferber hated it so much that she brought it up in two letters to Henry Ginsberg. On April 23, 1955, she made it perfectly clear how she felt. Of "the tea-drinking scene," she wrote, "I reject the whole thing. I find it appalling." And with regard to Leslie's compliment to Jett on his tea-making ability, Ferber declared, "I can't bear to read it, much less hear it." On May 27, she brought it up again: "The tea-drinking scene between Leslie and Jett is not clearly defined and is not—to me, at least—anything but dull." The explanation for her intense dislike of this invented scene is almost certainly attributable to her class bias. She also felt that Leslie was fading "into a somewhat pale character as the two leading male characters have taken on additional stature." And here, as elsewhere, Ferber objected to the words given to Leslie: "In many places, too, her dialogue is that of a Texan, not a woman born and reared as Leslie was." To her mind, a well-brought-up, educated, and altogether outstanding girl like Leslie would never stoop to have tea with a blue-collar déclassé stiff like Jett Rink. Ferber was deeply invested in class—it was a blind spot in her otherwise Edna-knows-best progressive hierarchy. It was a below-the-salt kind of thing. *Her* Leslie would never take tea in a workman's shack.

Some of the most memorable scenes in *Giant* are ones without dialogue. One of these was shot on June 22 (camera day 28). It involved Stevens, cinematographer William C. Mellor, a propman, Jimmy, and Bob Hinkle, the dialogue coach. It's the scene where Jett Rink claims possession of the land he inherited from Luz Benedict—which he names, tauntingly, Little Reata. They filmed the scene on a lonely ridgeline with a windmill nearby. Stevens gave instructions to Dean to walk toward the windmill, and the actor started out in an ordinary manner, as though it was nothing special. Stevens quickly yelled "Cut" and then, ripping a page out of his script, proceeded to tear off pieces and place them on the line where he wanted Dean to walk, weighting each one down with a stone. Then he asked Dean if he thought he could follow the markers. They were both getting on each other's nerves by now, and Dean shot back that he could. But what he did was to stride toward each piece of paper, pick it up, throw the rock away, and so on, until he had a bunch of paper in his hand, at which point he came back to confront Stevens.

"Now look, you're supposed to be the director. So direct. Tell me what you want me to do and I'll do it. If I need any marks, I'll put them down myself. But if you can't do that, then I'm going to get on an airplane and go back to Hollywood."

"So you think you can walk it off out there?"

"Just turn that damn camera on and watch me."

"All right, let's shoot it."

So Dean set out, angry as hell, to do it his way. This time, he emphasized the walk with his whole body, taking long, determined strides. He had talked to old-timers who'd measured their land in this manner.

"Stay on him," Stevens told Mellor.

"I got him."

When Dean reached the windmill, he climbed up on it and sat down, his arms crossed. Stevens hadn't said anything about climbing the windmill.

"You still got him, Bill?"

"I got him."

Stevens's commentary on the scene makes his intentions beautifully clear. He said that anybody looking at it would think, "Here's the most bereft piece of ground in the world." But the viewer would also recognize "the feeling within a man's heart for possessing things. It's like he owned Manhattan Island." Finally, there was the "fantastic skyscape," cloud formations that developed days later, after a brief rainstorm. Stevens took advantage of the storm's aftermath and shot the sky, and as he stated, "I had to put some wonderment in it." Stevens's gift for visual poetry was never more apparent.

The scene has drawn much praise, including this observation by James

Powers in 1996: "A single scene, where Dean paces out the first land he has ever owned, is unforgettable. . . . It has rhythm and beauty and says more than could a thousand words."

Cinematographer Mellor would later recall the indelible impressions that James Dean forged in front of the camera: "While we were making *Giant*, I think we all knew that young Jimmy Dean was giving a performance that not even the extreme adjectives of Hollywood could adequately sum up. It's not often a unit gets a feeling like that."

On June 24, Stevens and Ginsberg received a letter from Jack Warner. Its subjects were time and money. The last production report had worried Warner. It showed that the picture was eight days behind schedule and $200,000 ($1,812,231 today) over budget. Warner warned them that the company would spend no more than $2,549,000 ($23,096,888 today) for the completed picture. In the end, that figure would nearly double.

Although Stevens tried to shoot scenes in sequence whenever he could, it wasn't always possible.

The opening shot of the film, for example, wasn't shot until June 24 (camera day 30). A sizable herd of cattle press forward to drink from a large stock tank. As Stevens explained, "That big herd had been fenced up without water all day," and as a result they were naturally thirsty and made their way down to the water tank, "filling the entire screen just as we thought they would." Stevens always liked filming animals, and in scenes to follow, Bick Benedict takes his new bride to observe the spring roundup. It's hot, sweaty, dusty work, and Leslie watches with interest as her husband and the vaqueros rope and brand the calves. Stevens received letters urging him not to brand the cattle, but he ignored the animal rights advocates. The branding went on as it would have on Worth Evans's actual ranch. Clay Evans, J.W.'s brother, can be glimpsed riding a palomino in one shot.

The cattle didn't give Stevens any trouble, but James Dean did. He had a habit of driving a red Chevrolet onto the prairie where Stevens was filming cattle for background shots. It was irritating.

The cattle in the title sequence are Herefords, not longhorns, and the great cattle drives belong to the heroic past, celebrated in films like *Red*

River. This is modern Texas: The Comanches and Apaches have been defeated, the buffalo herds killed off, the cattle-drive era is only a memory among old trail drivers, and Reata, Bick Benedict's half-a-million-acre ranch, is a going concern where beef, breeding, and bullion order the cycle of the earth's turning—from a Texas rancher's perspective anyway.

In the finished film, the sweeping score of Russian-born composer Dimitri Tiomkin enhances the visual scale of size and epic history. Besides being a very successful composer, Tiomkin was something of a character, as expansive as the Russian steppes—or as the Texas plains. Stevens called him "our friend from Leningrad" and said he fit "the Texas milieu [because] he's got the same kind of exuberance that Texas is noted for." Tiomkin said much the same thing with reference to his love of the West: "While many modern composers seem to have been inspired by the subway train, blaring autohorns and the other sounds of city life, I get most excited by sounds like 10,000 cattle moving from left to right across the screen."

After this beginning, the first half of the film tracks the ranch operations and ends with a signature celebration of cattle breeding. The Benedicts and their rancher friends are on the front veranda. The day is hot, some of the womenfolk are fanning themselves, and the children look tired, as if it's past their naptime. They are all assembled to admire a huge bull displayed by Old Polo (Alexander Scourby) and presented formally to the assembled ranch royalty. The summary of the film in the Chronology of Shooting for July 5, 1955 (camera day 39), reads:

> Ext. Reata—Jett in truck comes to Reata, after his well came in. Tells Leslie she looks good enough to eat. This is continuation of prize bull sequence—large group on the veranda. Fight between Bick and Jett starts. Jett downs Bick. They fight. Jett exits in his truck.
> Wild sound track of truck of motor running to play over scene.

This spare description of the "prize bull sequence" only hints at the richness and significance of the scene.

The bull was a Brangus celebrity champion named Clear View Snuffy

76. Brought in from a ranch in Oklahoma at considerable expense, it weighed 2,050 pounds. Ferber had seen similarly sized beef behemoths at the King Ranch.

Bick Benedict has devoted his energies to breeding a superior beef-producing animal, typified here by King Tut, the bull's name in the film. This is another connection between the film and the facts stemming from the King Ranch. Although the legal department was concerned with all sorts of possible borrowings from the lives of the Klebergs and from the King Ranch background, this is one that they missed. The prize bull clearly echoes Bob Kleberg's experiments in breeding and his amazing bull Monkey. Seeking to improve the amount and quality of beef, Kleberg bred Brahma bulls with beef shorthorn cows. Monkey, born in 1920, was the most prepotent bull on the ranch, and the result was the Santa Gertrudis breed, a pinkish-colored cattle that produced excellent beef and were resistant to heat and parasites. It was the first new breed born in the United States.

The bull in the film appears only briefly, its meaty grandeur eclipsed by a cloud of dust on the near horizon, heralding the arrival of Jett Rink, ecstatic, elated, dripping with oil (actually molasses) from his face and clothes. Rink's noisy arrival in his old jalopy of a truck marks the end of the ranching empire's hegemony—at Reata, and in Texas. From this point onward, oil will dominate the rhythms and pulses of the Texas economy—and of the film.

Jett Rink knows it, too. He tumbles from his truck, announcing to the cattle barons on the porch, "I'm a rich boy, I'm a rich 'un. There's oil down there, Bick, there's more oil than you ever thought of, and I'm gonna get it. I'm gonna be richer than all of you stinkin' Benedicts." The language is perfect. "Stinkin' Benedicts" plays off "stinking rich," a common expression signifying wealth, and on sons of bitches signifying sons of bitches.

Jett then gets even more personal. He walks onto the porch and gazes admiringly at Bick's wife and pays her a compliment sure to cause trouble: "Miss Leslie, you look might near good enough to eat." Angered, Bick hits Jett, and as Jett recovers from that blow, he says, "You're as techy as an old cook, Bick," and then slams Bick hard in the gut as the rancher is being restrained by his friends. Elizabeth Taylor, incidentally, was knocked out by an accidental elbow from Monte Hale in the scrum around the falling Bick. Late in the film, in a very famous fistfight, Bick will take a beating from a techy cook, Sarge, owner of the roadside greasy spoon, Sarge's Place.

The scene of Jett Rink's disruption of the summer afternoon, one of the most compelling in *Giant,* signifies the end of the cattle industry's preeminence in Texas history. Bick Benedict doesn't know it yet, but the days of the old order are numbered. Uncle Bawley does, though, and his remark upon Jett Rink's departure is telling: "Bick, you oughta shot that boy a long time ago. Now he's too rich to kill."

J. Frank Dobie, authority on all things Texan, noted in 1950: "Oil is a tremendous fact in the economy of the world. A kind of oil culture dominates Texas with more force than cattle ever dominated it." Although oil displaced ranching in the state's pantheon of wealth, ranches still carried far more emotional power than oil wells, and the first thing lots of Texas oilmen did when their wells came in was to buy a ranch or two for the poetry of it. As the well-known couplet from a Texas poem puts it, "Other states were made or born/Texas grew from hide and horn."

In the second half of the film, we rarely see any ranch work being performed at all. The only time Bick is on horseback, he's watching, along with Old Polo, as Jett's oil tankers roll past the front gate of Reata. The only work performed in the second act is Jett Rink's overseeing of the expansion of his oil holdings into an empire of wealth. Almost all of the second act takes place indoors as the action shifts from western space to issues of race, feminism, generational change, and the future of modern Texas.

Though Stevens was getting the footage he wanted, Jack Warner wasn't so pleased. He sent a lengthy telegram to Stevens on July 5, complaining of "repetitious shooting of scene after scene." He was, of course, worried about the film's falling further behind schedule: "As I wrote you recently we never would have gone into this project if I thought for [a] moment the budget would be exceeded." Stevens answered him by telegraph that same day, "Deeply aware of the urgency expressed in your wire and most appreciate its humane tone. Doing utmost repeat utmost to pick up time."

On the very next day, July 6, Stevens began shooting a sequence that Warner and others would urge him to cut. But it meant as much to Stevens personally as anything he ever put on film.

⸙

The filming of *Giant* created an enormous daily spectacle attended by hundreds of onlookers, scores of press people from virtually every city in Texas, and a steady stream of columnists and movie scribes from L.A. It was an open set on a scale unlike that of any film of that era. Locals, outsiders, visitors from all over West Texas and beyond were welcome to observe the proceedings. The rules for visitors were simple: The public was to follow road directions, park in designated areas, stay behind the ropes, smoke in designated areas, and be quiet during rehearsals and shooting. But it didn't always work that way. Darlyne Freeman, a junior at Marfa High, recalled, "They kept some ropes up that spectators were supposed to be behind. But as soon as they took a break, the ropes would come down and everyone would rush around and ask for their photographs." The Marfa Chamber of Commerce provided placards—"Marfa is proud of George Stevens' *Giant*"—that made handy sunshades for journalists, tourists, cast, and crew.

Journalists and columnists came by plane, train, or automobile on junkets that promised good food, lots of liquor, and access to the set. Warner Bros. went all out in its publicity campaign. They provided press kits full of statistics, facts, and promotional spin. Members of the press talked to Stevens and any actors or worthies they found approachable. One reporter asked Boris Leven why they were shooting on location. He said people "wouldn't be fooled by a California background for a Texas locale." He also pointed out that "the Man," as he called Stevens, was "too meticulous to accept a shoddy compromise of second-best."

One of Stevens's cleverest publicity strategies was to invite amateur camera clubs to visit the set and snap away. Photographs were gold, and camera clubs from as far away as San Angelo, 256 miles distant, journeyed to the Ryan Ranch to make their own memories. Stevens set aside times when the amateur photographers could take photos.

The decision to have an open set continued to pay dividends in public relations. The folksy, down-home director who could do "Aw shucks" with the best of them regarded every visitor as a potential ambassador, and Warner Bros. cultivated goodwill every day. People from Marfa and all over West Texas and beyond showed up in droves as shooting went on all through June and into July. Earl Holliman recalled that every day planes carrying press people from distant places—New York, London, the West Coast— flew into Marfa. "They were fascinated with this location," he said. On weekends crowds of seven hundred to a thousand thronged to the set, and on weekdays there were always at least three hundred or so in attendance. Stevens told his cast, "All of these people are press agents."

If so, he had a lot of press agents. An estimated sixteen thousand citizens visited the set over the five and a half weeks of shooting.

All the reporters were impressed with the big show. On the streets of Marfa, the folks from Hollywood looked like part of the Raj, with their safari hats and riding boots. All they lacked was a swagger stick.

What impressed one reporter the most was the size and complexity of the whole undertaking: "Neither the stars nor the story dominate the location shooting of *Giant*. . . . It's the sheer magnitude of the operation that does it. It seems they came equipped for everything."

Reporters from near and far rolled into Marfa on a daily basis. Lowell E. Redelings, columnist for the *Hollywood Citizen–News*, described a typical visit to Marfa in his June 20 column, "The Hollywood Scene." Like most such reports, Redelings sprinkled his article with facts and factoids. Much of the reporting is too trivial to be of interest today—if it was then. Some points stand out, though. Rock Hudson, a favorite with autograph seekers, was "reluctantly cooperative." Elizabeth Taylor evinced a new maturity since becoming a mother and she is "now all woman." And the cattle "grazing in the background of the scenes adjacent to the big mansion may look real—but they're actually life-sized cardboard cutouts." Actually, the fake cattle were made of wood, not cardboard. This was another of Boris Leven's visual contributions. He thought up the fake cattle and overcame Stevens's objections. At first, Stevens thought the idea was ridiculous, but when they tried it, the fake cows were indistinguishable from real ones. There were plenty of real cattle around, too. Part of the contract with Worth Evans required the rancher to have one thousand head of cattle and three hundred horses penned up and at the ready in case they were needed.

Reporters packed their stories with stats. Frieda Halwe of the *Beaumont Enterprise* gave an excellent account of an afternoon's work. She watched Stevens rehearse the scene with James Dean and Elizabeth Taylor at the Little Reata shack. It took fifty men to set up everything for a scene with two actors. At the same time, ten miles away, Fred Guiol was shooting a brief scene with Rock Hudson and Alex Scourby sitting astride their horses at the Reata gate as they watched Jett Rink's trucks roll past. This brief scene required another thirty to forty men, including cowboys and doubles, along with the usual retinue of grips, soundmen, etc. Then Halwe was driven to the "big mansion, the truly fabulous evidence of art director Leven's genius." Here a crew of workers was tending to the greenery to keep it from dying in the heat and updating the driveway to match the span of years covered in the film. There were about twenty people involved in this preparation for upcoming scenes.

That evening at the Paisano Hotel, Halwe ate with the actors and technical chiefs. The "nerve center" adjacent to the dining room was extremely busy with "the Man" overseeing details involving the next day's shooting. Stevens orchestrated a personnel list of 236 people, which included ten production people, two art directors, two script supervisors, seventeen cameramen, twelve animal handlers, one Texas dialogue man (Robert Hinkle), and one Texas dialogue woman (Maryann Edwards, a former rodeo queen at the University of Texas). In all, there were 280 actors and technicians on the ground in Marfa. Warner Bros. rented forty-four cars, trucks, and buses from Marfa dealers. A "mammoth meal" was served on location every day: "The plates were loaded as for hungry thrash hands." The day ended at 11:00 P.M. At the end of her exhaustive account, Halwe was moved to a kind of poetry: "This project has the scope of the majestic sweep of mountain and mesa that is West Texas, parched by seven lean years of drought but still magnificent in a sort of protective coloration that has been taken on by the waterless land."

Of all the published accounts of visits to the set, the most insightful belongs to John Rosenfield, who wrote a retrospective essay published in the *Southwest Review* a year after his visit to the set of *Giant*. The first week in June, Rosenfield and the artist Ed Bearden, along with their wives, made the long 520-mile trek to Marfa. Bearden brought along his pencil and drew numerous sketches, which offer a valuable picture of the goings-on at the Ryan Ranch. One depicts a number of figures in various states of work or waiting. James Dean is sunning himself with his shirt off while waiting for the barbecue scene. The house looms in the background, the technical people are working with a boom and aluminum reflectors, and, perhaps best of all, a camera club lady is taking a photograph of a cowboy and a young woman who are among the extras on hand for the scene. There's another marvelous sketch of a "[s]ound truck with cameras and lights; an outdoor scene is being shot." The truck and attendants are in the foreground; in the background, two cowboys are on horseback and figures sit at wooden outdoor tables, with distant mountains against the skyline. He also drew sketches of Stevens, Taylor, McCambridge, and Charlie Watts (Judge Whiteside). He made three small studies of James Dean, as well. The only portrait that falls short is one of a shirtless Rock Hudson.

Rosenfield's observations are equally valuable. Here is how he describes Stevens at work: "He is tall and lumbering. He gives everybody a little time but not much. He talks patiently to everybody but not for long. His manners are impeccable and his concealment of his thoughts practically hermetic."

Among the actors, Elizabeth Taylor required the most direction, and Stevens gave her line readings before every take. He would tell her which register of emotion he wanted: wistful, surprised, angry, distressed, happy, whatever. According to Rosenfield, Stevens didn't worry about any conceptual understanding of the role on Taylor's part, concentrating instead on each take, and the technique worked perfectly.

On the personal side, Rosenfield found Taylor "a shrinking violet" but "genial, modest, and unassuming if you take the lead." Her conversation, he noted, ran mostly to clothes and family. Clay Evans formed a very different impression of the actress: "Aw, I remember Elizabeth Taylor. She cussed a lot and thought she was good lookin' but we didn't pay much attention to her."

Rock Hudson was a tougher nut to crack. Hudson often required retakes, and Rosenfield found the actor a "pathologically shy man" who was regarded as "upstage" or "supercilious," whereas Rock's friends defended him, saying he was apt to be "tongue-tied at the sight of strangers."

Old pros like Mercedes McCambridge, Chill Wills, and Jane Withers proved to be much more outgoing. "For a nickel," McCambridge would run upstairs to her hotel room and bring down a photo of Adlai Stevenson signed "Dear Mercedes."

Not surprisingly, it was James Dean who proved the most compelling figure. Although upon first meeting him, Rosenfield found him to be "ill mannered and uncommunicative" but he turned into "an easy interview subject" provided one took the lead and kept the conversation going. In contrast with Taylor and Hudson, Dean required little direction and his takes were "almost always right." Rosenfield was impressed with Dean's off-set dedication. He watched him gallop on a horse and toss his hat into an open car, then collect the hat and do it over and over until he was satisfied. There is no such scene in the film, but there might have been. Dean, who was alone most of the time, had "the self-absorption of the young and ambitious actor." And as for the director, "To others if not to Dean, Stevens was eloquently appreciative of his actor."

Rosenfield followed the whole process of a day's shooting, right down to the rushes at the Palace, which had been airmailed to the Warner Bros. laboratory two days before, after which they were screened at the theater across from the hotel. "One saw thirty different shots of Elizabeth Taylor leaving the train at the Benedict station, each with its virtues." The director, meantime, was in "intimate *sotto voce* conversation with his head cameraman and assistant directors." The next day and the next and on to the end of the location shooting in Texas, it would be the same. Stevens called the dailies the "owl show," and a Warner Bros. production note observed, "The locals loved it until they discovered how boring dailies really were!"

The "Marfa expedition" cost around a million dollars. Stevens would spare no expense to get his vision on the screen. Overall, Rosenfield thought

Giant was "probably the most eventful location trip in the history of pictures."

Elston Brooks of the *Fort Worth Star-Telegram* posted five stories from the front, and every one of them turned up a nugget or two. One piece dealt with the economic boom the film production produced. "Everyone, it seems, is working because of the picture," he wrote. This included visitors. Martha Kyger, for example, a seventeen-year-old from Fort Worth who visited the set one day, wound up playing Elizabeth Taylor's stand-in in one scene. In another posting, Brooks got some choice remarks from George Stevens regarding the differences between the film and the novel. "What we've done is humanized the book," he said. "All of the satiristic barbs have been removed from the script. I don't think there's anything cute about berating anyone." Stevens added that Ferber "was pleased with the screenplay, and she helped us on it." This was unusual; he almost never mentioned Ferber's connection with the screenplay.

Brooks didn't have as much success interviewing James Dean. He wrote of Dean, "Always sullen, he dismayed publicity men by refusing to grant interviews." He and some other reporters caught Dean resting in a car and managed to get a few reluctant responses from him.

When asked how it felt to be a "bobby-soxers' delight after one film," he replied, "What do you mean, how do I feel? I don't quit with one picture; I made another one and now I'm making this one. When I get through I'll make another one." Then he added, "You don't bury a man just because he's a success." And Brooks couldn't resist ending the piece, published two days after the actor's death, this way: "When he was killed in a California car wreck Friday night, he died a success. He'll be buried a success, too."

The local citizenry embraced the movie crowd, and business in Marfa was up by 30 to 50 percent. Obviously, the Paisano Hotel benefited, but so did other local businesses that provided services for the daily flood of sightseers coming through town to take in the action at the Ryan Ranch.

People flocked to the open set at the beginning and continued to come as word of mouth spread. For many Texans, it was a kind of mini vacation, something to do with the family. In those days, movies still had a mystery about them, a kind of magic. The average person knew next to nothing about how movies got made, and, besides that, how many times in one's life, especially if one lived in a small town in West Texas, would it be possible to observe the likes of Elizabeth Taylor, Rock Hudson, and James Dean in the flesh? There they were, strolling the sidewalks of Marfa or dining in the Paisano Hotel or at Elizabeth Taylor's favorite, the Old Borunda Café, a Mexican restaurant that, like everything else in Marfa, was in easy walking distance from the Paisano. As for common folk, they could watch the stars eat, and the next day they could watch them act. Teenage girls in Marfa would line up in cars parked in front of the Paisano to catch a glimpse of their favorite actors emerging from dining there most evenings.

The Big Bend Sentinel summed up the impact on Marfa in its issue of July 14, 1955: "Many local people, entirely too many to name, even if the names were available, took part in the actual filming of the picture—some in barbecue or other scenes requiring a number of individuals, others in bit parts where they were required to speak a few words."

⁓⸰⸰

In 1955, Stevens was a man still haunted by what he had seen in Europe a decade earlier.

Ten years after the end of World War II, he seemed driven in a way that hadn't been evident before. Like other directors, such as John Ford, Frank Capra, William Wellman, and John Huston, Stevens had suspended his professional and personal life to do his part in combating the forces of tyranny in faraway Europe. Though the filmmakers shot documentaries instead of guns, they were often in danger of being wounded or killed. They fought the war with their cameras, in Midway in the South Pacific, in the skies over Germany, and, in Stevens's case, on the ground at Nordhausen and Dachau.

The writer Irwin Shaw, who became a friend of Stevens in Europe, characterized those directors as "all very liberal men who had grown up with pacifistic ideas. And one and all they gave up very lucrative and prestigious careers and went right into the Army." Under the direction of the U.S. Army Signal Corps, these men, who had been artists and entertainers, were now required to become propagandists. In fact, it was a propaganda

film, Leni Riefenstahl's *Triumph of the Will*, that compelled both Stevens
and Frank Capra, among others, to go to war. When Capra saw it for the
first time, in 1942, he exclaimed, "We're dead. We're gone. We can't win
this war." Stevens saw it that same year and decided immediately to go
into the army. The film's impact made him think anew about the role of
filmmaking, and he reached the conclusion that "all film is propaganda"—
including his own. And in that light, looking back at *Gunga Din* (1939),
the movie that *Film India* (Bombay) had called "imperialist propaganda,"
Stevens had to agree: "The film is delightfully evil in the fascist sense. It
celebrates the rumble of the drums and the waving of the flags."

Once the war was over, Stevens had a very hard time recovering from
what he had experienced in Europe. Frank Capra thought that Stevens
"had the most difficult time of all finding his bearings." Some of it had
been glorious—the liberation of Paris, for example—but what Stevens saw
in Germany was almost too much to absorb. He shot footage at Nordhausen, where the ravaged bodies of slave workers bore the grim evidence of
starvation, torture, and murder. But Dachau was worse. There was nothing worse than Dachau. He shot boxcars packed with skeletal Jews; he shot
ditches filled with the dead. He was in a world of indescribable horror. "We
went to the woodpile outside the crematorium, and the woodpile was
people." He filmed the extinct and the living. He filmed German officers
and forced them to look at their handiwork, and he filmed German citizens, deniers all, in nearby villages, pretending they didn't know what had
been happening just down the road. He smelled the unbearable stench of
the sick and dying, and he saw signs of cannibalism among the heaped-up
bodies.

"After seeing the camps," he said, "I was an entirely different person."
And in one sickening moment, he saw himself in a way that he despised.
"You'd go into a block and move down the aisle and everybody is crawling
with lice, and your whole attitude is revulsion. You want to lash out, you
want to say, 'Halt! Get the hell away.' " He went on: "And you hate them. You
look at these people, and you despise them." He summed up by saying,
"You're disturbed by being of the human race." In late 1945, two documentary films made by Stevens, *The Nazi Plan* and *Nazi Concentration Camps*,

were admitted in evidence at the Nuremberg trials. They laid out Hitler's program of extermination of the Jews and revealed the conditions of places like Dachau.

In 1946, when he came home to the United States, he couldn't seem to find his way, much the same as Edna Ferber, who had gone into a period of deep depression over what she had witnessed in Europe. For a time, like Ferber, he couldn't work, and he became bitter about those who had stayed in L.A., making pictures during the war. He had a run-in with Cecil B. DeMille during the height of the McCarthy witch-hunt. When DeMille asked him what he'd been doing during the war, he replied, "I was up to my ass in mud at Bastogne, while you were fighting the battle of capital gains." He withdrew into himself and could not articulate the great anguish that was eating away at him. Although he had written his wife and son many letters from Europe, seeking to hold on to them as reminders of all that was good, once back, he simply couldn't embrace postwar normalcy. Instead of reentering the movie industry, he played golf every day for months. Silences and dark moods prevailed. "After the war," he said, "I don't think I was ever too hilarious again."

Old friends like Frank Capra felt that he "was not the same George Stevens." According to Capra, "The whole [war] became, for him, a kind of nightmare, a nightmare of the stupidity of man. He became hard to talk to—or maybe he just couldn't—express the horror he'd been through." Capra went on to say: "The films that he took of Dachau, the ovens, and the big, big piles of bones that nobody could believe existed . . . He had seen too much." And his wife, Yvonne, saw the lasting impact up close. "He was just shocked. He never got over it," she said.

His wartime experience would have a profound effect upon his career going forward. At a USA Film Festival held in Dallas in 1971, Stevens explained its impact: "I was more seriously engaged in films after I'd had three years of an unnatural experience, which was the war in Europe. And that changed my life and my thinking so seriously that it changed my professional instincts; I knew I wanted to do very different things than I'd done before."

By the end of the forties, Stevens was able to resume his lifetime's calling, and the period of his new seriousness began with *A Place in the Sun*, followed by *Shane* and *Giant*. Although he never made a war picture per se, he considered *Shane* in that light. He had observed something in Germany that he saw anew in America, the popularity of Westerns among young children, boys and girls wearing cowboy hats and practicing their fast draws with cap pistols; it was bang bang everywhere you looked. *Shane* is about a young boy's infatuation with a mythic gunfighter, and the movie is really, in Stevens's words, his "war picture." "In *Shane*," he said, "a gun shot, for our purposes, is a holocaust. And when a living being is shot, a life is over."

The intensity of feeling that the war held for Stevens is nowhere more apparent than in his dislike of General Eisenhower. Stevens hated Eisenhower. In Algiers in 1943, he attended a meeting with the Allied commander and asked him about a German general who had just been captured. Stevens wanted to know if General Eisenhower had talked to the German officer. Eisenhower's reply floored Stevens: "I'm here to kill Germans, not to talk to them." Stevens's reaction to that remark seems rather extreme: "That s.o.b. You've got to be eight years old, you know, to have your masters talk to you like that and not have it have an effect. All the time he was campaigning for president, many a time he was on the television, I would make that remark and lose a couple of votes for him. It wasn't enough."

Eisenhower, too, had seen those death camps close-up, and in his letters to his wife he described the horror and his fervent desire that the facts of what happened there never be lost or obscured in subsequent history. He blamed the Germans for the "immense destruction" wrought by the war and for continuing the war in the face of all reason. He wrote to his wife about his experience: "The other day I visited a German internment camp. I never dreamed that such cruelty, bestiality, and savagery could really exist in this world! It was horrible. The things I saw beggar description." He said that he went there to "give *first-hand* evidence of these things if ever, in the future, there develops a tendency to charge these allegations merely to 'propaganda.'"

In any event, Stevens continued over the years to repeat his negative reaction to meeting Eisenhower. Disliking Eisenhower was de rigueur among Hollywood liberals. Edna Ferber and Mercedes McCambridge both campaigned for Adlai Stevenson in his two runs—both unsuccessful—against Ike. America had twice elected a great man to be president, and Hollywood liberals couldn't see it. They preferred a man who gave eloquent speeches to a man who had shepherded the Allies to victory over the Nazis.

A decade later, the war still preyed on Stevens's mind, and in one sequence in the film, he brought that vision to life. The scene, which ran several minutes, was one that Jack Warner thought could be cut, and he was not alone. Edna Ferber agreed with him. Some members of preview audiences thought so, too, as did some theater owners. But Stevens, Ahab-like in his determination to make the picture in his mind, insisted it had to stay in.

On July 6 (camera day 40), the Chronology of Shooting reads:

Ext. Benedict Station (Ryan Siding)—Bob Dace comes home.
Ext. Benedict Station (Ryan Siding)—Angel Obregon comes home.

It's the return from World War II of two young men closely associated with Reata and the Benedict family. Bob Dace (Earl Holliman) is a neighboring cowboy who marries Judy, the twin of Jordan Benedict III. Bob wants to operate a new kind of ranch—one where bigness is replaced by more enlightened modern methods of producing better beef without destroying the grasslands. So committed is he to a new and better ranching ethos, he turns down Bick's offer to take over the running of Reata.

The scene was shot at the Ryan Siding, and half of Marfa was there to greet the returning soldier. Holliman was excited and nervous before the scene began (it was his only one on location in Texas) and asked Stevens, who came aboard the train, what emotion he should feel upon meeting the crowd. After a long pause, Stevens turned toward Holliman and "very slowly, in that wonderful sort of drawl he had, he said, 'I think he's glad to be home.'"

When Holliman steps down from the train, a noisy, rapturous crowd of

Studio head Jack L. Warner, novelist Edna Ferber, director George Stevens, and producer Henry Ginsberg—the Big Four looking as though they're about to break into a dance number. (*Courtesy of the Academy of Motion Picture Arts and Sciences*)

Set designer Boris Leven's sketch of the big house on the prairie captured Stevens's imagination. (*Courtesy of the Academy of Motion Picture Arts and Sciences*)

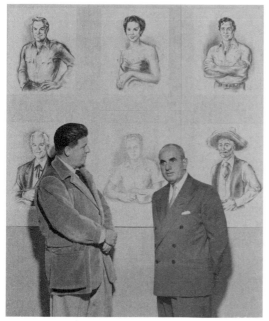

George Stevens and Henry Ginsberg in front of six character sketches by Dallas artist Edward Bearden that were influential in the director's thinking about casting. (*Courtesy of the Academy of Motion Picture Arts and Sciences*)

Henry Ginsberg, George Stevens, Elizabeth Taylor, Rock Hudson, and Dimitri Tiomkin at the Off-to-Texas Luncheon. (*Courtesy of the Academy of Motion Picture Arts and Sciences*)

Rod Taylor, Rock Hudson, and Elizabeth Taylor taking a break on location in Albermarle County, Virginia. (*Courtesy of the Academy of Motion Picture Arts and Sciences*)

One of the many times Texan dialogue coach Bob Hinkle and James Dean practiced roping. (*Courtesy of the Academy of Motion Picture Arts and Sciences*)

A typical day of shooting at the Ryan Ranch outside of Marfa, Texas. (*Courtesy of the Academy of Motion Picture Arts and Sciences*)

George Stevens with his son, George Stevens, Jr., on the set. (*Courtesy of the Academy of Motion Picture Arts and Sciences*)

James Dean alone on the lone prairie. (*Courtesy of the Academy of Motion Picture Arts and Sciences*)

Elizabeth Taylor ropes George Stevens while Mercedes McCambridge, Rock Hudson, and James Dean look on approvingly. (*Courtesy of the Academy of Motion Picture Arts and Sciences*)

George Stevens, Jane Withers, Edna Ferber, Elizabeth Taylor, Henry Ginsberg, Chill Wills, and Rock Hudson all dressed up for a group photo. (*Courtesy of the Academy of Motion Picture Arts and Sciences*)

Edna Ferber, James Dean, Victor Millan, and Mercedes McCambridge hanging out at Warner Bros. (*Courtesy of the Academy of Motion Picture Arts and Sciences*)

James Dean and Boris Leven studying oil field models. (*Courtesy of the Academy of Motion Picture Arts and Sciences*)

70-year-old Edna Ferber tries lassoing as Bob Hinkle and James Dean look on. (*Courtesy of the Academy of Motion Picture Arts and Sciences*)

The famous "Crucifixion" photograph, a publicity shot that Martin Sheen aped in his James Dean homage in Terrence Malick's *Badlands*. (*Courtesy of the Academy of Motion Picture Arts and Sciences*)

George Stevens, Jr., Elizabeth Taylor, James Dean, and George Stevens stand silhouetted against a barbed wire fence and a Texas sky. (*Courtesy of the Academy of Motion Picture Arts and Sciences*)

Jett Rink on Little Reata. (*Courtesy of the Academy of Motion Picture Arts and Sciences*)

Lengendary Texas wildcatter Glenn McCarthy, whose rags-to-riches story inspired the character of Jett Rink. (*Courtesy of Web Beard and Worth Beard*)

Madama and Jett shared an offscreen friendship in Marfa. (*Courtesy of the Academy of Motion Picture Arts and Sciences*)

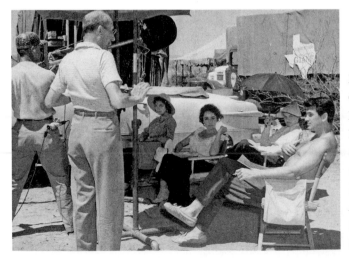

Elsa Cárdenas, Carroll Baker, Elizabeth Taylor, and Rock Hudson form a glamorous group on location in Texas. (*Courtesy of the Academy of Motion Picture Arts and Sciences*)

Dennis Hopper and Sal Mineo, two young actors from *Rebel Without a Cause*, joined their idol James Dean in *Giant*. (*Courtesy of the Academy of Motion Picture Arts and Sciences*)

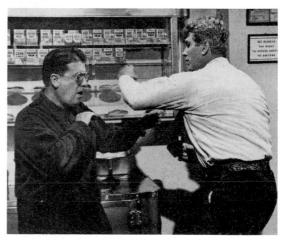

George Stevens showing Rock Hudson how to fight in the diner scene, with the infamous Jim Crow–era sign hanging on the wall. (*Courtesy of the Academy of Motion Picture Arts and Sciences*)

Screenwriter and good friend Fred Guiol and George Stevens in front of the painting that appears in the film and that hangs today in the Menger Hotel in San Antonio. (*Courtesy of the Academy of Motion Picture Arts and Sciences*)

An iconic photograph of James Dean and George Stevens on the prairie in front of the false-front Reata mansion. (*Courtesy of the Academy of Motion Picture Arts and Sciences*)

A contemporary photograph of downtown Marfa, Texas, the nerve center of *Giant* production in 1955. (*Courtesy of the Academy of Motion Picture Arts and Sciences*)

well-wishers is there to greet him, and the local high school band celebrates his return with a spirited version of "The Eyes of Texas." Local girls
Julie Nelson, Barbara Dawson, and Darlyne Freeman strutted their stuff.
Darlyne recalled, "We spent the entire day shooting that scene. Mr. Stevens would have us do it over and over."

The next shot is introduced by a newspaper headline, ANGEL OBREGON
COMES HOME TODAY. We see the same railroad siding for this soldier's return, but this time there is no music, no fanfare, no sound at all, just a
single flag-draped coffin lying alone on a flatcar. The only ones present
are his family. The quietness and solemnity are in stark contrast to Bob
Dace's homecoming.

Stevens had conceived of such a scene for a long time, having written
somewhat cryptically in the margins of the White Script: "Honda Knot
one of the great subjects of our times, big to mothers — wives—and young
men who are to die for their communities." What was *Honda Knot*? The
inspiration for the scene was a photograph in *Life* magazine of coffins on
the deck of a converted Army transport ship bringing back the remains of
3,028 American servicemen killed in the attack on Pearl Harbor. The
Honda Knot sailed into San Francisco Harbor on October 10, 1947. For
Americans who thought the war was over, the cargo on the funeral ship
told another story.

Those coffins brought home to Stevens the final outcome of the devas-
tation he had witnessed firsthand in Europe.

In an interview in 1964, he spoke movingly about the meaning of the
burial scene in *Giant*. He brought up the *Honda Knot* photograph, describing it as "this awful return, or this august return . . . something I thought
we should all pause and consider." He asked why we should care: "If it's
dust to dust in Europe, and dust to dust in the Pacific, why bring back this
ceremonial emblem, these remains?" Then he explained, "An explosive is so
far from home, but suddenly the *Honda Knot* delivered one, delivered it
with the same message that got you involved in the first place—the flag
and the symbolism—and here's what lured you away and here's how you
return, or your son returns, or your brother returns." In other words, the
war's impact lived on and on; it didn't stop in 1945. Stevens explained the

intention of the first shot of that sequence: "That boy on that baggage cart, and when the train pulls out, there it is. Even before the audience has the chance to say, 'Don't do that to me,' the film says, 'There it is, take a look at it.' " And finally, he said of the pictorial quality, "Suddenly it becomes like an evening in the west by Frederic Remington." To Stevens, the western spaces that he loved held a deep meaning: "People went to a place to live and be buried, they went to become a part of the soil."

Angel Obregón, the dead youth (played by Sal Mineo), was the most capable of the horsemen on the ranch. He could easily have taken over its management, and Bick Benedict at some level knows this, which is one reason he attends the funeral ceremony in the Mexican village, out of respect for Polo, Angel's grandfather, the oldest vaquero on the ranch, and Angel's father and family. After the soldiers hand a folded American flag to the Obregón family—a tradition at military funerals—Bick comes forward and gives them a Texas flag.

The burial of a Mexican-American soldier carried a particular weight in another sense, as well. After the war, there were several disgraceful incidents involving the interment of Mexican-Americans. The most notable was the case of Felix Longoria, a U.S. Army soldier from Three Rivers, Texas. Longoria was killed in the Philippines in 1945, but his remains were not returned to his family until 1948. The family intended to bury him in the "Mexican" section of the Three Rivers cemetery, separated from the white section by a barbed-wire fence, but first they wanted his remains to lie in state at the local funeral home. The funeral director, however, refused to permit a wake on the grounds that "The whites wouldn't like it." The incident sparked national attention after the Longorias contacted Dr. Héctor P. García of Corpus Christi, who organized a campaign to bring attention to the Three Rivers situation. Lyndon B. Johnson, the newly minted senator from Texas, arranged for Longoria to be buried at Arlington Cemetery with full military honors, a ceremony that took place on February 16, 1949.

In the film, the burial of Angel takes place in a Mexican-American cemetery without attention being drawn to the fact that death, like much else in Texas at that time, was segregated. Ferber's novel hewed more closely to the facts of segregation, and her Angel Obregón is much different from the character in the film. For one thing, he leaves Reata and works as a bellhop in a hotel in Vienciento (Corpus Christi). For another, he marries, and, even more interestingly, he embraces the *cholo* or pachuco rhetoric and dress of young urban Mexican-American males in the 1940s, best evidenced in the zoot suit phenomenon that led to riots in Los Angeles. As for the rest of his story, Ferber clearly had in mind the case of Felix Longoria. Angel goes to war, fights bravely in the South Pacific, and is awarded the Congressional Medal of Honor. Yet when his remains are returned to the town of Benedict, the local funeral director refuses to bury him in the white cemetery. It takes presidential action to right this wrong, and Angel is buried with full military honors in Arlington Cemetery.

Ferber didn't like Stevens's treatment of the Angel Obregón incident, and she told him so in a letter on May 27, 1955. "When Bick takes that flag off the wall and drapes it around the casket of Angel, I reject the act. It is a thing Leslie might do; Bick would not. Not yet, at least. It is a tear-jerker, but it is not the truth." To her, Bick was a benighted, unredeemable bigot—like 90 percent of Texas males. The only morally enlightened male Texan in the novel is Uncle Bawley, a kind of father confessor to Leslie. He has many long conversations with Leslie and shares liberal ideas that he keeps hidden from the rest of the family. Stevens softens Uncle Bawley's role in the film, making him more of an avuncular figure than the rather outspoken confidant of Leslie in the novel. But Bick's action, which demonstrates the expansion of his moral sensibility, is a crucial step toward the enlightened realization that occurs in the closing act of the film—the rousing fight in the diner.

The priest at the local St. Mary's Church in Marfa, Father José Santiago, advised Stevens on the protocols of such burials, and Stevens acquired the services of U.S. Army Reservists (Marfa Unit), mostly Hispanic, to play the GIs. Their crisp military demeanor lent an authenticity to the solemn military burial rites. They folded the American flag according to a time-honored tradition and solemnly honored the death of a fallen American—a moving ritual, as anybody who has ever attended a military funeral knows. In all, the burial scene took four days to film, finishing on July 9 (camera day 43).

The marriage ceremony of Jordan Benedict III to Juana Guerra was squeezed in on July 8 (camera day 42), performed in the small Catholic church in Marfa. Dennis Hopper (Jordy) finally got to be in a scene, and his bride, played by Elsa Cárdenas, also made her first appearance in the film. Cárdenas, nineteen and a native of Mexico, found herself surprised by the racial climate in Marfa. Because she was underage, she was accompanied by an Anglo chaperone and was shocked to learn that a local woman had asked Elsa's roommate how she could stand to sleep in the same room with a Mexican. In her eighties now, Cárdenas recalled her reaction to what she saw in Marfa: "I never felt this discrimination, I thought they were just scenes in the picture. When I learned it was the real thing, I was shocked, surprised and later sad and angry."

On a lighter note, Cárdenas was amused that for her role, her skin was darkened with makeup to make her appear more Mexican.

On July 9, the last outdoor footage was shot. The *Honda Knot* sequence was complete, and Stevens, the old warhorse, would resist any arguments in favor of cutting it from the film. Ferber wanted it cut, Jack Warner wanted it cut, and a number of viewers attending previews of the film the next summer wanted it cut. One wrote that he didn't see the point of another dead "wetback."

For Stevens, however, it was probably the most personal moment in the entire film, and it meant a great deal to him. Angel's homecoming played like a silent threnody on the big screen.

8

Duel in the Sun

Most journalists who met George Stevens described him in remarkably similar terms. To one, he was "a tall, broad shouldered man who speaks with quiet, friendly assurance like a college professor." Another cast him as "a rugged, modest down-to-earth fellow himself who has managed to remain completely human in the unreal world of Hollywood." *Time* magazine, in full alliterative mode, called him a "meaty, mild-mannered man." A writer for *The Christian Science Monitor* sounded a similar note: "George Stevens is a big, broad-shouldered man with a shrug like a barn door. He also gives the misleading impression of being somewhat casual and expressionless. But there is no one in Hollywood who is more passionately devoted to film as an art and as a carrier of ideas."

On the set at the Ryan Ranch, Stevens wore a cowboy hat, sunglasses, a western jacket, and a bandanna over his nose and mouth to protect him from the dust and hay fever.

But Stevens's affable, low-key public manner masked a sterner side to his character. His close friend director Frank Capra recalled, "He's not an easy man to push around; he certainly wasn't easy to be pushed around by his superiors."

Many ascribed Stevens's phlegmatic manner to his supposed American Indian background. A myth had grown up from Stevens's early association with Crow Indians in Wyoming that he was part Indian. In his autobiography, *A Life in the Movies,* Fred Zinnemann attributed Stevens's "Indian look" to his head of thick, dark hair and implacable demeanor, which seemed to fit the stereotype of the inscrutable noble savage. The supposed Indian identity lent further weight to his natural inclination to do what he wanted, on his terms, on his schedule. It was something he could use.

In the 1940s, when Stevens was working for Columbia Pictures, he had a clause in his contract forbidding studio head Harry Cohn from talking to him about his pictures. That same decade, he started wearing sunglasses so that no one could read his eyes.

The stoic persona was a part of the masking of his inner self that his biographer Marilyn Ann Moss described in a romantic light: "The lonesome, melancholy self was the essential Stevens." On his first serious feature film, *Alice Adams* (1935), Stevens ran headlong into a very formidable figure, Katharine Hepburn. They clashed over how to handle a scene showing Alice's emotions following a suitor's rejection. Hepburn wanted to fling herself on a bed, but Stevens thought it would be better if she walked to the window and looked at the rain and started crying as she stood there. She refused to do it, saying, "There's a limit to stupidity. I've put up with all of it I can. You dumb bastard, I'm going to cry on the bed." Stevens said he'd go back to making two-reel comedies before he'd give in. He prevailed, and upon viewing the result, she realized that he was right. She won an Academy Award nomination for her performance. Stevens, who had an affair with Hepburn, would later observe, "She was Jimmy Dean-ing before Jimmy Dean ever thought of it, and she wore slacks, too."

That breakthrough film gave him a lot of confidence: "Well, I'd had *Alice Adams,* and it had come off very well. Now I could be a pain in the ass." And so he remained for producers, studio heads, and corporate suits down through the years. As for his actors, he worked very successfully with many stars, including Spencer Tracy, Jimmy Stewart, Fred Astaire, Barbara Stanwyck, Jean Arthur, Joel McCrea, Ronald Colman, and Ginger

Rogers, a group that included some very robust egos. Jean Arthur said, "He was like the best cup of coffee you ever had."

Cary Grant, who starred in three of Stevens's films, admired the man's sense of purpose and focus: "Nothing and no one stopped him from accomplishing his purpose. Not other producers, not studio heads. He did it his way. Now, he might permit you to believe that you did it your way. But he was in control, and we all knew that. He was always dedicated to his purpose. If we got off the subject, he got right back to it."

In his approach to directing, Stevens saw himself as "a kind of host on the film set." By that he meant he had "to be able to explain to the actors everything they need to know about the characters they are playing, to create backgrounds for each person depicted in the story we are telling." He continued: "I have to help create very tangible and convincing people on the screen, and blend that with the actors' own interpretations of their roles so the story is as convincing as possible."

Stevens was known, too, for his extended silences. He had a habit of suspending a scene before it was done, walking off by himself, pipe clenched in his teeth, and continuing walking alone, thinking. Frank Capra thought he knew what these "periods of meditation" meant to Stevens: "He was mentally reviewing his whole picture—scene by scene—from beginning to end; analyzing the characters, their growth, their degradation, their effect on each other." Capra's explanation of Stevens's directorial style is probably as close as we can get to the purpose of those long silences, and Stevens himself never commented on this practice. Some actors were patient with these solitary exercises, and some were irritated. Once, during the making of a film with Ginger Rogers (with whom he also had an affair), Stevens went into his usual pipe-smoking, contemplative mode and left the cast waiting. After a time, Rogers shouted to the rest of the actors, "Eureka! I know what George is thinking when he paces like that—not a fucking thing!"

❈

There were those who felt that in the five years since *A Place in the Sun*, Stevens's manner had become "increasingly dictatorial." Elizabeth Taylor was one of them. The only actor in *Giant* to have a history with Stevens, she owed him a lot. Before he put her in *A Place in the Sun*, Taylor had been starring in a forgettable string of MGM assembly-line pieces like *Conspirator, Ivanhoe* ("a piece of cachou"), and *Beau Brummel*. "All I did," she wrote in her autobiography, "was just sort of whistle and hum my way through those films, powdering my nose and getting a great kick out of wearing pretty clothes—dying to wear more make-up, higher heels, lower-cut dresses." By her own account, she hero-worshipped Stevens for what he had gotten out of her in that film.

But in Texas things were not the same. Stevens seemed different from the patient man who'd shepherded her through *A Place in the Sun*. Perhaps she had forgotten those times when he'd belittled her by telling her she wasn't making *Lassie Comes Home to a Place in the Sun* or made her say lines she didn't want to. With *Giant*, she was no longer a protected teenager and she encountered a man who "could really be quite cold." They were bound to clash. Stevens had seen signs of a spirited disposition in the adolescent girl.

On her side, motherhood had increased her confidence, and she was no pushover (if she ever truly had been). There may also have been some postpartum emotionalism on Elizabeth's part resulting from a second cesarean birth only four months earlier. Brenda Maddox in her book *Who's Afraid of Elizabeth Taylor?* suggests just such a scenario: "Her postpartum mood, combined with the everyday paranoia of the star, made her feel that Stevens was deliberately trying to humiliate her." Whatever the reasons, Elizabeth and George fought a lot during the months it took to make the film.

One of their worst set-tos occurred near the end of filming in Texas, on July 7 (camera day 41). It had to do with something Elizabeth Taylor specialized in—how to dress. Leslie Benedict, upset with her husband's stubborn lack of sensitivity, decides to take a hiatus from her wifely duties and visit her family back in Maryland. And what she should wear upon departure ignited a firestorm. Stevens wanted her to "look desperate and sad and lonely," and to that end he costumed her in "thick brogue shoes, thick stockings, a long skirt, a man's slouch hat, and [her] hair in a tight bun."

On the face of it, this does seem like a terrible idea. A woman like Leslie would have wanted to look her best upon departing from her husband and upon meeting her family. Her appearance as she was leaving would make her husband feel the separation, the decision to return to her family, all the more. But dressed the way Stevens wanted, Taylor said she "felt like a damn fool and worse." She couldn't understand "why the girl, an utterly feminine woman, would deliberately put on a ludicrous getup that made her look like a lesbian in drag—or Charlie Chaplin."

When Taylor told Stevens what she thought, he exploded. He ridiculed her in front of cast and crew, exclaiming that all she ever cared about was how she looked and that she worried so much about being glamorous that she was never going to become an actress. It was a replay, but angrier, of the dressing-down she had taken back in L.A. the first week of shooting. It was quite a show, and Taylor, who had a temper of her own, fired back. She wiped all the makeup off her face, pulled her hair down, and then did the scene.

Taylor concluded that Stevens liked "having a patsy or two on a film." Besides her, the other patsy, of course, was James Dean. But at least, she felt, Stevens picked ones who could answer back—and usually did. "I think he prefers clay," she wrote—the very image that Rock Hudson used to praise Stevens. Rock was happy to make himself a piece of clay to be sculpted by the artist Stevens, and to the end of his days he always regarded *Giant* as the high point of his career. But in an unguarded moment years later, Hudson spoke about Stevens in a way he never had before. He stated that in filming *Giant*, Stevens wanted "to create a state of total dependency." "Elizabeth," he said, "could have accepted it easily. But George was a tyrant and she could be a termagant. Whenever they clashed, I stood well back."

⋈

Despite Stevens's confident manner and control of every aspect of the film, from script to final cut, his method of making a picture on the scale of *Giant* would encounter opposition and blowback. Just a week into shooting, production manager Ralph Black, a seasoned professional with a good record, quit and returned to L.A., explaining in his report to Warner Bros. that he could "no longer take the embarrassment of being abused before the entire company by Mr. Stevens." Besides Black, another production manager, along with Dick Moder, an assistant director, also left because of conflicts with Stevens. Dialogue coach Bob Hinkle put the reasons for their departures in earthy perspective: "He didn't go for any bullshit. And that's when a lot of guys got fired, because they tried to bullshit him." Stevens had his right-hand man, Fred Guiol, telephone Tom Andre, a well-regarded Warner Bros. manager, to come to Texas and take over the job vacated by Black.

Andre arrived on June 18, two weeks after the start of filming, and the first thing he did was seek advice from Boris Leven on how to handle Stevens. Leven told him, "Tom, if you want my advice, never say no. If he wants . . . I don't know . . . a *Titanic* or the *Queen Mary* or something right on this prairie, on this field, you say, 'Yes, sir, I'll do the best I can,' and forget it." Leven concluded, "Never say no to anything." There were rumblings of discontent among the makeup crew as well, though nothing ever came of it.

Without mentioning Stevens, Andre recalled the trying conditions of his job once on-site: "We'd get up about sun-up, 5 A.M. or so, and work all day until it got dark. It was hotter than Hades out there. Then we'd go back to the hotel, shower, have some dinner, watch the dailies, then try to get some sleep. The temperature would go down at night, but it didn't feel much cooler because it was so damn humid and we didn't have any air conditioning." He said they slept three to four in a room at the Paisano.

Stevens's tenacity and determination prompted Boris Leven to conclude, "I liked George and I hated him sometimes." Leven had started out a big fan of Stevens, but in Texas he became disillusioned: "The beginning was absolutely so fabulous and exciting and inspiring and what have you, and then the beginning of the marriage was very beautiful . . . then you got to know George, you know. He wasn't an easy person. I think he was a loner, and I think he was a very moody person, and often he was very hard on people."

Leven's memories of the days on location were anything but idyllic: "Things were tough . . . the weather and all kinds of conditions, you know, and it was a very big, large film that required many people." Tactical problems were "almost like moving an army. We had trucks and stuff. It was done on a big scale. I don't think they make films that way anymore." According to Leven, Stevens couldn't stand any inefficiency. Everything had to be done his way, according to his vision. He resisted advice. He had a picture in his head and he was going to shape everything to that end.

George Stevens, Jr., said that when his father made a decision, it was like the sun going down.

⚬

Stevens wanted to control everything on the set, but there was one actor whose behavior challenged his authority from early in the filming until near the end. Back in March, when James Dean was lobbying furiously for the Jett Rink role, he had gushed about Stevens in an interview in *The New York Times*: "Gadge (Kazan), of course, is one of the best. Then there's George Stevens, the greatest of them all. I'm supposed to do 'Giant' for him. This guy was born with the movies. So real, unassuming. You'll be talking to him, thinking he missed your point, and then—bang!—he has it." And then he added a typical bit of hip self-analysis: "The problem for this cat—myself—is not to get lost."

What started out so promising in Dean's first rush of enthusiasm at being cast in *Giant* collapsed pretty quickly. Stevens was no Kazan or Ray, no coddler of stars, although many actors considered him an actor's director. After Dean's near codirectorship with Nicholas Ray, it was almost inevitable that he would not share such closeness with Stevens, who was older and would be perceived as an establishment figure—the kind of man Dean typically did not like or respect. And unlike Ray, Stevens had little patience with erratic or rebellious behavior. There were more directors like Stevens than Ray in that regard—John Ford, William Wyler, Henry Hathaway, Otto Preminger, Alfred Hitchcock, to name a few. James Dean likely would have found none of them to his liking. They would have told him to go shit in his hat (a favorite Fordism) or something to that effect. Perhaps better than anyone, Hitchcock summed up a general view of actors held by many directors: "All actors are cattle."

Dean had been extremely lucky with his first two directors, but Stevens was something entirely different. Nick Ray himself wrote that "there were probably very few directors with whom Jimmy could ever have worked." According to Ray, Jimmy "had no hard professional shell." As a result, any "lack of sympathy, lack of understanding from a director or any of his staff disoriented him completely."

From the beginning Dean had problems with Stevens. Jimmy even asked his agent, Dick Clayton, to come to Texas because, Clayton explained, "[h]e was apprehensive about George Stevens, who he said had already been standoffish and giving him orders." Stevens was never going to devote the kind of personal attention and empathy that Jimmy had received from Kazan and Ray. Kazan alternately coddled and bullied Dean to get the performance he wanted, but Ray was like a brother, a buddy. Ray even approved of Jimmy's racing. "It was good for Jimmy to do something on his own with clarity and precision," he told Joe Hyams.

Dean's euphoria after winning the part quickly evaporated. Exhausted from finishing *Rebel Without a Cause*, he arrived by train in Texas on June 3, along with other cast members who had not been needed in the Virginia shoot. During the first week of shooting, Stevens came down hard on Jimmy and told a reporter that he was directing the picture, not Dean. Then, in typical Stevens fashion, he expressed confidence in Dean's abilities.

And Clayton did come to Marfa for a day or two, but it made no difference.

Only five days into filming, on Friday, June 10, Stevens and Dean clashed. Stevens required his actors to be in costume every day whether they appeared in a scene or not. He wanted them ready in case he had to shift some scenes because of unforeseen events. When Jimmy had to go three straight days in costume without any scenes, he failed to show on that Friday. According to Carroll Baker, on the next day, before shooting resumed, Stevens gave Jimmy a "severe scolding" in front of cast and crew. Baker admired Stevens as a "straightforward, no-nonsense, ex-Army officer" who wasn't a phony like some directors who would have praised Jimmy on the set and condemned him behind his back.

Stevens spent a lot of time talking to James Dean about particular scenes, to the point that the director sometimes became exasperated. Jimmy, he said, "had the ability to take a scene and break it down . . . into so many bits and pieces that I couldn't see the scene from the trees, so to speak. All in all it was a hell of a headache working with him." Like some other perceptive observers of the Dean phenomenon, Stevens detected a deliberate strategic element in Jimmy's behavior: "He seemed to practice, or emphasize, the immature aspects of his nature—perhaps with mature design."

And even though the role of Jett Rink was quite different, sociologically, from the close-to-his-heart autobiographical protagonists of both *East of Eden* and *Rebel Without a Cause,* the embittered figure in *Giant* was one that Dean could easily identify with. Consider this observation in the Ivan Moffat profile of Jett Rink: "Of all the people in our story, the only one who did not grow up, or mature, or become reconciled to this earth, was (in purely Texas terms) the most successful one of all: Jett Rink himself." This description eerily mirrored the real James Dean. Or take this characterization in a Warner Bros. preproduction sketch, which seems to have been tailored to fit Dean: "Perhaps the term 'man' is wrong in describing Jett. The angry boy persisted throughout."

Dennis Hopper, who plays Jordan Benedict III, came down on the train with Dean. They knew each other from working together on *Rebel Without a Cause.* The two weren't close, however. Dean considered the nineteen-year-old Hopper just another aspiring hanger-on who wanted to hitch a ride on Dean's meteor. Jimmy complained to John Gilmore that "this guy keeps following me around."

As for Hopper, he had been blown away by *East of Eden* and couldn't believe his eyes the first time he met Dean in the Warner Bros. commissary. "Here was this grubby guy in sneakers, an old turtleneck and glasses, sitting with a cup of coffee, pouring sugar into it, and watching the sugar dissolve." Upon being introduced to Hopper, Dean didn't acknowledge the younger actor in any way. Nonetheless, Hopper was fascinated by Dean and tried to get close to him. But he admitted that they never became "great buddies who went out drinking or anything like that."

Trained in classical stagecraft, Hopper later described himself as "an actor who'd come out of Shakespeare. My experience of acting was line reading, precise gestures, knowing what you were going to do next." But after he joined the cast of *Rebel Without a Cause* and saw James Dean in action, he knew there was a lot more to learn. "I thought I was potentially the best actor in the world," he said. "Then I saw Dean and realized I didn't know shit from shinola." Jimmy shared one piece of valuable advice during the making of *Rebel*: "Do things, don't show them. Stop the gestures. Well, if you're smoking a cigarette, just smoke it. You know, you feel like smoking, smoke it. It will be very difficult doing the simplest things at first, like drinking a cup of coffee." Hopper realized that he himself was "working externally," while Jimmy "was working internally"—which is basically a shorthand definition of Method acting.

In Marfa, their essential relationship remained the same, with Hopper as acolyte and apprentice. In the days ahead, Dean would share his views about acting, and Hopper would take on the coloration of Dean's persona. Dean came to Texas wanting to be a Texan for the duration of the film, and Hopper came wanting to be James Dean for the rest of his life.

Dean moved in with Chill Wills and Rock Hudson in a private home, while Hopper took a room in the Paisano. Putting antagonists in a film together was an old trick of directors, believing that proximity would intensify their antipathy on-screen. It probably did, but Dean and Hudson already didn't like each other. Although a photograph has survived of Dean, Hudson, and two other men playing cards, whatever camaraderie they had didn't last long. After about a week, Dean moved out, and according to one of his acquaintances, "Rock tried to 'queer' him, and when he resisted, Hudson became embittered and asked him to leave." Biographer Paul Alexander surmises that "Jimmy would have hated Rock for his fey ways and his penchant for drag. A part of the 'old' homosexual set, Rock would have been threatened by Jimmy's edgy and unconventional personality even as he was attracted by his sweet boyish looks." "Would haves" are not evidence, however. But there was certainly tension between the two men. Not only that, they both vied for the attention and company of one of Hollywood's most desirable actresses—Elizabeth Taylor.

Rock simmered while Dean pulled one offensive act after another. One morning, Dean and Hopper were walking past Rock's trailer as he was coming out, and Dean jumped onto Hudson and French-kissed him.

"Jimmy, I've seen you do some pretty crazy things, but what was that about?" Hopper asked, to which Dean replied, "Ah, he's a fairy." In a similar vein, Dean mocked Rock behind his back. Hanging out with local cowboys, he called himself "Rack." He had a name for Stevens, too: "Fatso."

Victor Millan (stage name for Joe Brown) was another actor in *Giant* who had known Dean before, at UCLA. The youth he remembered from college was a "very quiet, sensitive, kind person." But now Dean had put on weight and muscle and carried himself differently: "And I noticed what I call the New York Actors Studio slouch, all the mannerisms." He also noticed that "when he'd forget, he'd lose the mannerisms and then he'd remember that he had to have the mannerisms, and I noticed the key thing was the change in his speaking pattern. He would Steve McQueen it. Brando did that and then everybody did it."

Millan sensed that James Dean was playacting the role of Jimmy Dean. But he also admired Dean's "*tremendous concentration*." As time for a scene drew nearer, Dean ceased all the kidding around and focused with absolute intensity on getting himself ready. Yet that very intensity led some actors to criticize Dean, thinking he was showing off, trying to make them seem less serious than he was. Another actor who corroborated Dean's intense professionalism was Ronald Reagan, the host of *General Electric Theater*, on which Dean appeared twice in 1954. Said Reagan, who appeared with Dean in one episode, "The Dark, Dark Hours" (CBS, December 12, 1954), "He worked very hard at his craft, rehearsed with very much the same intensity that he gave the part on camera. . . . He seemed to go almost all out any time that he read his lines."

On *Giant*, there was hardly anything that Jimmy did on-camera that his costars liked, but Stevens knew that something was happening, that Dean was giving a performance that one could not stop watching. And so the highly organized old pro George Stevens was willing to put up with Dean's irritating juvenile behavior to get the footage the picture needed— up to a point, that is. But Jimmy, he said, "never understood that Jett Rink was only part of the film. . . . Edna Ferber in the book never intended Jett Rink to be the central figure." Nonetheless, Jimmy did everything he could to make Jett Rink the most important character in the film. He also tried to assert his own importance over that of the director. Stevens, of course, saw what was happening, and he didn't like it. "As Jimmy accuses me of interfering with his work, I can only say that I feel he is jeopardizing *my* work. And I am the one running the show . . . not Dean."

❧

Carroll Baker was the other Method actor in *Giant*, and she didn't cause anybody any trouble at all. *Giant* was technically her second film, and Stevens gave her second-tier star billing. He had chosen her partly on the basis of her performance in "The Treadmill," a TV drama in the CBS *Web* series (July 11, 1954). In *Giant*, she played Elizabeth Taylor's second daughter, Luz II, and at twenty-four she was one year older than her mother.

In her autobiography, *Baby Doll* (1983), Baker gives one of the best accounts of the cast at work and play in Marfa that summer of 1955. The town itself she dealt with in a sentence: "Everything was of an age gone by, with the exception of a movie house, a gas station, and the paved road." Nor were the accommodations anywhere near her expectations. She shared a "lonely clapboard house" with Jane Withers and Fran Bennett. One of the worst things about such lodgings was that there was no privacy for a spouse or boyfriend or husband.

The work schedule was grueling. Six days a week, the cast would gather at the El Paisano Hotel at 5:00 A.M. for wardrobe, makeup, and hairdressing to prepare for the day's shooting. Three hours later, the entire cast—thirty-nine strong—were transported to the Ryan Ranch, where shooting would begin.

This policy irritated a number of the players, but Rock Hudson and Elizabeth Taylor, veteran studio professionals, didn't let it bother them. And Carroll Baker, although she considered the demand "strenuous and inconsiderate," preferred it to staying in Marfa, where there was "absolutely nothing to do." She wrote, "On location, we could enjoy the camaraderie of our fellow actors, and each of us had a comfortable trailer where we could rest, out of that broiling sun." She also found ways to entertain herself. She played cards with Earl Holliman, who became a good friend, and she practiced riding horses with the help of the local cowboys, all very happy, one imagines, to lend a hand to such a beautiful young woman. She liked her days on the location site so much that she compared the time to a "paid vacation at an exclusive dude ranch." She is the only person on record to have felt that way.

But the thing she liked the most was the sumptuous daily buffet, catered by a firm from El Paso. She had been a starving artist long enough, and weighing 108 pounds, she considered herself underweight and ate to her heart's desire. And there was much to choose from: "caldrons of stews and curries; serving planks with roasts and fish and chicken; mashed, baked, boiled, and fried potatoes; a wide variety of vegetables and salads, assorted cheese, freshly baked rolls and bread; and dozens of yummy desserts." Reporters, always interested in a free lunch, also rhapsodized about the spread laid out each day at the Ryan Ranch.

Once the day's shooting was completed, around 6:00 P.M., the cast was taken back to Marfa, where they changed clothes and reassembled in the Paisano Hotel for dinner. T-bone steaks were usually on the menu. Elizabeth and Rock were always together and kept up a steady, intimate conversation, which made Baker and others envious. To Baker, it was kind of like high school. Everybody knew who the stars were, and those not included felt left out. James Dean wore his hat at the dinner table and played musical notes on the glassware with a spoon. Or he and Carroll would dine together and try to outdo each other in mocking Rock and Elizabeth. They laughed at their clothes, their status, and their self-involvement. Baker remembered that Jimmy's and her remarks were sometimes witty and always "cruel and cutting." When Dean jumped up to leave, Dennis Hopper always tried to grab his chair, but Earl Holliman always beat him to it. It was exactly like high school.

The dynamic among the foursome, Hudson and Taylor, Baker and Dean, changed as the days rolled by. As Jimmy started stealing more and more scenes, Rock and Elizabeth brought Carroll into their sphere. It was all part of a plan to undermine James Dean. Taylor's chauffeur drove the awestruck

Baker to Elizabeth's house, where Rock had a pitcher of martinis ready to kick the night off. The boredom of Marfa days and the intense work schedule were alleviated by nightly bouts of drinking and socializing. Rock was a very youthful twenty-nine and very sociable, Elizabeth could drink with the best of them, Carroll was like a teenager set down in a nocturnal world without boundaries, and Jimmy was a world-champion insomniac. But Jimmy was never a part of the Rock–Elizabeth insiders' circle.

Carroll was reduced to an "awed fan," given her sudden access to Rock and Elizabeth—"the luminous, untouchable stars of the first magnitude." And those two untouchables asked the novitiate to help them derail James Dean. Elizabeth angrily called him "an outrageous scene-stealer," and Rock agreed. He told Carroll that only another Actors Studio type could handle him. That proved to be accurate—up to a point—but it wouldn't be demonstrated until they returned to L.A., when Baker and Dean had their big scene together.

Baker was almost delirious to be invited inside the magic circle. One day, she walked into the Paisano with the two "radiant stars" and laughed and conspired with them while Dean sat alone at his table. She even snubbed her best friend, Earl Holliman. Later, at the rushes, she sat with the big three—Taylor, Hudson, and Stevens, whom she "also admired and adored."

The next day, she was invited to lunch in the separate structure that had been built on the location site at the Ryan Ranch for Stevens, Hudson, and Taylor. The table was draped with linen and the waiter wore a uniform. When Dean saw her, he turned without speaking and walked away. Other insider privileges included the all-night parties held at Rock's house.

Looking back at those times, Baker concluded that she and her new actor friends had all comported themselves "like a bunch of undisciplined, out-of-control adolescents." They were young, they didn't need sleep, they were confident that makeup would take care of any late-night wear and tear, and they were free to carry on "like absolute fools." And they did, all the way through the Marfa shoot.

After dinner, everybody would go across the street to the Palace to watch the previous day's rushes. Rock stayed glued to Elizabeth, and James Dean sat by himself in the balcony. Earl Holliman recalled endless hours of watching cattle gathering to drink from a stock tank.

Afterward, the players had some time to themselves. In *Elizabeth Takes Off,* a combination memoir and weight-loss program, the actress remembered, "The heat, humidity and dust were so thoroughly oppressive we had to bolster our spirits any way we could." Elizabeth and Rock used spirits to do the bolstering, and along the way they invented the best drink she had ever tasted: "a chocolate martini, made with vodka, Hershey's syrup and Kahlua. How we survived I'll never know."

The ebullient Jane Withers, the former child star, a veteran of forty-four films before *Giant,* knew full well the perils of boredom. She also realized upon arriving in West Texas that "there was nothing to do in Marfa." Installed in a private house, she created "Withers' USO," featuring snacks, board games, card games, records, and light refreshments (but no gambling or liquor). Withers made friends easily and was very impressed with Elizabeth Taylor and came to admire her wonderful sense of humor. She came to feel that "Liz is a great person."

The "USO" closed at 11:00 P.M., and it was only after hours that James Dean would drop by. He had a habit of climbing through a back window instead of using the front door, and several times Withers found him curled up asleep on her bed. This irritated her and she nailed the window shut so he had to come through the front door like any normal person. She liked Jimmy and listened sympathetically to the story of his little-boy sadness. She recognized his insecurities and gave him sound advice about trusting himself.

She recalled that sometimes they'd "just sit and talk, or . . . listen to music for a couple of hours at a time without saying a word. Sometimes he would dance . . . modern, interpretive things." She thought he had a "wonderful pantomimic gift. . . . He had a quality and style all his own." His unkempt appearance appealed to Withers's motherly instincts, and once after she'd seen him at the hotel wearing the same shirt for three weeks straight, she asked him if she could wash it for him, but he said, "No, I like this shirt the way it is."

But Jimmy couldn't stop being Jimmy, and when he took her for a ride in the red Chevy that Warner Bros. provided, he scared her to death with his fast, reckless driving. None of his mother figures could induce him to drive safely, and Stevens, who had already forbidden any racing, took the Chevy away from him because of his carelessness. Besides that, he had shot out the car's windows.

Another older woman that Jimmy became close to in Marfa, also a mother figure, was salty Mercedes McCambridge. Used to playing tough-as-boot-leather women in films like *All the King's Men* (for which she won an Oscar) and *Johnny Guitar,* she was an outspoken woman who hated just about everything in this little town. She complained about the food at the hotel, where the smell of frying fat permeated everything. She switched rooms with Fran Bennett so she could have one to herself and drink without having to deal with anybody unless she wanted to.

Besides drinking alone, her one solace, it seems, was Jimmy Dean. As usual, Dean was his charismatic, difficult, quirky self. She assessed his character accurately but liked him anyway: "Everybody seemed to have a lot of problems with Jimmy. Nobody had more problems with Jimmy than Jimmy had"—which is about as accurate a summing-up of Dean as anybody ever made. Years later, she called Jimmy the "runt of the litter of thoroughbreds. You could feel the loneliness beating out of him, and it hit you like a wave."

And Jimmy liked "Madama," her character's nickname in the film. They both had something in common; they didn't like George Stevens, whom McCambridge described as a "master editor, director, and not-always-benevolent dictator." One time when they were particularly mad at him, they binged like children, devouring a "full jar of peanut butter, a box of crackers, and six Milky Ways and . . . twelve Coca-Colas!" That would show Stevens!

Jimmy very much admired a beat-up old cowboy hat that Gary Cooper had given her back in L.A. Coop said it smelled of horse piss, a mark of authenticity, and Jimmy used every wile at his disposal to get it from Ma-dama, but she wouldn't let go of the hat and wore it with pride in the film.

Bored, Jimmy resorted to childish antics. One morning after breakfast in the hotel, he stuffed parts from a pecan roll into each nostril, and with the dough dangling out, he and Madama walked through the lobby, shocking three ranchers. Then he told Madama, "If anybody asks you, just say I am so rich I got dough coming out of my nose." This was the equivalent of Jimmy's old trick of yanking out his dental plate and plopping it down in restaurants. Wherever he happened to be, Jimmy often felt compelled to show that he was a Hoosier hick.

McCambridge couldn't wait to get out of Texas. One morning, she told a reporter, "Last night I dreamed that I might die today." And when she did die in the film, bucked off by War Winds (on June 23), she was free to return to L.A.

Jimmy worked hard to create a Texas persona. He could do it with as simple an object as a hat. Monte Hale, a country singer and western actor cast in a small part, recalled that Jimmy liked the way he removed his hat and copied him. McCambridge saw him spend hours removing his Stetson with one hand and flipping it onto the ground so it would land upright. He practiced until he could do it every time. Jimmy made the hat an essential part of his character as Jett Rink. He had a way of using physical objects to convey emotion. Lee Strasberg of the Actors Studio commented on the effectiveness of Dean's use of his hat in *Giant*: "You see every actor doing it now . . . pulling his hat down . . . it's become a style. But there was nothing loose about it . . . when Jim did it. Inside he was saying 'Gee, that blankety-blank,' but he couldn't quite say it. So he pulled down that hat."

Dean explained his approach: "I developed a program of understanding Jett and of doing the things he'd be likely to do. I didn't want any jarring notes in my characterization. Jett was a victim of his position in life. I want to play him sympathetically." For the first time in his brief career, he wasn't playing himself. The motivation had to come from other sources than Dean's private anguish. It had to have an economic and sociological dimension. It was the first film role in which Dean could play a character who was not drawn almost entirely out of his own guts.

Dean wanted to add every local detail to his repertoire in order to create the illusion of a Texas cowboy. The hat and the rope were integral to the building of his character of Jett Rink (who, ironically, we never see on horseback or doing any other work associated with a cowboy). Dean studied dozens of cowboys in Marfa and hung out with Worth Evans's two sons, Bub and Clay, at the Ryan Ranch. Bub and Clay were the real deal, very down-to-earth and very capable horsemen. Dean and Clay became buddies.

But it was Bob Hinkle, the Texas dialogue couch, with whom Jimmy spent the most time off the set. The friendship that began in L.A. only grew stronger in Texas. The Jimmy whom Hinkle knew wasn't like the one that a lot of others experienced. "People told me he was moody and hard to get along with, that he clammed up and wouldn't talk," Hinkle said. "That was a lot of nonsense. He could talk your arm off."

Jimmy and Bob constantly worked on rope tricks and practiced roping bales of hay, then moved on to calves, then on to people. Jimmy had been fascinated with ropes even before arriving in Texas. He'd fooled around with a rope during the filming of *East of Eden,* and there's a photograph of him with a rope encircling Julie Harris and Richard Davalos.

Monte Roberts, a wrangler on the film who also taught Jimmy some rope tricks, thought he saw what Jimmy was trying to do. "He really kind of aspired to be a Will Rogers type. He wanted to be quiet and occasionally say something intellectually deep while he twirled the rope."

Besides roping, Hinkle also taught Jimmy how to ride like a cowboy. He taught him how to saddle and unsaddle a horse and how to mount and dismount. Jimmy thought he would need these skills for any Westerns that lay in his future. But Jimmy must have known some of these things already, since he had bought a horse for himself, during the filming of *East of Eden.* Bob also taught him how to roll his own cigarettes. By the time he left Texas, Dean had achieved his goal of becoming a cowboy, a Texan whose accent was so tonally exact that other Texans considered him one of their own. People would ask Hinkle where Dean had grown up in Texas. Earl Holliman later made a shrewd observation: "In fact, Jimmy was kind of playing Bob Hinkle all through the movie, so to speak."

On many nights, Jimmy and Bob trekked into the countryside to hunt rabbits—an activity that alarmed some of Jimmy's friends. Jimmy had brought a lever-action .22 rifle with him from California, and Bob borrowed a .22 from the manager at the Paisano. Local ranchers applauded their efforts. Because of the drought, jackrabbits posed a real threat to grazing lands already under stress, and, in fact, bounties were paid in Marfa for jackrabbit ears. Jimmy and Bob bought .22 shells at Livingston's hardware store, and one rancher volunteered to pay for their shells if they'd hunt on his ranch.

They went out in a studio jeep most nights. Bob would drive, and Jimmy would bang away at rabbits caught in the glare of the headlights. It wasn't an entirely safe undertaking. Jackrabbits could be dangerous. Raoul Walsh had lost an eye when one jumped through the windshield of a jeep he was driving on location shooting in Arizona back in the silent era.

The two hunters used a spotlight to "freeze" the rabbits. Transfixed by the light, the rabbits would stand like furry statues, ears alert to danger. Jimmy and Bob would kill thirty or forty rabbits a night and cut off the ears and fill up a tow sack, then take them into town the next morning. Altogether, they killed 261 rabbits.

Jimmy couldn't get enough of rabbit hunting. But not everybody in the cast approved. When Jane Withers went along one night, as a kind of lark, she was sickened by what she saw. They came upon a wounded coyote tangled in a barbed-wire fence and Bob had to put it out of its misery; that was the last time Withers wanted any part of their rabbit safaris on the lone prairie. On another occasion, Mercedes McCambridge went on a similar hunt with Jimmy, but, like Withers, she was appalled by the results.

One time, Chill Wills was doing his level best to promote the film by having drinks with three visiting reporters at the house he shared with Dean and Hudson. Elston Brooks of the *Fort Worth Star-Telegram* described the scene: "The door opened and in came this character with a .22 rifle, a headlamp strapped onto his head, a big battery on his hip and smoke curling up around his temples from a cigarette dangling out of his mouth. It was James Dean." Out of the corner of his mouth, Wills remarked, "These Actor's [*sic*] Studio kids are a weird bunch." Wills had a habit of giving everybody nicknames. He called Hinkle "Buckle" because of a big champion rodeo buckle that he sometimes wore. He called Jimmy "the Spook," because he would always come into the kitchen in the morning wearing underwear, boots, and his cowboy hat.

⁂

Jimmy was at home in Marfa in a way that Rock Hudson and Elizabeth Taylor never were. It might have been partly because of his background and partly because he always tried to connect with locals on location. They were an audience, after all, and Jimmy was always performing. But he also felt comfortable with common people.

And he was certainly used to small towns. Fairmount (population 2,646 in 1950) was even smaller than Marfa, and the movie theater had the same name as the one in Marfa: the Palace. Jimmy ingratiated himself with children, high school–age kids, and the cowboys, ranchers, and workmen he met during the six weeks in Texas. He hung out with Clay Evans, and according to Clay, they did what cowboys do: drank beer and chased girls. Of course he also did things that shocked the locals—urinating in public, for example, and generally drawing attention to himself with his antics. But he was grounded in Marfa in a way that Rock Hudson and Elizabeth Taylor never tried to be. In Marfa, there was even a Dean Street, which intersected with Texas Street, and he and Bob Hinkle, of course, stole the signs. How could they not? Jimmy had several photographs taken of himself standing beside the signs—in one of which a very dour Rock Hudson is looking on in the background.

The small-town boy from Indiana related more closely with Marfa locals than any of the rest of the cast apart from native Chill Wills, Monte Hale, and Jane Withers, all of whom were very outgoing. Wills was always available for interaction with the community. He billed himself as "Mr. Texas" and was a very popular and enthusiastic ambassador for the film. The local paper summed it up: "Naturally, after all the nice things that Chill Wills has said about Marfa, Presidio County, and the Big Bend country, during his stay here . . . he has become the most popular, well-liked and often quoted of the Hollywood notables in Marfa."

Monte Hale (Bale Clinch, Bick Benedict's lawyer) and Jane Withers (Vashti Snythe) were also local favorites. A tall, friendly guy, Hale played the guitar most nights at the Paisano and sang everybody's favorite, "Cattle Call," which required some high yodeling. Jimmy loved to hear him sing that song and got Hale to try to teach him how to play a guitar.

Jimmy had his own local constituency. He connected with the high school–age girls, who oohed and aahed over his good looks and charisma. Lucy Garcia, a devoted Dean fan, recalled at the time, "He was very friendly. Liz and Rock would never pose for pictures, but Jimmy was always doing it. He even gave out autographs." She and her cousin Ofelia went to the El Paisano every night to try to catch a glimpse of Jimmy. Lucy said he talked a lot about his childhood. Both had photo albums filled with tiny black-and-white photos, and Ofelia had a photo of Jimmy in white skivvies, which revealed very muscular thighs.

Many years later, Lucy recalled, "I'm a little too much of an old lady to say this, but boy did Jimmy Dean have this sexy little giggle." She liked him so much, she formed a James Dean Fan Club.

Another girl, Darlyne Freeman, invited him to her birthday party. "He was very approachable," she said, "not stuck up or moody like the papers said he would be. Well, we didn't tell him that he was going to be the only boy there! He came into the room and was he surprised. He was very polite, but acted shy and uncomfortable. He left after a short time." It was the giggle that Darlyne always remembered.

Jimmy also bonded with Mexican-American children in Valentine, the dusty little town where the Mexican village was built. He and Bob Hinkle handed out Coca-Colas to the children.

Dean's popularity prompted Mexican-American girls in Marfa to form a softball team that summer named the Dizzy Deans, "after James Dean, who is here from Hollywood with Warner Bros.," the *Big Bend Sentinel* reported on June 23, 1955. Annie Marie Molina was manager, Lucile Polanco, captain, and Rosie Herrera, cocaptain, and all the players were Mexican-American. The outcomes of their games were reported the rest of that summer.

⁂

Elizabeth Taylor's relationship with Jimmy started out badly. He had no respect for her or for Rock Hudson; indeed, he held them in contempt. They were vassals of the studio system, while he was the new shiny Method actor. His view of Hudson never changed, but in time he became close to Elizabeth Taylor. On a professional level, she found him difficult at first. On camera, his Method mumblings and antics irritated her, and no wonder. His stuttering reading of lines, coupled with lack of eye contact and constant disregard of traditional marks, threw the two lead stars off pace. Particularly grating was his habit of interrupting a take by muttering, "Cut—I fucked it up." Dean had gotten away with this kind of behavior with his pal Nicholas Ray, but it infuriated Taylor and Hudson.

With Taylor, he was his usual rude self, which annoyed so many other actors trying to deal with him. He might appear approachable one day and the next he would cut her without a word of acknowledgment. Ordinary pleasantries—"Good morning," "Hello," "How are you?"—were the kinds of verbal greetings that Dean could not bring himself to utter. He knew how loutish he could be, and yet he would or could not change. He told one interviewer in L.A., "I'm a serious-minded and intense little devil, terribly gauche and so tense I don't see how people stay in the same room with me. I know I wouldn't tolerate myself." This statement suggests he may have been more pleased with himself than the remarks might at first suggest.

Jimmy's behavior was not lost on others. Composer Dimitri Tiomkin described his impressions of Dean to Leonard Rosenman: "I met your friend in Texas. Was very sensitive young actor, interesting person and big schmuck. Most of people in picture he bossed terribly. Insecure, I say."

Earl Holliman considered Jimmy a "strange boy, a strange young man. He could be charming and very likable, and yet if you didn't know him you couldn't figure out what the hell he was doing in his behavior toward people." According to Holliman, it was more important to Dean what he put up on the screen than how he treated other people.

When he wasn't in a scene, he'd entertain onlookers with a spot-on imitation of Charlie Chaplin impersonating Marlon Brando.

Dean's habit of overanalyzing a scene irritated Stevens. According to him, "I must admit that I sometimes underestimated him; and sometimes he overestimated the effects he thought he was getting." Dean's change-ability was disruptive: "He was always pulling and hauling, and he had developed this cultivated, designed irresponsibility." Stevens added, "From the director's angle that isn't the most delightful sort of fellow to work with." Another time, Stevens described how hard it was coping with Dean. "It was a hell of a headache to work with him," he said. Dean's attitude was, "It's tough on you, but I've just got to do it this way."

"As an actor," Stevens said, "Jimmy had the ability to reach people with movement. Using himself as a kind of clay, he could mold psychological impediments into his speech and into his movements. . . . Instinctively he seemed to understand all the impediments people have when they try to communicate with each other." Numerous observers felt that much of the physicality of a Dean performance, on-camera or onstage, resulted from his poor eyesight. His body was often out of alignment with every-body else's.

Stevens wanted it done his way, but Dean insisted on going it alone, approaching the character from his own angle. "Jimmy was never a cour-teous actor," Stevens recalled. "If he had a big scene, he would do his best to throw the actors playing with him. This was not because of a desire to star. It was because he felt that the scene belonged to his character." His unconventional physicality sometimes caused other actors to "loll and sway and shamble, too," Stevens said.

Even when Stevens commented positively on Dean, there was always a caveat: "Jimmy Dean could be tremendously winning. He was a little guy—mercurial. I had fun with him, but he was very much of the moment. He could turn on the charm or he could withdraw." Just about everybody had Jimmy's number.

Another thing about Dean that drove Stevens and the costars to dis-traction was his relentless pursuit of publicity. Every time a photographer showed up, Dean thrust himself into the composition, appearing in more publicity photos than Rock or Elizabeth. At other times, if it was just a re-porter and there weren't going to be any pictures, he'd walk away, refusing to be interviewed.

He injected himself into every opportunity to promote himself. Everybody on the set was aware of it. Carroll Baker pointed it out to Elizabeth Taylor. The public was beginning to get the idea that Dean was the costar with Taylor. Stevens was certainly aware of Jimmy's self-serving publicity tactics. Later, he would say that Dean "had a fine concept of how Jimmy Dean could be made popular, and he and his personally attached cameraman roamed around looking for the right people to be photographed with. He did this with Elizabeth Taylor, Edna Ferber (in L.A.), and many others." The cameraman that Stevens alluded to was Sanford Roth, on assignment from *Collier's*. He and Jimmy became good friends, and Roth would make the trip north to Salinas in Jimmy's little caravan on September 30.

Sometimes Jimmy's need for attention went too far. One day, the press was on hand, taking publicity photos of Taylor, when Jimmy sneaked up behind her, grabbed her, and flipped her upside down, showing her panties. She said she was glad she was wearing underwear that day, but the antic was embarrassing and it made her angry. Stevens reprimanded her and told her she should not let Dean treat her that way. "It certainly was undignified, Liz. Why do you allow Jimmy to do things like that?" Stevens made it seem as if it were her fault, which made her madder, and she stopped talking to Dean for a time.

But she didn't stay mad at him. One time, she even let him rope her without getting angry. Jimmy's rope was a constant on the set, and there is a lovely photograph of Elizabeth herself roping George Stevens in front of Reata's porch, with Mercedes, Rock, and Jimmy standing by watching.

Like numerous others, Elizabeth found herself drawn in by those same qualities that affected so many women who met Dean. He would emotionally seduce her with the exculpatory narrative of his life. Years later, she recalled, "We would sometimes sit up until three in the morning, and he would tell me about his past, his mother, minister, his loves, and the next day he would just look straight through me as if he'd given away or revealed too much." This was Dean's never-ending story, the one he told over and over, the one he could not escape. And after such an outpouring, it might take two or three days before he'd be friendly again with Elizabeth. "He was very afraid to give of himself," she said.

In any event, she couldn't stay mad at him for long, and she kept falling for his "little boy lost" narrative. In 1997, Taylor gave a fuller, more revealing account of Jimmy's innermost disclosures, one that zeroed in on something that many had wondered about—the relationship between the Reverend DeWeerd and Jimmy. According to Taylor, "When Jimmy was 11 and his mother passed away, he began to be molested by his minister. I think that haunted him the rest of his life. In fact, I know it did. We talked about it a lot. During *Giant* we'd stay up nights and talk and talk, and that was one of the things he confessed to me."

And a lot of people wondered about Jimmy's relationship with Elizabeth Taylor. Give Rock Hudson the final word on this: "Dean was a very depressed person and Liz took to him in a most motherly fashion. Whether she was in and out of his bed or he was in and out of her bed or whether no one was in anyone's bed is really no one's business but their own."

～⁂～

In the meantime, Elizabeth Taylor had other things going on in her life, as well—her marriage was growing colder by the day. At one point late in June, her husband, Michael Wilding, flew down to Texas to spend a few days with her. According to Wilding, "Liz" (a name she hated) had asked him to come to Texas, thinking he might "act as a referee" between her and Stevens and give her "a shoulder to cry on." Arriving dressed like a proper Englishman in a tweed suit and a bowler hat, Wilding quickly adapted, and the next day, seated in a canvas chair on the prairie, watching his wife at work, he was sporting casual dress and wearing a wide-brimmed western hat.

Elizabeth had asked him to come to Texas for support in the ongoing war between Stevens and Dean. She felt she was getting caught in the cross fire. On the set, Wilding witnessed the antagonism between a "brilliant director" and Dean, "such a good actor." He thought that Dean was sometimes right in yelling "Cut" and thus usurping the director's role, but he knew that neither would yield in what was "one long feud."

The press thought Wilding came to Texas for another reason—to quell rumors about his wife having an affair with Rock Hudson. They were spending many nights in each other's company, drinking and talking. Elizabeth had a habit of falling for her leading men, as she had told Wilding, and if Rock Hudson had been straight, she would doubtless have had an affair with him. Maybe she did anyway. He was very handsome, the very image of male virility, he liked women, and, another big plus, he had a great, bawdy sense of humor.

Besides that, her marriage to Wilding was lukewarm at best. Their age disparity had begun to be a problem (he was nineteen years her senior), and she had grown tired of his idleness, brought on by a decline in his film career after his move to the United States. For his part, Liz's shortcomings as a wife were manifest: She had no sense of time, she was colossally sloppy in her personal habits, and she let her love of pets—dogs, cats, a duck—turn their household into a smelly mess. Ultimately they were headed for a divorce, though neither had quite come to terms with that prospect yet. So now, with Wilding in Texas, he must have fully realized that things were not going to be set right in their marriage, affair or no affair. And upon meeting James Dean for the first time, he had something else to worry about when Jimmy said, "You'd better know right away, Mike, that I have fallen madly in love with your wife!"

Wilding found himself an observer of something that was beginning to take shape among the three leads. James Dean, always competitive, was slowly but inexorably taking Elizabeth Taylor away from Rock Hudson. It was as if the plot of the film they were making—Jett Rink's being hopelessly in love with Bick Benedict's wife—was being enacted off-camera as well as on, but with a different outcome. In the film, Jett does not succeed in stealing Leslie from Bick Benedict; he comes nowhere close. But in real life, out there on the prairie, Dean was in fact stealing Elizabeth Taylor from Rock Hudson. Toward the end of filming in Marfa, Taylor was spending those long nights in the company of James Dean instead of with Rock, but with the same results—lots of soulful talk leading to a deep friendship but in all likelihood no sexual consummation. James Dean had staying power for such late-night heart-to-hearts; he was, after all, one of the world's great insomniacs.

Wilding's trip to Texas changed nothing. He could feel his marriage and career slipping away and so he returned to L.A. and the house in Benedict Canyon to wait it out. Although Elizabeth missed her children and talked about them all the time, they never were brought to Texas to see their mother and she did not leave Texas during the Marfa shoot. It was as if everything was on hold in their marriage until the location shooting was finished.

❧

Although Rock Hudson had loved the verdant interlude in Virginia, Texas was another story. He found Marfa a "desolate place," the climate hot, the dust an irritation, the catered food monotonous, and there was nothing to do in the small town. In an interview late in his life, he recalled, "The weather just put its thumb on us and kept us right down into the ground." The only relief from the heat was a swimming pool in Alpine, twenty-six miles away.

But what most made Rock unhappy in Texas was James Dean. His antics, his scene stealing, his obsessive quest for publicity, his unpredictable demeanor, his courtship of Elizabeth Taylor's favors—all of this got under Rock's skin, and back in L.A., Rock's agent, Henry Willson, was disturbed to hear the stream of complaints pouring out of Texas. After all, Henry had shepherded his fast-rising client into a major motion picture with a prestigious director, and naturally he expected Rock to be happy and enjoy the ride to the top.

But as shooting continued, Rock stepped up his complaints. He felt that Dean was stealing the picture from him, and he was powerless to do anything about it. In scene after scene, Dean would find a way to get all the attention focused on him. He would fiddle with his hat or something, mumble a line, hitch his body off center, start fooling around with a rope; you never knew what was coming next. It was like trying to control a nervous animal; he was all twitches and stutters, all the time using that body of his to distract from a verbal exchange that should have featured the taller Rock towering over the squinting little guy but rarely did. Rock thought that acting was about giving and taking, but with Dean, he felt, it was all taking. Rock was not happy.

The woman in the middle, Elizabeth Taylor, confided in them both and adored both. She'd "sit up with one of them until 4 in the morning talking, then sit up with the other. Then go straight to work." But neither of them got along with the other. "Jimmy was 'thoroughly' Method." Rock, on the other hand, "was riddled with an inferiority complex." She also felt that Rock's looks "hurt him a lot. It was like being a beautiful woman in Hollywood. . . . If you were ugly as sin, people were taken seriously."

Five weeks in, Henry Willson dispatched his secretary to Marfa to try to calm his star client down. Henry had made Rock Hudson and he didn't want anything to tarnish the brightest star in his stable.

Phyllis Gates, though, was more than just a secretary. At her boss's urging, she had been seeing a lot of Rock. An attractive brunette from Minnesota, she had, like many Midwesterners, after a sojourn in New York, relocated to L.A., in thrall to the glamour and glitter of the movie industry. As Henry's secretary, she enjoyed many perks. Clients like Rock Hudson and Tab Hunter dropped by frequently, and Henry brought her into his lively social world, taking her to dinner at Ciro's and nightclubbing at the Mocambo, all the places to see and be seen in L.A. Henry also dished some of the best gossip this side of Hedda Hopper. Phyllis loved her job.

Unbeknownst to her, however, Willson had plans for her future. He envisioned her playing a significant part in Rock Hudson's life. In fact, Phyllis's role paralleled the uptick in Rock's career. When Rock landed the coveted role of Bick Benedict, Henry took the couple that night to the Mocambo to celebrate the news. Henry's date was Margaret Truman. His relationship with the daughter of the former president stirred talk in Hollywood of a possible marriage. It didn't fool anybody except perhaps Margaret Truman.

Henry was not only an agent; he was also a fixer and arranger. Phyllis liked working for him, but she was well aware of his manipulations and

wiles, as she wrote in her memoir, *My Husband: Rock Hudson* (1987): "Behind the façade of the witty bon vivant was a hard-boiled Machiavelli who would do anything to advance his clients' careers." She knew how he could kill a young actor's chance at a career if the actor offended him in some way. Willson, incidentally, hated James Dean.

Although she wasn't excited about going to a "godforsaken spot in the middle of Texas," Phyllis did her boss's bidding, arriving on July 5, five days before the end of filming. She was met at the train station by a "polite, clean-cut man in his early twenties." It was Dennis Hopper, and he told her he was "going crazy," having to wait around day after day without playing any scenes.

After shooting was finished that day, Rock went to her hotel room and embraced "Bunting," the special name they had for each other. According to her, they made passionate love. Afterward, they joined Stevens and the cast and crew to watch the dailies.

Once the screening was over, Rock introduced Phyllis to Stevens and his son and assistant, George, Jr., and to members of the cast. She found the director friendly and not at all like the "tough man" he was said to be on the set. Among the actors, she noted in particular Elizabeth Taylor's "flawless beauty" and James Dean's rather strange manner. "He was small and exceedingly shy. He gave me a weak handshake and then disappeared."

When she arose the next morning after sleeping late, Phyllis ran into Dean outside the hotel. He was twirling a rope on the sidewalk. Dean carried the rope with him everywhere, practicing intricate maneuvers. He spoke to her in his Texas drawl. Dean was quite friendly to Phyllis and invited her to take a few turns with the rope while he offered advice and guided her arms from behind. Then he asked her to go with him to the commissary and have a bowl of Texas chili. Walking into the dining room, Phyllis overheard Jane Withers say to another person, "I can't understand what Rock is going to do with her here."

The next day, Rock invited Phyllis to visit the set and watch the filming. She was excited. Nearing the site, she was struck by "the big Victorian mansion that George Stevens had built in the middle of nowhere." James Dean, who had been so warm to her the first time they met, now seemed

completely different. When she asked how he was, he touched his Stetson and, without ever looking at her, said in that James Dean way, "Mornin', ma'am, good to see ya," then wandered off.

On the other hand, George Stevens, garbed in cowboy duds—hat, jeans, plaid shirt—took time out to welcome her. She found him "warm and thoughtful." Elizabeth Taylor, however, seemed to be living in a cocoon, giving all of her time to those attending her, like her hairdresser and the makeup man. "She had little interest in anyone who wasn't in the movie business." Observing Rock and Elizabeth, Phyllis understood Jane Withers's overheard remark. They seemed to have a rapport that suggested some kind of intimacy. They joked around and seemed "almost childish with each other, talking a kind of baby talk and playing pranks like throwing water on each other." They appeared to be very good friends, but was there something else going on? Since Phyllis had no formal claim on Rock at that time, she didn't let the possibility of a fling between the two stars bother her. Or so she says. She also thought that Elizabeth Taylor was so beautiful, it would be difficult for any man not to have an affair with her if the opportunity arose.

Rock and Liz did not interact with the townspeople or the fans who came to watch the filming. According to Marcos Peña, who was working as a porter at the El Paisano, Taylor liked to eat a fruit plate for breakfast every morning and would tip him with bills she would pull out of a silver bowl. Hudson, on the other hand, was "a little bit more conservative, kind of like a snob," the porter remembered. Jimmy Dean was the friendliest and used to shoot pool with locals in the hotel basement.

During her weeklong stay, Dennis Hopper, at Rock's bidding, drove Phyllis to Mexico, fifty miles west, and the two spent the day shopping in the bazaars and markets in Ojinaga.

Phyllis got an earful of James Dean's behavior from Rock, who complained about Jimmy all the time. It wasn't the heat or the food or the isolation that caused Rock to be upset those long weeks in Texas; it was James Dean—his antics, his attitude, his rudeness, his overall demeanor. Privately, Phyllis thought that Rock was insecure. In any event, he was certainly angry.

Bob Hinkle was also aware of the rivalry and jealousy between Rock and Jimmy. "They never had words, but you could feel the jealousy," Hinkle said. "It would come out when Rock would say, 'How is Jimmy to work with?' or Dean would say, 'How do you like working with old Rock. You know, has he ever come on to you?'" For Rock, it was more than jealousy. He couldn't stand Dean's rudeness. Dean "was nasty, mean," Rock said. "I don't know what was eating him. If I said hello or good morning he snarled at me."

Rock feared that Stevens was "throwing the picture to Dean," he told Phyllis. Stevens was always taking Dean aside and talking to him, but he left Rock alone. Rock said that he'd worked mostly with hacks and never with someone of Stevens's "caliber" before. He felt that Stevens was ignoring him. With the director's approval, Rock believed, Dean was getting more close-ups.

Rock's anger extended to other actions by Dean, as well. He resented the attention the visiting press gave to Dean. James Dean was the hottest celebrity going, and Rock's studio style of acting—hit the mark, read the lines—could not match Dean's unpredictable Method style either on-camera or off. Dean kidded around with strangers, and Rock tended to loosen up only with close friends.

Over the years, Rock offered a bill of particulars regarding Dean's actions during the making of *Giant*. Dean, he said in one interview, "was always late and really very unprofessional." He behaved like "a Broadway actor who comes to California and deigns to make a motion picture." In another interview, Rock went further: "I didn't like him. Dean was hard to be around. He hated George Stevens, didn't think he was a good director, and was always angry and full of contempt. He never smiled, was sulky and had no manners." Rock also detailed Dean's selfishness as an actor: "While doing a scene, in the giving and taking, he was just a taker. He would suck everything out and never give back." Jimmy was also equally irritating before beginning a scene. According to Rock, "Before coming on set he used to warm up like a fighter before a contest. He never steeped [*sic*] into camera range without first jumping into the air with his knees up under his chin, or running at full speed around the set shrieking like a bird of prey." The Method could be very taxing to fellow actors.

In an interview near the end of his life, Hudson admitted that he had "never worked with an actor that had so much concentration." Gesturing toward a glass, he continued: "I mean, he could think about this piece of glass and that's it, nothing else would interfere; which, I felt, was brilliant." But Hudson thought Dean was not so strong as the older Jett Rink and believed that Montgomery Clift, whom Liz Taylor had originally wanted, would have done a much better job with the part. As for Dean himself, Hudson said, "Jimmy had a lot of faults. I didn't like him, personally." Continuing, he added, "He was a little guy, and thought little. He didn't have an expansive . . . he had blinders. He wasn't able to see sides, he channeled."

The week that Phyllis was there, Rock was with her all the time when he wasn't working. That left the perfect opening for Jimmy to seduce, metaphorically speaking, Elizabeth Taylor. And he did so the way he always did with women, especially mother figures. Taylor was an awfully young mother and she was very pretty, so she was just about a perfect audience for Dean's life narrative. Had she heard the one about the little boy who lost his mother when he was just nine years old and whose father was a coldhearted bastard who shunted the kid off to Indiana while he, the father, stayed in the Golden State? That story was always a grabber, and the saddest part of it all was that it was still so vividly and powerfully true, that at age twenty-four, the rising young star was still in the grips of that childhood trauma; he was still, as confidante after confidante testified, a little boy lost. Or maybe sometimes it was a con. There were those who thought so. Alec Wilder said Jimmy "bullshitted everybody to death." With Jimmy, nobody ever really knew what was going on or why.

In an interview in 1987, Taylor spoke about her relationship with both Hudson and Dean. "I was very connected to both Rock and Jimmy, but they had no personal connection at all. I was very connected to them— but it was like on the left side and the right side." She continued: "One on each side. I was in the middle, and it just would be like a matter of shifting my weight. I'd bounce from one to the other with total ease." She loved them both.

The first week in July, the *Giant* company caught a break. They got

Sunday off, as usual, but also Monday, July 4. There followed five more days of shooting. The last day of first-unit filming in Texas ended on July 9 (camera day 43). The final photography was a Frederic Remington–like shot of "Angel's funeral in progress far b.g."

The next day, Sunday, July 10, a chartered train carried most of the cast and crew back to L.A. Every train car bore a sign in the shape of Texas announcing the word GIANT. After thirty-eight days in the desert, everybody was happy to be heading home. But Rock Hudson was still upset and still complaining to Phyllis: "Dammit this is getting to be Jimmy Dean's picture. They're all trying to screw me." He also forbade her to spend time with the rest of the company, but by way of compensation, he made love to her. "It was wonderful," she remembered.

On the trip back, Elizabeth Taylor was surprised—and pleased—to see George Stevens loosen up. "He had this stoic demeanor," she remembered, "and when he released his affection and his sense of fun, it was an all-out kind of fun." Somewhere along the way, the train stopped for some reason, and the two of them got off the train and started picking yucca flowers and enjoying each other's company. "He was just a different man than the stern supervisor of the set."

⁓⁓⁓

Four days after Stevens and company departed for California, three inches of merciful rain fell on Presidio County. The long drought had broken, but the dreams of a uranium strike remained unfulfilled, and the ranchers and townspeople went on with their lives.

❧ 9 ❧

Being and Nothingness in L.A.

Once back in L.A. and the familiar confines of the studio in Burbank, everybody was presumably happy to be home, but much of the joy would dissipate in days to come. Flare-ups due to temperament and stressful moments began to escalate as the pressure to finish the film intensified. Perhaps the wide-open spaces of Texas had helped dissolve some of those tensions. Down there, the players at least had had physical distance from family distractions and worries, and virtually all of the scenes had been shot in the great outdoors. Warner Bros. might offer more comfortable amenities, but the studio could also feel claustrophobic, and studio watchdogs were everywhere. With every day over budget, the urgency to get the film finished increased.

Restored to home and hearth, Stevens, cast, and crew could sleep in their own beds, eat at their favorite restaurants, go to the beach, enjoy their family and friends—or not. There was a lot of emotional capital expended that July, August, September, and into the fall. In real time, the three stars would enact a cycle of adult life—marriage, divorce, death.

In early July, the second unit shot a series of pans of oil derricks in operation at Lost Hills, California, forty-two miles northwest of Bakersfield.

The Lost Hills Oil Field was huge, and shots of its densely populated derricks would appear in a brief sequence in the film illustrating the growth of Jett Rink's oil business, with his trucks carrying his oil, and Jett himself driving past a field of closely concentrated derricks.

James Dean did not return until July 13, having stayed behind in Texas for some second-unit photography of Jett Rink's discovery of oil, overseen by Fred Guiol. In a Warner Bros. press release, Dean commented on his sojourn in Texas: "It took me a while to accustom myself to the Texas way of life, but I regard the weeks as particularly well spent. In my desire to learn more about the character of Jett Rink, I learned much about Texas and Texans. I've gotten to like the state and the people so much I'm apt to talk like a proud Texan even after *Giant* is completed." When he wanted to, Jimmy knew exactly what to say.

According to Walter S. Ross, a publicity man at Warner Bros. who later wrote a novel about Jimmy, "Dean could behave intelligently when it suited him. If there was something important he wanted to talk to you about, he expressed himself clearly, but after he told you what he wanted, all you would get from him was mumbles. It made you wonder."

Filming in Burbank at the Warner studio resumed on Monday, July 11, the day after the arrival from Texas—no rest for the weary. The scene that day was the newlyweds' arrival at the ranch house where they will take up their married life. Once again, Leslie irritates Bick by thanking the Mexicans for carrying their luggage into the house. She is very kind and makes no distinction among people, but Bick does, telling her not to be too friendly to the servants, and Leslie responds by saying, "Elsewhere being gracious is acceptable."

That one word, *gracious,* sent Ferber into spirals of paroxysm. It is hard to understand her antipathy, but she wrote Henry Ginsberg a scorching letter upon seeing the offensive word in the script, back on April 23. She denounced the word *gracious* as "pure Bronx. It is Arthur Kober's Della [*sic*] Gross." The reference is to a Jewish humorist who had enjoyed some success in the twenties and thirties with caricatures of a Jewish husband hunter, whom he named Bella Gross. Ferber considered his work a travesty of Jewish experience. She told Ginsberg that she had removed the "sick-making word *gracious*" once, "but there it is, back again." It stayed in. Ferber's proprietary affection for Leslie remained a sore point in several scenes in which she thought the character's speech was not what *her* Leslie would have said.

❧

Stevens was laboring under the pressure of having fallen three weeks behind, and though this was not unusual for him, it created tension, and there was always the possibility that there would come a time when everything fell apart.

Immediately, problems in scheduling became an issue. Rock Hudson had to return to Universal for retakes on a film he'd made just before *Giant*, and in mid-July, Elizabeth Taylor came down with pharyngitis and cystitis and needed rest, according to her physician. Without it, she might miss a couple of weeks, which would be a very serious delay. Jack Warner was alarmed at the slowdowns. On July 18, he informed Stevens that he was way off schedule. Stevens plowed ahead.

There were golden moments in the filming, but more and more Stevens was running into trouble with Jimmy and Elizabeth.

Actress Noreen Nash, who had a small part as a rancher's wife, joined the cast in L.A., and she remembered that "by the time I got on the picture, director George Stevens and James Dean were at each other. Dean did his usual mumbling and Stevens kept saying, 'This script cost a lot of money. I want to hear those words.'"

During Taylor's absence, Stevens juggled the schedule, and on July 19 (camera day 51), he shot the encounter between Jett Rink and Bick Benedict and a chorus of good old boys. One of the signature scenes of the film— and of James Dean's career—it pitted poor boy Jett Rink against the ranching hierarchy. At issue is Luz Benedict's will, in which she bequeathed a patch of ground to Jett. Bick wants to appear to be generous and offers Jett $1,200 ($16,651 today) for the parcel of land, but he doesn't want to break up any of Reata's holdings, and he especially doesn't want Jett permanently in the picture. Bick places a dozen real one-hundred-dollar bills on the table, another example of Stevens's aesthetic of emphasizing the actual, the authentic. Jett doesn't pick up the money, although he does touch it with a finger, ever so lightly. In Texas, land was more important than just about anything else.

Before they began shooting, Jimmy told Bob Hinkle he was worried about the scene.

"Bob, what am I going to do? I just sit there while Rock and Chill and Monte put pressure on me. Rock's got the good lines."

After some thought, Bob replied, "Take that knotted rope in there with you. The whole time they're talking to you, just keep messing with that rope."

And with rope in hand, that was how Jimmy stole that scene. In the editing process the next year, Stevens let one take of that scene run for three minutes and forty-seven seconds. Ivan Moffat marveled at Dean's performance, and Stevens said it all: "Whoever is on the screen, it's Dean you watch—even if he has nothing to say!"

French critic Jean Queval focused on another memorable bit of business in that scene—the manner in which Dean departs from the room: "There is one gesture which is unforgettable—a gesture which recurs as the *leit-motive*. The right hand held out open, palm up, and insolently swung to the side—the gesture that says: 'count me out'; that indicates withdrawal. And the gesture is emphasized by blue eyes which mock rather than challenge; the gesture of one who is retreating deep into himself, misunderstood, arrogant, and invulnerable." Except that Queval gets it wrong; the palm is not up. But he is right about the effect of that gesture of adios and dismissal.

Despite Jimmy's triumph that day, just four days later he really ripped it with Stevens. Dean was growing increasingly restive at Stevens's insistence upon having him in makeup and costume and then not using him. A whole day would pass without his name being called. After three days in a row of waiting around for nothing, he failed to show up at all on Saturday, July 23. Warner Bros. did everything except hire bloodhounds to track him down. When a second-unit assistant director finally reached him at 4:00 P.M., Dean said he had been "too tired to work."

Actually, he had been busy all day, moving from an apartment to a small house in Sherman Oaks, using Bob Hinkle's pickup. The new dwelling looked like a hunter's lodge—lots of heavy dark wood. It would make a perfect setting for his favorite totems: a bloody matador's cape; a pair of bull horns; a noose (his favorite memento mori); his bongo drum; his cameras; his little library, including *The Complete Works of James Whitcomb Riley* (the Hoosier connection), *The Little Prince* (the Rogers Brackett connection), and *Death in the Afternoon* (which might have been the title of the last chapter of any biography of James Dean). Hedda Hopper noted that Dean was reading *The Note Book of Elbert Hubbard* that September, another indicator of Jimmy's untutored eclecticism.

Stevens was furious and asked staff to prepare a list of all the times Jimmy had caused delays based on "absences and/or tardiness." The list, dated August 1, 1955, ran from June 29 through August 1 and contained sixteen instances of tardiness, some as long as an hour, one as short as three minutes, when he showed up late in the company of Elizabeth Taylor. And of course there was the entry for July 23, the time he "did not come in all day."

On July 29, Dean was late again—thirty minutes. As it happened, Mercedes McCambridge had come to work that day despite having suffered a fall in her bathtub that morning that required stitches. The contrast with Dean's lack of professionalism was obvious, and Stevens let him have it in front of cast and crew. He denounced Dean's "inconsideration" of others and said he'd never seen anyone "go Hollywood" in such a short time. He said Dean would never appear "in another film I do."

The crew had had enough of Dean's tardiness, and although he apologized, they didn't respond. Finally, in the gathering silence, Dean said, "Maybe I better go to the moon," and one of them shot back, "We'll help you pack."

Jimmy was complaining all the time now about Stevens. He told Bill Bast, "Stevens has a method I call the 'around the clock system.' He's really no better than any other director, only he makes sure that he can't go wrong." Jimmy objected to Stevens's practice of shooting scenes "from every possible angle," a method that resulted in a lengthy period, a year sometimes, of editing. "And when they're through, surprise, another masterpiece! How the hell can you go wrong?"

Jimmy also spilled his anger to his improbable Hollywood advocate, Hedda Hopper: "I sat there for three days, made up and ready to work at nine o'clock every morning. By six o'clock I hadn't had a scene or a rehearsal. I sat there like a bump on a log watching that big lumpy Rock Hudson making love to Liz Taylor. I'm not going to take it anymore."

This outburst could be construed as just Jimmy being Jimmy, but, given the rivalry between Jimmy and Rock for Elizabeth Taylor's affection offscreen, it feels like a bleeding-over from script to a real ongoing competition/battle for her attention. Jimmy certainly didn't like and didn't respect Rock Hudson, and he doubtless resented the interaction between Rock and Liz. There is a telling photograph of the three of them on the Warner Bros. lot. Dean has that damned rope again, and Rock and Liz are facing each other, talking, and Dean is standing behind Liz with a little rope around her neck that he's fiddling with. With his glasses on, he looks like a small boy—or Jerry Lewis—intent on some mischief. It doesn't take a high-priced psychiatrist to figure out what the rope might signify.

Hedda Hopper, though, told Dean something that seems to have made an impression on him. She said that Henry Ginsberg and Edna Ferber stood to lose a lot of money if the film fell apart. She neglected to mention that the same situation applied to Stevens, but then, she seems not to have liked him very much. Taking Jimmy's side completely, she wrote in her memoir *The Whole Truth and Nothing But* (1963), "George Stevens is a martinet, a slow-moving hulk of a man who tried to force Jimmy to conform to George's interpretation of the role."

Whatever the cause, Dean did start arriving on time, and from then on Stevens didn't have any real problems with him, and despite his earlier troubles with Dean, Stevens always saw another side of Jimmy. "You were disturbed by him. Now you are dedicated to him."

During all of this turmoil, shooting continued, and on July 25 (camera day 56), Stevens shot the highly regarded showdown between Leslie Benedict and Bick and the boys talking politics. The men are huddled together in a bull session, no women allowed. They clam up when Leslie wants to join them, and when she persists, telling them she grew up around politics in Washington, Bick gets angry. He says, "This is men's stuff," and Leslie exclaims, "Men's stuff! Lord, have mercy! Set up my spinning wheel, girls. I'll join the harem section in a minute." Angry himself now, Bick draws himself up to his full height and tells her dismissively, "Leslie, you're tired." Her angry rejoinder carries a powerful feminist message: "That's right. Send the children on up to bed so the grown-ups can talk." This scene always surprises viewers seeing the film for the first time.

What is usually overlooked in this scene is the presence of a Mexican, a political boss named Gómez, who is there to confer with Bick and the other power brokers, lawyer, judge, and Uncle Bawley among them, to ensure the Mexican vote in the next election. This kind of machine politics along racial lines enabled Lyndon Johnson to be elected to the U.S. Senate in 1948 with a razor-thin margin of eighty-seven votes and earn the lasting nickname of "Landslide Lyndon."

On July 31, Elizabeth Taylor came down with a leg infection and would be out for a week, as her doctor informed Tom Andre. Stevens shifted his plans and during her absence moved the film crew from Warner Bros. to the Statler Hotel on Wilshire Boulevard. They shot establishing scenes at night to represent the Hotel Emperador, the film's version of Glenn McCarthy's Shamrock Hotel. McCarthy's, of course, was located in Houston, but in the strange geography of the film (and novel), it's in Hermoso, an imaginary city. The Warner Bros. publicity department printed a very strange map of Texas showing only three cities: Dallas, Houston, and Hermoso, located just north of the Big Bend. In fact, Hermoso in the film looks a lot like Burbank because it was Burbank, and the airport where all the fabulous airplanes of the wealthy land was the Lockheed Air Terminal in Burbank (now the Bob Hope Airport). On the map, Hermoso looks to be about twenty miles from Reata. The urban scenery and airport are completely generic, a point noted in some letters to Stevens lamenting the failure to capture the uniqueness of an actual Texas city.

As Jimmy got ready for his final scenes in the film, he didn't look like

James Dean anymore. He looked like an old man. They aged him by shaving off his hairline hair and slicking down the rest. They also gave him a little pencil mustache. In effect, they Howard Hughes'd him, making the actor look like the most famous oil baron in Hollywood. Sal Mineo was shocked when he saw his idol for the last time, "outside the commissary, a little old man with a mustache." Bill Bast said the same thing, and the ubiquitous Sanford Roth photographed him at a kendo match, where he looked old, like his future had caught up with him—a Dorian Gray in reverse. It might have spooked Jimmy a bit, imagining what the years might bring.

Jimmy was very worried about his performance as an aging man. He asked Dennis Hopper if he looked right, if he was convincing as an older man. Stevens wasn't worried. On August 2 (camera day 63) he got one of the best scenes in the film. In the Bottle Room of Jett Rink's new hotel, the Emperador, Jett is sitting at a table with Luz Benedict II, played by Carroll Baker. He is talking around the subject of marrying her, but it becomes clear that she is merely a surrogate for the woman he can never have and whom he will always love, her mother, Leslie Benedict. This would be a blow to any young girl. As for Luz, she has enjoyed Jett's attentions and likes being made love to on a flirtatious, strictly verbal basis.

Stevens had them do the scene over and over, and they never did the scene the same way twice. It was a tour de force between the only two Method actors in the cast. Each would add something, a tossing of the head, removing a rose from a vase. It was like a road show demonstration of the Actors Studio. For Carroll Baker, the scene was challenging: "There was always something new he would throw in. It was never exactly the same twice over, and I'd have to be listening and watching him just like the girl in the story—a bit tense and apprehensive." At one point, Dean went too far. "He slid one of his hands under the table. He clamped that hand right up between my legs and squeezed with all his mighty strength," Baker wrote. "I gasped. I wiped the tears of pain and humiliation from my glazed eyes." She looked at Stevens, who seemed impassive, and continued with the scene. Afterward, Stevens had praise only for her, and Dean gave her "a long, sad embrace." Overall, Baker considered Stevens "a grand master."

Stevens called it "a great boxing match between actors" and enjoyed playing the outtakes to friends.

Years later, Marlon Brando, Jimmy's idol and nemesis, would praise Dean's performance: "He was still developing when I first met him, but by the time he made *Giant*, he was no longer trying to imitate me. He still had his insecurities, but he had become his own man. He was awfully good in that last picture, and people identified with his pain and made him a cult hero."

The seventy-seventh camera day fell on August 22—the date that filming was supposed to be complete. But the end was not yet in sight. The "Christmas Sequence" at Reata took up six days, and scenes at Jett Rink's hotel carried through to the end of that month. Many of these scenes featured Dennis Hopper, who had largely been idle during filming in Texas. They focused on the conflicts with his father regarding his decision to become a doctor instead of assuming his designated role as heir and patriarch of Reata. And this is when Jimmy's acolyte got into trouble with Stevens. As filming went along, Hopper remained in thrall to James Dean. Following Dean's example, Hopper objected to the way Stevens had mapped out a scene, and Stevens shot back, "You've been watching that Dean guy again. You two guys are screwing me up." According to Hopper, Stevens and Dean "fought like dogs" and Stevens's irritation carried over to him: "Then he got on me, too, because everything that Dean did was somehow my fault." When all was said and done, Hopper considered Stevens "the most underestimated" of all the directors he had ever worked with. He said he "learned a lot from him on *Giant*, watching him. His way with actors. I had the most respect for him. Always did. His arguments were not wrong."

On September 1 (camera day 86), they shot a small scene at the Reata swimming pool (a result of Bick's new oil wealth from having made a deal with the devil, who is named Jett Rink). What happens in the scene probably passed right over the attention or understanding of hundreds of thousands of viewers of the film upon general release. Again it's Leslie who challenges the old-boy network. Sitting poolside, Bick's friends, Judge Whiteside and his cronies, are trumpeting the benefits of the 27.5 percent oil-depletion allowance, a tax shelter for the oil business. The depletion was based upon the idea of earnings being reduced by extraction of oil and the fact that many attempts failed and produced dusters instead. It was a hugely popular piece of legislation in Texas and other oil-producing states (like California), but petroleumless pilgrims in the Midwest and the Northeast hated it—along with progressives like Edna Ferber. Hearing its praise, Leslie points out that her father, a doctor, should receive a depletion allowance, considering he had given his life to the service of others.

James Dean's final scenes in the film carried special significance because they would be the last film images in Dean's career.

It took a week, starting September 2 (camera day 87), to shoot the entire banquet scene, when Jett Rink is to be honored on this night of nights for his rise to riches and civic prominence. The sequence includes his tipsy walk to the podium (accompanied by "The Eyes of Texas"), his lightning-quick fisticuffs with Jordy, and his comeuppance in the cellar scene and at the podium. Worried about the fight scene with Jett Rink, Dennis Hopper told his friend Steffi Sidney from *Rebel Without a Cause* that he wasn't a "violent person" and didn't know how to be one. The scene in question called for Hopper to smash a mirror in the hotel beauty parlor in Jett Rink's hotel because the women there had turned away his Mexican wife. "I just don't know how to do that," he said, and Steffi gave him the motivation he needed: "Well, just think of Nick Ray."

In the fight scene that doesn't happen, when Dean and Rock Hudson face off in the wine storeroom, Jett is too drunk to fight, and Bick Benedict walks away in disgust. But he does say what would turn out to be the last thing Rock Hudson ever said to James Dean: "You know, Jett, you're all through."

Edna Ferber, incidentally, did not like this scene. She didn't think that Jett would walk beside Bick to that place to fight. She is the only one who didn't like the scene, though the accidental cat that runs across the floor was never interviewed as to what it thought or why it departed the scene so fast.

In the podium scene, when Rink collapses facedown, unable to complete his speech, Dean was upset with his performance. Carroll Baker said that he was "terribly, terribly unhappy with himself in the older part." He asked Stevens to go through the scene with him, and they stayed late to work on it. Said Stevens later, "We did this darned thing for two nights, and then he came back to shoot it, and I think he did an excellent job with it—certainly as much as I felt the scene could do."

Dean seems to have drawn his portrait of creepy weirdness from a paragon of that style who was well known in Hollywood—Howard Hughes. Dean, in fact, had met Hughes at least once. Hughes, who pursued most of the young starlets in Hollywood at one time or another, had a thing for Ursula Andress, and one night when Jimmy went to her house, he learned that the man in the old car sitting out front was Hughes. Dean and Andress joined Hughes in the car, and at a stoplight, Hughes asked Jimmy to jump out and buy a pack of cigarettes for him. When Jimmy headed back with the cigarettes, Hughes sped away in the car.

Dean may also have drawn some details from Glenn McCarthy, who was also well known in Hollywood, having spent a lot of time partying there and gambling in Las Vegas. He and Hughes were friends, as well. Besides all that, the hard-drinking, free-spending, brawler-type Texas oilman was commonplace in L.A. Lots of high-rolling Texas millionaires found their way to L.A. sooner or later.

Dean's portrayal of the aging oilman is a problem for die-hard Deaners, who long for that rebel adolescent of his first two films. In truth, Dean's performance pointed the way for more adult roles. Looking older than his twenty-four years, he would have had to stop playing troubled teenagers at some point. When Dean mutters inaudibly his last lines in the film, those would be his last moments in a motion picture. Afterward, he told cinematographer William Mellor, "Take a good look at me. You may not get the chance again."

With the Dean issue contained, for the time being anyway, Elizabeth Taylor now became a problem—again. At the end of July, Taylor developed a leg infection and was expected to miss the week of August 1–5.

She returned to work on the next Monday, August 8, but two days later, she went home early with severe leg pain. Her doctor pronounced it sciatica, a very painful condition, but she managed to hobble in on crutches the next day. Her sick days were by no means over, though.

One of the most memorable scenes in the film, the fight at Sarge's Place, took six days to film, September 23 through September 28 (camera days 103–108). Stevens and his screenwriters had concocted a big, noisy, bruising scene for Bick Benedict in the closing minutes of the film. The scene in the novel is much different. Bick is not present during the visit to the "little roadside lunch room" and there is no fight. The unnamed racist owner comes over to Leslie, Luz II, Juana, and her little child and announces, "We don't serve Mexicans here." The women are stunned, and after he tells them they have to leave, Luz calls him a son of a bitch, and the man shouts, "Git! You and your greasers."

In the film, famously, there's a knock-down, drag-out fight between Bick and Sarge (Mickey Simpson), the big beefy man who owns the establishment, a racist who reluctantly serves Bick's little mixed-race group. When Bick orders ice cream for little Jordy, Sarge mutters, "ice—cream—thought that kid would want a tamale." Bick ignores this, trying to smooth over any hurt feelings, and then a small party of three Mexicans enters the diner, an old man, a woman, and their daughter. Sarge tells them they're in the wrong place and orders them to leave—"Let's go. Vamoose. Andale!"—at which point Bick comes forward to challenge the owner's action. "Look here," he tells Sarge, "I'd certainly appreciate it if you'd be more polite with these people." Then Bick tells him who he is, and Sarge's reply is not friendly, at which point Bick says, "The name Benedict has meant somethin' to people around here for a considerable time," and Sarge responds with another racial slur, "That there papoose, his name Benedict, too?" Then Bick makes a crucial public acknowledgment that, indeed, little Jordy, his grandson, is a Benedict. This is the first time he has accepted the undeniable fact that Jordan Benedict IV is half-Mexican. When Sarge turns to shove the Mexicans out of his establishment, the fight begins. Although Bick puts up a game effort, he is eventually pounded senseless by the younger man.

Stevens said in an interview that the film's length and its coverage of twenty-five years in the lives of the characters meant that the last twenty minutes required "intense excitement," that it needed a "series of climaxes which Edna was not required to have in the book." He gave a rather full account of his thinking in an interview with a *Christian Science Monitor* reporter. He described Bick as "legitimately and honestly reactionary, engaged in a noble fight to preserve his empire—in this case, a cattle ranch." He continued: "The physical thing is very important to him, and when he steps in for the underdog, it represents an awful mistake according to his old philosophy. He finds he's too old for it. There's no spring in his knees. He is beaten and he is humiliated."

Stevens held a strong belief in racial equality, and he meant *Giant* to tell a story that would compel viewers of the film to consider their own prejudices instead of blaming them on other people. In Stevens's mind, *Giant* would prompt people to examine their own hearts. Behind all this, though he didn't say so in this interview, lay the memory of Germany, of how ordinary Germans turned a blind eye to the lengths to which racial discrimination could be taken. Stevens clearly had in mind a World War II– inflected narrative directed at Texas and America.

Rock Hudson took something of a beating, too, in filming the fight scene. He was carrying around fifty pounds of extra weight—from a belt made to reflect his having grown older. He said he came home every night that week feeling as though "his arms were going to fall off any minute." Before beginning, he asked Stevens how an old man would fight, and Stevens said the same way a young man would but slower and perhaps more deliberately. As on other occasions, Hudson defended Stevens's method of shooting "an awful lot of film, an awful lot of angles." He reasoned, "I always thought that if he's going to be a sculptor, he better have enough clay with which to make the bust."

The sign that Sarge tosses on the fallen rancher, WE RESERVE THE RIGHT TO REFUSE SERVICE TO ANYONE, was the most famous emblem of racial discrimination in that era. The *Brown* v. *Board of Education* decision of 1954, overturning segregation, made everyone aware of the intention behind that sign. Another lesser-known Supreme Court decision that same year specifically addressed discrimination against Mexican-Americans. In *Hernán-*

dez v. *Texas*, the Court held that Mexican-Americans and all other racial or national groups were guaranteed equal protection under the Fourteenth Amendment of the U.S. Constitution.

Still, some filmgoers in 1956 believed that the sign applied only to blacks. Although caught up in the kinetic energy of the fight scene, they tended to disallow its historical authenticity. One of the respondents in a preview audience at the California Theatre in San Diego, May 22, 1956, reacted with indignation over the issue. "This could have been great if you'd shown negro discrimination. As a former Texan I never saw discrimination against the Mexican anywhere in the State. Bad propaganda." But another person at that same preview observed, "Racial situation well presented and <u>true</u>. (I lived in Texas a while.)" Quite a few respondents mentioned the racial theme. Said one, "Too strong re Mexicans." Another wrote, "This film is wonderfully done—but its implication of America (Texas, if you like) is bad publicity for our country." And another spoke more pointedly to the ideological spirit of the period: "Excellently done but tone down the message. This is good stuff for the commies."

But in reality, in Marfa and elsewhere in Texas, in the South, in the Midwest, in places all across the American landscape, that sign was intended to exclude, in the language of the day, Negroes, Mexicans, Orientals, etc. The Irish and other immigrant groups had received similar treatment in the previous century in citadels of higher thought, such as Boston and New York.

History confirmed the accuracy of Stevens's vision. Trains in South Texas as early as the 1890s bore signs reading FOR WHITES and FOR NEGROES, but as Richard Harding Davis, a well-known novelist of that era, noted in his book *The West from a Car-Window* (1892), "For Negroes" was read in the "south-west of Texas" . . . as "Mexicans."

In San Antonio, a city with a large Mexican-American population, there were establishments that posted signs like the following:

We Serve
Whites Only
No Spanish or Mexicans

One wonders how many Spaniards passed through San Antonio in any given year.

John Rechy, later famous for his novel *City of Night* (1963), saw a sign in the 1950s in a "two-bit run-down restaurant" in East Texas that read

We Do Not Serve Mexicans, Niggers, or Dogs.

Rechy wrote that in his hometown of El Paso, where the population was divided into North (white) and South (Mexican-Americans), "[p]rejudice against the Mexican is sometimes subtly, sometimes blatantly, manifest; whatever its form, it permeates the Southwest air as smog permeates downtown Los Angeles."

By using a lunch counter and that infamous sign, Stevens aimed at the maximum impact on the audience. Lunch counters were one of the most visible sites where civil rights demonstrations occurred in the wake of the Supreme Court decision of 1954, and Ferber had, in fact, told Stevens that the diner episode was based upon a real incident involving her friend Dr. Hector P. García. One of Stevens's notes in Ferber's White Script read "Edna's doctor in Corpus Christi; he knows all about the Mexican situation. Dr. Garcia. It was his little child that got kicked out of a Hamburger stand."

There were many instances of such discrimination in Texas in the 1940s and 1950s. In Mexico, the Comite Mexicano Contra el Racismo, founded in 1944, kept track of racial incidents involving discrimination against Mexicans in Texas. Committee members published the names of businesses and dates of racial incidents in their official publication, *Fraternidad*, identifying 150 Texas towns where such discrimination occurred.

During the year that *Giant* was being filmed, Ferber kept a sharp eye on newspaper reports about racial discrimination. She sent Ginsberg and Stevens an article detailing an incident at the Houston Airport—"Cafe Bars India Envoy as Negro." A woman restaurant manager at the airport placed a dark-skinned person in a special room, apart from the other diners. He was from India, but she thought he was a Negro, and the airport facilities, including dining areas and restrooms, were segregated.

On a second occasion around that same time, Ferber sent a newspaper clipping about a similar incident involving another foreign dignitary. In this instance, the Mexican consul general posted in San Antonio was turned away from a café in Boerne whose owner told the Mexican consul general and his party, "I serve even white trash in my place, but no Mexicans."

Ferber felt passionate about racial conditions in Texas: ". . . I thought this strange commonwealth exemplified the qualities which must not be permitted to infect the other forty-seven states if the whole of the United States as a great nation was to remain a whole country and a great nation." *Infect* is a pretty strong word. While writing her novel and afterward, she worried that the treatment of Mexican citizens in Texas presaged something like what had happened in Germany. She feared that as Texas had gone, so would the rest of the nation. Her fears, like those of Stevens, were deeply inflected by what she had seen in Germany in 1945. But Texas was not Germany, and Stevens was more optimistic than Ferber.

He lavished all of his attention on the diner scene. Through the windows of the diner, we see two iconic Texas images: oil wells in one, cattle in a truck on the way to market in the other. Both signify the source of Texas wealth as defined by the film. Inside the diner itself, perched on a shelf behind and above the work area of the counter, is a television set. It's almost startling to see one in a Warner Bros. picture. Jack Warner hated TV, regarding the "little black box" as an insidious threat to the motion picture industry. He banned any mention of TV or any actual TVs in Warner Bros. movies. But here it is in Sarge's diner, a nod on Stevens's part to the new reality and also a kind of inside joke on the Colonel.

The rousing jukebox recording of "The Yellow Rose of Texas," a song with deep roots in Texas history, made the scene unforgettable for many viewers. Considerable irony surrounds the original song's origins and meaning, and it's doubtful that anybody connected with *Giant* was familiar with that history. *Yellow rose* is a racialist term, which was widely known in the nineteenth century, less so now. A yellow rose was a metaphor for the expression "high yeller," which referred to a woman of mixed race, a mulatto. Such women had an erotic currency in the minds of men black and white. The song comes out of blackface minstrel shows, specifically the Christy Minstrels. The earliest known version, dated 1853, was quite explicit about the meaning of the term *yellow rose*:

> *There's a yellow girl in Texas*
> *That I'm going down to see;*
> *No other darkies know her*
> *No darkey, only me.*

The chorus underlines the explicit racial content:

> *She's the sweetest girl of colour*
> *That this darkey ever knew.*

Over the years, the song was modified, changing "darkey" to "soldier." The song still surfaces in odd contexts. A major grocery chain in Texas, H-E-B, sells a box of Kleenex decorated with yellow roses that contains these lines: "She's the sweetest rose of colour/ This soldier ever knew." It's doubtful that anybody in the H-E-B chain of command has ever noticed this racial echo of the minstrel song.

The version that Stevens used had been scrubbed of all racial content except in the use of the phrase Yellow Rose of Texas. Stevens chose the song because it was wildly popular the year he was filming *Giant*. In 1955, Mitch Miller's version topped the U.S. Billboard chart and sold a million copies. In Great Britain, it was number two. Stevens explained to an interviewer in 1967 his intentions behind its use: "Now, I've got those Texas people in the audience fighting for the minority." He continued: "I know these people. I know their bigotry. I know what they're proud of. . . . I think we could all be tarred with that brush." And he added, "Finally we took a moment and rubbed Bick's nose in it."

Following the big fight scene, the rest of the film traces the impact of that event upon the lives of Leslie and Bick. On September 30, Stevens began the final sequence, with husband and wife sitting together on the love seat where Luz had died with her boots on.

Above the love seat is the large painting of a western scene, evoking the vanished glory days of the cowboy and the open range. Stevens had seen the actual painting, *Venting Cattle on the Frisco System*, on one of his swings through Texas when he stopped at the Menger Hotel in downtown San Antonio, next door to the Alamo. The painting, done in 1902 by Frank Lewis Van Ness, hangs in the lobby to this day. It probably originally graced the wall of a train station or a post office on the railroad line. Stevens told his staff to secure permission to borrow the painting, and negotiations with the Menger and the San Antonio Chamber of Commerce over a three-month period brought the hotel around to loaning it out for five thousand dollars ($45,000 today). When Stevens learned that the painting had been acquired, he wrote a letter expressing his pleasure: "I think the character of this is a particularly excellent representation of the time and period that our film romanticizes. It will have a featured place in our principal setting." And it did. Its other appearance in the film is in the famous scene, where Jett Rink chooses land over Bick's buyout.

The decor of the house changes through the decades. There is a splendid account from *Retailing Daily* in 1956 that comments on the importance of the interior design features of the Reata house over the years. The first glimpse inside the "enormous Victorian oddity set against barren plains" reveals "dark and gloomy" interiors, with "dark leather upholstery, damask walls and heavy wood paneling." It is a wholly spartan, masculine interior space, cold and unwelcoming. By the end of the film, Leslie has transformed the house, giving it a more modern, middle-class decor: "As the family in the story becomes more opulent, the house becomes less ornate. As the house becomes more contemporary, it gains cheer but loses personality." In a perceptive essay upon the film's rerelease in 1996, Larry McMurtry pointed out that the changes in decor give one the feeling of reading a novel as the old is discarded and replaced by the new, a visual reminder of Leslie's influence upon the living quarters as well as the lives of those around her.

Leslie takes a phone call, and beside her on a table is a scale model of an oil derrick. Curiously, a similar model of an oil derrick appears in the last scene of *Written on the Wind*. In that film, the oil industry is the root of all evil, and in its closing scene, the daughter of the family that has built the oil empire inherits everything and has everything except love. She clutches the miniature oil derrick like an iron phallus, in her madness, her anguish at losing the love of her life—Mitch Wayne (Rock Hudson). Douglas Sirk thought he was portraying "the condition of society as a whole, at the time basking complacently under Eisenhower, while already disintegrating from within." Sirk's vision of a decomposing American society is embodied, he says, in the last shot of the film: "Malone, alone, sitting there, hugging that goddamned oil well, having nothing. The oil well which is, I think, a rather frightening symbol of American society." There it is, the most hated single symbol of Texas wealth: the oil well. It is hard to credit this view of American history—that the whole enterprise of the American Century was dying at its core during the Eisenhower era. But that is what Sirk and many others believed. The British historian Paul Johnson, in his recent book on Eisenhower, sums up the fifties as "a decade of unexampled prosperity and calm." Calling the decade "a golden age of American power," Johnson concludes "American prosperity acted as the parameters of a stable and peaceful world."

In *Giant*, the miniature oil derrick is a table decoration, fully domesticated by Leslie's taste. Oil's well that ends well.

Late in the afternoon of that day he was filming the final sequence, September 30, George Stevens, Elizabeth Taylor, Rock Hudson, and Carroll Baker were watching rushes when Stevens was called to the phone. Carroll Baker remembered that Stevens, "white and motionless," announced, "There's been a car crash. Jimmy Dean has been killed."

Everybody was stunned. Carroll Baker went numb. Elizabeth Taylor took it hardest of all. As she was going to her car, she came upon Stevens.

"I can't believe it, George. I can't believe it."

"I believe it. He had it coming to him. The way he drove, he had it coming," Stevens replied.

Taylor expected shooting to be suspended for the next day, October 1, a Saturday, but Stevens did not change the schedule. The film was thirty-four days behind schedule. She was supposed to report at 8:15 A.M. but didn't appear on the set until 11:45. Rock Hudson remembered that "Elizabeth, the Earth Mother, took Jimmy's death very, very hard. She was grief-stricken and crying and sobbing, and George made her work." According to a stuntman who was there that day, "Stevens seemed unnecessarily harsh on Elizabeth. She appeared highly upset and 'left' her breakfast in her dressing room. Once on the set—they were shooting interiors—she broke down and sobbed. She couldn't stop crying. She became semi-hysterical. Stevens became infuriated and forced her to finish the scene." Stevens had to shoot her from the back, but shoot her he did. She collapsed around four that afternoon and was taken to the hospital. A doctor's report on her condition emphasized two causes: the death of one of her coactors and the "extreme mental duress she was put under by the director at this time."

On October 3 she was still in the hospital, and when Warner Bros. got in touch with Michael Wilding, he said her release was up to the doctor. She reported for work the next day, but Tom Andre, in his report on October 4, recorded a still distraught Taylor who "performed her long shot scenes creditably but later in the afternoon, when we tried to get close ups of the scenes, she was still ill with nausea and said she was not feeling well." Later that afternoon, she was dismissed and again entered the hospital. She didn't return until a week later, on October 11. They couldn't go on without the star, and so no shooting took place for seven long days.

Finally, on October 11 (camera day 113), when shooting resumed, the discussion between Bick and Leslie following his defeat at the hands of Sarge continued. Bick considers himself a failure, his patriarchal dream of having his son carry forward the Reata legacy has failed, and instead he has a mixed-blood grandson. In his mind, there will be no pure-blood, 100 percent white Jordan Benedict V. His Texas is forevermore, by blood, implicated with Mexico. Bick feels his age now, too. Sarge saw to that. In his most poignant line in the film, Bick tells Leslie, "I feel like my saddle is turning out from under me." But with Leslie's help, he is learning to accept changes that he could never have imagined. His daughter, Luz II, is headed off to Hollywood to become an actress. Not one of Bick's children has followed his patriarchal design.

But to his amazement, Leslie has never been prouder of her husband. She pronounces his losing fight with Sarge "glorious" and says she has never been prouder of him in her life. He could not be more surprised than when she tells him that at long last the Benedict family is "a real big success." Ferber, incidentally, absolutely hated the word *big* in that line. In her long letter to Ginsberg on April, 23, 1955, she defined Leslie as "a woman of taste and education" who would never under any circumstances say "big." Then she quoted the line from her novel—"after a hundred years it looks as if the Benedict family is going to be a real success at last"—and concluded, "And that's what she'd say. Not because it's in the book. That's what she'd say." Then Ferber wrote a paragraph describing Leslie's character and asked Ginsberg to convey this to Elizabeth Taylor, ending it by saying, "As she grows older she learns that freedom dwells in the mind. That's why she says . . . the Benedict family is a real success at last." Ferber's objection seems almost pathological. It appears that she hated Texas' bigness so much she couldn't let her darling utter that word. Her objection to "big" did not, however, influence Stevens in the least. "Real big success" is in the film.

The end-of-picture sequence was finally shot on October 12 (camera day 114). The shot of the children and the calf and the lamb has seemed problematical to some viewers and critics over the years. It has been considered too obvious, too blatant. But for Stevens, it was necessary to drive the point home. And in one interview, he pointed to the idea underlying the coda. It went back to his experiences in the war. Referring to the two different babies, he said, "In contrast: one of pronounced Latin strain and one of the more Nordic, or if you please, 'pure Aryan strain.'" The word *Aryan* evoked the whole Nazi program, the camps, the Holocaust. Ferber once again weighed in; she had doubts about the need for two babies, and Stevens, digging in his heels, explained his reasoning to her, asking her to "consider the possible value of the two children in the playpen—in their innocence or wisdom, as you please—contemplating the past and the future." Then he added, "This could be the most significant thematic illustration we have in the film if we pull it off effectively." The key word in Stevens's riposte to Ferber is the *future*. He imagined a polyglot Texas and full citizenship rights for all. He advocated the end of racial discrimination. It wouldn't be until Lyndon Johnson's speech on voting rights in 1965 that as strong a voice as Stevens's would address the issue of full assimilation of Mexican-Americans into American society.

Some critics have fully understood Stevens's overarching structure. H. Wayne Schuth, for example, observes, "By accepting change, from the East, from the children, and from the culture, Bick Benedict and his family are indeed a success, and in fact, have become the embodiment of the romantic American dream."

With principal photography completed, the film had run thirty-seven days over its original schedule, and Warner executives had been very accurate in their predictions back in 1955. At a cost of $5,445,677 it was $3,000,000 over budget ($49,344,132 today).

Stevens closely followed the script in shooting *Giant*, a departure from his usual practice. Typically, he always spent a lot of time changing a script, rewriting at night and reshooting the scene the next day. But *Giant* was different. Sometime after completing the film, Stevens wrote Ivan Moffat a brief letter alluding to their work together on the script: "Thank God we worked as thoroughly . . . as we did because I wouldn't have had the energy down in Marfa, Texas to go through what we normally did."

The 114 days of shooting produced around 875,000 feet of film to edit, and it would take a year to do the job. The stars minus one went on with their lives, and Stevens began the editing process.

10

Love and Marriage

Back in L.A., Rock Hudson's life was getting more complicated by the day. Finishing up *Giant*, he had much to look forward to—megastardom, money, life at the top—but on the domestic front, he found himself facing a potentially career-ending problem. Journalistic interest in his bachelor's status was becoming more widespread. Questions about his unmarried status even reached him in Texas. One reporter asked him whether he intended to get married: "He's 29, says he has no plans for marriage, and remaining a bachelor this long 'was easy.'" Rock added, "I never stayed put long enough to get married."

He would be thirty in November, and at thirty a man needed to have a wife—or so the fan magazines believed. Nobody was more worried about it than Henry Willson. The main problem was close at hand—*Confidential* magazine, the scandal rag that specialized in exposing the private lives of stars. Founded in 1952, *Confidential* had become a must-read in Hollywood. According to the editor's son, the magazine's mission was to flip "over the rock of the sleepytime Eisenhower '50s" and expose "the creepy stuff underneath." Actor George Nader, a longtime gay friend of Rock's, said, "Every month, when *Confidential* came out, our stomachs began to turn."

Hollywood's newest heartthrob was a prime target, made even more so by his elevation to a starring role in one of the most ballyhooed films in years. The magazine had been on his trail since 1954, when two former lovers—Jack Navaar and Bob Preble—both former clients of Willson's— were offered ten thousand dollars ($89,554 today) each for the stories of their relationship with Rock. Although both remained loyal to Rock and turned down the cash, the danger was clear. Actor and agent had much to lose.

Another threat to his career earlier that year came when a man in possession of explosive sexual photographs of Hudson tried to blackmail Henry Willson. The blackmailer vowed to sell the photos if Willson didn't play along. But Henry, who had no intention of allowing this to happen, hired a private investigator to handle the case, and the PI, in turn, enlisted the aid of a strong-arm L.A. cop, who broke the blackmailer's nose and a few ribs and confiscated the compromising photos. In an only-in-L.A. twist, the blackmailer didn't want money; he wanted Henry to be his agent and make him a star. He said he could act better than Rock Hudson.

Fan magazines continued to raise questions about Rock's not being married, and sightings of Rock with Phyllis did not quell the drumbeat of questions about his future plans. In its October 3, 1955, issue, *Life,* the leading magazine of the period, pointedly called attention to Rock's bachelorhood: "Fans are urging twenty-nine-year-old Hudson to get married—or explain why not."

While Rock was on location in Texas, Henry Willson was concocting strategies to save his hottest client, and it is widely believed that Henry offered up two actors to *Confidential* to buy time, if nothing else. Rory Calhoun was an obvious candidate, since as a juvenile he had robbed jewelry stores and stolen a car, earning three years in prison. His story ran in May 1955, under the headline RORY CALHOUN, BUT FOR THE GRACE OF GOD, STILL A CONVICT. The bad publicity didn't hurt Calhoun very much though, because the story of his past was old news. Willson's second burnt offering was Tab Hunter, who, five years before, had attended a gay house party and was arrested along with dozens of others by L.A. police. There was a personal motive in Willson's choice because Hunter had fired him earlier that summer. "The Truth About Tab Hunter's Pajama Party" appeared in the September issue of *Confidential*.

The article on Hunter labeled him one of "the limp-wristed lads." He was also described as "one of the cute kids who haunt the studios by day and get their kicks in an unusual fashion by night." The account mentions "queer bars," "a gay joint," and "queer romps." It ends: "The vice squad said there were two dozen guys of the gayest and a pair of women in mannish attire." Jack Warner, whose studio was featuring Hunter in the soon-to-be-released *Battle Cry*, reassured the young actor: "Remember this: Today's headlines—tomorrow's toilet paper." Years later, Tab Hunter summed up the situation: "*Confidential* tarred 'fairies' with the same acid-dipped brush it used to vilify 'Commies.'"

George Nader considered it something of a miracle that Rock escaped in those years. If it was a miracle, it was Henry Willson's doing.

In view of the increasing danger of Rock's being exposed as gay, Henry Willson needed one more thing to happen if his star was to be safe. He needed Rock Hudson to marry Phyllis Gates.

Henry had urged Phyllis to go out to dinner with Rock as early as the fall of 1954, and they had done so. Phyllis had a lot of personality and a good sense of humor, and eventually she was introduced to Rock's "family"— George Nader and Mark Miller. Nader called her "bright, down-to-earth, no phony manners or pretensions of glamour like some of the actresses we knew." Nader added, "She accepted us immediately, which was unusual, because in that age, homosexuals were looked on as alien beings."

Rock told his friends that she was bisexual, and some of those friends said that they saw her in "lesbian situations."

In November 1954, Rock bought a two-bedroom house on Warbler Place, one of the so-called Bird Streets above the Sunset Strip, and shortly afterward Phyllis moved in with him, though she retained her apartment. This arrangement, unusual for that era, worked well through the next year, until the threat of exposure in *Confidential* required, in Henry Willson's view, a stronger measure—namely, marriage.

Right after *Giant* wrapped in early October, Henry urged Rock to take

Phyllis claimed that she was in the dark, that she didn't know what was going on, and she insisted that she never realized that Rock was gay until near the end of their relationship. Many in Hollywood found this hard to believe. Tab Hunter recalled their marriage in his memoir. He knew both Phyllis and Rock. He regarded Phyllis as "charming and intelligent" and speculated on their arrangement: "I'd certainly heard that Rock was gay, and I assumed Phyllis knew what she was getting into. Maybe they could work out some sort of arrangement that was, frankly, beyond my capabilities."

Phyllis didn't find out, she maintained, until after the filming of *A Farewell to Arms* in Italy. Hudson had been unfaithful in Italy, a friend told her. He had had an affair, and not just any affair; it was with another man. Not long afterward, she filed for divorce.

Rock's closest friends never did believe Phyllis's claim of innocence. When her memoir was published, Hudson insiders put the word out that Phyllis had to have known. How could she not have? After all, she had worked for Henry Willson and had seen many indications of Rock's sexual orientation—those all-male swimming parties, those strange phone calls from young men, plus the ongoing evidence of his lack of sexual interest in her.

Some insiders also insisted that Phyllis was a lesbian.

In an article in the *Advocate*, a gay rights magazine, Robert Hofler, Henry Willson's biographer, stated, "[Every] person I met who knew Gates called her a lesbian. Not straight, not bisexual, but lesbian." Perhaps she was as good an actor as the man she married.

In any event, Phyllis separated from Rock Hudson in 1957 and divorced him in 1958; she never remarried. Gates died in January 2006.

In 1959, Rock played the ultimate gay bachelor—in the older meaning of that word—in *Pillow Talk*, the first of his films to fully exploit his considerable comedic talent. Here he reprised his Texas accent from *Giant* as his character took on the persona of a rich Texan named Rex Stetson. In all, Hudson made thirty-two motion pictures after *Giant* and appeared in numerous TV shows, including starring in the hit series *McMillan & Wife* (1971–1977) and *Dynasty* (1984–1985). He died of

the next step, and, on November 9, 1955, Rock Hudson made Phyllis Gates his lawfully wedded wife. Henry arranged everything. He picked out the bridal bouquet, he found a church and a preacher, he arranged for a studio photographer to take pictures of the happy couple, and he made sure that the newlyweds placed calls to Louella Parsons and Hedda Hopper even before they informed their families.

Rock and Phyllis were happy at first, or so it seemed to the public, those who read the fan mags and saw the photos. There were loads of pics of a joyful Rock at the grill, Rock and Phyllis cooing and gazing into each other's eyes, all very cozy and homey. They weren't Ozzie and Harriet, and there wouldn't ever be the patter of little feet, but there was enough manufactured marital bliss to ensure the star's survival.

Phyllis relished the perks and luxuries of being married to a leading Hollywood actor. There was a great deal of travel, expensive clothes, expensive automobiles (a Cadillac for Phyllis), lagniappe (like free liquor and jewelry from studios), and the whole aura and privilege of living a life of celebrity. She especially enjoyed the parties, meeting luminaries like Humphrey Bogart, a man she came to adore. Their social life swept them up in a round of premieres, galas, charity events, and private parties at the homes of the rich and famous. They moved among the glitterati of Hollywood on the West Coast, and on one trip to New York, the couple had dinner with Edna Ferber at the Colony, the most exclusive restaurant Phyllis had ever been to. Ferber praised Rock's interpretation of Bick Benedict, and Phyllis enjoyed observing Ferber's grande dame manner.

As for Rock's view of Ferber, he considered her a "hell of a nice lady. I liked her." He also called her "a little tiger" and a "very homely old lady." He enjoyed her company and her storytelling ability, though he also said she "became kind of an angry and bitter woman," due, he thought, to the fact that she had never married and lived "a bit of a lonely life."

Socially, Rock had strict rules for Phyllis: She was never to talk to the press and especially never to Hedda Hopper or Louella Parsons, the arbiters of celebrity reputations, who could damage a career with a phrase. Phyllis was allowed to talk about the weather and other inconsequential things, but nothing personal, nothing about their life that might bring undue attention or stray from the picture-perfect domesticity of their married lives as purveyed in the fan mags.

And there was lovemaking, according to Phyllis Gates. Sometimes it was wonderful, but on average not so much. In her memoir, *My Husband, Rock Hudson*, published in 1987, two years after his death, she is quite candid about Rock's shortcomings in bed. He seemed to have a problem with premature ejaculation—not always, but often enough to bother his spouse. Against his will, she convinced him to talk to a woman psychiatrist about it, but that soon blew up, because the last thing Rock Hudson wanted to do was probe his inner life. The psychiatrist told Phyllis that Rock had the "emotional development of an eight-year-old boy." He was also moody and would sink into dark depths. At such times, he seemed unreachable.

Phyllis considered Rock a very simple man. She never saw him read a book. He didn't play golf or tennis or any sport. He liked to swim and water-ski. He liked gardening. He dressed badly, she thought. He smoked too much. He chewed his nails. Once, he bought several pairs of blue jeans, and she thought they looked ridiculous on him and threw them out. He liked to go without bathing and enjoyed his body odor, which she found disgusting. The disgust went both ways. He once told her, "All women are dirty. Their private parts remind me of cows."

Rock was faithful, in his fashion. There would be phone calls from young men, and Rock would disappear for a few hours and return without saying a word. There were swimming pool parties consisting entirely of young men, all of whom were California beach types, buff, suntanned bodies, blond hair, handsome lads but vacuous. Phyllis never liked attending such affairs.

After *Giant*'s success, Rock took on another dimension. With an Oscar nomination in hand, in 1957 he became the number-one box-office draw, an envious status he held for seven years in a row. A full-fledged star, he acted the part, to the bemusement and sometimes irritation of his old friends George Nader and Mark Miller. The couple itemized Rock's annoying new behavior in that period they called the "Impossible Years." They

started referring to him as "M.I."—matinee idol. Rock took to calling himself "Charlie Movie Star" and added the hint of a swagger to his walk. Everything had to be on his terms. He picked out the restaurants, and though he always paid, he treated waiters badly; he became arrogant in dealings with his friends; and he felt no obligations to his public. He would not sign autographs, nor would he ever open up or say anything authentic in interviews. One exception was a late interview in which he openly discussed his homosexuality. Asked what he thought about being called the "worst interview in town," he replied, "I'd rather be worst interview than worst lay." Typically, though, he preferred the cotton-candy fan mag stories, which bore little resemblance to the actual facts of his marriage and none at all to his secret gay life. When Phyllis told him he should sign autographs for his many fans, he refused and called them morons. Like James Dean, Rock had a bad case of success poisoning.

During a trip to Rome, courtesy of a studio-paid European tour, Rock acted like an entitled prince. He was ungrateful for all the perks, the expensive hotels, the top-tier restaurants. Phyllis was alarmed at his new bearing. "He expected everything to be done for him, swiftly and in the best style. He had lost the boyish wonder that I found so appealing in him."

The arrogance of a celebrity was one thing, but Rock's treatment of Phyllis turned quite ugly on that trip to Rome. One night, they were hanging out at a sidewalk café on the Via Veneto when a bronzed young Italian joined them. Rock, it turned out, knew him from a previous trip to Italy, and to Phyllis's unease, they seemed to dote on each other. Upon departing, the young Italian invited Rock—and, as an afterthought, Phyllis—to attend a luncheon for Anna Magnani the next day. Back at their hotel, Rock remarked that the luncheon sounded like fun, but Phyllis said she wasn't going. When pressed why not, she said, "Because he's a silly little fruitcake." In her memoir, she reported that Rock open-handed her in the face, smashing her necklace and causing her to burst into tears. Neither his own tears of apology the next day nor calling her "Bunting" assuaged her. She told him to go on to Africa, where *Something of Value* was to begin shooting, and said she wasn't going.

AIDS in October 1985, loyally supported by his old friend Elizabeth Taylor.

❧

Elizabeth Taylor's second marriage was on its last legs when she returned to L.A. from Texas. She knew it and her husband, Michael Wilding, knew it. She had grown increasingly tired of Wilding's British manner. "You're so goddamn British!" she would exclaim. "I'll bet if I told you I'd taken a lover your only reaction would be to ask him round for a cup of tea." He, in turn, could no longer stand her "volcanic" temper and became increasingly exasperated with her propensity for always being late and her incurable untidiness and total ineptitude as a housekeeper. And he never adjusted to animals and birds occupying and smelling up the house. Not least, his career was sinking fast.

They lived in a new home they had purchased the year before, a large ultramodern house replete with the requisite swimming pool. It was located in Beverly Hills, near the crest of Benedict Canyon, a name that surely would have resonated with Elizabeth. It was from this comfortable height that Wilding watched the impending dissolution of his marriage. "We sat on a hilltop in Hollywood, watching my career turn to ashes."

"We were so very different," Taylor recalled in her 1988 book, *Elizabeth Takes Off.* "He was extremely British, and in moving to Hollywood he had lost the star status he had achieved in England." The upshot of their years together was two handsome boys, a soaring career for Elizabeth, and an irreversible decline in Michael's movie fortune. According to Taylor, the result was "a brother/sister relationship" instead of a passionate marriage. All of this could have been foretold, but when has such prescience ever prevented nuptials?

They both still loved each other, but love wasn't enough. Once again, life was turning out to be so much different from an MGM script.

In June 1955, with Elizabeth in far-off Texas, her husband, along with a writer friend, began to frequent a burlesque joint named Strip City. The dancers were very friendly and accustomed to the attentions of celebrity visitors like Rock Hudson and Dean Martin. Two of the women, Jennie

Lee and Verena Dale, would visit with Michael and his friend at their table, and one night Wilding drove Verena home. On June 22, the two fans invited Jennie, Verena, and a male who worked at the strip joint to an after-hours spur-of-the-inebriated get-together at the Wildings' house on Beverly Estate Drive in Beverly Hills. The girls swam topless in the pool and Verena danced on a table. Sometime afterward, one of the girls sold the story to *Confidential*, and in mid-September, while *Giant* was still shooting, the November issue splashed a story certain to get everybody's attention: "When Liz Taylor's Away, Mike Will Play."

Although Elizabeth laughed it off, it wasn't the kind of publicity one wanted. She partly lessened its impact by an extended stay in the hospital—a way of both deflecting the scandal mag story and getting back at George Stevens. In years to come, Taylor's health problems, while mostly real, offered all sorts of strategic advantages in managing her life and career.

Whatever effect the negative publicity had, the tension between husband and wife intensified. One morning, she grabbed one of those crossword puzzles Michael was always working on and ripped it to pieces, daring him to hit her. "If only you would. That would prove you are flesh and blood instead of a stuffed dummy!" Wilding had his own health problems, too; he suffered from epilepsy, and Elizabeth blamed his low sexual drive on that.

It didn't seem the marriage could go on, but it did. Wilding had finally landed another picture, and the two of them traveled to Morocco in February 1956, for the filming of *Zarak*, a desert romance starring Victor Mature and Anita Ekberg. Elizabeth hated Morocco, and the film did nothing to help her husband's career or his marriage, especially when another *Confidential* headline, July 1956, blared out: WHEN MIKE WILDING CAUGHT LIZ TAYLOR AND VIC MATURE IN ROOM 106. It was all true, as Elizabeth later bragged to Eddie Fisher.

Still, the marriage limped along. In April 1956, Elizabeth began work on another epic-size film, *Raintree County*, costarring with her tortured friend, Montgomery Clift. Directed by Edward Dmytryk, the movie was like *Giant* in some respects. It involved a lot of expensive location shooting, it was set against a large historic panorama, it was slowed down on occasion by Taylor's intermittent health problems, it had a 110-day shooting schedule, and it was long—three hours and two minutes. And, as happened during the filming of *Giant*, its Method-acting star was involved in a devastating car crash. Clift didn't die, but he did disfigure himself for life.

The accident happened on the night of May 12, 1956. The Wildings threw a small party at their house in Benedict Canyon. Guests included Clift, Rock Hudson, his wife, Phyllis Gates, and Kevin McCarthy, an actor who was starring in *Invasion of the Body Snatchers* and with whom Elizabeth was having an affair. Clift and McCarthy may have been lovers, as well; those two inveterate gossips Tennessee Williams and Truman Capote thought so. Although Clift did not drink much at the party, he had been drinking all day, and he was always on pills. His private stock in New York was large enough to open a pharmacy. When he decided to leave in his leased sedan, Kevin McCarthy also left, telling Monty to follow him down the dark, twisting, treacherous canyon road. Driving on that "cork twister" of a road, as Elizabeth called it, Monty slammed into a utility pole, wrecking the car and permanently marring his appearance.

McCarthy raced back to the Wildings and told them to call an ambulance, and Elizabeth, Rock, and Phyllis rushed down the canyon to the scene of the wreck. Elizabeth managed to get inside the car, cradled Monty's head in her lap, and reached her hand in and pulled out three teeth that had been dislodged in the smashup, thereby probably saving him from choking to death. When the press showed up almost immediately, Elizabeth shouted, "Get those goddamned cameras out of here," and followed that up with "Get the hell away or I'll make certain none of you ever works in Hollywood again!" They scattered like a flock of grackles. Monty's injuries delayed work on *Raintree County* for nine weeks, and Monty himself was never quite the same following the accident. Already addicted to alcohol and drugs, he had few resources to overcome a deep-seated unhappiness that darkened and overwhelmed him. He died in 1966, at the age of forty-five.

Like many episodes in Taylor's life, her next marriage happened very fast. In late June 1956, she met, quite literally, her match. His name was Avrom Hirsch Goldbogen, but the world knew him as Mike Todd. Like

Wilding, Todd was considerably older than Taylor, but there the resemblances ceased.

Even Edna Ferber was bowled over by Mike Todd when she ran into him in Paris in 1945. She was familiar with his success on Broadway (seventeen productions in all), and upon meeting him in the flesh, she found herself in the presence of a "dynamic human engine." It took a string of adjectives to capture him: "Restless, dynamic, improbable, amusing, preposterous, handsome, a disarming showman." She reckoned him a "high-voltage electric wire." She thought he would be "almost exhausting to any companion." But he certainly wasn't exhausting to Elizabeth Taylor. No wonder she fell for him. He could promise the world and he could deliver. He was a boisterous, unstoppable force of nature, and he wooed her with diamonds galore.

A funny, brash, ultra-alpha male Jewish millionaire, he shocked her mother, calling Elizabeth "my fat little Jewish broad, Lizzie Schwartzkopf." Or he'd stick his hand down her blouse and exclaim, "Boy these little Jewish gals sure have big tits, don't they?"

Following that first meeting on his yacht off the California coast, Taylor had filed for divorce by October 4. It was granted on January 31, 1957, in Acapulco, Mexico. Ever the gentleman, Michael Wilding had flown to Mexico to facilitate the decree. Eddie Fisher (husband number four) and Debbie Reynolds, close friends of the couple, were present to witness the marriage.

Beginning on August 9, 1955, while *Giant* was still being shot, Todd produced his own epic film, an improbable adventure action comedy based loosely on Jules Verne's *Around the World in Eighty Days*. Todd's version, under the same title, used his own Todd-AO wide-screen film format and featured over forty cameos by actors, including Sir John Gielgud, Marlene Dietrich, Frank Sinatra, Buster Keaton, and Peter Lorre. Edna Ferber, usually a severe critic, saw it twice and pronounced it "enchanting and preposterous." It succeeded in beating out *Giant* and other contenders for the Best Picture Oscar and won four other Academy Awards. Thus, a film about nothing took the garland from a film about life in Texas. It also earned $42 million at the box office.

Raintree County, which is not one of the "1001 Movies You Must See Before You Die," brought Elizabeth Taylor her first Academy Award nomination for Best Actress. She should have received one for *Giant*. Finally, Elizabeth Taylor was beginning to be appreciated for her acting and not just for her beauty.

In her next film, she racked up a strong performance costarring with Paul Newman in *Cat on a Hot Tin Roof* (1958), based on a play by Tennessee Williams, and received another nomination for Best Actress. In her next film, based on another Tennessee Williams play, *Suddenly, Last Summer* (1959), she was paired again with Montgomery Clift and again garnered an Oscar nomination. Finally, she received the Oscar for Best Actress for *Butterfield 8* (1960), a film she hated. Based on a John O'Hara novel, it told the dark story of a high-priced Manhattan prostitute, and Taylor, upon walking behind the curtain after receiving her Oscar, said spiritedly, "I still think it's a piece of shit." There was a second Oscar in her future, in her earthy portrayal of Martha in *Who's Afraid of Virginia Woolf?* (1966).

The run from *Giant* to *Butterfield 8* was phenomenal—three Oscar nominations in a row, three box-office hits, and four nuanced and compelling feminist-inflected portrayals of women carving out a life of meaning in a world dominated by men. It was a story she knew well, because it was essentially the story of her life in the movie industry and beyond. Elizabeth Taylor charmed, cajoled, seduced, threatened, schemed, and fought her way to a remarkable career in one of the most chauvinistic enclaves in America—Hollywood. She possessed the beauty of Cleopatra and the bawdy humor and life force of the Wife of Bath. There was never a more likable, funnier, or lovelier Hollywood star. She outlasted most of the *Giant* players, dying on March 23, 2011.

11

Last Days at the Villa Capri

Before that fatal day of September 30, 1955, James Dean had, as the cliché goes, everything to live for. Apart from his troubled relationship with Stevens and his anxieties about playing an aging tycoon, Dean savored his return to L.A. following the time in Texas, and in his private life he picked up right where he had left off in late May.

He had dropped the Googie's hangout that spring for another venue, the Villa Capri restaurant at 1735 North McCadden Place, smack in the heart of Hollywood. He became friends with the Romano family, who owned the small stucco restaurant. They let him enter through the kitchen and mostly condoned his eccentric behavior. Despite its indifferent cuisine, the Villa Capri enjoyed an A-list clientele. Frank Sinatra and the Rat Pack were regulars, and Sammy Davis, Jr., became a big fan of the rising star. Jimmy often took his dates to the restaurant.

In July, he started going around with another foreign beauty, Ursula Andress, who was from Switzerland. Friends were astonished; the two of them looked like twins. They both wore jeans and white T-shirts, and with their blond hair (hers was cut short) and general appearance, there was a strong resemblance. Dressed up, they made a glamorous couple attending the Thalian Ball at Ciro's on August 29, Jimmy in a resplendent tux and Ursula in a chic black evening dress.

Like most of the women who dated Jimmy, Andress had his number. Her account of a night with Jimmy is one of the best on record. She told Jimmy's friend Joe Hyams, "Jimmy a nice boy but he come by my house one hour late. He come in room like animal in cage. Walk around and sniff of things like an animal. I don' like. We go hear jazz music and he leave table. Say he going play drums. He no play drums, no come back." Abandoned, she returned home alone. Later that night, Jimmy returned to her place on his motorcycle and invited her to look at it. They sat outside talking until five. She summed up Jimmy in a succinct sentence: "He nice but only boy." Ursula, who was in love with actor John Derek and later married him, went on to achieve movie immortality with her role as Honey Ryder, James Bond's girlfriend, in *Doctor No* (1962).

One day in August, Joe Hyams appeared on the set of *Giant* in search of Jimmy, but instead he ran into "a tiny woman with white, freshly waved hair." It was Edna Ferber, in town to watch some of the filming. Naturally, they talked about Jimmy. Ferber and Jimmy had hit it off immediately. He snared her and she enjoyed his eccentric manner—while at the same time shrewdly taking his measure—this boy "who performed like a gifted angel and behaved like a juvenile delinquent." She told Hyams that in her view Jimmy was suffering from "success poisoning," a condition she had experienced decades before when she had had two successive hits on Broadway. Later, she wrote a thumbnail sketch of the figure she considered an original. Dean was "impish, compelling, magnetic; utterly winning one moment, obnoxious the next. Definitely gifted. Frequently maddening."

Maybe success *was* spoiling Jimmy Dean. His friend Rod Steiger from the Actors Studio days saw signs of it that August. Around the time Jimmy was having so many problems with Stevens, Jimmy invited Steiger to lunch to talk about it. Steiger suggested using tact rather than emotional confrontation, but what happened at the end of the lunch irked him. Calling the waitress over, Jimmy told her he didn't like the steak. When she pointed out that he had eaten three-fourths of it, he replied, "Honey, this is Hollywood. Take it back." Steiger recalled, "This was the only time I heard

Jimmy say something that bothered me. I looked at him, surrounded by a lot of people, and I thought, 'We're going to destroy him.' " Kazan and others had earlier seen signs of this kind of self-centered "I'm a star" behavior.

On September 17, while Jimmy was still working on *Giant*, Warner Bros. executive William Orr sought him out in his dressing room. Orr wasn't just another suit; he was also Jack Warner's son-in-law. Orr wanted Jimmy to do a National Safety Council interview. It wouldn't take five minutes, but Jimmy told him flat out no, he didn't want to do it, and Orr had had enough. He pushed Jimmy down on a small couch and let him have it. "Listen to me, you little son of a bitch. You are going to do it. You've been nasty to a lot of people around here, but you're not going to be nasty to the whole country. You're going to go down and make this damned public service announcement, or I'll stand here until you do!"

So Jimmy did it. Gig Young, the actor who had made the promo for *Giant* back in the spring, conducted the interview. Dressed in suit and tie, Young queried James Dean, garbed in his Jett Rink ranch-hand outfit and carrying, of course, that little rope. He asked Jimmy about his interest in racing, and Jimmy allowed that he'd rather take his chances on the racetrack than on a highway. Then, just before exiting the two-minute interview, he smiled and rendered his own version of familiar words known to all in the 1950s, "Drive safely, the life you save may be your own." Instead, Jimmy gave the slogan a different spin: "Take it easy driving, the life you might save might be mine."

James Dean showed that summer the same mercurial personality that had marked his ascent from obscurity to stardom apparent to observers in New York and L.A. during the previous eighteen months. On August 16, at a party for Sinatra held at the Villa Capri, Jimmy ran into Steffi Sidney, a sweet girl who'd had a bit part in *Rebel Without a Cause*. She recalled his appearance that night: "I don't know whether he was drunk when he came, but he sure was drunk by the time he left. He came wandering over to me. His fly was open." He was told to leave after ten minutes because of his "unruly behavior." Before leaving, he insisted on having a picture taken with Steffi, and the photographs were delivered to her house a few weeks later, on September 30.

Sometime in September, Dean had a falling-out with one of his friends from New York, composer Leonard Rosenman. Jimmy "was in a period of his life where he drank a good deal. And he was kind of drunk and disorderly, and I had just outgrown that kind of thing," said Rosenman. Like many others, Rosenman traced much of Jimmy's difficulties to insecurity: Rosenman was also quite upset about Dean's driving. He'd been in Jimmy's MG, roaring down Mulholland Drive, once and they'd smashed into garbage cans outside a house. Jimmy begged his friend not to tell anybody, and Rosenman didn't, but he also refused to ride with him ever again.

Eventually, Rosenman just got tired of Jimmy's reckless behavior.

That summer, Jimmy renewed his friendship with Lew Bracker, whom Jimmy had met back in 1954 through, ironically enough, Len Rosenman, who had married Bracker's sister. Bracker was an insurance salesman, a regular guy who was close to his family, and Jimmy loved dropping by his friend's home to have a meal and hang out. The atmosphere there provided him relief from pressures at Warner Bros. and a warm family environment, as well.

In his recent memoir, *Jimmie & Me, A Personal Memoir of a Great Friendship*, Bracker recounts the first time he met Dean. It was at the Green Room with Rosenman. When Lew asked Dean why the Green Room was called that, Jimmy quipped, "Because everyone here is jealous of somebody else." Talk shifted to Jack Warner and his private dining room, which was closed off from the Green Room. It was where the Colonel held forth each day, presiding over a kind of royal court of insiders summoned to please the whims of his majesty. Asked what he'd do if he were invited, Jimmy said, "I'd go right in there, sit next to Jack Warner, take my teeth out, put them right in front of him, and say let's eat!"

But Lew also saw at that luncheon another side of Jimmy that often surfaced, a kind of "half-smile/half-smirk" that came over him, a condescension toward those to whom he felt superior. Paul Newman dropped by the table to say hello, taking a break from *The Silver Chalice*, dressed in costume, and Jimmy did not pass up the opportunity to lord it over him: "You win some, you lose some, but you do look cute in that dress." Later, when Lew met Dick Davalos, he saw the same note of superiority and condescension in Jimmy's treatment of his costar.

The friendship between the two men ripened in the period between *East of Eden* and *Rebel Without a Cause*, and Lew began to hear rumors about Jimmy's past. Photographer Dennis Stock, for example, cautioned against getting "too close." But throughout his memoir, written a half century later, Bracker maintains, "I can say unequivocally that he never gave me any indication, or reason to think, that he was gay, and we were alone quite a bit at Jimmy's place, our house—and we even shared a bedroom once." Instead, he says, they talked about girls a lot. It seems that James Dean was very much a chameleon, able to adapt himself to the needs—and sexuality—of persons he was close to, whether from affection or professional ambition, it was often impossible to say.

Although Lew dismissed any idea of James Dean's bisexuality, he was certainly aware of other males being drawn to Jimmy. Lew noticed a lot of competition to be Jimmy's friend on *Rebel Without a Cause*. The most blatant was Nick Adams, who became very jealous of the friendship between Lew and Jimmy. And later, when Dean was in Texas shooting *Giant*, Nick sent him numerous postcards.

Cars were a big part of the men's friendship. When Jimmy traded in his MG for a Porsche Super 1500 in February 1955, it was the first Porsche Lew had ever seen. Although it looked "like an imported bathtub on wheels," Lew became fascinated with the car's speed and "Spartan interior." Jimmy took him on fast runs up and down Laurel Canyon. Lew had never thought about racing and never attended the three races that Jimmy was in, but he wound up being captivated by the idea and bought himself a Porsche Speedster and entered a race on September 3, 1955, in Santa Barbara.

He and Jimmy talked about more than cars, however. Jimmy wanted Lew to produce the films that he wanted to direct in the future. He had in mind a film of *The Little Prince* and a motorcycle racing film, *The Flying Mantuan*, based upon an Italian racer named Tazio Nuvolari. He wanted somebody he could trust. He also turned over the care of his horse, Cisco, to Lew, whose family owned a ranch in Santa Barbara.

Not surprisingly, it was Bracker who told Jimmy about the new Porsche Spyder 500 on display at a sports-car dealership. This was on September 18, and Jimmy fell instantly in love with the "bomb," as he called it, a curvy, low-slung racer that looked like a bathtub designed by Henry Moore, if Henry Moore had been into designing bathtubs. Jimmy pounced on the car, bought it, and immediately had the name LITTLE BASTARD painted on the back. Nobody is certain why he did that. Jack Warner had called him a little bastard once, and probably so had a lot of other people. He and Bill Hickman, a friend and stuntman-actor, joshed each other, using the names "Little Bastard" and "Big Bastard." But it's entirely possible that Dean meant the name more literally, referring to himself as a bastard by birth, perhaps another way of striking back at his father.

With his work on *Giant* done, except for one day of mopping up scheduled for October 4—some still photos, a do-over with Taylor, and a bit of dialogue looping—James Dean was free to do whatever he wished, and he spent his final days busy with a number of things.

On September 21, Dean drove the Spyder up to Bracker's house. Lew turned around and bought Jimmy's Super from the dealer. According to Bracker, he and Jimmy talked extensively about the future, the two of them setting up a Porsche/VW dealership, Jimmy buying a house, marrying, having his own family, and, the coup de grâce, racing.

On September 23, Jimmy dined, as usual, at the Villa Capri. His companion that night was Lew Bracker. While Jimmy was going through the menu, Bracker noticed that Alec Guinness had entered the restaurant. When he told Jimmy, Dean jumped up and ran over to Guinness, introduced himself, and took him outside to see his car. Jimmy had to show off his newest gem to everybody. But Guinness did not react with awe and admiration. Instead, he experienced a powerful psychic moment, as he related in his autobiography *Blessing in Disguise*. He thought the car looked "sinister" and heard himself saying in a strange voice, "Please, never get in it." Then he added, "It is now ten o'clock, Friday the 23rd of September, 1955. If you get in that car, you will be found dead in it by this time next week." Jimmy just laughed it off and returned to the restaurant.

Guinness was not the only one for whom the Porsche portended disaster. Patsy D'Amore, the manager of the Villa Capri, told Jimmy the same thing. "I tell him he die in that car," she recalled saying after he showed it to her.

But Jimmy brushed aside such fears, and he couldn't wait to show off his newest toy. One of his first stops was Warner Bros., where he pulled George Stevens away from a meeting to take a quick spin with him. Stevens said the car looked like "a turtle with a cockpit cut into it." Jimmy took him for "a ride around the lot on two wheels." Stevens recalled, "By the time we got back, the studio guards had also come over and said, 'You can never drive this car on the lot again; you're gonna kill a carpenter or an actor or somebody.'" Jimmy bid good-bye to Stevens, saying, "So long, I think I'll let the Spyder out," and that was the last time Stevens saw him.

Producer Henry Ginsberg, who was sympathetic toward Jimmy, had a spin in the new car, too. Afterward, he told the Warner Bros. production department, "If you have any loose ends, you better tie them up quick. The way this kid's handling that car I don't think he's going to be around much longer."

Freed from *Giant*, Jimmy had time to think about the future, and that future looked very bright indeed. Warner Bros. signed him to a nine-film contract for a million dollars. His next outing was to be *Somebody Up There Likes Me*, a boxing biopic based on the life of Rocky Graziano, in which Jimmy would get to muscle up and play another underdog against the world. It was right in his wheelhouse. Instead, it helped turn Paul Newman into a star. The next after that was a Western, and not just any Western, but a moody, psychological oater based on the teleplay by Gore Vidal. *The Left Handed Gun*, he called it, partly to hint at a gay interpretation of that famous little killer, Billy the Kid, and according to studio publicity, "James Dean is reading all available books on Billy the Kid. Dean, now portraying a Texan in 'Giant,' wants to do an authentic film on the New York born bandit."

Paul Newman again replaced Dean, but *The Left Handed Gun* had flop d'estime written all over it, and indeed, when it got made in 1958, that's what happened. Could Jimmy Dean have endured a box-office bust? Perhaps he could have taken solace from abroad. The French are the only ones who liked Arthur Penn's offbeat Western.

But before making any new film, Jimmy wanted to take some time off. It had been an exhausting eighteen months during his ride to the top.

Jimmy's friend Lew Bracker urged him to take out an insurance policy now that he was going to be making big money. So Jimmy bought a
$100,000 policy, divvying up the payout among his family in Indiana:
$85,000 to Marcus and Ortense Winslow, who had raised him; $10,000 to
Marcus, Jr., for his education; and $5,000 to his grandparents. He left
nothing to his father.

He saw a good deal of his friends the Roths, Sandy and Beulah, an older
intellectual couple with whom he had a stable relationship. Roth was famous for his photographs of French artists like Picasso and his circle, and
Dean wanted very much to go to Europe and soak up some culture. They
talked about it a lot.

On paper, Jimmy was not as disorganized as his behavior often suggested.
The last week of his life, for example, he made notes on an envelope, listing
appointments he needed to make: "oculist, dentist, doc-body, doc-head."
On September 27, Dean's medical doctor, Irving S. Berman, certified that
he was "in excellent health" and therefore "physically qualified to engage
in competitive automobile racing." There is no record of whether Dean saw
the "doc-head" that week or not.

During the last week of his life, Dean attended a preview screening of
Rebel Without a Cause. He was very pleased with his performance, but
not so much with Nick Ray's Hitchcockian "I'm the director!" cameo at
the picture's end. Afterward, he and the old gang, Natalie, Nick Adams,
and Sal, gathered at Googie's for a nostalgic evening recalling old times—
old meaning April and May of that year.

Eartha Kitt, a close friend of Jimmy's, sensed something unsettling in
her last encounter with him. Her friendship with "Jamie," as she called
him, went back to their days in New York, where they had become like
brother and sister, sharing a deep interest in music, dance, and playing
drums. She had become one of his favorite sounding boards, and as the
problems with George Stevens escalated, he had poured out his grievances
and unhappiness to her. "Jamie's biggest personal trial came while filming
Giant," she wrote. "He'd call almost every night, so upset with the film—
and apparently so at odds with the director—that each day he dreaded
going before the cameras. He vowed that when the film was completed,

he'd never go to see it." She added, "He felt a bit insulted, too, at being sand-wiched between what he referred to as 'surface actors' and 'two of the weak-est actors in the business': Elizabeth Taylor and Rock Hudson." He considered it merely a "slick epic film." Besides the predawn telephone calls, he took her on motorcycle rides in the hushed streets of L.A. during hours when everybody except members of the Night Watch was in bed asleep.

On September 25, she attended a party for Jimmy at the Chateau Mar-mont, hosted by his agent, Jane Deacy. When Kitt saw Jamie, she hugged him but felt "a strange emptiness."

"What's happened to you? Something's wrong. You're not here."

"Oh, Kitt, you're running one of your spiritual numbers on me again," he replied. In her autobiography *Alone with Me,* she spelled it out: "I had had the distinct impression that his spirit had already left him. I know that sounds weird, but it happened."

Sometime between September 25 and 29, Jimmy had dinner with Nick Ray. They were still close and talked of plans for a new project, *He-roic Love.* Then, in typical fashion, Jimmy dropped by Ray's bungalow at the Chateau Marmont at 3:00 A.M. to borrow a book on cats. Elizabeth Tay-lor had given him a Siamese kitten as a memento of their time together on *Giant,* and Jimmy named the cat Marcus, after the young Marcus Win-slow back in Indiana.

On the afternoon of Wednesday, September 28, Dean, Bracker, and Ur-sula Andress went to see *I Am a Camera,* a film version of Christopher Isherwood's *The Berlin Stories.* The English author lived in Santa Mon-ica, and Dean claimed to be a friend of his, but he wasn't; he had never met Isherwood. With Jimmy, appearance was reality, and he was always acting.

That night, he dropped in on Jeanette Miller, a sometimes girlfriend, to ask her if she was going to go to Monterey with him on Saturday. She was sick, however, and upon seeing her in that condition, Jimmy began to cry. She couldn't understand why but believed that "something very emo-tional was going on in Jimmy's life at the time." Or her condition might have been a heartbreaking reminder of his mother's illness and death, which he could still not deal with.

The next morning, he stopped by Jeanette's place again, this time with Marcus, the Siamese cat, in tow. He had concluded that he led such an unpredictable life, he had better not assume the responsibility of taking care of a kitten, but he did give Jeanette detailed instructions on what to feed Marcus.

Later that day, he drove to Ursula Andress's place and asked her to go with him to the car race. But she was tied up with John Derek and declined—which she probably would have in any case. He asked other friends. Mercedes McCambridge said no; she was skittish about his racing and told him so. Dennis Stock at first said yes, then reversed himself because of some inner prompting. Even Lew Bracker turned him down. He was going to the USC–University of Texas football game. The last words Jimmy spoke to him were, "Okay, but it's your funeral."

Jimmy knew Willam Bast wouldn't go, but he took the Spyder around for him to see anyway. Bast was surprised to hear that Jimmy had given the kitten away, and Jimmy said he might not come back. The Roths were surprised to hear about the cat as well.

His father also said no, though he did join his son for coffee and doughnuts around noon on the morning of the thirtieth, before Jimmy left for the seven-hour drive north. By chance, family members Marcus and Ortense Winslow, on a trip west from Fairmount, and an uncle were also on hand that day.

Racing the new Porsche so soon didn't make much sense. The decision to drive it instead of towing it—the original plan—was flawed. Up to the time he left that morning, he had put only five hundred miles on the car. It wasn't even broken in properly, and given its small size and visibility problems (it was hard to see on a highway), it should have been towed, or, better yet, Jimmy should have waited for a later date to race the car. It was never meant for highway driving. It was strictly a racing car, as anybody could see.

And so the small caravan headed north: Jimmy driving the bomb; his German mechanic, Rolf Wütherich, sitting beside him; and Jimmy's new station wagon trailing behind, driven by Bill Hickman ("Big Bastard"), who was accompanied by photographer and friend Sanford Roth, whom he had met on location in Texas. The mechanic's main job was to light Jimmy's Chesterfields as he chain-smoked his way down the highway. Jimmy ignored his own safety advice and got a speeding ticket—65 mph in a 45 mph zone—as did the pair in the station wagon. The policeman didn't know who James Dean was, but he was fascinated by the car.

And so they drove on in the waning light of that early-fall day. They were traveling through largely empty country near the site of Cholame, in San Luis Obispo County, about 175 miles south of Salinas. The terrain and history were much like that of the Marfa region: a small, obscure unincorporated community on land that had originally belonged to Indians and later was part of a mid-nineteenth-century Mexican land grant. The area remains a working cattle ranch.

Near the junction of state highways 41 and 46, Dean's Porsche Spyder slammed into a big Ford sedan driven by a college student named Donald Turnupseed. Nobody knows how fast Dean was driving. The Ford was making a left turn into the path of the Porsche Spyder, and Turnupseed maintained that he never saw the approaching car. It would have been hard to see the small, low-slung, silver racer in the late-afternoon haze. Dean did everything he could to brake in time, but it was not enough. He was killed instantly and Rolf Wütherich was thrown into the ditch alongside the road, severely injured. Dean was not wearing his seat belt, and the passenger's side did not have a seat belt.

The final irony of Dean's death in the racing car is that it possibly wasn't his fault. Though legally cleared of any responsibility, Turnupseed continued to be the target of many Dean enthusiasts who believed that the college student had been partly, if not wholly, at fault.

Late that afternoon, Mercedes McCambridge and her husband, on their way to a vacation in San Francisco (she, too, was celebrating the end of the long shoot), were driving along an isolated highway in a rather desolate area that reminded her of the "*Giant* country in Texas." At one point they stopped at a run-down gas station to fill up, and a fat woman announced, "We have James Dean's sports car in the garage." When McCambridge saw it, she burst out, "Oh, my God." The car was "a crumpled mechano-set and the blood was everywhere."

Earlier that week, Edna Ferber had written Dean a letter, thanking him for a studio photograph of himself that he had sent her. She compared his visage to that of John Barrymore: "It really is startlingly similar." And, she added, "But then, your automobile racing will probably soon take care of that."

He had inscribed the photograph: "Dear Edna, it seems that gentleness is always respected and remembered in the cruel man." This was how Dean could sound when he was trying to impress somebody. It always has to be remembered that his favorite poet was the minor Hoosier household versifier, James Whitcomb Riley, whose rustic poems he could quote by the yard. He had a very thin, scattered knowledge of literature. He dabbled in photography, music, painting, sculpture, and poetry. He had one true art: himself.

News of his demise spread fast throughout Dean's world, from L.A. to New York. Nobody was surprised. Elia Kazan, when John Steinbeck called him, said, "That figures." Lee Strasberg of the Actors Studio, from whose criticism Dean had recoiled, commented, "It somehow was what I expected." And one of his old New York girlfriends, Barbara Glenn, said she knew it was "imminent." She knew that "someday he was never coming back."

Nicholas Ray was in London when he received the phone call. He immediately left for Germany, where for the next two weeks he wept and drank, sharing his grief with a longtime friend, Hanne Axman. Back in London, where he screened a copy of *Rebel Without a Cause* for a British censorship official, he wrote Steve Trilling of Warner Bros. that "it's a little like going to a funeral." Roger Donoghue, a former boxer and friend, believed that Dean's death marked the beginning of a long decline in Ray's career as the hippest director in Hollywood drifted more and more into drink, dissipation, and drugs. The French *Cahiers du Cinéma* crowd never forsook him; Truffaut and company always placed him high in their auteur pantheon.

Dennis Hopper was also cut up badly by his idol's death. He was attending a play with his agent, who received the news by telephone in the lobby, and when the agent returned to tell Hopper, Hopper lashed out, hitting him and calling him a liar. Hopper picked up the mantle of rebellion and carried it into the next decade, climaxing with his hippie motorcycle masterpiece, *Easy Rider*. A steady diet of anger, alcohol, and a wide array of drugs nearly destroyed his career as an actor. Hopper admitted, "My life was confused and disoriented for years by his passing." A drug-laced Western shot in Peru almost finished him off, but a decade later he rebounded, got sober, and rebuilt a solid career in films like *Blue Velvet* and *Hoosiers*. He abandoned Dean's lifestyle, but he never abandoned Dean. He talked about him his entire life.

In New York that night, a clutch of Jimmy's friends—Nick Adams, Natalie Wood, and Sal Mineo—went to see Richard Davalos in Arthur Miller's *A View from the Bridge*. They had wanted Jimmy to go with them that weekend. Afterward, they talked about Jimmy's racing. Nick Adams was the first to learn of Jimmy's death, but he was advised not to tell the others until the next morning. Curiously, all three—Adams, Mineo, and Wood— would die violent deaths in the coming decades.

Lee Strasberg, a bigger fan of Jimmy than Jimmy was of him, said he didn't cry at the time, but he did when he saw *Giant*, which he regarded as Dean's best film: "What I cried at was the waste, the waste," he later said.

According to Phyllis Gates, Rock told her that he had wanted Dean to die: "I was jealous of him because I was afraid he was stealing the picture from me. I've been wishing him dead ever since we were in Texas. And now he's gone!" He wept copious tears, said Gates.

But Rock's agent, Henry Willson, shed no tears over Dean's death. He hadn't liked Dean from the start, and said, "He would not have lasted in Hollywood." Sounding a lot like Willy Loman, Willson explained that "Jimmy Dean was not well liked, and to last in this town you have to be well liked."

Humphrey Bogart observed, "Dean died at just the right time. He left behind a legend. If he had lived, he'd never have been able to live up to his publicity."

The news shattered the groupies who hung out at Googie's. They named the banquette at the back of the coffee shop "the James Dean Banquette."

The funeral was held in Fairmount on October 8. James Byron Dean came home to Fairmount as his mother had fifteen years earlier. Only a few friends from L.A. attended the funeral, Henry Ginsberg, Lew Bracker, Jack Simmons, and Dennis Stock. Elizabeth Taylor and Edna Ferber sent flowers. The Reverend DeWeerd delivered a eulogy. Seeing the closed coffin, Dennis Stock later wrote, "For all I knew, it was the same coffin he had foolishly posed in a few months before."

After the service, Stock introduced Lew Bracker to Winton Dean. The first thing out of Jimmy's father's mouth was, "Oh yes, you're the insurance man. Do you know when I will be getting the check?" It turned out that Jimmy had not made a will, and so, though absent almost all of his son's life, the father walked away with $100,000 ($906,115 today), not a cent of which he ever gave to the Winslow family, who had cared for Jimmy from age nine through high school.

❧ 12 ❧

Fanfare

When *Rebel Without a Cause* premiered on October 26, 1955, twenty-six days after James Dean's death, a lot of young people felt that their idol couldn't be dead; there he was on the screen in living CinemaScope—the angst-ridden, tortured teenager who was just like them, their hero, their voice. The cult of James Dean soon morphed into things so weird that countless articles and numerous books have been written exclusively about the supposed paranormal phenomena surrounding his death. Typical magazine articles had titles like "Jimmy Dean Is Not Dead," "Where is Jimmy Dean?," "Jimmy Dean Fights Back from the Grave," "Did Jimmy Dean's Spirit Haunt the Studio?," "The Boy Who Didn't Die," "Elvis Hears from James Dean," and "How Jimmy Dean Still Works Miracles for Others."

And believing he wasn't dead, believing it was all a publicity ploy engineered by Warner Bros., they wrote letters to Jimmy. Seven thousand a month poured into Burbank, and nobody had ever seen anything like it. They wrote Jim Backus, who played his father in *Rebel*, and it was clear to Backus that they thought Jim Stark and James Dean were the same and that he was Jimmy's father. The avalanche of letters far outpaced the passionate response to Valentino's death, for those old enough to remember that star's early demise. Fan club membership in the United States soared to 3,800,000 paying members.

And they wrote George Stevens; they sent him death threats, menacing missives in scrawled cursive, warning him not to cut a single foot of James Dean's performance. Stevens found the letters unsettling: "It's absolutely weird, the most uncomfortable stuff I've ever read." Even without the threats, Stevens was keenly aware of the special nature of this undertaking. He'd never been in the position before of editing posthumously an actor's work in one of his pictures. So he was doubly aware of the burden placed upon him. It turned out that James Dean dead was as disruptive and demanding and compelling as James Dean alive.

A preview comment showed the kind of pressure Stevens was under: "I don't know how possible it is, but the studio almost <u>owes</u> its audience as much of James Dean as can be squeezed in." Stevens certainly felt the pressure of Jimmy's presence. Early in the process, he observed, "I spent six hours today with Jimmy Dean, as I have most of the days in these past two months. He is always up there on the projection-room screen in front of me, challenging me not to like any part of him in the picture. And there is no part of Jimmy I don't like, no part of him that hasn't always the attraction that goes with complete naturalness."

In some ways, Stevens was confronting a ghost: "There was a poetic presence in his every word and gesture. He seemed to be dreaming of some lost tenderness. . . . I can see him now, blinking behind his glasses after having been guilty of some preposterous bit of behavior and revealing by his very cast of defiance that he felt some sense of unworthiness." On another occasion, Stevens summed up his view of Dean: "He wasn't always a joy to work with, but find me any actors who aren't difficult." Then, sounding like Jett Rink himself, Stevens added, "You gamble along with young people and hope their performance comes off. We gambled with Dean and we won."

To Stevens, Dean was "like a magnet. You watch him: Even when he's not doing anything, you watch him and not the others." Twenty years later, Stevens paid homage to Dean's acting by recalling a scene in the film when he and Jimmy disagreed about a particular act. The scene called for Jett Rink, after entering the Benedict house, where a party for Leslie is being held, to go up to the bar and pour himself a drink of whiskey. But Jimmy objected, believing that his character should pull a flask from his pocket instead of drinking Bick's whiskey. Stevens insisted that Dean should play the scene as written, but all these years later he realized that Dean was right: Jett Rink "was *too proud* to take a drink from their table." Stevens added, "His idea was too damn smart, and he didn't explain it to me, so I didn't get it then. But he really *knew* that character, and that's the best tribute I can pay to his talent as an artist."

The editing process, with over 800,000 feet of footage to go through, went on for a full year, typical of Stevens's meticulousness. In an interview in September 1955, when he was just beginning the process, he spoke of his intentions. "I want height and I want to be able to edit freely. Height because the movie is a world of upright things and tall men." He went on to say that he was "telling a story that goes through three generations and it has to roll along." But he also said he was aiming at a two-and-a-half-hour running time. This last remark might have been for Jack Warner's consumption, because that was the maximum length that the Colonel could imagine.

But Stevens was obsessive in the editing room, and even his son, George, Jr., who spent time there with his dad, thought his father was excessively devoted to the process. "I became impatient with his meticulousness," he recalled. "We'd had three previews with enthusiastic audience response, but he was still switching one close-up for another to refine performances, trimming frames off shots and sliding soundtracks to sharpen scenes." At one point he told his father, "Dad, you have a great picture. Why don't you lock it up?" His reply was, "When you think about how many man-hours people will spend watching this picture, don't you think it's worth a little more of our time to make it as good as we can?"

The preview responses were crucial in Stevens's conception of the final cut. Everybody, including the director, expected an intermission in a film with a running time of over three hours. Intermissions were a structural means of signifying importance. The logical place for such a break, Stevens thought, would be "the end of the first act . . . when Jett Rink's oil well comes in." But preview audiences were so receptive to the story's pace that they watched enthralled, and although some suggested an intermission, many did not. An early screening on May 22, 1956, ran three hours and thirty-five minutes. No one walked out and there was a big ovation at the end. Another preview, on June 29, ran three hours and twenty-one minutes, and in an audience of 1,096 people, only 5 walked out, a couple with a sleepy child and three who had to be at work early. Of the 500 cards collected, 492 rated the film excellent and 8 good. It received no "fair" responses (the lowest rating). An interoffice memo from Chuck Cochard to Stevens (June 29, 1956) must have pleased Stevens: "In the final cut it is the greatness of GIANT which answers all of the questions regarding its length and the very fact that no one gets up and walks out of the theatre is proof." Cochard ended on a frequent note that came up in preview screenings— that *Giant* "equals and many times surpasses 'Gone With the Wind.'"

There was, however, a clamor for a specific cut coming from a powerful lobby that strongly objected to the 27.5 percent depletion allowance. On April 12, 1956, Bob O'Donnell, the powerful head of the Interstate Theatres, sent copies of articles championing the depletion allowance to both Stevens and Ferber. John O'Melveny, a tax lawyer, wrote Ginsberg on July 10, stating that "our oil people are considerably upset." As late as October 18, Jake L. Hamon, an executive for the American Petroleum Institute, sent a letter to Giant Productions arguing that including the scene would "do irreparable harm" and concluded, "I am sure that you must realize that there must be a sound reason for this provision in the tax laws and its elimination would be a death blow to our industry, and would make gasoline much more expensive to the consumer." Needless to say, Jack Warner was very concerned. According to George Stevens, Jr., Warner told his father that "Warner had exhibitors pressing him" and said loans "were being pulled in retaliation," to which Stevens replied, "Jack, you just have to tell them I can't do it." The footage stayed in. Stevens argued that "it was important only to sophisticated people and the people who thought the depletion allowance was a damned good thing." Stevens certainly knew where Edna Ferber stood. She predicted in a letter to him in 1954 that in five to ten years the "oil and gas millionaires will be anachronisms like the dear old covered wagons and the California gold-rush boys."

Cheered by the overwhelmingly positive preview response and, as usual, following his own judgment, Stevens decided to let the story roll on to its final cut of three hours and eighteen minutes. Stevens felt that *Giant* earned its length because of its "excellent structure design, which has to do with the audience anticipating and looking some distance ahead all the way to the finish, which is a reversal on how this kind of story would normally end—the hero is heroic." As he explained, *Giant* was different in that respect: "Here the hero is beaten, but his gal likes him. It's the first time she's ever really respected him because he's developed a kind of humility—not instinctive, but beaten into him."

And in running the film to that three hour–plus length, Stevens had once again, and decisively, ignored Jack Warner's advice.

After Warner saw the more than three-hour film, he posted a note to Stevens specifying what should be cut. This included the burial scene, the oil-depletion allowance scene, and bits of several other scenes. But with the Colonel, there was one thing that trumped all else, and that was success. *Giant*—without an intermission—met that criterion splendidly.

In an interview that year, Stevens defined *Giant* in a particular way that has largely gone unnoticed. "The reflective film," he said, "is the service we can perform as against this other visual medium television, which has to move fast and tell its story within extremely limited time." Like Jack Warner, and like the whole movie industry at that crucial turning point in the history of the business, Stevens wanted to overcome the pernicious effects of the little black box that threatened, or so it was widely felt, Hollywood's very existence. He wanted to give moviegoers an entertainment and an experience that television couldn't give them, one that they wouldn't forget. He wanted to make a difference, and he believed that a big "reflective" film like *Giant* was the means to do it.

⁓

Finally, in the fall of 1956, the film was ready to be released to the public, and Warner Bros. went into high gear. The TV campaign stressed "The big stars. The big story. The big emotions . . . The two big stars. The only picture big enough to bring them together." Radio pounded the message home: "It's a big story of big feelings and big things. Liz and Rock, Liz and Rock, Liz and Rock, *Giant!*" There was no mention of James Dean in the Warner Bros. publicity campaign.

On October 10, 1956, *Giant* premiered at the Roxy Theatre in New York.

There was some worry that James Dean's legion of fans might be a problem. Thirteen months out, many refused to believe that he had died at all. The most rabid believed that Jimmy's death was an elaborate publicity stunt. In their crazed idolatry, they were sure that their teenage icon was the only person in America, and in the world, who understood them, and who, on this night, would appear in the flesh.

The truth is that if James Dean hadn't been killed, he quite possibly would not have attended the premiere in the first place. After all, he had skipped the premiere of *East of Eden* in New York on March 9, 1955, a no-show that infuriated the Warner Bros. publicity team. It was a grand affair, with part of the proceeds going to the Actors Studio—another reason Dean should have attended. "Ushers" for the event included Marlene Dietrich, Margaret Truman, Fleur Cowles, Anita Loos, and a resplendent Marilyn Monroe, who captivated the crowd.

When the limos pulled up to the curb in front of the Roxy, the stars met a crescendo of cheers and excitement, followed by something very different and very threatening. A kamikaze cult of Dean enthusiasts had stationed themselves closest to the red-carpet aisle. They "were thrashing against the barriers, letting out menacing eerie cries; they had red, distorted, lunatic-like faces," wrote Carroll Baker. The frenzy of noise increased and a dangerous kinetic energy roiled the mass of bodies. Jack Garfein, Carroll Baker's husband, feared for his wife's safety because she was pregnant, but his cries of "Stop! Stop! My wife is pregnant!" had no effect. The maddened Dean cultists grew crazier and broke through the barriers and frightened the photographers and the actors. It threatened to get worse. Jane Withers was thrown to her knees, and, bizarrely, three girls attacked Elizabeth Taylor's hair. In the chaos of the moment, she lost one of her ten-thousand-dollar earrings. She wanted to look for it, but Mike

Todd knew they had to get inside the building before somebody got seriously hurt. Eventually, they all managed to push through the crowd and join Stevens and the others who had arrived early and were safe inside the lobby. They were all concerned with Carroll's condition, but she said she didn't need to see a doctor.

Jane Withers, whose knees were badly skinned and raw, suffered the worst physically. Rock Hudson's shirt was torn, his bow tie was missing, and he'd lost a cuff link. After some brandy and corned beef sandwiches that Mike Todd had ordered, they all recovered, and Elizabeth Taylor made everybody laugh with her impersonation of Groucho Marx. The Roxy melee hadn't dampened their spirits. And Mike told Liz, who wouldn't be quiet about the missing earring, to "shut up," adding that he had already ordered another pair. That was the kind of man she liked—a take-charge guy who was commanding and rich.

Surviving footage of the premiere at the Roxy shows a typical excited crowd but none of the physical harassment and fear unleashed by the Dean cultists.

The hosts were Jane Meadows, a well-known TV personality, and Chill Wills, who called everybody cousin, the way he always did. Jack Warner, wearing his usual tux, bow tie, and pocket handkerchief, upon being introduced to Meadows, cracked, "I remember when you were a field." As usual, his attempt at humor fell flat. Henry Willson sported a tux and, on his arm, Natalie Wood. George Stevens was accompanied by his son.

The only actor unnerved by the screening itself was Rock Hudson. The audience hissed and booed him on several occasions, and it wasn't until it was over that he realized they had been upset at the racism his character exhibited. When he fought for racial justice at the end, they cheered him.

Reviews were generally great from coast to coast. *Time* proclaimed it "an act of artistic courage." *The Chicago Daily News* pronounced it "as intimate as a letter from home." Bosley Crowther at *The New York Times* praised it. One sour note was John McCartin's supercilious and snarky review in *The New Yorker,* titled "Southwestern Primitives." Most reviews cited James Dean's performance as exemplary. George Christian, who would later serve as LBJ's press secretary, wrote in the *Houston Press*, "James Dean's talent glows like an oilfield flare."

A week later, the film premiered at Hollywood's Grauman's Chinese Theater without incident. Most of Hollywood royalty was there, but the rabid cultists were not a problem, apparently dispirited by Dean's no-show in New York. It was beginning to dawn on them that he was really dead.

Giant was hugely popular in Germany, Italy, and France, though French critics associated with the *Cahiers du Cinéma* crowd didn't like the film at all. François Truffaut in particular hated it, calling it "three hours and twenty minutes of deadly boredom tinted with disgust!" He preferred *Written on the Wind*, "a small, successfully done *Giant*." Most Americans didn't give a damn what the French critics thought (and didn't read what they wrote).

In Mexico, the reception really irritated Stevens. The censors in that country cut all scenes showing discrimination against Mexicans, over thirty minutes in all. In essence, they gutted the film. In Canada, they cut any scenes involving the drinking of alcohol—which seems passingly strange.

Although Bob O'Donnell had hoped to premiere *Giant* in Texas, it didn't happen. There was, however, a private screening in Houston in the Cork Room of Glenn McCarthy's hotel, now, in 1956, a part of the Hilton chain. The legendary wildcatter bore no animus regarding the film. Indeed, he embraced it. Chill Wills was invited to the event and later wrote Stevens about the evening. He said it reminded him a little bit of the hotel scene in *Giant*: "Minks dragging minks, arm-weary women lifting diamonds— quite a display. I sang Mr. Tiomkin's song 'Giant'—the crowd stood up and cheered it at the finish." When the film opened at the Majestic, it broke the one-week attendance record.

The Hollywood trades were enthusiastic about the film's quality and its box-office prospects. *Variety* wondered about the film's reception in Texas because of its "powerful indictment of the Texas superiority complex" but concluded, "Texas apart, 'Giant' rates as sock box office." They needn't have worried about Texas. Any ill feelings directed at Ferber's novel fell away in the brilliant light of the epic's glow. Stevens asked for a report on the film's reception in Texas, and the results were very gratifying. The report told of record sellout attendance in Houston, Austin, Dallas, Fort Worth, San Antonio, in smaller towns like Odessa, Midland, San Angelo, and in little towns like Weslaco, Monahans, and Marfa. The returns from Marfa indicated that almost everyone in the town saw the picture. John Connally would use the sound track in his successful campaign for governor in 1961.

Giant quickly became the "national film of Texas," or, as drive-in movie critic Joe Bob Briggs later put it, the "state religion." Overall, it would rate third that year in box-office receipts, after *The Ten Commandments* and *Around the World in 80 Days*. Only God and Mike Todd, it seemed, could outsell Texas.

⁓੪⁓

By the time *Giant* was released, Glenn McCarthy's greatest days were over. Yet in the aftermath of the film, he was still considered newsworthy. In July 1957, he appeared on *The Mike Wallace Interview* (ABC). Dressed in a suit and tie, with his trademark sunglasses and mustache, he bore a strong resemblance to his friend Errol Flynn.

The ostensible reason that Wallace had McCarthy on his show was the renewed attention that the oilman had received as a result of *Giant*, which both men at one time or another called "the Giant." But the real reason seems to have been Wallace's determination to attack him for his wealth (already diminished) and his swashbuckling lifestyle.

After a lengthy paean to the pleasures of smoking Philip Morris cigarettes—the "manly cigarette" and the "most natural" tobacco on the market—Wallace lit into McCarthy. "Why the quest for money, for great wealth?" he asked in that blunt, in-your-face style. Without waiting for an answer, Wallace quoted an unnamed friend of McCarthy's who said that the oilman's motive was a "grudge" against the family of the "rich girl" he married. McCarthy answered by agreeing that he had grown up in a family that didn't have "the luxuries of life" and that he had wanted some of those things for himself and his own family.

But Wallace wouldn't let up. Returning to the grudge motive, he added the early part of the century, and he invited high-wattage guests like Gary Cooper, Bing Crosby, Conrad Hilton, and Fred Astaire to lend star power. Edith Piaf provided the entertainment, adding a note of class. All told, the party cost $125,000 ($1,115,988 today) and everybody had a grand time, but as one press report observed, "By 2 A.M. of Jan. 1, 1957, when the party started dwindling, the movie looked pretty authentic."

On a trip to Saint Thomas in the late 1950s, the doughty Mercedes McCambridge encountered some people from Dallas staying in an expensive hotel. "They were noisy. They were Neiman-Marcused and all they did was talk about things back home." The Texans were quite traveled. "In the summah, Paris is like a morgue," intoned one. They laughed—loudly—a lot. "Things didn't have to be funny, just loud," McCambridge wrote. And so it went, boorishness upon boorishness. They were Texans and so what else could one expect?

In 1961, John Bainbridge, a *New Yorker* writer, published a kind of nonfiction sequel to *Giant*. He called it *The Super-Americans: A Picture of Life in the United States, as Brought into Focus, Bigger Than Life, in the Land of the Millionaires—Texas*. Texas reviewers like Lon Tinkle, who had lambasted Ferber's novel, embraced this book, though it confirmed and sometimes amplified many of the things he and others disliked about Ferber's portrait of the state. In fact, Tinkle later wrote a rave introduction for a new edition of *The Super-Americans*.

In 1963, *The Wheeler Dealers*, a comedy starring James Garner as a Texas wildcatter, opened in Dallas the week of November 22. It reincarnated the comic Texans from *A Texas Steer*: Yell, Bragg, and Blow became Jay Ray, Ray Jay, and J.R. Jay Ray and J.R. were played by two actors from *Giant*: Chill Wills and Charles Watts. The noisy, lovable braggarts wind up investing in Abstract Expressionist paintings instead of oil wells, and James Garner turns out to be an Ivy League graduate who is just impersonating a Texan in order to make money.

The old stereotypes proved to be a hearty perennial. In 1964, during the early days of the Lyndon Johnson administration, British journalist Alistair Cooke received a cable from his editor regarding a piece on the

that the "friend" said the rich girl's family didn't like him. McCarthy calmly and deliberately, in a voice inflected with an East Texas southern drawl, replied that it was understandable that a family might be upset over a daughter who gets married at age sixteen. (Exactly the same thing had happened in McCarthy's own family a few years before, in 1950, when his seventeen-year-old daughter married against her parents' wishes. She eloped with a handsome, penniless Greek immigrant, whom the McCarthy family, in time, came to accept.)

When Wallace hammered away at McCarthy's possible motives for pursuing great wealth, McCarthy replied that he didn't think it was just the money, that it was "more of achievement." Then Wallace shifted the line of questioning to the film and its depiction of James Dean's being ostracized by Texas "aristocracy." McCarthy responded by saying that he didn't like Edna Ferber's portrayal of Texas and that a lot of writers "try to pick Texas apart." Interestingly, he also saw himself in Bick Benedict, a successful man who has a "fine family," while the other side—Jett Rink—represents a "brawler-type operation."

Once again, Wallace brought the discussion around to his main line of attack—"what happens when people gain great wealth." Then he quoted Scripture: " 'No man can serve two masters; you cannot serve God and Mammon.' Do you think Christ was wrong?" It's hard to imagine Mike Wallace questioning the sources of wealth of the junior senator from Massachusetts, John F. Kennedy, along the same lines. Why McCarthy even agreed to sit down with Wallace is puzzling.

In 1987, the Shamrock met its end, reduced to a pile of rubble by a demolition crew. Hundreds of Houstonians watched as the structure came tumbling down. Among them was the old wildcatter himself. Glenn McCarthy died a year later, one day after his eighty-first birthday.

❧

Although the *Daily Worker* rated *Giant* the top film of 1956, the Academy of Motion Pictures Arts and Sciences did not. Instead, the Oscar for Best Film went to Mike Todd's celebrity-laden *Around the World in 80 Days*. *Giant* received ten nominations but racked up only one win: George Stevens for Best Director. Both Rock Hudson and James Dean were nominated for Best Actor; logically, it seems to have been a mistake to have them competing against each other. Yul Brynner won for his screen-chewing turn in *The King and I*. Elizabeth Taylor was not nominated for Best Actress, though she should have been. Mercedes McCambridge lost a Best Supporting Actress nomination to Dorothy Malone for *Written on the Wind*. And so it went on down the list: Best Adapted Screenplay, Best Music Score of a Dramatic or Comedy Picture, Best Art Direction–Set Decoration; Best Costume Design, and Best Film Editing—all lost.

But Warner Bros. had every reason to be pleased with the box-office success of *Giant*. By August 31, 1957, the film had racked up $15,000,000 ($128,117,614 today) in grosses.

᷁ᵗ

In 1957, as the Senate Permanent Subcommittee on Investigations ground on, Edna Ferber's novel "The Giant," as Roy Cohn called it, came under scrutiny. Mr. M. G. Horneffer of the French Voice of America was questioned concerning a review of Ferber's novel by a French journalist, Marcelle Henry. Her review had been broadcast five years earlier, on December 2, 1952. If all of this sounds like beating a dead horse, it was. The committee wanted to know what Miss Henry had said about the novel.

MR. COHN: Did she first state: Miss Ferber knows the Texans well, whatever the Texans may say to the contrary?

MR. HORNEFFER: She did.

MR. COHN: And then did she go on to say that as far as the whole Texas group are concerned, the men drink bourbon by the gallon, the women are nitwits who talk but say practically nothing, and there are also a lot of Mexican peons who work on the ranches and in the homes as servants, and who live harsh and difficult lives?

MR. HORNEFFER: That is correct.

CHAIRMAN: Would you consider that good anti-Communist propaganda?

MR. HORNEFFER: I would say it is the best anti-American propaganda.

SENATOR MUNDT: It is also a slur, Mr. Chairman, on the great Republican state of Texas.

SENATOR McCARTHY: If I were a member of the Communist Party, and I wanted to discredit America and further the Communist cause, could you think of any better job I could do helping out the Communist cause than by beaming to Europe the type of material which you have just described?

Although Horneffer admitted that he had not read the novel, he obviously knew how to answer the questions to the committee's satisfaction. It seems odd that nobody on the committee mentioned the film.

There is no evidence that any of the principals—Stevens, Guiol, Moffat, Ferber—ever knew anything about this episode. Ferber would have been both angry and elated at being singled out by Senator McCarthy and Roy Cohn. She considered McCarthy, who hailed from her beloved Appleton, Wisconsin, a "would-be Führer." Perhaps she just didn't like men named McCarthy.

᷁ᵗ

Ferber had discovered black gold in Texas. By 1956, 25 million copies of *Giant* had been sold. And in 1958, Ferber's share of Giant Productions clocked in at $1,500,000 ($12,604,100 today). Her well had come in. Film stock, incidentally, is a by-product of petroleum.

᷁ᵗ

The stereotyping of Texas and its citizens continued unabated, and Texans often played right into the hands of the Texas bashers. D. D. "Tex" Feldman, a Dallas oilman, threw a big New Year's Eve party in Hollywood at the end of 1956 to disprove the caricatures in *Giant*. "I wanted to show the world that Texans can compete with the best in gentility," Feldman told the press. He spent some money, too; he paid $75,000 to have an L.A. restaurant redecorated in the style of New York's famed Delmonico's from

new president. It read: "Would Appreciate Article on Texas as Backgrounder Johnson Stop Cowboys Comma Oil Comma Millionaires Comma Huge Ranches Comma General Crassness Bad Manners Etc."

Dallas, the wildly successful TV soap opera that ran from 1978 to 1991, owed much to *Giant*. It projected the image of oil and cattle into homes all over the world, and its leading figure, oilman J. R. Ewing, was a comic rogue version of Jett Rink, a wheeler-dealer whose charm overcomes all obstacles—even murder. In the episode "Who Shot J.R.?" (November 21, 1980—notice that calculated date), 350 million people in fifty-seven countries tuned in. In fact, *Dallas*, with all its glamour and wealth, helped the nation move beyond the anger directed at the city of Dallas in the wake of the Kennedy assassination.

-ᚷ-

In 1958, Ferber published her last novel, *Ice Palace*, and it, too, became a bestseller and it, too, was turned into a film. She had made a pile of money off the biggest state in the union and now, as her friend Senator Ernest Gruening attested, she had helped Alaska achieve statehood and kick vainglorious Texas into second place in size. Alaskans considered Ferber their Harriet Beecher Stowe.

She thought she had one more novel in her, and she made several trips to New Mexico and Arizona to gather material for a story about Indians, or Native Americans, as they would be referred to in the future. She wearied of the task, though, because the passivity of Indian men irritated her beyond the saying of it.

But her health was beginning to fail, and after *Ice Palace*, she published only one more book. *A Kind of Magic* (1963) would turn out to be slimmer and less impressive than *A Peculiar Treasure* (1939), but it would reveal the ongoing impact Texas had on her: "Texas was to have a staggering effect on my life—my health, finances, emotions, work." In all her travels, only Israel could match what she had experienced in Texas: an "attitude of insularity on the part of its people toward the rest of the world; an arrogance, a braggadocio, an assumption of superiority." Despite vast differences in size, the "temperament of its people, their disregard for the achieve-ments or importance of all other geographical regions, was startlingly similar."

She came to the obvious conclusion: "Israel was a sort of Jewish Texas; without oil wells."

Edna Ferber died of stomach cancer in 1968.

⚘

After the success of *Giant,* Stevens turned directly to World War II, which still loomed so large in his consciousness, and filmed *The Diary of Anne Frank* (1959). It garnered eight Academy Award nominations and three wins, including one for Best Cinematography, which went to Stevens's long-time friend Bill Mellor. Nominated for Best Director again, Stevens lost to William Wyler for the latter's sensational Biblical epic, *Ben-Hur.*

The Greatest Story Ever Told (1965) marked a return to the epic scale of *Giant*. Filmed in various sites in the West, with Arizona, California, Nevada, and Utah standing in for the Middle East, the biblical tale received poor reviews and failed at the box office. Even worse, Bill Mellor, who had been with Stevens during the war, had a heart attack and died on location.

Stevens ended his directorial career with *The Only Game in Town* (1970), a small, rather claustrophobic comedy starring Elizabeth Taylor and War-ren Beatty. This was Taylor's third outing with Stevens, and, unlike the first two, quite negligible. Beatty admired Stevens and called him "Super Chief."

Stevens died five years later, in 1975.

❦ 13 ❧

Meta-Marfasis

After the nymphs departed, the false-front mansion remained, a fragile trompe l'oeil that continued to capture the imagination of passersby. Worth Evans had most of the boards removed and made into a barn, which *The New York Times* called "the fanciest hay barn in all Texas." Thirty years later, all that remained of the house was telephone poles rising akimbo above the grasslands, a scattering of graying wooden boards, and a few pieces of iron slowly oxidizing into the desert floor. Cows grazed around the margins of the site without any sense of historical resonance.

During those years, *Giant* inspired two Hollywood films. *Come Back to the 5 & Dime Jimmy Dean, Jimmy Dean* (1982), from Ed Graczyk's play of the same title (1976), paid homage to the film by dramatizing its lasting impact on a group of women living in a nearby fictional town. *Fandango* (1985), which featured Kevin Costner in his first starring role, traced the journey of four University of Texas graduates who travel to the ranch and spend a night on the land near the remains of Reata.

Marfa grew used to pilgrims and journalists visiting their town to try to relive some of the magic of *Giant*. Deaners came to Texas to see if they could find any last traces of their idol. They sought out locals who had appeared in the film and went out to the ranch and looked at the decaying site; they were excited when they saw the iron posts that announced LITTLE REATA; they studied the haunting little cemetery in Valentine. But whatever magic and mystery had once flickered there in the desert was proving as elusive as the Marfa Lights.

In town, the Palace Theatre was closed down. The coming of television had seen to that. And the El Paisano Hotel fell into decline in the 1960s and 1970s. The sixty-five rooms were converted into nine time-share condominiums, and when that failed, the building was abandoned, until its reopening in 2004 under the name Hotel Paisano. As the years unfolded, fewer and fewer people came to celebrate *Giant.* Three decades on, there just wasn't that much to see, and an attempt by some locals to celebrate the film's thirtieth anniversary sputtered out. There was a halfhearted rodeo, with a few motley drug dealers on the sidelines offering their wares, and Clay Evans, now middle-aged, showed that he could still ride with the best of the younger cowboys. There was supposed to be a screening of the film, but as the girl at a ticket office in town told inquirers, it didn't never arrive from California.

In 1956, Stevens told his son, who'd worked as a production assistant on *Giant,* "We will have a better idea what kind of film this is in about twenty-five years." He needn't have worried. The film lived on. It neither faded away nor was forgotten. Warner Bros. kept *Giant* alive with rereleases in 1963, 1970, 1996 (also on DVD), 2003, and 2013 (Blu-ray). And George, Jr., who has had a long and distinguished career as a producer, as founder of the American Film Institute, and as head of the Kennedy Center Honors, proved to be an extraordinary curator of his father's work. In *George Stevens: A Filmmaker's Journey* (1984), he traced his father's life from the silent era through World War II—including footage shot in Europe during the war—and on through his major postwar films.

More documentaries followed. In 1996, Kirby Warnock, a native of nearby Fort Stockton, produced and wrote an excellent documentary on the making of the film, *Return to Giant,* directed by Jim Brennan. *Return to Giant* paid homage to the film's greatness and its impact on Marfa. It drew upon archival footage and interviews with a number of cast members and others close to the production, including George Stevens, Jr., and Robert Hinkle; numerous locals, who related their stories about that magical summer; and a handful of commentators, who dilated on the meaning and importance of the film. Don Henley narrated.

Two years later, in *Memories of Giant,* George, Jr., stitched together more interviews with principal actors in the film, including footage from those deceased.

Another documentary on the making of the film, Hector Galán's *Children of Giant,* appeared in 2015. It focused on the lives of Mexican-Americans in the 1950s, with an emphasis on the segregated Blackwell School in Marfa. Henry Cisneros, former mayor of San Antonio, narrated the film. Galán combined archival footage with interviews of actors and locals, including several of the same figures who had appeared in *Return to Giant.* The most important new interview was with Elsa Cárdenas of Mexico. Galán's picture of racial conditions in Texas during that period garnered widespread attention in national media, and both *Return to Giant* and *Children of Giant* continue to attract new audiences to the film.

⁓⁑⁓

Critically, *Giant* fared better with the public than it did with the French-inflected American auteur critics. In his influential book *The American Cinema* (1968), Andrew Sarris ranked directors according to their vision and style. Sarris placed fourteen directors in the pantheon, the top-ranking, including John Ford, Howard Hawks, Alfred Hitchcock, and Orson Welles. Sarris dubbed the second rank as "The Far Side of Paradise," defined rather archly as those "directors who fall short of the Pantheon either because of a fragmentation of their personal vision or because of disruptive career problems." Sarris put Stevens in this category, sandwiched between Douglas Sirk (Hans Detlef Sierck) and Erich von Stroheim. "George Stevens was a minor director with major virtues before *A Place in the Sun,* and a major director with minor virtues after," declared Sarris. As for Stevens's three major post–WWII films, Sarris was quite dismissive: "The technique of Stevens' American Dream *Sun-Shane-Giant* trilogy that once seemed accomplished now seems labored." Other arbiters of film, like David Thomson, have followed suit, objecting to the film's epic ambitions and execution.

The auteur theory is predicated on the assumption that the director has the same status as the author of a work of literature—thus the film becomes part of a personal vision and each film displays the auteur's signature style and viewpoint. Stevens commented on the theory himself in one interview: "The 'auteur' concept is certainly the most desirable form of filmmaking, from my point of view." But as Thomas Schatz has shown in his influential book *The Genius of the System* (1988), the studio method of making films offers a better explanation of style and content than the "genius" theory behind auteurism.

Borrowing from Schatz, one might speak of the genius of Stevens's system. For in films like *Giant*, Stevens certainly presented a viewpoint and a vision. James Dean never liked Stevens's system; he preferred auteurs he could manipulate. But audiences didn't read auteur criticism and they didn't study the styles of different studios, they just went to the movies or not, and in the case of *Giant*, those who went remembered the film, and many saw it more than once. Over the years, *Giant* hauled in $39 million in box-office receipts. It proved to be a movie not soon forgotten.

Among directors, Stevens had his contemporary admirers: Fred Zinnemann, John Huston, John Ford, William Wyler, and Frank Capra. Ford, who famously edited with his camera, nonetheless applauded Stevens's quite different approach: "George Stevens," Ford stated, "can take an ordinary performance and edit it into a brilliant one, the way a good newspaperman trims a reporter's story to make it read better." More recently, Steven Spielberg has expressed admiration for Stevens: "We admire Stevens today because he never pushed his images, casting long spells on us, only asking us to be patient with him—and when we were, he would reward us with one indelible moment after the other."

Stevens himself seemed to back away from thinking of *Giant* as an epic. "The title embarrassed us when shooting," he told Joe Hyams. "It is interested in small things, smaller than usual, because the Texas background is so vast. The spotlight is on people with the background as a setting." For

Stevens, the film was always about a marriage. It was "simply this story of what happens ever after. So many of our romantic pictures just led up to the altar and leave you with a general assumption of inevitable happiness. But this is a story about the hazards of the marriage relationship." Critics who don't like the concept of an epic prefer the first half of the film—which expresses its most epic qualities scenically and thematically— more than the second, the more domestic, more indoor, more intimate half. They vent their displeasure by dismissing the second half as family melodrama. But critic Stephen Farber rightly calls the film "an intimate epic."

One of the best reevaluations of *Giant* comes from Richard Schickel. Writing in *The New York Times* in 2003, Schickel invoked the power of the controlling image of the film: "In all of movie history no single shot surpasses our first glimpse of that sober, nutty encrustation on an innocent land in its ability to symbolize, in a few seconds of screen time, the essence (and the ambition) of the film in which it appears." Granting that "*Giant* has not fared terribly well with film historians" who think of it like those "big, fin-tailed Cadillacs of the 50's, excessive without being very exuberant," Schickel instead found himself "—all twitchy intellectualism aside— liking it enormously." He also praised the intimate scenes between Rock Hudson and Elizabeth and singled out Taylor as a "premature feminist" whose performance represents "star acting at its best." He gave similar praise to Rock Hudson's Bick, especially the scene at the end when he defends "his little wetback (yes, he uses that word, but with a grandfather's self-mocking affection)." He proclaimed, "It was a great scene in 1956. . . . It remains a great scene 47 years later—maybe because liberalism is now so whining and unmuscular."

Six decades later, *Giant* still has the power to surprise. Critics approach it like an archaeological dig. Rebecca Solnit, environmentalist and cultural critic, reports her findings in *Harper's* (September 2016): "It's a freak: a wildly successful mid-1950's Technicolor film about race, class, and gender from a radical perspective, with a charismatic, unsubjugated woman at the center." And the film's overturning of patriarchal power is astonishing, too: "The shift is not just from cows to crude, but from patriarchy to some kind of negotiated reshuffling of everything, the beginning of our contested contemporary era." Or to put it another way, "the king has fallen—as he does, literally, in the diner—and everything is fine. That's what makes it radical." Solnit's insights are the latest word on *Giant* but surely not the last; the film keeps finding new ways to speak to Americans across the decades.

❧

The status today of the three stars in *Giant* is historically off-kilter. Rock Hudson has faded terribly, Elizabeth Taylor has had stronger staying power and keeps attracting the attention of feminists in particular, but the only actor who has survived intact from that era is, of course, James Dean.

Dallas Buyers Club (2013), for example, begins with remarks about Rock Hudson. Rodeo cowboy Matthew McConaughey points to a newspaper headline announcing the actor's death from AIDS in 1985, and his buddies have the following exchange:

"Who's Rock Hudson?"

"He's an actor, dumbass."

"Have you ever seen *North by Northwest?*"

This back-and-forth underlines the erasure of Rock Hudson from public awareness, and in the millennial generation it is rare to find any knowledge of Rock Hudson at all. Still, his work in *Giant* has rightly earned appreciation from critics like Kevin Thomas, writing in 1996: "More than anyone else it is Hudson who holds the film together, a rugged, handsome Benedict to match cinematographer William C. Mellor's endless Texas vista and to match the astonishing beauty and quick wit of Taylor's Leslie."

Elizabeth Taylor has fared better. M. G. Lord's *The Accidental Feminist: How Elizabeth Taylor Raised Our Consciousness and We Were Too Distracted by Her Beauty to Notice* (2012) makes a timely case for Taylor's role in *Giant* and numerous other films as a remarkable anticipation of modern feminism.

But James Dean belongs in another category altogether. In a recent poem, James Franco acknowledges Dean's lasting impact: "Dean's ghost never stopped, launched from that moment, off the back of his image, and shot through every generation thereafter."

Literary authors have been drawn to Dean from the very beginning. New York confessional poet Frank O'Hara wrote a poem titled "Obit Dean, September 30, 1955" right after Dean's death. And in 1961, John Dos Passos, a major American novelist of the Modernist era, wrote a powerful biographical sketch about Dean and his youthful adherents. In "The Sinister Adolescent," Dos Passos concluded, "The teenagers found it hard to believe that James Dean was dead. There he was right on the screen when they saw his old pictures. The promoters had been struggling hard to blow up the story that millions wouldn't believe he was dead, but when they released a picture on his life nobody went to see it. James Dean was dead sure enough." The picture Dos Passos referred to was *The James Dean Story,* a documentary directed by Robert Altman and George B. George. Released in 1957, it sank like a stone. Its narrative voice-over (delivered in an exaggerated, portentous manner by actor Martin Gabel) is one of many reasons why. "He [Dean] took his envy to the beach. He looked at the ocean and he was jealous of its power. He envied the gulls for having found each other. He envied them their freedom and their solitary flights. Suddenly he knew that as an actor he could be the ocean and flood everything with his power. As an actor he could be a gull." By contrast, in 1976 the ubiquitous William Bast wrote an excellent TV drama titled simply *James Dean* (ABC). Actor Stephen McHattie gave a strong performance, which for the first time publically suggested Dean's openness to homosexual experience.

❊

George Stevens reacted vigorously to the phenomenon of Dean's ascendancy when *Giant* was released. Embarrassed by *Giant*'s being called "the late Mr. Dean's 'masterpiece,'" Stevens wanted to correct the record: "There are a lot of other people besides Jimmy involved in this project. They are being overlooked." And, he added, "To concentrate on him would have made the whole movie very negative; it's about people who have adapted and changed, and I wanted to show that in a positive light."

⁖

But novels, poems, documentaries, biographies, memoirs, and movies about James Dean kept pouring out through the decades, until finally, it seemed, he towered over everybody from that era. There are scores of books about James Dean. Two came out in 2016. Eventually, the memoirs will stop. The latest appeared in 2013, from Lew Bracker. The first novel about Dean, *The Immortal*, was published in 1958 by Walter Ross, who had worked at Warner Bros. during Dean's time with the studio. Edwin Corley's *Farewell, My Slightly Tarnished Hero* (1971) tells the story of a hot young actor from the Midwest who made three pictures—*Paradise Gate, Chicken Run*, and *Texas*—but spends little time with the "Texas" section, which he places in Amarillo.

So, too, in the numerous films made about Dean, *Giant* invariably receives less attention than do other segments of his life. More than one film concentrates on the lost-love narrative of Jimmy's affair with Pier Angeli— *James Dean Forever Young* (2005) and *James Dean* (2012). *James Dean: Race with Destiny* (1997) also stresses the romantic theme but devotes some time to Dean's clashes with George Stevens (played by Robert Mitchum in his last screen appearance). The two most recent films on Dean are *Joshua Tree, 1951: A Portrait of James Dean* (2012) and *Life* (2015). Beautifully shot in black and white, *Joshua Tree* offers a brooding portrait of the hungry, sometime gay young actor and his relationships with William Bast and Rogers Brackett in L.A. before he left for New York. *Life* (2015) focuses on Dean's friendship with photographer Dennis Stock and the famous photographic shoot in Fairmount, Indiana, early in the last year of the actor's life.

⁖

As for Dean's relationship with *Giant*, he expended all of his energy and guile in trying to usurp the film, to wrest it from Stevens and the two stars ahead of him in the credits. Elizabeth Taylor, listed first, earned the highest salary, $175,000 ($1,562,383 today), Rock Hudson, $100,000 ($892,790 today), and James Dean, a paltry $21,000 ($187,485 today). Chill Wills made more than Dean did. Yet in the erosion wrought by the years, James Dean now "owns" *Giant*. In the 2013 Blu-ray edition of the film, his is the largest image looming over the title and the much smaller images of Taylor and Hudson. Anybody looking at it without knowing anything about the film would conclude that he is the star of *Giant*. And many contemporary journalists and bloggers freely assume that this is so. Typical is this headline from a news report on Hector Galán's *Children of Giant* in 2015: HOW '50s JAMES DEAN MOVIE DARED SHOW RACISM AGAINST MEXICAN-AMERICANS. The author calls Dean the star of *Giant* but misses entirely the fact that Dean's character is the worst racist in the film.

For the Deaners who are still around, things are complicated. They're very loyal to the teenage-angst dramas *East of Eden* and *Rebel Without a Cause*—both of which have dated badly—and they almost invariably favor those two films over *Giant*. They don't like seeing Jimmy old and they don't like his being on-camera only about one-third of the time in *Giant*.

⁂

Marfa as a site associated with *Giant* draws a much smaller percentage of pilgrims and seekers these days. Instead, most of the visitors—hipsters from New York or Austin or wherever hipsters come from—account for current tourism in the little town, its population now shrunk to 1,981. Along with visitors from England, Germany, France, Greece, and other European countries, most of those who make the long journey to Marfa come to view the abstract installations of Donald Judd, one of the most celebrated post-modern artists. A cranky visionary, Judd started buying up properties in Marfa in the 1970s, along with acres of desert land south of town. He gutted the buildings in town and installed his abstract geometric forms—squares and rectangular shapes—an impersonal art, a kind of geometrical aesthetic. In the desert, he adapted gun sheds and hangars from the abandoned army base Fort D. A. Russell, as spaces to exhibit massive abstract installations. He situated some of his larger constructions on the desert floor and left it up to the viewer to ponder what the shapes might signify.

In a *New Yorker* piece, art critic and poet Peter Schjeldahl tagged Marfa the "Xanadu of Minimalism" and pointed out that Judd had turned a bank, a supermarket, and various other abandoned buildings "into an austere utopia of concrete, metal, glass, Sheetrock, brick, and adobe." The works of Judd and his disciples represented, Schjeldahl wrote, "the twentieth century's fixations on rational process and aesthetic purification. As such, it has an air of being entirely too good for mere human beings." Perhaps so, but human beings continue to stream into Marfa to see what Judd and his acolytes have wrought.

Judd was all about light and space, and Marfa had both of those in abundance. He was drawn to Texas, he wrote, because "the land was pretty empty, defined only by the names in the stories about Texas by J. Frank Dobie." He settled upon Marfa in 1971 for reasons similar to those of Stevens two decades earlier. "I chose the town of Marfa (population 2,466) because it was the best looking and most practical." Both Judd and Stevens were drawn to the primal features of desert, light, and sky. Judd was the emperor of Minimalism and Stevens of Maximalism: in the former, the object drained of meaning, and in the latter, the screen filled to abundance. They both needed Marfa, and Marfa needed them.

The tension between the two artists is caught perfectly in a large wall mural that adorned one side of Frank Restaurant, an upscale hot dog venue in Austin, a few years back. It pictured James Dean sitting in the Duesenberg and Stevens standing outside the car. In back of them, instead of the Reata mansion, are two large box-shaped structures. Dean in a cartoon balloon says, "Donald Judd," and Stevens says, "Never heard of 'em." Thus spake Zarathustra: Dean is always the coolest cat in any group.

Following in the wake of Judd, numerous artists have been drawn to Marfa, and there is no dearth of postmodern offerings. The artist and poet Carl Andre, for example, presents us with a "poem" consisting of one word run together—breathbreathbreathbreathbreath—repeated exactly the same in fourteen lines, and asks us to accept this as a sonnet. For some, Marfa is where avant-garde art soars; for others, it's where it dies in the desert.

Tourism founded on the art of Judd and his acolytes has made the town into something like a smaller Santa Fe or, better yet, Taos—a destination site unparalleled in Texas. Marfa is about meta-Marfasis: gas stations transformed into art galleries, the Palace Theater into an art studio, old houses into repositories of sculpture, a church chapel from 1886 into a part-time gallery and studio, another gas station into a PBS studio, etc. Among other artistic pursuits, Marfa today offers a writer residency program, two film festivals, public radio, a theater, a first-rate bookstore, and loads of pop-up events. There is nearly always something quirky going on in Marfa, and in 2005, Prada Marfa, a postmodern installation by two German artists, was erected on U.S. 90 near the little town of Valentine, west of Marfa. Yvonne Force Villareal, one of the producers of Prada Marfa, was excited at the prospect of a piece of art that would not need to be maintained. If somebody spray-painted it or a cowboy shot it full of holes, the point was that it would be a part of history. And sure enough, about eight or nine years later, somebody did deface it, but it has since been restored to its original irrelevance. The installation has taken on a life of its own, as indicated by a canvas print that hangs in an Austin art gallery. It reads *Prada Marfa 1837 miles*, a distance that closely approximates the distance from the nation's capital to the remote little oases of Marfa and Valentine.

The only vestiges of *Giant* in Marfa these days may be seen in the lobby and an adjacent room in the Hotel Paisano, where, in addition to photographs of the stars, a small-screen television plays a DVD of *Giant*. Food and drink are available in Jett's Grill. One morning, a few years back, Neville Hoad, an English professor from South Africa who teaches at the University of Texas, was having an eye-opener in Jett's Grill when the woman sitting next to him turned and introduced herself. "I'm Yoko," she said. Which proves you never know just who you're going to run into in Marfa, Texas.

⁓ͼ⁓

Despite its remove from 1955, *Giant* remains a seminal event in Marfa's history. Robin Lambaria, founder of the Marfa Film Festival, said in February 2016, "*Giant* is important to Marfa because it was this area's first real taste of Hollywood, and the region's real debut on the big screen to such a huge audience. Without *Giant* I don't know if we'd all be in this town today."

And as ever, the desert still exerts its austere majesty. After a recent bicycle trip through that country, John Burnett, a PBS reporter, remarked, "West Texas is so intense. It's like a different republic out there."

⁂

Contemporary Texas presents a very diverse population of 27 million, 4 million of whom live in Houston, whose black mayor has recently proclaimed his city as the fourth most diverse population in the United States. One wonders what Edna Ferber would think about this state of mind.

The Latino population of Texas is expected to surpass that of Anglos early in this century.

⁂

Stevens and his favorite cameraman, Bill Mellor, often asked each other which was tougher, World War II or *Giant*.

ACKNOWLEDGMENTS

The George Stevens Papers at Margaret Herrick Library of the Academy of Motion Picture Arts and Sciences contain a wealth of materials relating to the making of *Giant*: scripts, memos, contracts, location data, casting lists, correspondence, newspaper clippings, interviews, etc. They even have the actual prop sign used in the famous diner scene: WE RESERVE THE RIGHT TO REFUSE SERVICE TO ANYONE. Anybody seeking to understand the movie's origins and its production owes a large debt to Stevens, his son, George, Jr., and everybody associated with the Margaret Herrick Library. I specifically wish to thank Jenny Romero, head of Reference and Public Services, for her generous aid, along with Christina Ha and Louise Hilton and indeed everybody at the library.

I am especially grateful for the brilliant research skills of Barbara Hall, an independent researcher whose knowledge of the Stevens collection is indispensable. Barbara performed a lot of invaluable research for me and spared me a lot of air travel.

I also wish to thank Val Almendariz for supplying an important nugget from the George Stevens Papers.

And thanks to Mary K. Huelsbeck of the Wisconsin Center for Film and Theater Research at the University of Wisconsin for making available documents, notes, and other printed materials from the Edna Ferber Papers.

Teri Heydari of the DeGolyer Library at Southern Methodist University was very helpful in granting me access to interviews of Rock Hudson, Jane Withers, and Earl Holliman that were conducted by Ronald L. Davis. Thanks also to Sam Ratcliffe, head of the Bywaters Special Collections at Hamon Arts Library, and Ellen Niewyk, curator of the Bywaters Special Collections. Michael V. Hazel of Dallas was also helpful. Martha Utterback, assistant director of the Daughters of the Republic of Texas Library, also offered expert help on a painting that appears in the film.

Don Carlton's staff at the Dolph Briscoe Center for American History at the University of Texas was helpful, as always.

I would also like to thank Dr. Elizabeth Cullingford, chair of the Department of English at UT-Austin, for a departmental summer research fellowship in 2015. Also thanks to Liza Scarborough of the Office of the Vice President for Research for a special research grant.

Several people in Marfa provided useful information. These include Vicki Lynn Barge, general manager of the Hotel Paisano, Lupita Rivera, Lucy Garcia, and, back in 1986, Clay Evans.

Robert Halpern, editor of the *Big Bend Sentinel,* was very helpful, as was staff writer Sarah M. Vasquez.

Historian Lonn Taylor of Fort Davis generously supplied some facts about Presidio County in the 1950s.

Travis Bubenik, a former student of mine who was the *Morning Edition* host and reporter at Marfa Public Radio, offered valuable advice and information.

I owe the greatest debt to Kirby F. Warnock of Fort Stockton. I first met Kirby in 1996, when he was making his excellent documentary *Return to Giant.* We became friends, and when I launched this project, I turned to him, and he never failed to be an invaluable source of information, advice, and encouragement.

Sarah Little deserves special mention. A former student and now good friend, "Little" helped on several fronts—assisting with computer problems, chasing down *Giant*-related details, and being a great asset on a fact-finding trip to Marfa with the Betsola and myself.

Other friends and compadres who helped along the way include Keith Sharman, Barbara Dawson, Stephen Michaud, Skip Hollandsworth, David Montejano, Hector Galán, James F. Green, Mike Felder, Elizabeth Abrams, Chris Morris, Henry Anderson, Jeffrey Boruszak, Matthew Arias, Web Beard, Worth Beard, Gina Sopuch, Philipp Meyer, K. C. Sinclair, Nick Almeida Miller, David and Martha Wilkinson, Adena Rivera-Dundas, Delia Byrnes, Joyce Dormandy, Ann Gaines Rodriguez, James Magnuson, Marla Akins, Debbie DeWees, Matthew E. Rebhorn, Lesley Brown, Barry Maxwell, Jené K. Gutierrez, and Katie Stacy.

Thanks also to Garrett Cannon D'Entrement for an especially helpful bit of research and to Helen Kleberg Groves, who shared with me her memories of a tense dinner with Edna Ferber at the King Ranch in 1948.

Among colleagues at the University of Texas, I am grateful to the following: Heather Houser, Charles Ramírez Berg, Tom Schatz, Chad Bennett, Lars Hinrich, John Ruskiewicz, Kurt Heinzelman, and Peter LaSalle.

Author James L. Haley gave me good counsel regarding his publishing experiences.

Others who offered advice along the way include Mark Busby, Dickie M. Heaberlin, W. K. "Kip" Stratton, and Paul Seydor.

Jim Hornfischer, agent and author in his own right, deserves a lot of credit for his expert advice in shaping the proposal from idea to completion and in his unwavering support throughout this project.

Editor Charlie Spicer and associate editor April Osborn are the best, and visiting them in their offices in the Flatiron Building was a special treat. I very much appreciate their expertise, patience, good sense, and enthusiastic support.

I am also very grateful to Elizabeth Curione and Frances Sayers, of St. Martin's Press, whose copyediting expertise proved to be invaluable, and to John Karle, associate director of publicity for St. Martin's Press, whose tireless advocacy for the book I deeply appreciate.

Finally, I want to thank my wonderful wife, Betsy Berry, for all her help, love, and advice. An author and teacher of writing, Betsy pored over final drafts and offered insights into everything from chapter titles to Elizabeth Taylor's greatness. She also provided invaluable assistance in my ongoing challenges with computer technology. I couldn't have done it without her.

Upon finishing this book, I am reminded of the injunction printed on the interoffice communication memo forms used by Warner Bros. Pictures. Inc.:

Verbal Messages Cause Misunderstanding and Delays

(Please Put Them in Writing)

NOTES

PROLOGUE

1 "Chuck Wagon": George Stevens Papers, 56-f.692, Margaret Herrick Library, Academy of Motion Picture Arts and Sciences, Beverly Hills, CA. Hereafter cited as GSP.

2 "Jack Warner would rather": Bob Thomas, *The Clown Prince of Hollywood*, 156.

2 "Madame, I have only one thing": Carroll Baker, *Baby Doll*, 111.

2 "This is really a kind of homage": Peter Biskind, *Easy Riders, Raging Bulls*, 35.

2 "I know I won't have to tell you": Mike Connolly, "Rambling Reporter," *The Hollywood Reporter*, May 19, 1955; GSP, 54-f.680.

2 "I want to thank you all": Army Archerd, "Just for Variety," *Variety*, May 19, 1955; GSP, 54-f.680. Archerd, a longtime columnist for *Variety*, was the first journalist to break the story, in July 1985, that Rock Hudson was undergoing treatment for AIDS.

2 "Is there some way in your rewriting": Jack Warner to George Stevens, February 11, 1955, GSP, 57-f.719.

3 "a sort of pope": George Stevens, Jr., *Conversations with the Great Moviemakers of Hollywood's Golden Age*, 220.

3 "the giant behind *Giant*": Trevor Willsmer, *George Stevens' Giant*, 6.

3 "Henry and George and all you boys and girls": Edna Ferber, Western Union telegram, May 17, 1955, GSP, 56-f.692.

3–4 "There's better than an even chance": Lowell E. Redelings, "Notes About People 'n' Things," *Hollywood Citizen-News*, May 1955; GSP, 54-f.680.

4 "Oh, he's just the end": Kendis Rochlen, "A 'Giant' Feast," *Los Angeles Mirror and Daily News*, May 20, 1955; GSP, 54-f.680.

4 "a summer dream": Edith Gwynn, "Hollywood Party Line," fan scrapbooks by Lon Busch, 1955, GSP, 54-f.680.

4 "looked as unbelievably beautiful": Rochlen, "A 'Giant' Feast"; GSP, 54-f.680.

5 "Instead, he squirmed a bit": ibid.

6 "What counts to the artist": David Dalton, *James Dean*, 267.

6 "That's typical of the guy": ibid., 266–67.

7 "Just can't get any goddamned sleep": Joe Hyams, with Jay Hyams, *James Dean*, 199.

7 "miserable, a squinty-eyed runt": John Gilmore, *Live Fast—Die Young*, 109.

1. LONG STORY SHORT

9 "The Giant": "Edna Ferber Denies Film Studios Peek At Her New Novel," *Variety*, May 21, 1952.

9 "blanket 'no' ": GSP, 35-f.458.

9 "based on character sketches": ibid.

10 "All of this bombast": Joanne L. Yeck, " '*Giant*': Wild Success Outraged Texas," *Senior*, March 1997.

10 "Despite their fierce pride in their state": Associated Press, "Director Vs. Texans," Edna Ferber Papers, Wisconsin Center for Film and Theater Research, Madison, WI. Hereafter cited as EFP.

11 "If you make and show": Don Graham, *Cowboys and Cadillacs*, 62.

11 "shoddy piece of defamatory merchandise": Carl Victor Little, "Takes Edna Ferber 18 Months to Sell Giant to the Movies," *Houston Press*, July 31, 1953; GSP, 54-f.676.

12 "a man of taste": Julie Gilbert, *Ferber*, 155.

12 "Shall I produce '*Giant*' ": John Rosenfield, " 'Giant' Enroute, Warts and All," *Dallas Morning News*, March 24, 1954.

12 "tall slim girl": Edna Ferber, *Giant*, 72.

12 "State of mind" and "a world in itself": ibid., 110.

12 "Who gets hold": ibid., 215.

13 "after a hundred years": ibid., 447.

13 "admittedly a provocative book": George Stevens, "Filming of 'Giant' Holds Challenge," EFP.

14 "moderating influence on George": Trevor Willsmer, *George Stevens' Giant*, 12.

15 "associate producer can mean": "Ivan Moffat obituary," *The Times* (London), July 26, 2002.

16 "Most of the writing": Ivan Moffat, *The Ivan Moffat File*, 272.

16 "For Fred Guiol you might read": Willsmer, *George Stevens' Giant*, 12.

16 "mordant tongue, a bluestocking": This and the following quotations are from GSP, 35-f.456 and 35-f.457. These contain George Stevens's extensive annotations of Ferber's novel.

17 "Woman of the year": ibid.

17 "Make This One Hell": ibid.

17 "Bick comes in just in time": ibid.

17 "Bick is old": ibid.

17 "Memorable line": ibid.

17 "Aha! Oil" and "War": ibid.

18 "aint's, gonnas, and you was-es"; Edna Ferber to George Stevens, December 7, 1954, GSP, 51-f.614.

18 "powerful, dramatic and often compelling": Edna Ferber to Henry Ginsberg, April 23, 1954, GSP, 51-f.614.

18 "a funny, frisky woman": Willsmer, *George Stevens' Giant*, 13.

18 "wake scene at the ranch": Moffat, *The Ivan Moffat File*, 273.

18 "He is 36": Edna Ferber to Henry Ginsberg, May 27, 1955, GSP, 51-f.614.

19 "We might use": GSP, 37-f.472.

19 "This scene with the boy": ibid.

19 "Honda Knot one of the great": GSP, 37.f-472.

20 "They never did fit me": Marilyn Ann Moss, *Giant*, 212.

20 "Let the picture say this" and Stevens's subsequent notations on the script: ibid.

20 "strengthening": Edna Ferber to George Stevens, December 7, 1954, GSP, 51-f.614.

21 "a bit expository": "Notes from F. Zinnemann's Office re: 'Giant' Estimating Script. Via telephone—12/16/54," GSP, 38-f.479.

21 "night clothes": Geoffrey M. Shurlock to J. L. Warner, December 13, 1954, quoted in *James Dean*, Leith Adams and ed. Keith Burns, 131.

21 "sadistic love of brutality": ibid., 132.

21 "specially worrisome property": Adams and ed. Burns, *James Dean*, 133.

21 "in the public mind": ibid.

22 "disguise": ibid., 135.

22 "We were having dinner": Ferber, *Giant*, 437.

23 "The saga of three generations": "Product Information for 1972," GSP, 56-f.697.

23 "I believe that once the green light": Moss, *Giant*, 216.

23 "[s]hort pictures also": Willsmer, *George Stevens' Giant*, 24.

23 "the information on a map": ibid., 33.

2. BEEFCAKE BARON

24 "walking in clouds": Robert Hofler, *The Man Who Invented Rock Hudson*, xi.

24 "Texas of the 1930s and 1940s": Julie Gilbert, *Ferber*, 314.

25 "You know, I don't know": John Rosenfield, "Texas-Size *Giant*," *Southwest Review* 41, no. 4 (Autumn 1956): 375.

26 "He has the great robust charm": Trevor Willsmer, *George Stevens' Giant*, 16.

26 "It's easier to believe": ibid.

27 "I wish you a lot of luck": Bob Thomas, *Golden Boy*, 129.

27 "every actor in town": Willsmer, *George Stevens' Giant*, 16.

27 "He so inundated himself": Rock Hudson and Sara Davidson, *Rock Hudson*, 57.

27 "Just make yourself a piece of putty": Willsmer, *George Stevens' Giant*, 32.

29 "I tried to think of something": Jerry Oppenheimer and Jack Vitek, *Idol*, 21.

29 "He convinced unsure talent": Tab Hunter, with Eddie Muller, *Tab Hunter Confidential*, 47.

29 "His face was a misshapen mask": Phyllis Gates and Bob Thomas, *My Husband, Rock Hudson*, 21.

30 "beefy, tough-talking, chronically phobic": Hofler, *The Man Who Invented Rock Hudson*, 3.

30 "sought sexual favors": ibid., 6.

30 "Everybody who went with him": ibid., 189.

30 "It was awful": Hofler, *The Man Who Invented Rock Hudson*, 189.

30 "grossly unethical": Robert Wagner, with Scott Eyman, *You Must Remember This*, 182.

30 "the most powerful agent": ibid., 7.

31 "Mr. Texas": Willsmer, *George Stevens' Giant*, 22.

31 "Even Rock Hudson calls me Uncle": ibid., 21.

31 "about fifty years of age": Robert Hinkle, with Mike Ferris, *Call Me Lucky*, 5.

31 "like a Randolph Scott–type character": ibid., 6.

31 "looked like a stereotype of the Jewish movie executive": ibid.

32 "Do you think . . . damn accent": ibid.

32 "Hell yes, I can teach": ibid., 7.

32 "She has a tendency sometimes": ibid., 37.

33 "a real live Texan": ibid., 41.

33 "When we run the test": ibid.

33 "had come from the flat plains": ibid.

34 "When I do *Giant*": Willsmer, *George Stevens' Giant*, 21.

34 "wasn't much of a part": ibid.

34 "Well, I went up to Warner Brothers": ibid.

34 "He was so charming": ibid.

34 "Texas Girl": GSP, 49-f.594.

34 "strong acting quality": ibid.

35 "You don't know much, do you": Hoflar, *The Man Who Invented Rock Hudson*, 15.

35 "How old am I?": Mark Bego, *Rock Hudson*, 34.

35 "We used to do whole scenes": Richard Hubler, "How to Create a Movie Star," *The Saturday Evening Post*, September 27, 1952.

36 "Pretty soon, you're going": ibid., 35.

36 "*Thank goodness I've already*": Hunter, with Muller, *Tab Hunter Confidential*, 46.

36 "I had it lucky": Bego, *Rock Hudson*, 38.

37 "Rock Hudson!": Gates and Thomas, *My Husband, Rock Hudson*, 39.

37 "The camera sees with its own eye": Jon Halliday, *Sirk on Sirk*, 86–87.

37 "Taza will build Oona": Brenda Scott Royce, *Rock Hudson*, 8.

37 "looked like Joe College": Hudson and Davidson, *Rock Hudson*, 37.

37 "I had seen him on the screen": Gates and Thomas, *My Husband, Rock Hudson*, 22.

37 "He had good looks": Bob Dorian, "Rock Solid: The Stepping Stones of Mr. Hudson's Career," *American Movie Classics Magazine*, February 2000.

38 "as a straight, good-looking American guy": Michael Stern, *Douglas Sirk*, 77.

38 "Don't ever let a man": Hofler, *The Man Who Invented Rock Hudson*, 227.

39 "it wouldn't have been unusual": John Gilmore, *Live Fast—Die Young*, 168.

39 "Before a Rock Hudson party was over": Paul Alexander, *Boulevard of Broken Dreams*, 199.

3. TELL MAMA ALL

40 "It was like a big": Jonathan Cott, "Elizabeth Taylor: The Lost Interview," *Rolling Stone*, March 29, 2011.

40 "I don't remember": William J. Mann, *How to Be a Movie Star*, 40.

41 "can bring before us": George Stevens to Audrey Hepburn, July 9, 1954; GSP, 49-f.596.

41 "helpful in final development": ibid.

42 "is practically described by Ferber": Letter to George Stevens; GSP, 49-f.594.

42 "Liz Taylor cast herself": Trevor Willsmer, *George Stevens' Giant*, 19.

42 "the most important female star": ibid.

42 "She has extraordinary talent": ibid., 20.

42 "A rather curiously not-so-good picture": C. David Heymann, *Liz*, 130.

42 "off-beat with mercurial": ibid.

43 "So many of our romantic pictures": Willsmer, *George Stevens' Giant*, 10.

43 "The character development herein": Marilyn Ann Moss, *Giant*, 223.

43 "Do you really think": J. E. Smyth, *Edna Ferber's Hollywood*, 194.

43 "She was soon to discover that Texas": Ivan Moffat, *The Ivan Moffat File*, 279.

44 "alarmed her terribly": Elizabeth Taylor, *Elizabeth Taylor*, 15.

44 "the executives tell you": ibid., 14.

44 "When I read *Lolita*": Barbara Leaming, *Orson Welles*, 260.

44 "Draped head to toe": Heymann, *Liz*, 75.

44 "I never understood why people": ibid., 82.

45 "When she first came into": Moffat, *The Ivan Moffat File*, 258.

45 "She was not one to read": Kitty Kelley, *Elizabeth Taylor*, 49.

45 "I want someone": Donald Spoto, *A Passion for Life*, 50.

45 "was totally split sexually": Patricia Bosworth, *Montgomery Clift*, 165.

46 "She looked ravishing": ibid., 177.

46 "The combination of their beauty": ibid., 179.

47 "a real pain in the ass": Kelley, *Elizabeth Taylor*, 47.

47 "Oh, hello, Mr. Moffat": ibid., 55.

47 "I once began kissing her": Moffat, *The Ivan Moffat File*, 55.

47 "She wore an awful lot of makeup": Bosworth, *Monty Clift*, 201.

47 "The fun thing about her": Kelley, *Elizabeth Taylor,* 82.

47 "fuck": Bosworth, *Monty Clift,* 105.

48 "Your tits are fantastic": Kelley, *Elizabeth Taylor,* 57.

48 "he communicated with them": Heymann, *Liz,* 83.

49 "Forgive me, but": Kelley, *Elizabeth Taylor,* 54.

49 "Elizabeth dissolved when": Bosworth, *Monty Clift,* 185.

49 "With that one radiant scene": Mann, *How to Be a Movie Star,* 126.

49 "overrides our prefrontal cortex": M. G. Lord, *The Accidental Feminist,* 34.

49 "If she thought I was more severe": Ruth Waterbury, with Gene Arceri, *Elizabeth Taylor,* 89.

49 "The only thing was to prod her": ibid., 83.

49 "The first time I ever considered *acting*": Taylor, *Elizabeth Taylor,* 48.

50 "They evidently sort of work themselves": ibid., 49.

50 "He didn't make me feel like": Spoto, *A Passion for Life,* 62–63.

50 "[h]e would just say": ibid., 63.

50 "She has been kept in a cocoon": Heymann, *Liz,* 86.

51 "Tell that madman to stay away": ibid., 76.

51 "sexual athlete": ibid., 108.

51 "I told her myself": Kelley, *Elizabeth Taylor,* 62.

52 "Nick kind of got a kick": *Larry King Live,* January 15, 2001.

52 "I saw Elizabeth at the St. Regis": Kelley, *Elizabeth Taylor,* 90.

53 "Dear Mr. Shilly-shally": Spoto, *A Passion for Life,* 85.

53 "I believe Michael Wilding": Michael Wilding, *Apple Sauce,* 103.

53 "In 1952 Hollywood was still the film capital": ibid., 102.

53 "Our home is like": Alexander Walker, *Elizabeth,* 159.

54 "What an allegation to make": Wilding, *Apple Sauce,* 108.

4. PLANTATION LIFE

55–56 "And there it was, in sections": Rock Hudson and Sara Davidson, *Rock Hudson,* 92.

56 "Well, Victorian": ibid.

56 "Well, it was": ibid.

56 "He was like a god": ibid., 91.

56 "I was rich and strong and bigoted": ibid.

56 "soft, petulant": Ivan Moffat, audio commentary on *Giant* DVD (1996).

56–57 "He spoke quietly to me": Hudson and Davidson, 93.

57 "Why, we really stole Texas": Edna Ferber, *Giant,* 89. In the film, Stevens includes a shot of Leslie reading books at night. One is predictably generic, *The Alamo,* but the other is a long-forgotten volume, *Texas, the Marvellous,* a celebratory travel book by Nevin O. Winter, published in 1916 and reissued during the Texas Centennial of 1936. Winter's take on Texas is rhapsodic: "This marvelous State of illimitable

distances, which is primarily an agricultural domain, is becoming a commonwealth with great and progressive cities" (p. xviii). The book's appearance in the film is another example of Stevens's passion for authenticity.

57 "Rock overacted a bit": Robert Hinkle, with Mike Ferris, *Call Me Lucky*, 56.

57 "Liz, for her part": ibid.

57 "Damn it, George": ibid., 57.

57 "Bick Benedict was royally PO'd": ibid., 58–59.

57 "had taken the edge off": ibid., 59.

57 "master psychologist": ibid., 55.

57 "*allowing* people to do": ibid.

57 "I'm never gonna question": ibid., 59.

58 "How can you stand": Hudson and Davidson, *Rock Hudson*, 93.

58 "All the women on the set": Rock Hudson interview with Ronald L. Davis, August 24, 1983, tape no. 276, Oral History Collection, DeGolyer Library, Southern Methodist University, Dallas, TX.

59 "Just who the hell": Brenda Maddox, *Who's Afraid of Elizabeth Taylor?*, 110.

59 "all that deliberately": ibid.

59 "I daz": Hudson and Davidson, 93.

63 "It is a touchy sort of story": Trevor Willsmer, *George Stevens' Giant*, 32.

63 "liked least of all" and "I found Taylor a simpering mess": Edna Ferber to Henry Ginsberg, August 15, 1955; GSP, 51-f.614.

64 "difficult to enunciate": ibid.

5. LONE STAR

65 "Of all the roles": John Rosenfield, "Texans from Inside Out," *Dallas Morning News*, November, 23, 1954.

65 "I learned more about acting": Beverly Linet, *Ladd*, 150.

66 "You know, you could have": ibid., 188.

66 "I have worked at": Marilyn Ann Moss, *Giant*, 215.

66 "Mitchum any good": Edna Ferber to Henry Ginsberg, May 4, 1954; GSP, 51-f.614.

66 "against type": ibid.

67 "My secretary, Leona": Trevor Willsmer, *George Stevens' Giant*, 18.

67 "Physically and temperamentally": George Turner, "*Giant* Still Towers," *American Cinematographer*, October 1996.

67 "That's me, that's me": Marceau Devillers, *James Dean*, trans. Jonathan Marks, 43.

67 "autocratic ways": Lew Bracker, *Jimmie & Me*, 57.

68 "There were many things": Ronald Martinetti, *The James Dean Story*, 147.

68 "There is a lot": Van Holley, *James Dean*, 240.

68 "Discontented, cheated out of his birthright": Donald Spoto, *Rebel*, 230.

69 "brilliant senior guard": Randall Riese, *The Unabridged James Dean*, 59.

71 "Jimmy never mentioned": Paul Alexander, *Boulevard of Broken Dreams*, 44.

71 "homosexual relationship": Joe Hyams, with Jay Hyams, *James Dean*, 20. Other biographers, such as Donald Spoto, have rejected this charge on the basis of lack of evidence.

71 "I knew within five minutes": John Gilmore, *Live Fast—Die Young*, 49.

71 "terrible": Holley, *James Dean*, 49.

71 "He was too eccentric": ibid., 56.

72 "couldn't take the tea-sipping": ibid., 60.

72 "the worst mannered": Gilmore, *Live Fast—Die Young*, 60.

73 "Go fuck yourself": Holley, *James Dean*, 64.

73 "mixed-up misfit": Gilmore, *Live Fast—Die Young*, 65.

73 "an elegant, Clifton Webb type": ed. Peter L. Winkler, *The Real James Dean*, 118.

73 "Here was Jimmy": Gilmore, *Live Fast—Die Young*, 67.

73 "an arch, pompous villain": William Bast, *Surviving James Dean*, 82.

73 "life was never the same": ibid., 84.

74 "I asked him": Holley, *James Dean*, 73.

74 "Rogers did manage": Bast, *Surviving James Dean*, 85.

75 "there seemed to be a barrier": John Gilmore, *The Real James Dean*, 54.

75 "It was after his first day": Bast, *Surviving James Dean*, 89.

75 "Rejoice!": Riese, *The Unabridged James Dean*, 231.

76 "an ill-mannered, boorish young fellow": Gilmore, *Live Fast—Die Young*, 68.

76 "I did a little": Bast, *Surviving James Dean*, 123.

76 "My primary interest": Riese, *The Unabridged James Dean*, 60.

76 "Rogers Brackett did not": Spoto, *Rebel*, 88.

76 "felt that he was above": Alexander, *Boulevard of Broken Dreams*, 86.

77 "Jim (Brando Clift) Dean": Spoto, *Rebel*, 160.

77 "He said he had Clift": Dennis Hopper, "Introduction," in *James Dean*, Leith Adams and ed. Keith Burns, 9.

77 "Shit, man, Stevens": Gilmore, *Live Fast—Die Young*, 22.

77 "It's the Little Prince": Holley, *James Dean*, 84.

78 "It is only": Liz Sheridan, *Dizzy & Jimmy*, 117.

78 "He was short, physically strong": Holley, *James Dean*, 85.

78 "a pleasant companion": ibid.

78 "mother hens": Hyams, *James Dean*, 52.

78 "Marshmellow Brando": Holley, *James Dean*, 153.

78 "agony": ibid., 151.

78 "Depending on which of his ex-lovers": Hyams, *James Dean*, 5.

78 "Well, I'm certainly not": Riese, *The Unabridged James Dean*, 239.

79 "He's the type of guy": Alexander, *Boulevard of Broken Dreams*, 102.

79 "He always had": ibid.

79 "if this shy, mumbling": Sheridan, *Dizzy & Jimmy*, 31.

79 "with some child": ibid., 139.

80 "came on": ibid., 144.

80 "I succumbed to him": ibid., 145.

80 "I knew Jimmy": ibid.

80 "the greatest sex": ibid., 160.

80 "I keep telling him": ibid., 163.

80 "Rogers babied Jimmy": Gilmore, *Live Fast—Die Young*, 88.

80 "a building famous for": Sheridan, *Dizzy & Jimmy*, 164.

80 "Rogers Brackett was color-coordinated": ibid., 165.

80 "was really like an old woman": Gilmore, *Live Fast—Die Young*, 82.

80 "Brackett seemed to fade": Sheridan, *Dizzy & Jimmy*, 170.

80 "I don't believe": ibid.

81 "One of his favorite roles": ibid., 174.

81 "It was so evident": ibid., 175.

81 "Nurturing was really the thing": Holley, *James Dean*, 171.

81 "Later I came to understand": ibid., 201.

81 "I believed his mannerisms": ibid.

81 "in a sort of poutish mess": Alexander, *Boulevard of Broken Dreams*, 111.

82 "There was no sign": Sheridan, *Dizzy & Jimmy*, 217.

82 "Jimmy later conceded": Bast, *Surviving James Dean*, 150.

82 "You know, I've had my cock": Gilmore, *The Real James Dean*, 94.

83 "knew instinctively that": Bast, *Surviving James Dean*, 145.

83 "Undisciplined": Spoto, *Rebel*, 197.

84 "This young man": ibid., 196.

84 "The little son of a bitch": ibid., 141.

84 "cut more and more": Gilmore, *Live Fast—Die Young*, 138.

84 "Jimmy played Bachir": Holley, *James Dean*, 12.

84 "I often saw him": Spoto, *Rebel*, 114.

85 "You know, I was shocked": *Larry King Live*, December 3, 2005; in *The Real James Dean*, ed. Peter L. Winkler, 126.

85 "What a shock": Roy Schatt, *James Dean*, 1.

85 "small lump": ibid., 2.

85 "I just wanted to spark": ibid., 4.

85 "I had a motorbike": ibid., 12.

85 "a man with a great": ibid., 1.

85 "Well, maybe": ibid., 13.

85 "I'm not going to": ibid., 5.

86 "slouched at the end": Elia Kazan, *A Life*, 534.

86 "He was guarded, sullen, suspicious": *Los Angeles Times*, September 29, 1985.

86 "conversation was not": Kazan, *A Life*, 534.

86 "I looked thru a lot": Elia Kazan, *The Selected Letters of Elia Kazan*, ed. Albert J. Devlin, with Marlene J. Devlin, 259.

86 "John thought Dean": Kazan, *A Life*, 534.

87 "stay off that": Bast, *Surviving James Dean*, 178–79.

87 "had no definition and made no impression": Kazan, *A Life*, 535.

87 "Well, then, there now": Bast, *Surviving James Dean*, 183.

87 "All right, you two": *Tab Hunter Confidential* (documentary, 2015).

88 "Jimmy is inventive" and "He'll be": Kazan, *The Selected Letters of Elia Kazan*, 266.

88 "angel": Kazan, *A Life*, 538.

88 "She would adjust": ibid.

88 "Are you going": Holley, *James Dean*, 208.

88 "Jimmy never knew his lines": Raymond Massey, *A Hundred Different Lives*, 376.

89 "Jimmy's got to get to hate": ibid., 377.

89 "Must I always be": Riese, *The Unabridged James Dean*, 411.

89 "he was constantly fucking himself": Holley, *James Dean*, 252.

90 "boffing": Kazan, *A Life*, 537.

90 "decades-long myth": Bast, *Surviving James Dean*, 197.

91 "Now I had Jimmy": Kazan, *A Life*, 587.

91 "goddamn contact sheets": ibid., 537–38.

91 "twisted": Gilmore, *Live Fast—Die Young*, 161.

91 "In this business": Spoto, *Rebel*, 169.

91 "Their life's experience": Kazan, *A Life*, 541.

92 "was so adoring that": ibid., 538.

92 "Because I do it": Peter Manso, *Brando*, 390.

92 "sick": ibid.

92 "He was hypersensitive": Marlon Brando, with Robert Lindsey, *Songs My Mother Taught Me*, 224.

93 "Len, why don't you": Spoto, *Rebel*, 171.

93 "a technique": Kazan, *A Life*, 535.

93 "It grated on me": Brando, with Lindsey, *Songs My Mother Taught Me*, 223.

93 "an extreme grotesque of a boy": Alexander, *Boulevard of Broken Dreams*, 153.

93 "I got to know him": Gilmore, *Live Fast—Die Young*, 135.

94 "He has been absolutely impossible": Adams and ed. Burns, *James Dean*, 69.

94 "My God": Hyams, *James Dean*, 182.

94 "So, kid, you're now a movie star": ibid.

94 "It's my belief that": quoted on back of book jacket of Holley's *James Dean*.

94 "You always knew when he was around": Wes D. Gehring, *James Dean*, 195.

94 "The latest genius sauntered in": Hedda Hopper and James Brough, *The Whole Truth and Nothing But*, 168.

95 "supreme egotist": ibid., 98.

95 "I loved Jimmy": Riese, *The Unabridged James Dean*, 192.

95 "friend in court": Hyams, *James Dean*, 171.

96 "To me, his sex appeal": Holley, *James Dean*, 191.

96 "[m]any of the movements": ed. Peter L. Winkler, *The Real James Dean*, 26.

96 "I had just watched": Bast, *Surviving James Dean*, 199.

97 "I got fed up": Bernard Eisenschitz, *Nicholas Ray*, trans. Tom Milne, 235.

97 "The only thing to do with a Siamese cat": ed. Winkler, *The Real James Dean*, 248.

97 "There sat in the corner": Eisenschitz, *Nicholas Ray*, trans. Milne, 527.

98 "highly egocentric gesture" and "acted like a spoiled kid": Spoto, *Rebel*, 206–207.

98 "let him fool around": ibid., 208.

99 "American director in whom greatness": David Thomson, *The New Biographical Dictionary of Film*, 6th ed., 855.

99 "nuts" and "I don't know": Riese, *The Unabridged James Dean*, 430.

100 "an odd bird": John Gilmore, *Laid Bare*, 73.

100 "Jack was gay": Lawrence Frascella and Al Weisel, *Live Fast, Die Young*, 80.

100 "I did feel there was something": Gilmore, *Live Fast—Die Young*, 184.

100 "practically a co-director": Patrick McGilligan, *Nicholas Ray*, 302.

101 "We had never seen": ibid., 301.

101 "Look, junior, I've been around": Frascella and Weisel, *Live Fast, Die Young*, 140.

101 "Well, God doesn't care": ibid., 140–41.

102 "But I think Nick": Eisenschitz, *Nicholas Ray*, 247.

102 "James Dean directed *Rebel Without a Cause*": McGilligan, *Nicholas Ray*, 302.

102 "Goddamn it, Nick!": Frascella and Weisel, *Live Fast, Die Young*, 115.

102 "special kind of climate": ed. Winkler, *The Real James Dean*, 33.

102 "would stand there": Frascella and Weisel, *Live Fast, Die Young*, 141.

103 "When you saw *Rebel Without a Cause*": ed. Joseph Humphreys, *Jimmy Dean on Jimmy Dean*, 105.

103 "the Night Watch" . . . "a crew of creeps": Gilmore, *Live Fast—Die Young*, 169.

103 "I don't go out with witches": Riese, *The Unabridged James Dean*, 365.

103 "ran his fingers over the scars": Toni Lee Scott, *A Kind of Loving*, ed. Curt Gentry, 79.

103 "It's beautiful": ibid.

103 "there was friendship": ibid., 81.

103 "opportunistic explorer": ed. Winkler, *The Real James Dean*, 93.

104 "Bad boys playing bad boys": Gilmore, *Live Fast—Die Young*, 121. The blow-by-blow account of their experimentation is given in explicit detail and extends over several pages.

104 "sex assorted with beatings": Alexander, *Boulevard of Broken Dreams*, 101.

104 "had a dinner date": Hyams, *James Dean*, 207.

104 "strictly platonic and spiritual": Eartha Kitt, *Alone with Me*, 224.

105 "a solemn, intense, and troubled": ibid., 225.

105 "virtually impossible" and "He had no discipline": Spoto, *Rebel*, 194.

105 "deadly game": ed. Winkler, *The Real James Dean*, 243.

105 "stood there like a little boy": ibid.

106 "It scared the shit": Holley, *James Dean*, 243.

106 "murdercycle": ed. Winkler, *The Real James Dean*, 245.

106 "That night I swore": Bast, *Surviving James Dean*, 206.

107 "a small face peeked out": Carroll Baker, *Baby Doll*, 97.

107 "It's his place": ibid., 121.

107 "He looked up only briefly": ibid.

108 "I want you to help": Robert Hinkle, with Mike Farris, *Call Me Lucky*, 45.

108 "That's why I like": ibid., 46.

108 "ease up a bit": ibid., 52.

108 "You've got to treat": Baker, *Baby Doll*, 97.

108 "Really filthy, with heavy dandruff": Spoto, *Rebel*, 205.

108 "Hell no" Hinkle, *Call Me Lucky*, 44.

109 "Then I say something": Hyams, *James Dean*, 125.

109 "He could be warm": ed. Winkler, *The Real James Dean*, ix.

109 "Those of us who knew Dean": Douglas L. Rathgeb, *The Making of Rebel Without a Cause*, 180.

109 "Fame made him": ibid.

109 "his almost pathological vulnerability": ed. Winkler, *The Real James Dean*, 240.

109 "Verging on thirty": ibid., 152.

109 "For all the supernal light": ibid., 153.

109 "Jimmy lived a complex": Holley, *James Dean*, 236.

109 "magic creature" and "He was never pulled together": Venable Herndon, *James Dean: A Short Life*, 158.

109 "Don't ever put my fucking picture": Gilmore, *Live Fast—Die Young*, 190–91.

6. WEST OF THE PECOS

111 "In the valleys of the foothills": Zane Grey, *The Lone Star Ranger*, 174. Stephen Harrigan gives a good account of the size and diversity of the desert's plant and animal life in his essay "Going into the Desert," declaring, "It is not so much a place as it is a condition." See Harrigan, *A Natural State*, 99.

111 "When I was a kid": Marilyn Ann Moss, *Giant*, 56.

112 "Custer adventure": ibid., 16.

112 "The point about location filming": Alvin H. Marill, *Katharine Hepburn*, 90.

112 "The one thing that's continually": ed. Paul Cronin, *George Stevens: Interviews*, 99.

112 "These visuals go beyond": ibid.

112 "Nothing is more pleasant for me": ibid., 73.

112 "The story's so hot": Trevor Willsmer, *George Stevens' Giant*, 26.

112 "copious rains": GSP, 51-f.625.

113 "Tenny Wright suggests we might solve": ibid.

113 "The giant kingdom that was the Reata Ranch": Edna Ferber, *Giant*, 12.

115 "was better suited for": Willsmer, *George Stevens' Giant*, 24.

115 "the question is whether": Andrew Dowdy, *The Films of the Fifties*, 55.

115 "man's aspirations": Willsmer, *George Stevens' Giant*, 24.

115 "a real ranch house in which the Benedicts lived": Susan Winslow interview with Boris Leven, May 20, 1982. George Stevens Collection: "A Filmmaker's Journey" Box 2.f-39.

115 "Ten Beautiful Days in Texas": GSP, 48-f.576. The subsequent details and quotations are from this report.

116 "old beauty": Winslow interview with Leven. In February 2016, Stan Kroenke, owner of the L.A. Rams, bought the Waggoner Ranch for $725 million. See Steve Brown, "L.A. Rams Owner Stan Kroenke Buys Legendary Texas Ranch That Spans 535,000-Acres Over Six Counties," available at www.dallasnews.com/business /2016/02/09/fabled-w-t-waggoner-texas-ranch-sells-to-sports-team-owner-who -has-lots-of-dallas-ties.

116 "I saw quite a number of these sort": Willsmer, *George Stevens' Giant*, 27.

117 "Partner, this is the best damn thing": ibid., 28.

118 "It has a natural beauty": Lowell E. Redelings, "On Location in Marfa," *Hollywood Citizen-News*, June 20, 1955; GSP, 55-f.681.

118 "in the summer it is often": Lee Bennett, "Marfa," *The Handbook of Texas Online*, available at https://tshaonline.org/handbook/online/articles/hjm04.

120 "I have my own ideas": Willsmer, *George Stevens' Giant*, 28.

120 "sun-drenched gem of the West": ibid.

121 "dropped visibility to zero" and "smattering of hail": "Last Week's Storm Did More Good than Harm Say Ranchers," *Big Bend Sentinel*, June 9, 1955.

121 "a fine rain which greatly benefited": ibid.

121 "spellbound": "Talk on Uranium Holds Local Chamber Meeting Spellbound," *Big Bend Sentinel*, June 2, 1955. In the hope-springs-eternal department, the discovery of the Alpine High field in 2016, located in parts of Reeves and Jeff Davis counties northeast of Marfa, has certainly quickened pulses in Presidio County. See no. 24 (2016) in the annual Christmas oil field series from the law firm of Osborn, Griffith & Hargrove, Austin, TX.

122 "THE PAISANO HOTEL of Marfa, Texas, is pleased": *Big Bend Sentinel*, June 2, 1955.

122 "notables of the film industry": "Stars Arrive from Hollywood for Filming of Giant," *Big Bend Sentinel*, June 9, 1955.

122 "Benedict Manor": photo caption, *Big Bend Sentinel*, June 16, 1955.

123 "James Dean Must Be Seen": *Big Bend Sentinel*, June 9, 1955.

123 "Where are we?": Carroll Baker quoting Taylor in the documentary *Memories of "Giant"* (1998).

123 "dusty one-horse town": ibid.

123 "the ugliest landscape on the face of the earth": Mercedes McCambridge, *The Quality of Mercy*, 206.

124 "I want you" and subsequent dialogue: "Chaney Chosen for Part in 'The Giant,'" *Big Bend Sentinel*, June 9, 1955.

124 "Chaney had taken his share of the kidding": ibid.

7. PLEIN AIR

126 "Benedict siding": "Only in Reel Life," *Big Bend Sentinel*, June 16, 1955.

127 "Everyone strained to catch sight": Billy Lee Brammer, *The Gay Place*, 416.

128 "Cut" and subsequent dialogue: Elston Brooks, "Cast of 'Giant' Getting Real Workout in Filming of Movie in Marfa Area," *Fort Worth Star-Telegram*, June 19, 1955.

128 "Before it's over": ibid.

128 "In *Giant* there is": ed. Paul Cronin, *George Stevens: Interviews*, 43.

128 "the eyes of the audience": ibid.

128 "Nothing has told them": ibid., 44.

129 "included everything": Helen Kleberg Groves, with Bill Benson, *Bob & Helen Kleberg of King Ranch*, 111.

129 "Then we'd be dressed": Art Chapman, "*Giant* Fans Trek to Marfa Celebration," *Fort Worth Star-Telegram*, May 28, 1995.

129 "Mr. Stevens would": Mel Dellar to Art Klein, February 16, 1955; GSP, 53-f.667.

130 "long beforehand": ed. Cronin, *George Stevens: Interviews*, 103.

130 "I wanted to go from the extreme long shot": ibid.

130 "I will wager that 5,000 feet": Trevor Willsmer, *George Stevens' Giant*, 38.

131 "Jimmy was doing his first scene": John Howlett, *James Dean, A Biography*, 144.

131 "got half-way, unzipped his pants": ibid.

131 "It was Elizabeth Taylor": Peter L. Winkler, *Dennis Hopper*, 39.

131 "I did it because": Mercedes McCambridge, *The Quality of Mercy*, 109.

132 "Jimmy has never been more vulnerable": Barney Hoskyns, *James Dean*, 178–79.

132 "the tea-drinking scene": Edna Ferber to Henry Ginsberg, April 23, 1955; GSP, 37-f.470.

132 "The tea-drinking scene between Leslie and Jett": Edna Ferber to Henry Ginsberg, May 27, 1955; GSP, 51-f.614.

132 "Cut": Robert Hinkle, with Mike Farris, *Call Me Lucky*, 94.

133 "Now look, you're supposed to be the director" and subsequent dialogue: ibid., 95–96.

133 "Here's the most bereft piece of ground": Willsmer, *George Stevens' Giant*, 42.

133 "I had to put some wonderment": ibid.

134 "A single scene": James Powers, "Déjà Review: 'Giant,'" *Hollywood Reporter*, September 15, 1996.

134 "While we were making *Giant*": Randall Riese, *The Unabridged James Dean*, 207.

134 "That big herd had been fenced up": Willsmer, *George Stevens' Giant*, 37.

135 "our friend from Leningrad": ibid., 66.

135 "While many modern composers": ibid.

137 "Oil is a tremendous fact": J. Frank Dobie, "The Writer and His Region," *Southwest Review* 35, no. 1 (Winter 1950): 81.

137 "Other states were made or born": quoted in Don Graham, *Kings of Texas*, 1.

137 "repetitive shooting of scene after scene": Jack Warner to George Stevens, July 2, 1955; GSP; 57-f.719.

137 "Deeply aware of the urgency": George Stevens to Jack Warner, July 5, 1955; GSP, ibid.

138 "They kept some ropes up": Kirby Warnock, " 'Giant' and That Texas State of Mind," D Magazine, September 1996.

138 "Marfa is proud": Lowell E. Redelings, "On Location in Marfa," Hollywood Citizen-News, June 20, 1955; GSP, 55-f.681.

138 "wouldn't be fooled": Frieda Halwe, "Ferber's 'Giant' Is Striding Across Plains of West Texas," Beaumont Enterprise, July 3, 1955; GSP, 55-f.681.

139 "They were fascinated": Earl Holliman interview with Ronald L. Davis, July 24, 1989, tape no. 459, Oral History Collection, DeGolyer Library, Southern Methodist University, Dallas, TX.

139 "All of these people": Earl Holliman, Children of Giant documentary (2015).

139 "Neither the stars nor the story": Bill Brammer, "A Circus Breaks Down on the Prairie," Texas Observer, July 4, 1955.

139 "reluctantly cooperative": Redelings, "On Location in Marfa"; GSP, 55-f.681.

139 "grazing in the background": ibid.

140 "big mansion, the truly fabulous": Halwe, "Ferber's 'Giant' Is Striding Across the Plains of West Texas"; GSP, 55-f.681.

140 "nerve center" and subsequent Halwe quotes: ibid.

141 "[s]ound truck with cameras": The drawings can be found in John Rosenfield, "Texas-Size Giant," Southwest Review 41, no. 4 (Autumn 1956): 370–79.

141 "He is tall and lumbering": ibid., 373.

141 "a shrinking violet": ibid., 378.

141 "Aw, I remember Elizabeth Taylor": John Burnett, "On Location: 50 Years of Movie Magic in Marfa, Texas," NPR All Things Considered, July 15, 2011.

142 "pathologically shy man": Rosenfield, "Texas-Size Giant," 378.

142 "For a nickel": ibid.

142 "ill mannered and uncommunicative": ibid., 379.

142 "To others if not to Dean": ibid.

142 "One saw thirty different shots": ibid.

142 "owl show": Warner Bros. production material, 1972; GSP, 56-f.697.

142 "The locals loved it": ibid.

142 "Marfa expedition": Rosenfield, "Texas-Size Giant," 371.

143 "probably the most eventful location trip": ibid.

143 "Everyone, it seems, is working": Elston Brooks, "Marfa Having Boom with Film Production," Fort Worth Star-Telegram, June 17, 1955.

143 "What we've done is humanized": Elston Brooks, "Humanizing of Ferber Novel 'Giant' Stressed by Producer on Location," Fort Worth Star-Telegram, June 18, 1955.

143 "Always sullen, he dismayed publicity men": Elston Brooks, "James Dean Gloomed His Way—Like Brando," Fort Worth Star-Telegram, October 2, 1955.

143 "bobby-soxers' delight": ibid.

143 "When he was killed": ibid.

144 "Many local people": " 'Giant' Filming Is Completed Here This Week," *Big Bend Sentinel*, July 14, 1955.

144 "all very liberal men": Mark Harris, *Five Came Back*, 193. In March 2017, Netflix released a three-part series based on Harris's book. The third episode vividly depicts Stevens's experiences from Normandy to Dachau and the lasting impact the war had upon him for the rest of his career.

145 "We're dead. We're gone": ibid., 141.

145 "all film is propaganda": ibid., 6.

145 "imperialist propaganda": Marilyn Ann Moss, *Giant*, 61.

145 "The film is delightfully": ed. Cronin, *George Stevens: Interviews*, 100.

145 "had the most difficult time": Frank Capra, *The Name Above the Title*, 378.

145 "We went to the woodpile": ed. Cronin, *George Stevens: Interviews*, 66.

145 "After seeing the camps": ibid., 65.

145 "You're disturbed by being": ibid., 66.

146 "I was up to my ass in mud": ibid., xiii.

146 "After the war I don't think": ibid., 418.

146 "was not the same": ibid., 415.

146 "The whole [war] became": ibid.

146 "The films that he took": ibid., 418.

146 "He was just shocked": ibid.

146 "I was more seriously engaged": George Stevens interview with Robert Hughes, February 1967; GSP, 59-f.695.

147 "In *Shane* a gun shot": ed. Cronin, *George Stevens: Interviews*, 116.

147 "I'm here to kill Germans": ibid., 113.

147 "That s.o.b.": ibid.

147 "immense destruction": Stephen Ambrose, *Eisenhower*, vol. 1, 400.

147 "The other day I visited": ibid.

147 "give *first-hand* evidence": ibid.

148 "very slowly, in that wonderful sort": Willsmer, *George Stevens' Giant*, 46.

149 "We spent the entire day": Kirby Warnock, "Going Hollywood," *Big Bend Quarterly*, May 1996.

149 "this awful return": ed. Cronin, *George Stevens: Interviews*, 45. The arrival of the *Honda Knot* was described in "Nation Mourns Pacific War Dead Coming Home in 'Operation Taps,' " *San Francisco Chronicle*, October 10, 1947.

149 "An explosive is so far": ibid.

150 "That boy on that baggage cart": ibid.

150 "Suddenly it becomes": ibid., 46.

150 "People went to a place": ibid.

150 "The whites wouldn't like it": Carl Allsup, "Felix Longoria Affair," *The Handbook of Texas Online*, available at https://tshaonline.org/handbook/articles/vefol.

151 "When Bick takes that flag off the wall": Edna Ferber letter to George Stevens,

May 27, 1955; GSP, 51-f.614. The burial scene received local newspaper coverage in "Marfa Unit US Army Reserve Took Part in Filming Giant," *Big Bend Sentinel,* July 14, 1955.

152 "wetback": Willsmer, *George Stevens' Giant,* 47.

8. DUEL IN THE SUN

153 "a tall, broad shouldered man": Harold Hutchings, "Stevens Gives His Appraisal of Jim Dean," *Chicago Sunday Tribune,* October 31, 1956; GSP, 55 f.682.

153 "a rugged, modest down-to-earth fellow": ed. Paul Cronin, *George Stevens: Interviews,* 13.

153 "meaty, mild-mannered man": "The New Pictures," *Time,* October 22, 1956.

153 "George Stevens is a big, broad-shouldered man": Trevor Willsmer, *George Stevens' Giant,* 6.

153 "He's not an easy man": Marilyn Ann Moss, *Giant,* 106.

154 "Indian look": Fred Zinnemann, *A Life in the Movies,* 53.

154 "The lonesome, melancholy self": Moss, *Giant,* 194.

154 "There's a limit to stupidity": Anne Edwards, *A Remarkable Woman,* 137.

154 "She was Jimmy Dean-ing": ed. Cronin, *George Stevens: Interviews,* 61.

154 "Well, I'd had *Alice Adams*": Moss, *Giant,* 59.

155 "He was like the best cup of coffee": ibid., 68.

155 "Nothing and no one stopped him": Nancy Nelson, *Evenings with Cary Grant,* 128.

155 "a kind of host on the film set": ed. Cronin, *George Stevens: Interviews,* 27.

155 "periods of meditation": Frank Capra, *The Name Above the Title,* 245.

155 "Eureka! I know": Edwards, *A Remarkable Woman,* 150.

155 "increasingly dictatorial": William J. Mann, *How to Be a Movie Star,* 127.

156 "a piece of cachou": Elizabeth Taylor, *Elizabeth Taylor,* 33.

156 "All I did": ibid., 48.

156 "could really be quite cold": Donald Spoto, *A Passion for Life,* 102.

156 "Her postpartum mood": Brenda Maddox, *Who's Afraid of Elizabeth Taylor?,* 109.

156 "look desperate and sad and lonely": Taylor, *Elizabeth Taylor,* 51.

157 "felt like a damn fool and worse": ibid.

157 "why the girl, an utterly feminine woman": ibid.

157 "having a patsy or two": ibid., 50–51.

157 "I think he prefers": ibid., 51.

157 "to create a state of total dependency": Alexander Walker, *Elizabeth,* 162.

158 "no longer take the embarrassment": Mann, *How to Be a Movie Star,* 127.

158 "He didn't go for any bullshit": Willsmer, *George Stevens' Giant,* 38.

158 "Tom, if you want my advice": Susan Winslow interview with Boris Leven, May 20, 1982. George Stevens Collection: "A Filmmaker's Journey." Box 2.f-39.

158 "We'd get up about sun-up": David Dalton, *James Dean: The Mutant King,* 296.

158 "Things were tough": ibid.

159 "Gadge (Kazan), of course, is one of the best": Howard Thompson, "Another Dean Hits the Big Leagues," *New York Times,* March 13, 1955.

159 "All actors are cattle": Joe Gross, " 'Hitchcock/Truffaut': An Artist in His Moment," *Austin-American Statesman,* February 26, 2016.

160 "there were probably very few directors": ed. Peter Winkler, *The Real James Dean,* 252.

160 "had no hard professional shell": ibid., 251.

160 "[h]e was apprehensive about George Stevens": Van Holley, *James Dean,* 269.

160 "It was good for Jimmy": Joe Hyams, *James Dean,* 201.

160 "a severe scolding": Carroll Baker, *Baby Doll,* 124.

160 "a straightforward, no-nonsense": ibid.

161 "had the ability to take a scene": ed. Joseph Humpreys, *Jimmy Dean on Jimmy Dean,* 120.

161 "He seemed to practice, or emphasize": Harold Hutchings, "Stevens Gives His Appraisal of Jim Dean," *Chicago Sunday Tribune,* October 31, 1956; GSP, 55-f.682.

161 "Of all the people in our story": Ivan Moffat, *The Ivan Moffat File,* 278.

161 "Perhaps the term 'man' ": Randall Riese, *The Unabridged James Dean,* 197.

161 "this guy keeps following": John Gilmore, *Live Fast—Die Young,* 191.

161 "Here was this grubby guy": ed. Nick Dawson, *Dennis Hopper: Interviews,* 44.

161 "great buddies who went": ibid., 198.

162 "an actor who'd come out of Shakespeare": Peter L. Winkler, *Dennis Hopper,* 33–34.

162 "I thought I was potentially": ed. Dawson, *Dennis Hopper: Interviews,* 106.

162 "Do things, don't show them": Winkler, *Dennis Hopper,* 35.

162 "working externally": ibid., 33.

162 "Rock tried to 'queer' him": C. David Heymann, *Liz,* 136.

162 "Jimmy would have hated Rock": Paul Alexander, *Boulevard of Broken Dreams,* 215.

163 "Jimmy, I've seen you": Winkler, *Dennis Hopper,* 40.

163 "very quiet, sensitive, kind": Venable Herndon, *James Dean,* 143.

163 "when he'd forget, he'd lose": ibid.

163 *"tremendous concentration":* ibid.

163 "He worked very hard at his craft": Ronald Martinetti, *The James Dean Story,* 100.

163 "never understood that Jett Rink": Riese, *The Unabridged James Dean,* 509.

164 "As Jimmy accuses me": Gilmore, *Live Fast—Die Young,* 221.

164 "Everything was of an age gone by": Baker, *Baby Doll,* 122.

164 "strenuous and inconsiderate": ibid., 123.

164 "On location": ibid., 124.

165 "paid vacation": ibid., 125.

165 "caldrons of stews and curries": ibid.

165 "cruel and cutting": ibid., 126.

166 "awed fan" and "the luminous, untouchable stars": ibid., 127.

166 "an outrageous scene-stealer": ibid.

166 "radiant stars": ibid., 128.

166 "also admired": ibid.

166 "like a bunch of undisciplined": ibid., 126.

166 "like absolute fools": ibid.

167 "The heat, humidity and dust": Elizabeth Taylor, *Elizabeth Takes Off,* 69.

167 "a chocolate martini": ibid.

167 "there was nothing to do": Mann, *How to Be a Movie Star,* 128.

167 "Withers' USO": Herndon, *James Dean,* 144.

167 "just sit and talk": Riese, *The Unabridged James Dean,* 564.

167 "No, I like this shirt the way it is": Riese, 565.

168 "Everybody seemed to have a lot of problems": Mercedes McCambridge, *The Quality of Mercy,* 205.

168 "runt of the litter": Martinetti, *The James Dean Story,* 147.

168 "master editor, director": McCambridge, *The Quality of Mercy,* 204–205.

168 "full jar of peanut butter": ibid., 205.

169 "If anybody asks you": ibid., 210.

169 "Last night I dreamed": Keith Elliott, "Marfa 'Swamped' by Film Makers," *San Antonio Express News,* June 1955.

169 "You see every actor doing it now": Timothy Jacobs, *James Dean,* 70.

169 "I developed a program": Riese, *The Unabridged James Dean,* 414.

170 "People told me he was moody": Martinetti, *The James Dean Story,* 146.

170 "He really kind of aspired": Hyams, *James Dean,* 222.

170 "In fact, Jimmy was": Earl Holliman interview with Ronald L. Davis, July 24, 1989, tape no. 459, Oral History Collection, DeGolyer Library, Southern Methodist University, Dallas, TX.

171 "The door opened and in came this character": Kirby F. Warnock, "Going Hollywood," *Big Bend Quarterly,* May 1995.

171 "These Actor's [*sic*] Studio kids": ibid.

171 "Buckle" and "the Spook": Robert Hinkle, with Mike Farris, *Call Me Lucky,* 69.

172 "Naturally, after all the nice things": "Chill Wills Knows How to Rough It," *Big Bend Sentinel,* June 30, 1955.

173 "He was very friendly": Magdalin Leonardo, "The Ruins of Reata: Theatrical Archaeology," available at http://our.tentativetimes.net/marfa/reatarun.html.

173 "I'm a little too much of an old lady": Simon Romero, "A Texas Town Holds Fast to Its Ties to a Classic," *New York Times,* June 9, 2003.

173 "He was very approachable": *Return to Giant* (documentary, 1996).

173 "after James Dean, who is here": "Dizzey Deans Baseball Team Organized Here; Will Play Ft. Stockton," *Big Bend Sentinel,* June 23, 1955. It is curious that in this account there is no mention of the famous baseball announcer and Hall of Famer, pitcher Dizzy Dean.

174 "Cut—I fucked it up": Walker, *Elizabeth*, 162.

174 "I'm a serious-minded": Martinetti, *The James Dean Story*, 99.

174 "I met your friend in Texas": Donald Spoto, *Rebel*, 235.

174 "strange boy, a strange young man": Earl Holliman interview with Ronald L. Davis.

174 "I must admit": ed. Humphreys, *Jimmy Dean on Jimmy Dean*, 120.

175 "He was always pulling and hauling": ibid.

175 "As an actor": George Turner, "*Giant* Still Towers," *American Cinematographer*, October 1996.

175 "Jimmy was never a courteous actor": ibid., 89.

175 "Jimmy Dean could be tremendously winning": "Young Hollywood Through the Decades," *People*, November 11, 1996.

176 "had a fine concept of how Jimmy Dean": Spoto, *Rebel*, 236.

176 "It certainly was undignified, Liz": Baker, *Baby Doll*, 130.

176 "We would sometimes sit up": Heymann, *Liz*, 137.

177 "He was very afraid": ibid.

177 "When Jimmy was 11": ed. Winkler, *The Real James Dean*, 120.

177 "Dean was a very depressed person": Gilmore, *Live Fast—Die Young*, 225–26.

177 "act as a referee": Michael Wilding, *Apple Sauce*, 114.

177 "brilliant director": ibid.

177 "one long feud": ibid.

178 "You'd better know right away": ibid., 113.

179 "desolate place": Rock Hudson interview with Ronald L. Davis, August 24, 1983, tape no. 276, Oral History Collection, DeGolyer Library, Southern Methodist University, Dallas, TX.

179 "The weather just put": ibid.

180 "sit up with one of them" and subsequent quotes in this paragraph: "Growing up in the Spotlight," *Newsweek*, June 18, 1992.

181 "Behind the façade": Phyllis Gates and Bob Thomas, *My Husband, Rock Hudson*, 76.

181 "godforsaken spot": ibid., 61.

181 "polite, clean-cut man": ibid.

181 "tough man": ibid., 62.

181 "flawless beauty": ibid.

181 "He was small and exceedingly shy": ibid., 63.

181 "I can't understand": ibid.

181 "the big Victorian mansion": ibid., 65.

182 "Mornin', ma'am": ibid.

182 "almost childish with each other": ibid., 66.

182 "a little bit more conservative": Romero, "A Texas Town Holds Fast to Its Ties to a Classic," *New York Times*, June 9, 2003.

183 "They never had words": ed. Winkler, *The Real James Dean*, 295.

183 "was nasty, mean": ed. Humphreys, *Jimmy Dean on Jimmy Dean*, 113.

183 "was always late": Spoto, *Rebel*, 234.

183 "I didn't like him": Ray Loynd, "Some Unsentimental Memories of James Dean by Rock Hudson," *Hollywood Reporter*, August 9, 1968.

183 "Before coming on set": ed. Humphreys, *Jimmy Dean on Jimmy Dean*, 116.

184 "never worked with an actor": Rock Hudson interview with Ronald L. Davis.

184 "Jimmy had a lot of faults": ibid.

184 "I was very connected to both Rock and Jimmy": Jonathan Cott, "Elizabeth Taylor: The Lost Interview," *Rolling Stone*, March 29, 2011.

185 "Dammit this is getting to be Jimmy Dean's picture": Gates, and Thomas, *My Husband, Rock Hudson*, 67.

185 "It was wonderful": ibid.

185 "He had this stoic demeanor": Willsmer, *George Stevens' Giant*, 49.

185 "He was just a different man": ibid.

9. BEING AND NOTHINGNESS IN L.A.

187 "It took me a while": Lee Raskin, *James Dean*, 91.

187 "Dean could behave intelligently": Ronald Martinetti, *The James Dean Story*, 135–36.

187 "pure Bronx": Edna Ferber to Henry Ginsberg, April 23, 1955; GSP, 51-f.614.

188 "sick-making word": ibid.

188 "by the time I got on the picture": Mike Fitzgerald, "Noreen Nash: An Interview," at www.westernclippings.com/interview/noreennash_interview.shtml.

189 "Bob, what am I going to do": Robert Hinkle, with Mike Farris, *Call Me Lucky*, 92.

189 "Whoever is on the screen": Trevor Willsmer, *George Stevens' Giant*, 48.

189 "There is one gesture": John Howlett, *James Dean*, 137.

189 "too tired to work": Leith Adams and ed. Keith Burns, *James Dean*, 136.

190 "absences and/or tardiness": Randall Riese, *The Unabridged James Dean*, 202.

190 "did not come in all day": ibid.

190 "inconsideration": Martinetti, *The James Dean Story*, 153.

190 "in another film I do": ibid.

190 "Maybe I better go to the moon": John Howlett, *James Dean*, 133.

190 "Stevens has a method": William Bast, *Surviving James Dean*, 220.

191 "I sat there for three days": Hedda Hopper and James Brough, *The Whole Truth and Nothing But*, 175.

191 "George Stevens is a martinet": ibid.

191 "You were disturbed by him": ed. Joseph Humpreys, *Jimmy Dean on Jimmy Dean*, 115.

193 "outside the commissary": David Dalton, *James Dean*, 131.

193 "There was always something new": Howlett, *James Dean*, 126.

193 "He slid one of his hands": Carroll Baker, *Baby Doll*, 139.

194 "a long, sad embrace": ibid.

194 "a grand master": Willsmer, *George Stevens' Giant*, 21.

194 "a great boxing match": Baker, *Baby Doll*, 138.

194 "He was still developing": Marlon Brando, with Robert Lindsey, *Songs My Mother Taught Me*, 224.

194 "You've been watching that Dean guy" and subsequent remarks by Hopper: ed. Peter L. Winkler, *Dennis Hopper*, 42.

195 "violent person": Riese, *The Unabridged James Dean*, 240.

196 "terribly, terribly unhappy": Willsmer, *George Stevens' Giant*, 50.

196 "We did this darned thing": ibid.

196 "Take a good look at me": Riese, *The Unabridged James Dean*, 418.

197 "little roadside lunch room": Edna Ferber, *Giant*, 437–40.

198 "intense excitement": Willsmer, *George Stevens' Giant*, 53.

198 "legitimately and honestly reactionary": ibid.

198 "his arms were going to fall off": Willsmer, *George Stevens' Giant*, 54.

198 "an awful lot of film": ibid.

198 "I always thought that": ibid.

199 "This could have been great" and subsequent viewers' comments: GSP, 53-f.661. The Stevens collection contains three boxes of *Giant* preview cards, a very high percentage of which rated the film excellent.

199 "For Negroes": Richard Harding Davis, *The West from a Car-Window*, 27. A later novelist, Graham Greene, passed through San Antonio on his way to Mexico in 1938, and he, too, was struck with the fact that "Texas seemed to be half Mexico already— and half Will Rogers" (*The Lawless Roads*, 25). Greene also pointed out the deplorable living conditions in the "dreary hovels of the Mexican West Side" in San Antonio and concluded, "Nowhere in Mexico did I see quite so extreme a poverty" (27).

200 "two-bit run-down restaurant": John Rechy, "Jim Crow Wears a Sombrero," *The Nation*, October 10, 1959.

200 "[p]rejudice against the Mexican": ibid., 211. Lewis W. Gillenson, in an article in *Look* in 1951, described the plight of Mexican-Americans in stark terms: "Texas tub thumpers enjoy shouting about the state's bumper crop of millionaires. But there is an awkward silence when conversation veers to the subject of the million and a half Texans of Mexican descent who comprise 'the Mexican problem.' The silence becomes eloquent when the facts of 'the Mexican problem' are known. The truth is simply this: Nowhere else in America is a group of people so downtrodden and defenseless, and nowhere are human dignity and life held in such low regard."

201 "I serve even white trash": "San Antonio Consul Charges Boerne Café Denied Him Service," EFP, Wisconsin Center for Film and Theater Research, Madison, WI.

202 *There's a yellow girl in Texas*: Jeffrey D. Dunn and James Lutzweiler, "The Yellow Rose of Texas," *The Handbook of Texas Online*, available at https://tshaonline.org /handbook/online/articles/xey01. It is a part of Texas lore that the Yellow Rose

was a free mulatto named Emily D. West (sometimes Emily Morgan, after her employer). According to legend, Emily West was in General Santa Anna's tent for a dalliance on the afternoon of April 21, 1836, when Sam Houston's Texas army attacked and won the Battle of San Jacinto. Margaret Swett Henson, "Emily D. West," https://tshaonline.org/handbook/online/articles/fwe41.

202 "Now, I've got those Texas people in the audience": Willsmer, *George Stevens' Giant*, 54.

203 "I think the character of this": George Stevens to Tom Andre, April 11, 1955; GSP, 52-f.640.

203 "enormous Victorian oddity": Lynn Bloom, "Home Fashions from New Films: Two Distinctive Houses Add Meaning to 'Giant,'" *Retailing Daily*, October 11, 1956.

203 "As the family": ibid.

204 "the condition of society as a whole": Jon Halliday, *Sirk on Sirk*, 10.

204 "Malone, alone": ibid., 119.

204 "a decade of unexampled prosperity and calm": Paul Johnson, *Eisenhower*, 122.

204 "The 1950s are now seen": ibid., 123.

204 "white and motionless": Baker, *Baby Doll*, 140.

204 "I can't believe it": Elizabeth Taylor, *Elizabeth Taylor*, 56.

205 "Elizabeth, the Earth Mother": Willsmer, *George Stevens' Giant*, 59.

205 "Stevens seemed unnecessarily harsh": C. David Heymann, *Liz*, 138.

205 "extreme mental duress": statement by Dr. John H. Davis, October 1, 1955; GSP, 49-f.596.

205 "performed her long shot scenes": Tom Andre memo to Eric Stacey; GSP, 49-f.596.

206 "a woman of taste and education": Edna Ferber to Henry Ginsberg, April 23, 1955; GSP, 51-f.614.

206 "In contrast": Marilyn Ann Moss, *Giant*, 213.

206 "consider the possible value": ibid.

207 "Thank God we worked": Willsmer, *George Stevens' Giant*, 13.

10. LOVE AND MARRIAGE

208 "He's 29": Elston Brooks, "Cast of Giant Getting Real Workout in Filming of Movie in Marfa Area," *Fort Worth Star-Telegram*, June 19, 1955.

208 "over the rock": William J. Mann, *How to Be a Movie Star*, 153.

208 "Every month": Robert Hofler, *The Man Who Invented Rock Hudson*, 244.

209 "Fans are urging": ibid., 242.

210 "the limp-wristed lads": Tab Hunter, with Eddie Muller, *Tab Hunter Confidential*, 116.

210 "one of the cute kids": Hofler, *The Man Who Invented Rock Hudson*, 262.

210 "The vice squad said": ibid.

210 "Remember this": Hunter, with Muller, *Tab Hunter Confidential*, 122.

210 "*Confidential* tarred 'fairies'": ibid., 117.

210 "bright, down-to earth": Rock Hudson and Sara Davidson, *Rock Hudson*, 80.

210 "She accepted us immediately": ibid.

210 "lesbian situations": ibid., 89.

211 "hell of a nice lady": Rock Hudson interview with Ronald L. Davis, August 2, 1983, tape no. 276, Oral History Collection, DeGolyer Library, Southern Methodist University, Dallas, TX.

212 "emotional development": Hudson and Davidson, *Rock Hudson*, 104.

212 "All women are dirty": Phyllis Gates and Bob Thomas, *My Husband, Rock Hudson*, 129.

212 "Impossible Years": Hudson and Davidson, *Rock Hudson*, 101.

213 "Charlie Movie Star": ibid.

213 "He expected everything": Gates and Thomas, *My Husband, Rock Hudson*, 143.

213 "Because he's a silly": ibid., 139.

214 "charming and intelligent": Hunter, with Muller, *Tab Hunter Confidential*, 172.

214 "[Every] person I met": "1955: Rock Hudson Marries," at www.playgroundtothestars .com/timeline/1955-rock-hudson-marries-phyllis-gates/. Retrieved February 16, 2015.

215 "You're so goddamn British!": Michael Wilding, *Apple Sauce*, 111.

215 "I'll bet if I told you": ibid., 112.

215 "We sat on a hilltop": Donald Spoto, *A Passion for Life*, 92.

215 "We were so very": Elizabeth Taylor, *Elizabeth Takes Off*, 69.

216 "When Liz Taylor's Away": Mann, *How to Be a Movie Star*, 154.

216 "If only you would": ibid., 156.

216 WHEN MIKE WILDING: ibid.

217 "Get those goddamned cameras": C. David Heymann, *Liz*, 146.

218 "dynamic human engine": Edna Ferber, *A Kind of Magic*, 209.

218 "Restless, dynamic, improbable": ibid., 210.

218 "my fat little Jewish broad": Kitty Kelley, *Elizabeth Taylor*, 122.

218 "Boy these little Jewish": ibid.

218 "enchanting and preposterous": Ferber, *A Kind of Magic*, 209.

219 "I still think": Spoto, *A Passion for Life*, 181. John McPhee's recent recollection of his impressions of Taylor in the 1960s is very much worth considering: "In comparison with a great many of the actresses I had met in my years of writing about show business, she was not even half full of herself. She seemed curious, sophisticated, and unpretentious, and compared with people I had known in universities she seemed to have been particularly well educated" ("Elicitation," *The New Yorker*, April 7, 2014).

11. LAST DAYS AT THE VILLA CAPRI

221 "Jimmy a nice boy": Joe Hyams, *James Dean*, 229.

221 "a tiny woman": ibid., 231.

221 "who performed like a gifted angel": Edna Ferber, *A Kind of Magic*, 267.

221 "success poisoning": Hyams, *James Dean*, 231.

221 "impish, compelling, magnetic": Ferber, *A Kind of Magic*, 266.

221 "Honey, this is Hollywood": Hyams, *James Dean*, 224.

222 "Listen to me, you little son of a bitch": Donald Spoto, *Rebel*, 243.

222 "Take it easy driving": [https://www.youtube.com/watch?v=vz3W87uWcx8] Many writers misquote Dean's version of the famous slogan.

222 "I don't know whether he was drunk": Randall Riese, *The Unabridged James Dean*, 493.

222 "unruly behavior": Spoto, *Rebel*, 242.

223 "was in a period": Riese, *The Unabridged James Dean*, 466.

223 "Because everyone here is jealous": Lew Bracker, *Jimmie & Me*, 8.

223 "I'd go right in there": ibid., 9.

223 "half-smile/half-smirk": ibid.

223 "You win some, you lose some": ibid.

224 "I can say unequivocally": ibid., 44.

225 "sinister": Riese, *The Unabridged James Dean*, 218.

225 "I tell him he die": Hyams, *James Dean*, 236.

226 "a turtle with a cockpit": Lee Raskin, *James Dean*, 105.

226 "a ride around the lot": David Dalton, *James Dean*, 277.

226 "You can never drive": Hyams, *James Dean*, 236.

226 "So long, I think": George Stevens, "A Tenderness Lost," *Modern Screen*, January 1956.

226 "If you have any loose ends": Ronald Martinetti, *The James Dean Story*, 167.

226 "James Dean is reading": Leith Adams and ed. Keith Burns, *James Dean*, 137.

227 "oculist, dentist": Raskin, *James Dean*, 102.

227 "in excellent health": ibid., 105.

227 "Jamie's biggest personal trial": Eartha Kitt, *Alone with Me*, 227.

228 "strange emptiness" and subsequent remarks by Kitt: ibid., 228.

228 "something very emotional": Hyams, *James Dean*, 240.

229 "Okay, but it's your funeral": Bracker, *Jimmie & Me*, 126.

230 "*Giant* country": Mercedes McCambridge, *The Quality of Mercy*, 215.

230 "We have James Dean's": ibid., 216.

231 "It really is": Ferber, *A Kind of Magic*, 269.

231 "Dear Edna, it seems": Julie Gilbert, *Ferber: Edna Ferber and Her Circle*, 9.

231 "That figures": Van Holley, *James Dean*, 277.

231 "It somehow was what": ibid.

231 "imminent": ibid.

231 "it's a little like": Patrick McGilligan, *Nicholas Ray*, 316.

232 "My life was confused and disoriented": Dennis Hopper, "Introduction" in *James Dean*, Leith Adams and ed. Keith Burns, 11.

232 "What I cried at": Riese, *The Unabridged James Dean*, 513.

232 "I was jealous of him": Phyllis Gates and Bob Thomas, *My Husband, Rock Hudson*, 69.

232 "He would not have lasted": Robert Hofler, *The Man Who Invented Rock Hudson*, 321.

232 "Dean died at just": Martinetti, *The James Dean Story*, xi.

233 "For all I knew": Dennis Stock, *James Dean Revisited*, 137.

233 "Oh yes, you're the insurance man": Bracker, *Jimmie & Me*, 137.

12. FANFARE

234 "Jimmy Dean Is Not": Randall Riese, *The Unabridged James Dean*, 343.

234 "Jimmy Dean Fights Back": ibid., 346.

234 "Elvis Hears from": ibid., 347.

235 "It's absolutely weird": Wes D. Gehring, *James Dean*, 252.

235 "I don't know how": GSP, 53-f.661.

235 "I spent six hours today": George Stevens, "A Tenderness Lost," *Modern Screen*, January 1956.

235 "There was a poetic presence": ibid.

235 "He wasn't always a joy": Paul Alexander, *Boulevard of Broken Dreams*, 277.

236 "was *too proud* to take a drink": Dalton, *James Dean*, 304.

236 "I want height and I want": Philip K. Scheuer, "A Town Called Hollywood: Stevens Finds Big Scopes Restrict His Film Editing," *Los Angeles Times*, September 18, 1955.

236 "I became impatient": Jason Fraley, "Giant 1956," August 13, 2013, available at http://thefilmspectrum.com/?p=18730.

236 "Dad, you have a great picture": ibid. Others in the film industry were keenly aware of Stevens's meticulous attention to editing. Joe Mankiewicz, for example, the producer of *Woman of the Year*, said of Stevens, "After the actors and the technicians were gone, there was nothing left but George and his film" (ibid.).

237 "the end of the first act": ed. Paul Cronin, *George Stevens: Interviews*, 102.

237 "In the final cut": Chuck Cochard to George Stevens, June 29, 1956; GSP, 53-f.662.

237 "our oil people": John O'Melveny to Henry Ginsberg, July 10, 1955; GSP, 52-f.653. The oil-depletion allowance was almost sacred in Texas, according to Stanley Marcus (of Neiman Marcus), who wrote in his memoir, *Minding the Store* (1974), "The fact that Kennedy was a Catholic was not discussed, but worse than being a papist, he was suspected of being against the oil depletion allowance, which was a cardinal sin in the petroleum and country clubs of the state" (179).

237 "do irreparable harm": ibid. Jake L. Hamon to Giant Productions.

237 "Warner had exhibitors": Myron Meisel, " '*Giant*' Reawakens," *Film Journal International*, 2013.

237 "it was important only": Trevor Willsmer, *George Stevens' Giant*, 71.

238 "oil and gas millionaires": Edna Ferber to George Stevens, December 7, 1954; GSP, 51-f.614.

238 "excellent structure design": ed. Cronin, *George Stevens: Interviews*, 102.

238 "The reflective film": Harold Hutchings, "Stevens Gives His Appraisal of Jim Dean," *Chicago Sunday Tribune*, October 31, 1956.

238–239 "The big stars": William J. Mann, *How to Be a Movie Star*, 171.

239 "were thrashing against the barriers": Carroll Baker, *Baby Doll*, 169.

239 "Stop! Stop!": ibid.

240 "shut up": ibid., 171.

240 "I remember when you": *Memories of Giant* (documentary, 1998).

240 "an act of": Joanne L. Yeck, " '*Giant*': Wild Success Outraged Texas," *Senior*, March 1997.

240 "as intimate as a letter": ibid.

241 "James Dean's talent": George Christian, review of *Giant*, *Houston Press*, October 26, 1956.

241 "three hours and twenty minutes": "*Giant (Géant)*," ed. Wheeler Winston Dixon, *The Early Film Criticism of François Truffaut*, 85.

241 "a small, successfully done *Giant*": ibid., 87.

241 "Minks dragging minks": Willsmer, *George Stevens' Giant*, 70. An internal Warner Bros. report on February 23, 1957, detailed tremendous box-office results in Texas cities and small towns, including Marfa: "This is almost every one in the town seeing the picture"; GSP, 53 f.667.

241 "powerful indictment": Fred Hift, "Giant," *Variety*, October 10, 1956.

242 "state religion": Kirby F. Warnock, "*Giant* and That Texas State of Mind," *D Magazine*, September 1996.

242 "Why the quest for money, for great wealth?": This and the subsequent quotes are from Glenn McCarthy's interview with Mike Wallace. See www.hrc.utexas.edu /collections/film/holdings/wallace.

244 "Did she first state": For these exchanges with the Senate investigative committee, see Ann Shapiro, "When Edna Ferber Was Accused of Communist Propaganda," *Studies in American Jewish Literature* 27 (2008): 16–22. Ida Mercedes Muse Darden, a staunch conservative Texas author, also attacked Ferber's novel for purveying Communist propaganda. Darden objected particularly to Ferber's portrayal of children who disavowed their parents' wealth and denigrated their fathers by marrying beneath them. See George N. Green, "Darden, Ida Mercedes Muse," *Handbook of Texas Online*, available at https://tshaonline.org/handbook/online/articles/fda59.

245 "would-be Führer": Edna Ferber, *A Kind of Magic*, 301.

245 "I wanted to show": George Fuermann, *Reluctant Empire*, 85.

246 "By 2 A.M.": ibid.

246 "They were noisy": Mercedes McCambridge, *The Two of Us*, 25.

246 "Things didn't have to be": ibid.

247 "Would Appreciate Article": Alistair Cooke, *Letter from America*, 127.

247 "Texas was to have": Ferber, *A Kind of Magic*, 308.

247 "attitude of insularity": ibid.

248 "Israel was a sort": ibid.

13. META-MARFASIS

249 "the fanciest hay barn": *New York Times,* September 4, 1955.

250 "We will have a better idea": Susan King, "George Stevens Jr. and His 'Giant' Undertaking," *Los Angeles Times,* September 15, 1996.

251 "The Far Side of Paradise": Andrew Sarris, *The American Cinema,* 83.

251 "George Stevens was a minor director with": ibid., 110.

251 "The technique of": ibid., 111.

252 "The 'auteur' concept": ed. Paul Cronin, *George Stevens: Interviews,* x.

252 "George Stevens": ed. Gerald Peary, *John Ford: Interviews,* 149.

252 "We admire Stevens today": "George Stevens, Jr.," *Conservations with the Great Moviemakers of Hollywood's Golden Age,* 220.

252 "The title embarrassed us": Joe Hyams, " 'Giant' a Film Story of Small Things," *New York Herald Tribune,* July 31, 1956.

253 "simply this story of what happens": Bruce Petri, *A Theory of American Film,* 180–81.

253 "an intimate epic": Stephen Farber, commentary on *Giant* DVD (1996).

253 "In all of movie history": Richard Schickel, "A Movie Whose Ambitions Were as Big as All Outdoors," *New York Times,* May 25, 2003.

253 "It's a freak": Rebecca Solnit, "Giantess," *Harper's,* September 2016.

254 "The shift is not just from cows to crude": ibid., 7.

254 "More than anyone else": Kevin Thomas, " 'Giant' Doesn't Quite Live up to Its Legend," *Los Angeles Times,* September 27, 1996.

255 "Dean's ghost never stopped": James Franco, "New Rebel," in *Straight James/Gay James,* 29.

255 "The teenagers found it hard": John Dos Passos, "The Sinister Adolescents," in *Midcentury,* 486.

255 "He [Dean] took his envy": *The James Dean Story* (documentary, 1957).

255 "the late Mr. Dean's 'masterpiece' ": Hyams, " 'Giant' a Film Story of Small Things."

258 "Xanadu of Minimalism": Peter Schjeldahl, "Light in Juddland," *The New Yorker,* September 25, 2000.

258 "the twentieth century's fixations": ibid., 99.

258 "the land was pretty empty": ed. Marianne Stockebrand, *Chinati,* 277.

258 "I chose the town of Marfa": ibid., 278.

259 "*Giant* is important to Marfa": Michael Hoinski, "On the Shoulders of Giants," *Texas Monthly,* February 2016.

260 "West Texas is so intense": Pam LeBlanc, "Pedaling for Education," *Austin American-Statesman,* May 2, 2016.

BIBLIOGRAPHY

❦

BOOKS

Adams, Leith, and Keith Burns, ed. *James Dean: Behind the Lines*. New York: Carol Publication Group, 1990.

Alexander, Paul. *Boulevard of Broken Dreams: The Life, Times, and Legend of James Dean*. New York: Plume, 1997.

Ambrose, Stephen. *Eisenhower*. Vol 1. New York: Simon & Schuster, 1983.

Bainbridge, John. *The Super-Americans: A Picture of Life in the United States, as Brought into Focus, Bigger Than Life, in the Land of the Millionaires—Texas*. New York: Holt, Rinehart and Winston, 1961.

Baker, Carroll. *Baby Doll: An Autobiography*. New York: Arbor House, 1983.

Baker, J. I. *James Dean: A Rebel's Life in Pictures*. Des Moines, IA: Life Books, 2014.

Barrett, Ross, and Daniel Worden, eds. *Oil Culture*. Minneapolis: University of Minnesota Press, 2014.

Bast, William. *James Dean: A Biography*. New York: Ballantine Books, 1956.

———. *Surviving James Dean*. Fort Lee, NJ: Barricade Books, 2006.

Baxter, Monique James. "*Giant* Helps America Recognize the Cost of Discrimination: A Lesson of World War II." In *Hollywood's West*, edited by Peter Rollins and John E. O'Connor. Lexington: University of Kentucky, 2005.

Beath, Warren, with Paula Wheeldon. *James Dean in Death: A Popular Encyclopedia of a Celebrity Phenomenon*. Jefferson, NC: McFarland & Company, 2005.

Bego, Mark. *Rock Hudson: Public and Private, An Unauthorized Biography*. New York: New American Library, 1986.

Behlmer, Rudy, ed. *Inside Warner Bros. (1935–1951)*. New York: Simon & Schuster, 1985.

Biskind, Peter. *Easy Riders, Raging Bulls: How the Sex-Drugs-and-Rock 'n Roll Generation Saved Hollywood*. New York: Simon & Schuster, 1988.

————. *Seeing Is Believing: How Hollywood Taught Us to Stop Worrying and Love the Fifties*. New York: Pantheon Books, 1983.

————. *Star: How Warren Beatty Seduced America*. New York: Simon & Schuster, 2011.

Bonds, Laura and Shawn Conners, eds. *Bon Bons Bourbon and Bon Mots: Stories from the Algonquin Round Table*. El Paso, TX: Traveling Press, 2010.

Bosworth, Patricia. *Marlon Brando*. New York: Viking Penguin, 2001.

————. *Montgomery Clift: A Biography*. New York: Harcourt Brace Jovanovich, 1978.

Bracker, Lew. *Jimmie & Me: A Personal Memoir of a Great Friendship*. Santa Fe: Fulcorte Press, 2013.

Brando, Marlon, with Robert Lindsey. *Songs My Mother Taught Me*. New York: Random House, 1994.

Burrough, Bryan. *The Big Rich: The Rise and Fall of the Greatest Texas Oil Fortunes*. New York: Penguin, 2009.

Buscombe, Edward. "*Giant*." In *1001 Movies You Must See Before You Die*, edited by Steven Jay Schneider. Hauppage, NY: Barron's, 2015.

Capra, Frank. *The Name Above the Title: An Autobiography*. New York: Vintage, 1985.

Christopher, James. *Elizabeth Taylor: A Biography*. Bath, England: Chivers Press, 2000.

Cohen, Julie. "*Giant*." In *Latinas in the United States: A Historical Encyclopedia*, vol. 1, edited by Vicki L. Ruiz and Virginia Sanchez Korrol. Bloomington: Indiana University Press, 2006.

Cooke, Alistair. *Letter from America: 1946–2004*. New York: Penguin, 2004.

Cronin, Paul, ed. *George Stevens: Interviews*. Jackson: University Press of Mississippi, 2004.

Dalton, David. *James Dean: American Icon*. New York: St. Martin's Press, 1984.

————. *James Dean: The Mutant King*. San Francisco: Straight Arrow Books, 1974.

Dawson, Nick, ed. *Dennis Hopper: Interviews*. Jackson: University Press of Mississippi, 2012.

De La Hoz, Cindy. *Elizabeth Taylor: A Shining Legacy on Film*. Philadelphia: Running Press, 2012.

Devillers, Marceau. *James Dean*. Translated by Jonathan Marks. London: Sidgwick & Jackson, 1987.

Dixon, Wheeler Winston, ed. *The Early Film Criticism of François Truffaut*. Bloomington: Indiana University Press, 1993.

Dowdy, Andrew. *The Films of the Fifties: The American State of Mind*. New York: William Morrow, 1975.

Edwards, Anne. *A Remarkable Woman: A Biography of Katharine Hepburn*. New York: William Morrow, 1985.

Eisenschitz, Bernard. *Nicholas Ray: An American Journey*. Translated by Tom Milne. Minneapolis: University of Minnesota Press, 1993.

Eyman, Scott. *Print the Legend: The Life and Times of John Ford*. New York: Simon & Schuster, 1999.

Fehrenbach, T. R. *Lone Star: A History of Texas and the Texans*. New York: Macmillan, 1968.

Ferber, Edna. *A Kind of Magic.* London: Victor Gollancz, 1963.

———. *Giant.* Garden City, NY: Doubleday & Company, 1952.

———. *A Peculiar Treasure.* New York: Doubleday, Doran & Company, 1939.

Feurmann, George. *Houston: Land of the Big Rich.* Garden City, NY: Doubleday & Company, 1951.

———. *Reluctant Empire: The Mind of Texas.* Garden City, NY: Doubleday & Company, 1957.

Folsom, Tom. *Hopper: A Journey into the American Dream.* New York: HarperCollins, 2013.

Frankel, Glenn. *The Searchers: The Making of an American Legend.* New York: Bloomsbury, 2013.

Frascella, Lawrence, and Al Weisel. *Live Fast, Die Young: The Wild Ride of Making Rebel Without a Cause.* New York: Simon & Schuster, 2005.

Fuchs, Wolfgang J. *James Dean: Footsteps of a Giant.* Translated by Hugh Beyer. Berlin: TACO, 1986.

Gates, Phyllis, and Bob Thomas. *My Husband, Rock Hudson: The Real Story of Rock Hudson's Marriage to Phyllis Gates.* New York: Doubleday, 1987.

Gehring, Wes D. *James Dean: Rebel with a Cause.* Indianapolis: Indiana Historical Society Press, 2005.

Geraghty, Christine. *Now a Major Motion Picture: Film Adaptations of Literature and Drama.* Lanham, MD: Rowman & Littlefield, 2008.

Gilbert, Julie. *Ferber: Edna Ferber and Her Circle, a Biography.* New York: Applause Books, 1999.

Gilmore, John. *Laid Bare: A Memoir of Wrecked Lives and the Hollywood Death Trip.* Los Angeles: Amok Books, 1997.

———. *Live Fast—Die Young: Remembering the Short Life of James Dean.* New York: Thunder's Mouth Press, 1997.

———. *The Real James Dean.* New York: Pyramid Books, 1975.

González, John Morán. *Border Renaissance: The Texas Centennial and the Emergence of Mexican American Literature.* Austin: University of Texas Press, 2009.

Goodwyn, Frank. *Lone-Star Land: Twentieth-Century Texas in Perspective.* New York: Alfred A. Knopf, 1955.

Graham, Don. *Cowboys & Cadillacs: How Hollywood Looks at Texas.* Austin: Texas Monthly Press, 1983.

———. Introduction to *The Gay Place,* by Billy Lee Brammer. Austin: University of Texas Press, 1995.

———. *Giant Country: Essays on Texas.* Fort Worth: TCU Press, 1998.

———. *Kings of Texas: The 150-Year Saga of an American Ranching Empire.* Hoboken, NJ: John Wiley & Sons, 2003.

Greenberg, Keith Elliot. *Too Fast to Live, Too Young to Die: James Dean's Final Hours.* Milwaukee: Applause Books, 2015.

Greene, Graham. *The Lawless Roads.* New York: Viking, 1982. Originally published in 1939 under the title *Another Mexico.*

Grey, Zane. *The Lone Star Ranger.* Roslyn, NY: Walter J. Black, 1915.

———. *West of the Pecos.* Roslyn, NY: Walter J. Black, 1937.

Groves, Helen Kleberg, with Bill Benson. *Bob & Helen Kleberg of King Ranch.* Houston: Bright Sky Press, 2004.

Gunther, John. *Inside U.S.A.* New York: New Press, 1997.

Halberstam, David. *The Fifties.* New York: Villard Books, 1993.

Hall, William. *James Dean.* Guernsey, Channel Islands: Sutton Publishing, 1999.

Halliday, Jon. *Sirk on Sirk: Interviews with Jon Halliday.* New York: Viking, 1972.

Harrigan, Stephen. *A Natural State: Essays on Texas.* Austin: University of Texas Press, 1988.

Harris, Mark. *Five Came Back: A Story of Hollywood and the Second World War.* New York: Penguin, 2014.

Hay, James. "Shamrock: Houston's Green Promise." In *Cinema and the City: Film and Urban Societies in a Global Context,* edited by Mark Shiel and Tony Fitzmaurice. Oxford: Blackwell Publishers, 2001.

Hendler, June. *Best Sellers and Their Film Adaptations in Postwar America.* New York: Peter Lang, 2001.

Herman, Jan. *A Talent for Trouble: The Life of Hollywood's Most Acclaimed Director, William Wyler.* New York: G. P. Putnam's Sons, 1996.

Herndon, Venable. *James Dean: A Short Life.* New York: New American Library, 1974.

Heymann, C. David. *Liz: An Intimate Biography of Elizabeth Taylor.* New York: Atria, 2011.

Hinkle, Robert, with Mike Farris. *Call Me Lucky: A Texan in Hollywood.* Norman: University of Oklahoma Press, 2009.

Hofler, Robert. *The Man Who Invented Rock Hudson: The Pretty Boys and Dirty Deals of Henry Willson.* New York: Carroll & Graf, 2005.

Hofstede, David. *James Dean: A Bio-Bibliography.* Westport, CT: Greenwood Press, 1996.

Holley, Van. *James Dean: The Biography.* New York: St. Martin's Press, 1995.

Hopper, Hedda, and James Brough. *The Whole Truth and Nothing But.* Garden City, NY: Doubleday & Company, 1963.

Hoskyns, Barney. *James Dean: Shooting Star.* London: Bloomsbury, 1989.

House, Boyce. *Texas Laughs.* Dallas: Naylor, 1950.

Howlett, John. *James Dean: A Biography.* London: Plexus, 2005.

Hudson, Rock, and Sara Davidson. *Rock Hudson: His Story.* New York: William Morrow, 1986.

Humphreys, Joseph, ed. *Jimmy Dean on Jimmy Dean.* London: Plexus, 1990.

Hunter, Tab, with Eddie Muller. *Tab Hunter Confidential: The Making of a Movie Star.* Chapel Hill, NC: Algonquin Books, 2006.

Hyams, Joe, with Jay Hyams. *James Dean: Little Boy Lost.* New York: Warner Books, 1992.

Jacobs, Timothy. *James Dean.* Lombard, IL: Mallard Press, 1991.

Jeffers, H. Paul. *Sal Mineo: His Life, Murder, and Mystery.* New York: Carroll & Graf, 2000.

Johnson, Paul. *Eisenhower: A Life*. New York: Viking, 2014.

Kaplowitz, Craig. *LULAC, Mexican Americans, and National Policy*. College Station: Texas A&M University Press, 2005.

Kazan, Elia. *A Life*. New York: Alfred A. Knopf, 1988.

———. *The Selected Letters of Elia Kazan*. Edited by Albert J. Devlin, with Marlene J. Devlin. New York: Alfred A. Knopf, 2014.

Kelley, Kitty. *Elizabeth Taylor: The Last Star*. New York: Simon & Schuster, 1981.

Kitt, Eartha. *Alone with Me: A New Autobiography*. Chicago: Henry Regnery, 1976.

Lamour, Dorothy. *My Side of the Road*, as told to Dick McInnes. Englewood Cliffs, NJ: Prentice-Hall, 1980.

Leaming, Barbara. *Orson Welles: A Biography*. New York: Viking, 1985.

Levene, Bruce, ed. *James Dean in Mendocino: The Filming of East of Eden*. Mendocino, CA: Pacific Transcriptions, 1994.

Levy, Shawn. *Paul Newman: A Life*. New York: Three Rivers Press, 2009.

Limón, José E. *American Encounters: Greater Mexico, the United States, and the Erotics of Culture*. Boston: Beacon Press, 1998.

Linet, Beverly. *Ladd: The Life, the Legend, the Legacy of Alan Ladd*. New York: Arbor House, 1979.

Lord, M. G. *The Accidental Feminist: How Elizabeth Taylor Raised Our Consciousness and We Were Too Distracted by Her Beauty to Notice*. New York: Walker, 2012.

Maddox, Brenda. *Who's Afraid of Elizabeth Taylor?* New York: M. Evans, 1977.

Mann, William J. *How to Be a Movie Star: Elizabeth Taylor in Hollywood*. Boston: Houghton Mifflin, 2009.

Manso, Peter. *Brando: The Biography*. New York: Hyperion, 1994.

Marcos, Stanley. *Minding the Store: A Memoir*. New York: New American Library, 1974.

Marill, Alvin H. *Katharine Hepburn*. New York: Galahad Books, 1973.

Martinetti, Ronald. *The James Dean Story: A Myth-Shattering Biography of an Icon*. New York: Birch Lane Press, 1995.

Massey, Raymond. *A Hundred Different Lives: An Autobiography*. Boston: Little, Brown, 1979.

McBride, Joseph. *Searching for John Ford: A Life*. New York: St. Martin's Press, 2001.

McCambridge, Mercedes. *The Quality of Mercy: An Autobiography*. New York: Times Books, 1981.

———. *The Two of Us*. London: Peter Davies, 1960.

McDanield, H. F., and N. A. Taylor. *The Coming Empire; or, Two Thousand Miles in Texas on Horseback*. New York: A. S. Barnes, 1878.

McGilligan, Patrick. *Nicholas Ray: The Glorious Failure of an American Director*. New York: HarperCollins, 2011.

McGraw, Eliza. *Edna Ferber's America*. Baton Rouge: Louisiana State University Press, 2013.

McWilliams, Carey. *North from Mexico: The Spanish-Speaking People of the United States*. Philadelphia: J. B. Lippincott, 1948.

Meade, Marion. *Bobbed Hair and Bathtub Gin: Writers Running Wild in the Twenties.* Orlando, FL: Harcourt, 2004.

Michaud, Michael Gregg. *Sal: A Biography.* New York: Crown, 2010.

Miller, Ann, with Norma Lee Browning. *Miller's High Life.* Garden City, NY: Doubleday & Company, 1972.

Mizruchi, Susan L. *Brando's Smile: His Life, Thought, and Work.* New York: W. W. Norton, 2014.

Moffat, Ivan. *The Ivan Moffat File: Life Among the Beautiful and Damned in London, Paris, New York, and Hollywood.* Edited by Gavin Lambert. New York: Pantheon Books, 2004.

Montejano, David. *Anglos and Mexicans in the Making of Texas, 1836–1986.* Austin: University of Texas Press, 1987.

Morella, Joe, and Edward Z. Epstein. *Rebels: The Rebel Hero in Films.* New York: Citadel Press, 1971.

Moss, Marilyn Ann. *Giant: George Stevens, a Life on Film.* Milwaukee: University of Wisconsin Press, 2004.

Nelson, Nancy. *Evenings with Cary Grant: Recollections in His Own Words and by Those Who Knew Him Best.* New York: Applause Books, 2012.

Oakley, J. Ronald. *God's Country: America in the Fifties.* New York: Dembner Books, 1986.

O'Connor, Louise S., and Cecilia Thompson. *Marfa.* Charleston, SC: Arcadia, 2009.

Oppenheimer, Jerry, and Jack Vitek. *Idol: The True Story of an American Film Hero.* New York: Villard Books, 1986.

Parker, John. *Five for Hollywood.* New York: Carol Publishing Group, 1991.

Parrish, Robert. *Growing up in Hollywood.* New York: Harcourt Brace Jovanovich, 1976.

Peary, Gerald, ed. *John Ford: Interviews.* Jackson: University Press of Mississippi, 2001.

Pérez-Torres, Rafael. *Mestizaje: Critical Uses of Race in Chicano Culture.* Minneapolis: University of Minnesota Press, 2006.

Perry, George. *James Dean.* New York: DK Publishing, 2005.

Perry, George Sessions. *Texas: A World in Itself.* Gretna, LA: Pelican, 1975.

Petersen, Anne Helen. *Scandals of Classic Hollywood: Sex, Deviance, and Drama from the Golden Age of Hollywood Cinema.* New York: Plume, 2014.

Petri, Bruce. *A Theory of American Film: The Films and Techniques of George Stevens.* New York: Garland, 1987.

Phillips, Gene D. *The Movie Makers: Artists in an Industry.* Chicago: Burnham, 1973.

Pilkington, Tom. *State of Mind: Texas Literature and Culture.* College Station: Texas A&M University Press, 1998.

Raskin, Lee. *James Dean: At Speed.* Phoenix: David Bull, 2005.

Rathgeb, Douglas L. *The Making of Rebel Without a Cause.* Jefferson, NC: McFarland, 2004.

Rees, Robert R. *James Dean's Trail: One Fan's Journey.* Katy, TX: Empire, 1995.

Richie, Donald. *George Stevens: An American Romantic*. New York: Museum of Modern Art, 1970.

Riese, Randall. *The Unabridged James Dean: His Life and Legacy from A to Z*. Chicago: Contemporary Books, 1991.

Rodriguez, Elena. *Dennis Hopper: A Madness to His Method*. New York: St. Martin's Press, 1988.

Roth, Beulah. *James Dean*. Corte Madera, CA: Pomegranate Artbooks, 1983.

Royce, Brenda Scott. *Rock Hudson: A Bio-Bibliography*. Westport, CT: Greenwood Press, 1995.

Sarris, Andrew. *The American Cinema: Directors and Directions 1929–1968*. New York: E. P. Dutton, 1968.

Schatt, Roy. *James Dean: A Portrait*. New York: Delilah Books, 1983.

Schatz, Tom. *The Genius of the System: Hollywood Filmmaking in the Studio Era*. New York: Pantheon Books, 1988.

Schickel, Richard. *The Men Who Made the Movies*. New York: Atheneum, 1975.

Schuth, H. Wayne. "*Giant.*" In *International Dictionary of Films and Filmmakers*, 3rd ed., edited by Nicolet V. Elvert and Aruna Vasudelan. Detroit: St. James Press, 1997.

Scott, Toni Lee. *A Kind of Loving*. Edited by Curt Gentry. New York: World Publishing Company, 1970.

Seydor, Paul. *Peckinpah: The Western Films—A Reconsideration*. Urbana: University of Illinois Press, 1997.

Shaughnessy, Mary Rose. *Women and Success in American Society in the Works of Edna Ferber*. New York: Gordon Press, 1977.

Sheppard, Dick. *Elizabeth: The Life and Career of Elizabeth Taylor*. New York: Doubleday & Company, 1974.

Sheridan, Liz. *Dizzy & Jimmy: My Life with James Dean*. New York: Regan Books, 2000.

Smyth, J. E. *Edna Ferber's Hollywood: American Fictions of Gender, Race, and History*. Austin: University of Texas Press, 2010.

Spoto, Donald. *A Passion for Life: The Biography of Elizabeth Taylor*. New York: HarperCollins, 1995.

———. *Rebel: The Life and Legend of James Dean*. New York: HarperCollins, 1996.

Spratt, John Stricklin. *The Road to Spindletop: Economic Change in Texas, 1875–1901*. Austin: University of Texas Press, 1955.

Springer, Claudia. *James Dean Transfigured: The Many Faces of Rebel Iconography*. Austin: University of Texas Press, 2007.

Steinbeck, John. *Travels with Charley: In Search of America*. New York: Penguin, 1997.

Stern, Michael. *Douglas Sirk*. Boston: Twayne, 1979.

Stevens, George, Jr. *Conversations with the Great Moviemakers of Hollywood's Golden Age*. New York: Alfred A. Knopf, 2006.

Stock, Dennis. *James Dean Revisited*. New York: Penguin, 1978.

Stockebrand, Marianne, ed. *Chinati: The Vision of Donald Judd.* New Haven: Yale University Press, 2010.

Tanitch, Robert. *The Unknown James Dean.* London: Betsford, 1997.

Taraborrelli, J. Randy. *Elizabeth.* New York: Rose Books, 2006.

Taylor, Elizabeth. *Elizabeth Takes Off.* New York: G. P. Putnam's Sons, 1988.

———. *Elizabeth Taylor: An Informal Memoir.* New York: Harper & Row, 1965.

Texas Almanac—1945–1946. Dallas: A. H. Belo, 1945.

Texas Almanac—1947–1948. Dallas: A. H. Belo, 1947.

Thomas, Bob. *The Clown Prince of Hollywood: The Antic Life and Times of Jack L. Warner.* New York: McGraw-Hill, 1990.

———. *Golden Boy: The Untold Story of William Holden.* New York: Berkley Press, 1984.

Thompson, Helen. *Marfa Modern: Artistic Interiors of the West Texas High Desert.* New York: Monacelli Press, 2016.

Thomson, David. *The New Biographical Dictionary of Film*, 6th ed. New York: Alfred A. Knopf, 2014.

Vagg, Stephen. *Rod Taylor: An Aussie in Hollywood.* Duncan, OK: BearMania Media, 2010.

Vinciguerra, Thomas. *Cast of Characters: Wolcott Gibbs, E. B. White, James Thurber, and the Golden Age of The New Yorker.* New York: W. W. Norton, 2016.

Vineberg, Steve. *Method Actors: Three Generations of an American Acting Style.* New York: Macmillan, 1991.

Wagner, Robert, with Scott Eyman. *You Must Remember This: Life and Style in Hollywood's Golden Age.* New York: Viking, 2014.

Walker, Alexander. *Elizabeth: The Life of Elizabeth Taylor.* New York: Grove Press, 1997.

Warner, Jack L., with Dean Jennings. *My First Hundred Years in Hollywood.* New York: Random House, 1964.

Waterbury, Ruth, with Gene Arceri. *Elizabeth Taylor: Her Life, Her Loves, Her Future.* New York: Bantam, 1964.

Wilding, Michael. *Apple Sauce: The Story of My Life.* London: George Allen & Uwin, 1982.

Willsmer, Trevor. *George Stevens' Giant: The Making of an Epic Motion Picture.* Collector's Edition. Los Angeles: Warner Bros., 1996.

Winkler, Peter L. *Dennis Hopper: The Wild Ride of a Hollywood Rebel.* Fort Lee, NJ: Barricade Books, 2011.

———, ed. *The Real James Dean: Intimate Memories from Those Who Knew Him Best.* Chicago: Chicago Review Press, 2016.

Winter, Nevin O. *Texas: The Marvellous—The State of the Six Flags.* Garden City, NY: Garden City Publishing Co., 1936.

Woolley, Bryan. *Mythic Texas: Essays on the State and Its People.* Plano, TX: Republic of Texas Press, 2000.

Zinnemann, Fred. *A Life in the Movies.* New York: Charles Scribner's Sons, 1992.

Zuckoff, Mitchell. *Robert Altman: The Oral Biography.* New York: Alfred A. Knopf, 2009.

ARTICLES AND RADIO BROADCASTS

Agresta, Michael. "Miracle in the Desert." *Texas Monthly,* July 2016.

"A Legacy of Division in Marfa's Cemeteries." KRTS 93.5 FM Marfa, October 17, 2014.

Allsup, Carl. "Felix Longoria Affair." https://tshaonline.org/handbook/online/articles /vef01.

———. "Hernández v. Texas." www.tshaonline.org./handbook/online/articles/jrh01.

"An Unofficial Film Fest Event, 'Return to Giant' Screens at Hotel Paisano." *Big Bend Sentinel,* July 14, 2016.

Archerd, Army. "Just for Variety." *Variety,* May 19, 1955.

Ayala, Elaine. "Movie 'Giant' Exposed Ugliness." *Houston Chronicle,* February 24, 2015.

Babout, Lee. "Troubling White Benevolence: Four Takes on a Scene from *Giant.*" *Melus* 36, no. 3 (Fall 2011).

Barkham, John. "Where It's the Biggest and Bestest." *New York Times Book Review,* September 28, 1952.

Barnes, Jeanne. "Edna Ferber's 'Big' Indictment of Texas Really Too True in Spots." *San Antonio Express,* September 28, 1952.

Barnes, Michael. "Life and Death on the Border 100 Years Ago." *Austin American-Statesman,* February 22, 2016.

Barron, David. " 'Children of Giant' Examines Iconic Film as Backdrop of Changing Culture." *Houston Chronicle,* April 16, 2015.

B.B. "On Rereading 'Giant'—'Enormous,' But 'Incredible.' " *Texas Observer,* July 4, 1955.

Bedell, W. D. "Texas Bigness Seen with a Bitterness." *Houston Post,* September 28, 1952.

Bennett, Lee. "Marfa," *Handbook of Texas Online.* https://tshaonline.org/handbook /online/articles/hjm04.

"Big Time in Houston." *Fortune,* May 1949.

Blakely, Sam. " 'The Giant.' " *Texas Sun Enterprise* (Beaumont), October 12, 1952.

Bloom, Lynn. "Home Fashions from New Films: Two Distinctive Houses Add Meaning to 'Giant.' " *Retailing Daily,* October 11, 1956.

Brammer, Bill. "A Circus Breaks Down on the Prairie." *Texas Observer,* July 4, 1955.

———. "Unworldly Little Marfa." *Texas Observer,* June 27, 1955.

Brooks, Elston. "Cast of 'Giant' Getting Real Workout in Filming of Movie in Marfa Area." *Fort Worth Star-Telegram,* June 19, 1955.

———. "Humanizing of Ferber Novel 'Giant' Stressed by Producer on Location." *Fort Worth Star-Telegram,* June 18, 1955.

———. "James Dean Gloomed His Way—Like Brando." *Fort Worth Star-Telegram,* October 2, 1955.

———. "James Dean Shoots Rabbits Along Highway." *Fort-Worth Star-Telegram,* June 17, 1955.

———. "Jane Withers Happy to Be Working Again." *Fort-Worth Star-Telegram,* June 18, 1955.

————. "Marfa Having Boom with Film Production." *Fort Worth Star-Telegram*, June 17, 1955.

————. "2 Top Supporting Stars Give 'Giant' Big Boost." *Fort Worth Star-Telegram*, June 20, 1955.

Broyles, Willam, Jr. "The Last Empire." *Texas Monthly*, October 1980.

Burnett, John. "On Location: 50 Years of Movie Magic in Marfa, Texas." NPR, *All Things Considered*, July 15, 2011. www.npr.org/2011/07/15/138163048/on-location -50-years-of-movie-magic-in-marfa-texas.

Bustin, John. "Tiny Marfa Poses 'Giant' Hardships." *Austin American-Statesman*, June 26, 1955.

Butcher, Fanny. "Edna Ferber's 'Texians' Made into Literary Giant." *Chicago Sun Tribune*, September 28, 1952.

Butcher, Sterry, "Something in the Air." *Texas Monthly*, February 2016.

Byrne, Joseph E. " 'Giant': Divisions in the Heart of Texas." https://engl245umd .wordpress.com/2013/09/23/giant-divisions-in-the-heart-of-texas/.

Calhoun, Claudia. "Where Houston Met Hollywood: *Giant*, Glenn McCarthy, and the Construction of a Modern City." *Journal of Urban History*. https://www.academia .edu/11975168/Where_Houston_Met_Hollywood_Giant_Glenn_McCarthy_and _the_Construction_of_a_Modern_City_Journal_of_Urban_History_.

"Californians to Ship House to Texas (Howzat!) Film Site." *Mirror and Daily News* (Los Angeles), April 11, 1955.

Calvo, Dana. "A 'Giant' Effort to Keep a Legacy Alive." *Los Angeles Times*, June 9, 2003.

Carrigan, William D., and Clive Webb. "When Americans Lynched Mexicans." *New York Times*, February 20, 2015.

Castillo, Juan. "How '50s James Dean Movie Dared Show Racism Against Mexican Americans." http://nbcnews.com/news/latino/how-50s-james-dean-movie-dared -show-racism-against-mexican-n341501.

"Chaney Chosen for Part in 'The Giant.' " *Big Bend Sentinel*, June 9, 1955.

Chapman, Art. "*Giant* Fans Trek to Marfa Celebration." *Fort Worth Star-Telegram*, May 28, 1995.

"Chill Wills Knows How to Rough It." *Big Bend Sentinel*, June 30, 1955.

"Chill Wills Sees Cubs Drubbed by Kilowatt Kids." *Big Bend Sentinel*, June 23, 1955.

Christian, George. Review of *Giant*. *Houston Press*, October 26, 1956.

Cogburn, Anne. "The Natives Are Mad: Edna Ferber's 'Giant' Story of Texas' Growth." *Atlanta Journal*, 1952.

Cohen, Jason. "Fightin' Words: Larry McMurtry v. the People of Marfa." *Texas Monthly*, April 17, 2012. www.texasmonthly.com/the-culture/fightin-words-larry-mcmurtry -v-the-people-of-marfa/.

Connolly, Mike. "Rambling Reporter." *Hollywood Reporter*, May 19, 1955.

Connor, Geoff. "Bigger Than Life." thesocietydiaries.com/bigger-than-life/.

Contreras, Russell. "LBJ Linked Latinos, Civil Rights in 1965 'Selma' Speech." *Austin American-Statesman*, March 8, 2015.

Cott, Jonathan. "Elizabeth Taylor: The Lost Interview." *Rolling Stone*, March 29, 2011. www.rollingstone.com/culture/news/elizabeth-taylor-the-lost-interview-20110329.

Crowther, Bosley. "Screen: Fashion Show in Boom Town; Lucy Gallant Wins Texan at Victoria Producing Team Makes Concession to Women." *New York Times*, October 21, 1955.

———. "Screen: Large Subject; the Cast." *New York Times*, October 11, 1956.

Davies, Erin. "The Biggest Ranches: From the Fabled King to the Formidable 06, the Twenty Most Storied Spreads in Texas." *Texas Monthly*, August 1998.

Davis, Steven L. "Mining Dobie: Cormac McCarthy's Debt to J. Frank Dobie in *The Crossing*." *Southwestern American Literature* 38, no. 2 (Spring 2013).

Debruge, Peter. "Film Review: 'Five Came Back.'" *Variety*, April 1, 2017.

Dillin, John. "How Eisenhower Solved Illegal Border Crossings from Mexico." *Christian Science Monitor*, July 6, 2006. www.csmonitor.com/2006/0706/p09s01-coop.html.

"Dizzey Deans Baseball Team Organized Here; Will Play Ft. Stockton." *Big Bend Sentinel*, June 23, 1955.

Dobie, J. Frank. "The Writer and His Region," *Southwest Review* 35, no. 1 (Winter 1950).

Dorian, Bob. "Rock Solid: The Stepping Stones of Mr. Hudson's Career." *American Movie Classics Magazine*, February 2000.

Ealy, Charles. "'Giant': From Mexican-American Viewpoint." *Austin American-Statesman*, April 12, 2015.

Ebert, Roger. *George Stevens: A Filmmaker's Journey* (1984). www.rogerebert.com /reviews/george-stevens-a-filmmakers-journey-1984.

Eder, Bruce. "'Giant': Review Summary." *New York Times*, January 16, 2016.

"Edna Ferber." *New York Herald Tribune Book Review*, October 5, 1952.

"Edna Ferber Brings Shrieks of Anguish from Land of Texas." *Jackson Sun* (Tennessee), November 9, 1952.

"Edna Ferber Denies Film Studios Peek at Her New Novel." *Variety*, May 21, 1952.

"Edward Carpenter Bearden (AM. 1919–1980)." http://daviddike.com/artists/66-artist .html.

"Elizabeth Taylor, Mike Todd Wed in Mexico." *Toledo Blade*, February 3, 1956.

Elliott, Keith. "Marfa 'Swamped' by Film Makers." *San Antonio Express-News*, June 1955.

Ellis, Ryan. "Ryan's Vintage Review: Giant (1956)." https://top100project.files.wordpress .com/2013/03/giant.jpg.

"Empire of Cattle: The King Ranch of Texas." *Fortune*, December 8, 1933.

England, Jim. "Edna Ferber's 'Giant' Is Guidebook, History and Sociology of Texas." *Salt Lake City Tribune*, October 5, 1952.

Erickson, Hal. "Fred Guiol." *New York Times*, December 21, 2014.

Essoe, Gabe. "Elizabeth Taylor Still Has a Chance to Escape from the Obvious." *Films in Review* 11 (August–September 1970).

"Evans" (obituary). *Big Bend Quarterly*, October 29, 2015.

"Ferber's Big Book on Texas Overdoes Even Zealot's Role." *San Angelo Standard*, September 28, 1952.

Fernandez, Manny. "The Texas-Shaped World." *New York Times,* September 29, 2016.

Fitzgerald, Mike. "Noreen Nash: An Interview." www.westernclippings.com/interview /noreennash_interview.shtml.

Fletcher, Joseph. "Vandal of Prada Marfa Installation Pleads Guilty, Will Pay to Restore Piece." *Austin American-Stateman,* November 14, 2014.

Fraley, Jason. "Giant (1956)." Thefilmspectrum.com/?p=18730.

"Fred Guiol" (obituary). *Variety,* May 26, 1964.

Gard, Wayne. " 'Giant.' " *Evening Sun* (Baltimore), October 7, 1952.

" 'Giant.' " *Catholic World,* December 1956.

" 'Giant' Filming Is Completed Here This Week." *Big Bend Sentinel,* July 14, 1955.

" 'Giant,' Mysteries, Westerns Lead Best Sellers at Library." *Big Bend Sentinel,* July 14, 1955.

" 'Giant' (1956) Review." http://felicelog.blogspot.com/2015/04/giant-1956-review.html.

" 'Giant' Rolls Today After Party Sendoff." *Hollywood Reporter,* May 19, 1955.

Gillienson, Lewis, W. "Texas' Forgotten People: A Million and a Half Mexican-Americans Live on Little More Than Hope." *Look,* March 27, 1951.

"Glenn McCarthy: Colorful Oilman." Associated Press (obituary), December 29, 1988.

Gotheim, Christie. "Marfa, TX: A World of Art Way Out West." www.travelmag.com /articles/marfa-a-world-of-art.

Graham, Don. "Deep in the Heart of Texas." *American Movie Classics,* February 2000.

————. "Movie of the Century: *Giant.*" *Texas Monthly,* November 1999.

Green, George N. "Darden, Ida Mercedes Muse." *Handbook of Texas Online.* https:// tshaonline.org/handbook/online/articles/fda59.

Griffith, Albert J. "The Scion, the Senorita, and the Texas Ranch Epic: Hispanic Images in Film." *Bilingual Review* 16 (1991).

Gross, Joe. " 'Hitchcock/Truffaut': An Artist in His Moment." *Austin-American Statesman,* February 26, 2016.

"Growing Up in the Spotlight." *Newsweek,* June 18, 1992.

Hall, Michael. "The Buzz About Marfa Is Just Crazy." *Texas Monthly,* September 2004.

Hall, Mordaunt. "The Screen; The Showman" (review of *A Texas Steer*). *New York Times,* January 2, 1928.

Halwe, Freda. "Ferber's 'Giant' Is Striding Across Plains of West Texas." *Beaumont Enterprise,* July 3, 1955.

Harford, Margaret. "Texans Laud Friendliness of Their Movieland Guests." *Los Angeles Mirror-News,* July 7, 1955.

————. "Texas Cattle Town Booms as Hollywood Invades It." *Los Angeles Mirror-News,* July 6, 1955.

Hartung, Philip T. "The Screen: Lone Star State of Mind." *The Commonweal,* October 26, 1956.

Heineman, Ben W., Jr., and Cristine Russell. "Elizabeth Taylor's Feisty, Feminist Turn in *Giant.*" *The Atlantic,* November 5, 2013.

Herman, Ken. "Count Me Out for This Run to the Border." *Austin American-Statesman*, November 20, 2015.

Hift, Fred. "Giant." *Variety*, October 10, 1956.

Hinojosa, Gilbert. " 'Texan' Myth a 'Giant' Story of Money, Power, and Strength." *San Antonio Express-News*, December 1, 1996.

Hoinski, Michael. "On the Shoulders of Giants." *Texas Monthly*, July 15, 2016.

Hollandsworth, Skip. "The King's Palace." *Texas Monthly*, February 2016.

Hopper, Hedda. "Jane Withers." "Hedda Hopper's Hollywood," syndicated column, April 1, 1956.

"Houston Airport Café Bars India Envoy as Negro." *New York Evening Post*, August 23, 1955.

Houston, Penelope. *"Giant." Sight & Sound* (Winter 1956).

Howe, Mary Burke. "Deep in the Heart of Texas," *America*, October 11, 1952.

Hubler, Richard. "How to Create a Movie Star." *The Saturday Evening Post*, September 27, 1952.

Hutchings, Harold. "Stevens Gives His Appraisal of Jim Dean." *Chicago Sunday Tribune*, October 31, 1956.

Hyams, Joe. " 'Giant' a Film Story of Small Things." *New York Herald Tribune*, July 31, 1956.

"Ivan Moffat" (obituary). *The Times* (London), July 26, 2002.

"Jake Brisbin Jr." (obituary). *El Paso Times*, September 15, 2008.

"Jane Withers." classiccinemagold.com/jane-withers/jane-withers.

JP, "Texas' Own 'Gone With the Wind': George Stevens' 1956 Epic—'Giant.' " selvedgeyard .com/2010/12/29/texas-own-gone-with-the-wind-george-stevens-1955-epic-giant/.

Kelly, Christopher. "No Country for Bad Movies." *Texas Monthly*, June 2011.

Kelly, Hubert. "America's Forbidden Kingdom." *Reader's Digest*, May 1938.

"King of the Wildcatters." *Time*, February 13, 1950.

King, Susan. "A 'Giant' Legacy in a Tiny West Texas Town." *Los Angeles Times*, April 12, 2015.

———. "Classic Hollywood: 'Children of Giant' Explores Legacy of 'Giant' in Marfa, Texas." www.latimes.com/entertainment/classichollywood/la-et-mn-ca-classic -hollywood-children-giant-20150412-story.html.

———. "George Stevens Jr. and His 'Giant' Undertaking." *Los Angeles Times*, September 15, 1996.

Knecht, Lyndsay. "Pivotal Scene in *Giant* a Complicated First for Mexican-Americans," North Texas Public Broadcast, KERA, April 16, 2015. http://keranews.org/post /pivotal-scene-giant-complicated-first-mexican-americans.

Koestler, Fred L. "Operation Wetback." https://tshaonline.org/handbook/online/articles /pq0.

"Last Week's Storm Did More Good Than Harm Say Ranchers." *Big Bend Sentinel*, June 9, 1955.

LeBlanc, Pam. "Hang Out with the Hipsters in Funky Marfa." *Austin American-Statesman*, February 1, 2015.

———. "Pedaling for Education." *Austin American-Statesman*, May 2, 2016.

———. "Sleek Hotel Rises in West Texas Outpost of Marfa." *Austin American-Statesman*, April 2, 2016.

Leleux, Robert. "Giant Scandal." *Texas Observer*, August 22, 2011.

Levy, Emanuel. "*Giant* (1956): George Stevens Epic Starring Rock Hudson, Elizabeth Taylor, and James Dean in His Last Role." Emanuellevy.com/review/giant-4/.

Little, Carl Victor. "Book Stores Offered Big Bonus to Push Ferber's 'Giant' into Best Seller Lists." *Houston Press*, August 23, 1952.

———. "By-The-Way Discusses Ferber's New Book, 'Midget'; Or: I Say It's Spinach and the Heck with It." *Houston Press*, September 13, 1952.

———. "By-The-Way Hacked Anew by the Sweetheart of Texas; Or: So Ferber Claims We Ain't Got No Culture, Eh?" *Houston Press*, August 2, 1952.

———. "Ferber's Big Bust: She Fills Texas Air with Private 4-Engine Jobs." *Houston Press*, June 20, 1952.

———. "Meet Ferber's Texan Who Kills Man to Get Barbecue Sauce Recipe." *Houston Press*, June 24, 1952.

———. "Takes Edna Ferber 18 Months to Sell Giant to the Movies." *Houston Press*, July 31, 1953.

Long, Christian. "'Giant' Gave James Dean a Final Role That Suggested Untapped Potential." http://uproxx.com/movies/giant-gave-james-dean-a-final-role-that-suggested-untapped-potential/#comments.

Lopez, Gabriel R. "Giant 1956." https://filmproject.wikispaces.com/Giant+1956.

Lord, M. G. "Dennis Hopper, a Movie Giant." *Los Angeles Times*, June 6, 2010. articles.latimes.com/2010/jun/06/opinion/la-oe-lord-hopper-20100606.

———. "I Am Liz, Hear Me Roar." *W*, February 1, 2012.

Loynd, Ray. "Some Unsentimental Memories of James Dean by Rock Hudson." *Hollywood Reporter*, August 9, 1968.

MacCormack, John. "Findings Shed New Light on 1918 Porvenir Massacre." *Houston Chronicle*, April 3, 2016.

———. "Quirky Marfa Feels Growing Pains." *San Antonio Express-News*, July 12, 2014.

"Marfa, Texas: The Capital of Quirkiness." *60 Minutes*, April 14, 2013.

"Marfa Unit US Army Reserve Took Part in Filming Giant." *Big Bend Sentinel*, July 14, 1955.

Maurer, David. "Giant Effort to Make It in Movies." *Charlottesville Daily Progress*, March 9, 2013.

McCartin, John. "The Current Cinema: Southwestern Primitives." *The New Yorker*, October 20, 1956.

McDermott, William F. "McDermott on 'Giant': Tremendous . . . Colossal . . . Huge—
That's Texans' View of Texas Before Miss Ferber's Alamo." *Cleveland Plain Dealer*,
January 14, 1953.

McMurtry, Larry. "Men Swaggered, Women Warred, Oil Flowed." *New York Times*,
September 29, 1996.

McNeil, Elizabeth. "The Untold Story: Rock Hudson's Final Days." *People*, April 27,
2015.

McWilliams, Carey. "Oilmen Invade Hollywood." *Nation*, October 16, 1948.

"Man Finds Car Lost Twelve Years in King Ranch." *Corpus Christi Caller*, November 6, 1948.

Meisel, Myron. "*Giant* Reawakens." *Film Journal International*, 2013.

Meyers, Sim. "Edna Ferber Unleashes Furor with Publication of 'Giant.'" *Avalanche-Journal* (Lubbock), September 28, 1952.

Michael, Tom. "Marfa's Mexican-Americans Remember 'Giant' and Southwest Segregation." *All Things Considered*, NPR, April 24, 2015.

"Military Rites for Dead." *Sun*, October 7, 1947.

"Monty Hale for 'Giant.'" *Hollywood Reporter*, May 19, 1955.

"Morgan Starts Core Drill Tests for Uranium on Claim on Hubbard Ranch Near Marfa."
Big Bend Sentinel, June 23, 1955.

"Nation Mourns Pacific War Dead Coming Home in 'Operation Taps.'" *San Francisco Chronicle*, October 10, 1947.

O'Connor, John J. "What '*Giant*' Did to Texas." *New York Times*, May 24, 1997.

"On Location: Sketches of the film *Giant* by Ed Bearden." Mildred Hawn Exhibition
Gallery, Hamon Arts Library, Southern Methodist University, January 27–April 28,
2006. https://sites.smu.edu/cul/hamon/gallery/2006/Giant/index.htm.

Pitts, Martin. "Ivan Moffat: The Making of *Giant*." http://www.americanlegends.com
/interviews/dean_moffat.htm.

Powers, James. "Déjà Review: 'Giant.'" *Hollywood Reporter*, September 15, 1996.

Rechy, John. "Jim Crow Wears a Sombrero." *The Nation*, October 10, 1959.

Redelings, Lowell E. "Notes About People 'n' Things." *Hollywood Citizen-News*,
May 19, 1955.

———. "On Location in Marfa." *Hollywood Citizen-News*, June 20, 1955.

Rees, Robert R. "Vampira and James Dean: Cult vs. Occult." *Screen* 5 (1994).

Reinhold, Robert. "Houston Hotel Sale Signifies Fading of Oil Wealth." *New York Times*, December 29, 1985.

"Review: *Giant*." *Variety*, October 10, 1956.

Review of *Giant*, *Dallas Times Herald*, December 28, 1952.

Rivas-Rodriguez, Maggie. "Mexican-Americans of WWII Era Fought Civil Right
Battles and Won." *Austin American-Statesman*, April 9, 2014.

Rochlen, Kendis. "A 'Giant' Feast." *Los Angeles Mirror and Daily News*, May 20, 1955.

"Rock On Espanol." *Valley Times* (North Hollywood), April 12, 1955.

Rogers, Lisa Waller. "How Liz Taylor Saved Monty Clift's Life." lisawallerrogers.com /tag/benedict-canyon/.

Rogers, W. G. "Excitingly Unfair." *Omaha World-Herald,* October 5, 1952.

Rogers, Will. "Mr. Rogers Finds a Real Ranch and Real Cow Hands in Texas." *New York Times,* November 6, 1931.

Romero, Simon. "A Texas Town Holds Fast to Its Ties to a Classic." *New York Times,* June 9, 2003.

Rosenfield, John. " 'Giant' Enroute, Warts and All." *Dallas Morning News,* March 24, 1954.

———. "Marfa Needs It and Gets It from 'Giant.' " *Dallas Morning News,* June 11, 1955.

———. "Texans from Inside Out." *Dallas Morning News,* November 23, 1954. (The six influential sketches of major characters by artist Ed Bearden illustrate this article.)

———. "Texas-Size *Giant." Southwest Review* 41, no. 4 (Autumn 1956).

Scheuer, Philip K. "A Town Called Hollywood: Stevens Finds Big Scopes Restrict His Film Editing." *Los Angeles Times,* September 18, 1955.

Schickel, Richard. "All the Raw Materials for a Life in the Spotlight." *Los Angeles Times Book Review,* October 10, 2004.

———. "A Movie Whose Ambitions Were as Big as All Outdoors." *New York Times,* May 25, 2003.

Schjeldahl, Peter. "Light in Juddland." *The New Yorker,* September 25, 2000.

"Screening: *Giant." The Clearing House* 31, no. 7 (March 1957). http://www.jstor.org /stable/30187549.

Shapiro, Ann. "When Edna Ferber Was Accused of Communist Propaganda." *Studies in American Jewish Literature* 27 (2008).

Smyth, J. E. "Jim Crow, Jett Rink, and James Dean: Reconstructing Ferber's *Giant* (1952–1956)." *American Studies* 48, no. 3 (2007).

Solnit, Rebecca. "Giantess." *Harper's,* September 2016.

Sorkin, Amy Davidson. "How Elizabeth Taylor and James Dean Grew Old." *The New Yorker,* March 24, 2011. https://www.newyorker.com/news/amy-davidson/how -elizabeth-taylor-and-james-dean-grew-old.

Stafford, Jeff. "Giant: Overview Article." tcm.com.

Stern, Michael. "Interview with Douglas Sirk." *Bright Lights* 6 (Winter 1977–78).

Stevens, George. "A Tenderness Lost." *Modern Screen,* January 1956.

Stevens, George, Jr. "A *Giant* Step in Film Restoration." *DGA Magazine,* September–October, 1996.

Stewart, Lloyd. "Blond Fort Worth Debutante Sparkles in TV and Movies." *Fort Worth Star-Telegram,* June 9, 1955. http://nl.newsbank.com/nl-search-/we/Archives/?p _product=KRHA-FW&p_theme=histpap . . .

"Study of 'Giant': Killer of B.O. Blues." *Variety,* March 6, 1957.

"Talk on Uranium Holds Local Chamber Meeting Spellbound." *Big Bend Sentinel,* June 9, 1955.

"Television Unit Making Publicity Film This Week." *Big Bend Sentinel,* July 23, 1955,

"Texans Have 'Beef' About Prize Bull." *Pittsburgh Press,* October 3, 1955.

The Mike Wallace Interview, July 21, 1957. Transcript at Harry Ransom Center, University of Texas at Austin. www.hrc.utexas.edu/collections/film/holdings /wallace/.

Thomas, Bob. "Texas' Reaction to Book Violent, Novelist Says." *Albuquerque Tribune,* July 31, 1953.

Thomas, Kevin. " 'Giant' Doesn't Quite Live up to Its Legend." *Los Angeles Times,* September 27, 1996.

Thompson, Howard. "Another Dean Hits the Big Leagues." *New York Times,* March 13, 1955.

Tinkle, Lon. "Reading and Writing: Ferber Goes Both Native and Berserk: Parody, Not Portrait, of Texas Life." *Dallas News,* September 28, 1952.

Treviño, Jésus Salvador. "Latino Portrayals in Film and Television." *Jump Cut: A Review of Contemporary Media* 30 (1985).

Turner, George. "*Giant* Still Towers." *American Cinematographer,* October 1996.

Vasquez, Sarah M. "Film Reveals *Giant* Director's Take on Racism of the Times." *Big Bend Sentinel,* March 5, 2015.

Warnock, Kirby F. "*Giant* and That Texas State of Mind." *D Magazine,* September 1996.

———. "Going Hollywood." *Big Bend Quarterly,* May 1995.

Warren, Mia. "A Legacy of Division in Marfa's Cemeteries." KRTS 93.5 FM, Marfa, October 17, 2014.

Waterbury, Ruth. "On Location with 'Giant.' " *Tempo & Quick,* July 25, 1955.

Wells, Stephen. "Pastoral Landscapes and Upscale Retreats." *New York Times,* October 24, 2008.

West, Richard. "The Last Frontier: What Texas Once Was, Marfa Still Is." *Texas Monthly,* November 1977.

"Wide Spread Rains Cover County and Highland Area During Week." *Big Bend Sentinel,* July 21, 1955.

Wilonsky, Robert. "For Sale: A 1960s Pencil Sketch of City's Skyline by a Member of the Dallas Nine, Ed Bearden." *Dallas Observer,* August 14, 2011.

Worden, Daniel. "Fossil-Fuel Futurity: Oil in *Giant.*" *Journal of American Studies* 46, no. 2 (May 2012).

Yardley, Jonathan. "Ferber's 'Giant' Cut Down to Size." *Washington Post,* May 8, 2006.

Yeck, Joanne L. " '*Giant*': Wild Success Outraged Texas." *Senior,* March 1997.

Yen, Hope. "Census Bureau: U.S. Whites Will Be a Minority by 2043." *Austin American-Statesman,* June 14, 2013.

"Young Hollywood Through the Decades." *People,* November 11, 1996.

Young, Neil. "Joshua Tree, 1951: A Portrait of James Dean: Film Review." www .hollywoodreporter.com/review/joshua-tree-1951-portrait-james-dean-matthew -mishory-338556.

GIANT'S LONG REACH: CREATIVE RESPONSES

Brammer, Billy Lee. *The Gay Place*. New York: Houghton Mifflin 1961.

Children of Giant (2015). Galán Productions. Documentary. Director: Hector Galán. Cast: Henry Cisneros, Elsa Cárdenas, Robert Hinkle, Earl Holliman, George Stevens, Jr. Running time: 86 minutes.

Come Back to the 5 & Dime, Jimmy Dean, Jimmy Dean (1982). Mark Goodson Productions. Director: Robert Altman. Cast: Sandy Dennis, Cher, Karen Black, Sudie Bond, Kathy Bates. Running time: 109 minutes.

Corley, Edwin. *Farewell, My Slightly Tarnished Hero*. New York: Dodd, Mead, 1971.

Dallas (1978–1991). Created by David Jacobs. Cast: Larry Hagman, Linda Gray, Barbara Bel Geddes, Patrick Duffy, Jim Davis, Victoria Principal. CBS TV series.

Dean, James. "Texas." In *Rebel with a Pen: The Poetry of James Dean*, edited by Carlton Hayes. Chicago: Dover Press, 2008.

Dos Passos, John. "The Sinister Adolescents." In *Midcentury*. Boston: Houghton Mifflin, 1961.

Ebersol, Lucinda, and Richard Peabody, eds. *Mondo James Dean: A Collection of Stories and Poems about James Dean*. New York: St. Martin's Press, 1996.

Fandango (1985). Amblin Entertainment. Director: Kevin Reynolds. Cast: Kevin Costner, Judd Nelson, Sam Robards, Chuck Bush, Brian Cesak. Running time: 91 minutes.

Forever James Dean (1988). Chelsea Communications. Director: Ara Chekmayan. Cast: William Bast, Bob Gunton, Bob Roth, Frank Worth, Jack Grinnage. Running time: 60 minutes.

Franco, James. "James Dean on Havenhurst." In *Directing Herbert White: Poems*. Minneapolis: Graywolf Press, 2014.

———. "New Rebel." In *Straight James/Gay James*. East Brunswick, NJ: Hansen Publishing Group, 2016.

George Stevens: A Filmmaker's Journey (1984). Director, writer, and producer: George Stevens, Jr. Producers: Antonio Vellani and Susan Winslow. Cast: Jean Arthur, Fred Astaire, Montgomery Clift, James Dean. Running time: 111 minutes.

Giant (musical). Lyrics by Michael John LaChiusa; book by Sybille Pearson. Premiered at Signature Theatre, Arlington, Virginia, 2009. Off-Broadway, Public Theater, New York, 2012. Dallas Theater Center, 2012. Illinois Wesleyan University, Bloomington, Illinois, 2015.

Graczyk, Ed. *Come Back to the 5 & Dime, Jimmy Dean, Jimmy Dean*. New York: Samuel French, 1976.

Graham, Don, and Betsy Berry. "Giant Country." In *New Texas 95: Poetry & Fiction*, edited by Katherine S. McGuire and James Ward Lee. Denton: Center for Texas Studies, 1995. Revised version collected in Graham, Don. *Giant Country: Essays on Texas*. Fort Worth: TCU Press, 1998.

Heinzelman, Kurt. "The Marfa Lights." In *The Names They Found There*. San Antonio: Pecan Grove Press, 2011.

Ifkovic, Ed. *Lone Star: An Edna Ferber Mystery.* Scottsdale, AZ: Poisoned Pen Press, 2009.

James Dean (2012). Warner Home Video. Director: Mark Rydell. Writer: Israel Horovitz. Cast: James Franco, Michael Moriarty, Enrico Colatoni, Valentina Cervi, Edward Heerman. Running time: 96 minutes.

James Dean Forever Young (2005). Warner Bros. Pictures. Director: Michael J. Sheridan. Writers: Michael J. Sheridan and Kevin J. Sheridan. Cast: Martin Sheen, Corey Allen, Pier Angeli, Ed Begly. Running time: 88 minutes.

James Dean: Race with Destiny (1997). Director: Mardi Rustam. Writer: Daniel L. Sefton. Cast: Casper Van Dien, Carrie Mitchum, Diane Ladd, Mike Connors, Robert Mitchum, Connie Stevens. Running time: 94 minutes.

James Dean: Sense Memories (2005). *American Masters,* PBS. Director and writer: Gail Levin. Cast: Mark Rydell, Martin Landau, Eli Wallach, William Bast, George Stevens, Jr. Running time: 53 minutes.

Joshua Tree, 1951: A Portrait of James Dean (2012). Iconoclastic Features. Director and writer: Matthew Mishory. Cast: James Preston, Dan Glenn, Clare Grant, Ed Singletary, Dalilah Rain. Running time: 93 minutes.

Life (2015). Barry Films. Director: Anton Corbijn. Writer: Luke Davies. Cast: Robert Pattinson, Dane DeHaan, Alessandra Mastronard, Ben Kingsley, Joel Edgerton. Running time: 111 minutes.

Memories of Giant (2003). Warner Home Video. Cast: Carroll Baker, Earl Holliman, Rock Hudson, George Stevens, Jr. Running time: 52 minutes.

Meyer, Philipp. *The Son.* New York: Ecco, 2013.

Ogawa, Ai. "James Dean." In *Fate.* New York: Houghton Mifflin, 1991.

O'Hara, Frank. "Obit Dean, September 30, 1955." In *The Collected Poems of Frank O'Hara,* edited by Donald Allen. Berkeley: University of California Press, 1995.

Return to Giant (1996). Trans Pecos Productions. Documentary. Director: Jim Brennan. Producer and writer: Kirby F. Warnock. Cast: Don Henley, Don Graham, Earl Holliman, Bryan Woolley, Carroll Baker, George Stevens, Jr. Running time: 55 minutes.

Rock Hudson: A Life Shrouded in Mystery (2007). Konigsberg/Sanitsky Company Production. Director: John Nicolella. Cast: Daphne Ashbrook, Mathieu Carrire, Michael Ensign, Don Galloway, Jean Kasem. Running time: 94 minutes.

Ross, Walter. *The Immortal.* New York: Simon & Schuster, 1958.

Selena (1997). Q-Productions. Director: Gregory Nava. Writer: Gregory Nava. Cast: Jennifer Lopez, Edward James Olmos, Jon Seda, Constance Marie. Running time: 127 minutes.

Sinclair, K. C. "Palabras Muertas." http//www.texasobserver.org/short-story-contest-finalist-palabras-muertas/.

Stratton, W. K., "Dennis Hopper ii." In *Dreaming Sam Peckinpah.* Temple, TX: Ink Brush Press, 2011.

Teresa Hubbard/Alexander Birchler. *Giant,* 2014. Installation. 30-minute loop. Blanton Museum, University of Texas, July 9, 2017–October 1, 2017.

The James Dean Story (1957). Warner Bros. Directors: Robert Altman and George W.

George. Writer: Stewart Stern. Cast: Martin Gabel, James Dean, Lew Bracker, Patsy D'Amore. Running time: 81 minutes.

"This Old Porch." Words and music by Lyle Lovett and Robert Earl Keen Jr. 1986.

Thomas, T. T. *I, James Dean.* New York: Popular Library, 1957.

Urrea, Luis Alberto. *In Search of Snow.* Tucson: University of Arizona Press, 1994.

Villanueva, Tino. *Scene from the Movie Giant.* Willimantic, CT: Curbstone Press, 1993.

Wiggerman, Scott. "At the Paisano." *Southwestern American Literature* 37, no. 1 (Fall 2011).